BTEC NATIONAL STUDY GUIDE

Engineering

Compiled from

BTEC National Engineering

By Mike Tooley and Lloyd Dingle

Mechanical Engineering: BTEC National option units

By Alan Darbyshire

Electrical and Electronic Principles and Technology

By John Bird

PEARSON

Custom
Publishing

Edexcel Learning
80 The Strand
London
WC2R 0RL

Part of the Pearson group of companies throughout the world

This Edexcel Learning Edition first published 2005

Compiled from

BTEC National Engineering
By Mike Tooley and Lloyd Dingle, published by Newnes
ISBN 0 7506 5166 0
© Mike Tooley and Lloyd Dingle 2002

Mechanical Engineering: BTEC National option units
By Alan Darbyshire, published by Newnes
ISBN 0 7506 5761 8
© Alan Darbyshire 2003

Electrical and Electronic Principles and Technology
By John Bird
ISBN 0 7506 6550 5
© John Bird 2003

ISBN-10: 1-84479-585-3
ISBN-13: 978-1-84479-585-7

Printed and bound in Great Britain by Henry Ling Limited at the Dorset Press, Dorchester DT1 1HD

Contents

BASIC ELECTRICAL AND ELECTRONIC ENGINEERING PRINCIPLES

Electrical and Electronic Principles and Technology by John Bird

Preface

This Study Guide for the BTEC National in Engineering has been published to give you a flavour of the resources that are available to support your course.

A good textbook fulfils many roles. If you have forgotten something your tutor told you in class, you can look it up in the book. If there is something you are not quite sure about or don't quite understand, you can get to grips with it at your own pace and in your own time. If you are unfortunate to miss a class then you can probably read about the topic you missed in the textbook.

Texts also have activities and case studies for you to do so you can see how much you have understood. If you realise you need help, you can then go back to your tutor. Activities also give you the opportunity to practise the skills you will need for assessment.

And most texts will take you beyond their covers! They give you useful websites to explore, they will suggest journals and magazines that will widen your researches and they will have lists of other books to read if you want to explore an issue in greater depth. Make the most of all these leads to broaden your horizons. You will enjoy your course more and you are likely to get better grades.

This Study Guide covers one of the core units you will study for your BTEC National and gives you support for some of the option units you may study. We hope you will find the Guide useful and will want to make further use of the books that are presented here.

THE SMART WAY TO ACHIEVE YOUR BTEC NATIONAL

We all know people who seem to do well almost effortlessly – at work, at college and even when they are just enjoying themselves. Some of them may be clever or talented but not all of them – so what is their secret? And how does this relate to your BTEC National course?

Every year thousands of students enrol on BTEC National courses. Most are successful and obtain the full qualification. A few do not - either because they don't complete the course or because they don't achieve all the units they need. In some cases students who are successful are still disappointed because they don't achieve the grades they wanted. This can have serious consequences if their offers of a university place are based on the achievement of specific final grades.

The difference between students who don't do as well as they had hoped, and those who do well, rarely has anything to do with brain power. After all, they were all accepted as suitable for the course in the first place. The difference is usually because some work efficiently and some do not. In fact, some students seem to go through college continually making life difficult for themselves – and then wonder why they have problems!

Students who work efficiently are **smart**. The strategies they use mean they are more likely to stay on the course (even if they have problems) and they regularly achieve better grades than other students.

So what do *you* need to do to be smart? First: read this guide. Second: follow it! Third: keep it safely and re-read it at regular intervals to refresh your memory.

The smart way to learn to be smart

1

BTEC National Study Guide: Engineering. See page 325 for order details of individual texts

1

In a nutshell

Working in a smart way means you are more likely to stay on your course, even if you have problems. You will also achieve better grades for doing the same amount of work!

Be smart about your course

There may be quite a gap between your interview at college and the date you start on your BTEC National course. In that time you will probably have forgotten a lot about what you were told. So the first thing to do is to refresh your memory and find out *exactly* what your course entails. You can do this by re-reading college information and also by logging onto the Edexcel website at www.edexcel.org.uk.

* There are three types of BTEC National qualifications and each has a different number of units.

    - The BTEC National Award has 6 units
    - The BTEC National Certificate has 12 units
    - The BTEC National Diploma has 18 units

    You should already know which type of BTEC National you are taking and how long your course lasts. It is useful to find out how many units you will study each term and how many units you will complete each year if you are on a two-year course.

* Every BTEC National qualification has a set number of **core units**. These are the compulsory units which every student must complete. There is also a range of **specialist units** from which you may be able to make a choice. These enable you to study particular areas in more depth. You need to check:

    - the title of each core unit and the topics it contains
    - the title of each specialist unit and the area it covers
    - whether you can choose any specialist units you want, or whether your choice is restricted. This may be because of the structure of the qualification or because your college does not offer the full range.

Knowing all about your course means that you are more likely to choose the most appropriate specialist units for your own needs and interests. You will be more mentally prepared and know what to expect. This also enables you to relate your everyday experiences to the topics you will be learning. You can then be alert to information that relates to your studies, whether you are watching television, reading an article, talking to your family or working – even in a part-time job a few hours a week. The more alert you are to these types of opportunities, the more you will benefit.

In a nutshell

Log on to www.edexcel.org.uk and check the exact content of your BTEC National course. Download the *Student's Guide* for your course which describes the course structure and the unit titles and check with your tutor which you will study each term. Check the course specification to find out the exact content of each unit and check the specialist units that are offered at your college before you select your specialist units. Always be alert to all sources of useful information that relate to your course.

Be smart about resources

A resource is anything that helps you to achieve your goal and so, generally speaking, the more you have the better! You will be introduced to many college resources during your induction, such as the library, the learning resource centre(s) and the computer network. However, most students never actually sit down and list all the resources they have. This is worthwhile because you will probably have far more than you realise. The easiest way is to divide up your resources into different categories and make a list under each heading.

BTEC National Study Guide: Engineering. See page 325 for order details of individual texts

There are two aspects to resources. Knowing what they are and using them properly! The main types of resources to consider are given below.

- **Course materials**   These include this Student Guide, all the materials on the Edexcel website, all the information given to you during induction, the textbook(s) you use for particular units, the handouts you are given in class and the notes you make in class. They also include resources you are asked to provide yourself, such as lined paper, folders for storing notes, dividers for sub-dividing topics in your folders, pens, pencils, a hole punch, calculator and a good dictionary. These, by the way, are all essential resources – not optional extras you can scrounge from someone else!

If you are smart then you always have the right resources for each lesson or session because you get organised in advance. You also file handouts and notes *promptly* in the right place in the right folder so that you can find them again quickly. You have clearly labelled dividers and your notes have a clear heading so that you can find information easily. If you are writing up your own notes from research then you will have made a clear note of the source of your information. How to do this is given in the IVA guide *Ten Steps to a Great IVA*.

- **Equipment and facilities**   These include your college library and learning resource centre(s); the college computer network; other college equipment you can use, such as laptop computers and photocopiers; electronic information resources, such as Internet access, electronic journals and CDs; equipment you have at home – such as a computer; specialist equipment and facilities relevant to your particular course.

Libraries can be baffling if you don't understand the system used to store books: your college computer network is of limited use if you don't know the difference between an Intranet and the Internet or realise that information is stored on CDs as well as in books. Library and resource centre staff are employed to give you help and advice if you need it – so don't hesitate to ask them! You also need to find the recommended way to transfer data between your home computer and college if your options are limited because of IT security. It is also very important that you check the regulations or guidelines on using the Internet and computers in your college so that you make the most of the equipment without falling foul of any of the rules that apply.

- **People**   These include your tutor(s), specialist staff (such as library and resource centre staff), your employer and your colleagues at work, your relatives and friends who have particular skills or who work in the same area you are studying.

Smart students have their own resources

BTEC National Study Guide: Engineering. See page 325 for order details of individual texts

Most people will be keen to help you if you are courteous, well prepared and are not trying to get them to do the work for you! Prepare a list of open questions if you want to interview someone. These are questions that can't be answered with a 'yes' or 'no'. Work down your list but aim to get the person talking freely whilst you make notes. Unless they wander far from the topic you will find out more this way. Then do a final check that you have covered all the areas on your list and get a contact number in case you need to speak to them again. Don't forget to say thank you – and try not to overuse one particular person.

One word of warning! Be careful about asking for help from a friend who has already done the same course and *never* be tempted to borrow their assignments. Tutors can soon tell if the work isn't in your own personal style, or if it varies in style. In addition, assignments are normally changed each year and answers are expected to be up-to-date, so an answer from a previous year is unlikely to be of much use.

- **Your own skills and abilities**   Obviously if you have excellent IT skills then you will produce your written assignments more easily. You will also be better at researching online if you know and understand how to use the Internet and have included useful sites in your Favourites list. Other vital skills include being able to recognise and extract key information from a book, being able to summarise and able to type up your work relatively quickly and accurately. As you will see as you work through this Guide being well-organised and using your time wisely are also invaluable skills and can make all the difference to your final grades.

You can assess yourself as you read this Guide by listing those areas in which you are weak and need to improve your skills. Then talk to your tutor about the best way to do this.

In a nutshell

Resources are vital because they help you to succeed. If you list your resources you may find there are more than you think. Then you must use them wisely. This includes storing handouts safely and thanking people who help you. You also need to develop skills and abilities which will help you to work more easily – such as improving your Internet and typing skills.

Be smart about time

Some weeks you may find you have very little to do – so you can manage your workload easily. Then everything changes. In a short period of time you seem to be overwhelmed with work to do. If you are unlucky, this will coincide with a time when you also have family, personal or work commitments as well. So – how do you juggle everything and still stay in control?

There are several skills you need to be able to do this.

- **Record important dates in advance**   Keep a homework diary or (even better) a wall chart and mark all key dates in colour. You can devise your own system but it is useful to enter assignment review dates with your tutor in one colour and final deadline dates in another. Keep your chart up-to-date by adding any new dates promptly every time you are given another task or assignment. This gives you prior warning when important dates are looming and, if nothing else, stops you from planning a heavy social week for the same time!

- **Prioritise your work**   This means doing the most important and urgent task first. This is normally the task or assignment with the nearest deadline. The exception is when you have to allow for the availability of other people or other resources. For example, if you have two assignments to do and one involves interviewing three people, it is sensible to schedule the interviews first. If you need to send off for information it is also sensible to do this promptly, to allow plenty of time for it to arrive. It also means allowing enough time to print out your assignment well before the deadline – unless you are prepared to join the long queues of students who have the same deadline as you and who are all trying to print out their work at the last minute!

- **Plan your work**   This means analysing each task and estimating how long it will take. For example, you may estimate that an assignment will take you one hour to plan, six hours to research, four hours to type up

BTEC National Study Guide: Engineering. See page 325 for order details of individual texts

4

Be smart about time

and one hour to check. In this case you need *at least* twelve hours to do the work. If you are sensible you will allow a little more, in case you encounter any problems or difficulties. It is wise to schedule fixed times to work and then plan to give yourself time off when you have completed a task or are 'between' tasks or assignments.

- **Regularly review your progress**   You need to check regularly that you are on schedule. It is easy to spend much longer than you think on some tasks – either because you get bogged down or because you become too absorbed. This will mean you have to do the rest of the work in a rush and this may affect your grade.

- **Be smart – but be kind to yourself too!**   If you are over-conscientious you may be tempted to burn the midnight oil to keep up-to-date. This isn't wise on a regular basis because no-one does their best work when they are over-tired. In this case remember to *target* your efforts where they will count most – rather than try to have everything perfect. Schedule in some breaks and relaxation time too; you are allowed a treat from time to time! If your problem is just the opposite – and you struggle to stay focused if you're not in the mood for work – then you need to practise a little more self-discipline. One trick is to find an aspect of a task that you will find easy or really enjoy. Then start with this to get yourself going. Aim to complete a fixed amount of work before you give yourself a small reward – such as a fifteen-minute break or a bar of chocolate!

You can find more detailed information on planning your work and reviewing your progress in the IVA Guide *Ten Steps to a Great IVA*.

BTEC National Study Guide: Engineering. See page 325 for order details of individual texts

5

We all need a treat from time to time

In a nutshell

Your workload may be unpredictable and some weeks will be worse than others. You will cope better if you note down all key dates in advance, prioritise properly, plan realistically the time work will take and regularly review your progress. Target your efforts so that you can take sensible breaks and start with tasks you enjoy to motivate yourself.

Be smart about assignments

Assignments are the main method of assessment on all BTEC National courses. Edexcel specifies the exact **assessment criteria** for each unit in a grid. In plain English, this is the list of skills and knowledge you must demonstrate to achieve a pass, merit or distinction. You will find these in your course specification immediately after the content of each unit.

There are two types of assignments.

- There are those that are **internally set**. In this case the assignments are set and marked by your own tutors. Each assignment will include tasks and activities that enable you to produce evidence directly linked to the assessment criteria for a particular unit. Most units have internally set and assessed assignments.

- Alternatively there are **externally set** assignments. In this case an **Integrated Vocational Assignment (IVA)** is set by Edexcel.

In both cases Edexcel checks that centres are assessing assignments correctly and that all centres have the same standards.

Many people panic at the thought of assignments, but being smart means you are well-prepared and won't break any golden rules!

- Always check the assessment criteria grid for the unit in advance, so that you know what to expect.

- The grid is divided into three main columns which state what you must do to achieve a pass, a merit and a distinction grade. The main word, which tells you what to do, is called a **command word**. You must understand the command word *and obey it* to obtain a specific grade. This is dealt with in more detail in the next section.

- Read the assignment brief *thoroughly* and query anything you do not understand with your tutor.

- Check those tasks which must be all your own work and which (if any) you will complete as a member of a group. If you are asked to do any work as a member of a team then you must always identify your own individual contribution to each task.

BTEC National Study Guide: Engineering. See page 325 for order details of individual texts

6

- *Always* remember that plagiarism (copying someone else's work) is an extremely serious offence and will result in disciplinary action. *Never* be tempted to share your work (or your disks or CDs) with anyone else and don't ask to borrow theirs!

- Check the other rules that apply. These will include
  - whether you can discuss your research or draft answers with your tutor – and when you must do this
  - the college-set deadline date for submission – and the penalties for handing in work late (this might mean your assignment not being assessed)
  - what to do if you are absent when the assignment is due or have a serious personal problem which affects your ability to complete the work on time. There is normally an official procedure for obtaining an extension. This is only when mitigating circumstances apply and can't be used just because you fail to plan properly!

- Make sure you answer every question fully and present your information according to the instructions. You may, for instance, have to provide information in a table or report rather than simply answering questions. You will get a lower grade if you ignore important presentation instructions.

In a nutshell

The assessment criteria grid for each unit states what you must provide evidence against to achieve a pass, merit or distinction grade. It is important that you read and understand this, as well as the assignment brief, and obey all the instructions. Check you know any other rules that apply, such as how to apply for an extension to the deadline if you have a serious personal problem. Then answer the questions fully and present the work as required.

Sadly, over-sleeping doesn't count as a serious personal problem

BTEC National Study Guide: Engineering. See page 325 for order details of individual texts

Be smart about command words

Command words are used to specify how a question must be answered, eg 'describe', 'explain' or 'analyse'. These words are often related to the level of answer required. You will therefore find these command words in the assessment grid and you will usually see, for example, that 'describe' will get you a pass grade. However, you would need to do more than give a straightforward description to get a merit or distinction grade.

Many students don't get the grades they should for an assignment because they do not realise the difference between these words. Instead of applying their knowledge (for a merit grade) they simply give a brief explanation or a list. Just listing *more* facts will not improve your grade; you must show you can use your knowledge.

The chart below shows you what is usually required when you see a particular command word. You can use this, and the answers below, to identify the difference between the types of answers required for each grade. Remember these are just *examples* of acceptable answers to help you. The exact response required will often depend upon the way a question is worded so check with your tutor if you are unsure what it is you have to do.

To obtain a pass grade you must prove your knowledge and understanding by giving the relevant facts clearly and concisely.	
If it says:	This means you should:
Describe	Give a clear description that includes all the relevant features. You might want to think of this as 'painting a picture in words'.
Define	Clearly explain what a particular term means and give an example, if appropriate, to show what you mean.
Design*	Create a plan, proposal or outline to illustrate a straightforward concept or idea.
Explain how/why	Set out in detail the meaning of something, with reasons. This is more difficult than 'describing' or 'listing' so it can often help to give an example to show what you mean. Start by introducing the topic and then give the 'how' or 'why'.
Identify	Point out (ie choose the right one) or give a list of the main features.
Illustrate	Include examples or a diagram to show what you mean.
Interpret	Define or explain the meaning of something.
List	Provide the information in a list, rather than in continuous writing.
Outline	Write a clear description but not a detailed one.
Plan	Work out and explain how you would carry out a task or activity.
State	Write a clear and full account.
Summarise	Write down the main points or essential features.

Q   Describe the Apple iPod.

Below is an example answer that would achieve a pass grade.

A   The Apple iPod is a digital player on which music can be stored and played without the need for CDs or tapes. Music is stored on an iPod by transferring MP3 music files that have been downloaded from the Internet or copied from a CD. The Apple iPod with the largest capacity will store up to 10,000 songs and costs about £420. A mini version is much cheaper but stores far fewer – about 1,000 – for about £180. Both have been praised in reviews for their excellent sound quality, ease of use and stylish design.

* You may also find the word 'design' at merit level, as you will see below.

BTEC National Study Guide: Engineering. See page 325 for order details of individual texts

8

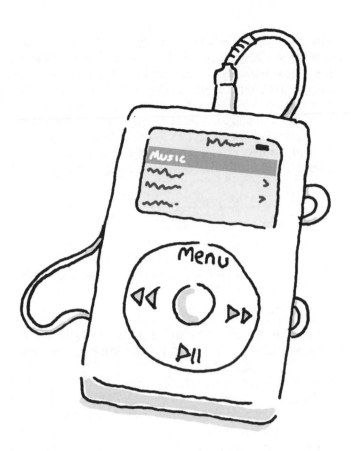

To obtain a merit grade you must prove you can apply your knowledge in a specific way.	
If it says:	This means you should:
Analyse	Identify separate factors, say how they are related and how each one contributes to the topic. This is one step up from the explanation you gave at pass level.
Compare/contrast	Identify the main factors that apply in two or more situations and explain the similarities and differences or advantages and disadvantages.
Demonstrate	Provide several relevant examples or related evidence which clearly support the arguments you are making. If you are doing a practical subject, this might be, e.g. showing your computer or coaching skills.
Design	Create a plan, proposal or outline to illustrate a relatively complex concept or idea.
Assess	Give careful consideration to all the factors or events that apply and identify which are the most important and relevant.
Explain in detail	Provide details and give reasons and/or evidence to clearly support the argument you are making.
how/why Justify	Give reasons or evidence to support your opinion or view to show how you arrived at these conclusions.

Q   Analyse why Apple iPods are so popular.

Below is an example answer that would achieve a merit grade.

A   Apple is one of several brands of MP3 players on the market. Rivals include the iAudio player and the Sony net walkman. Some rivals are cheaper than the iPod, so price is not the main reason for Apple iPod popularity. The iPod took off because its stylish design looked so good and there was some great

BTEC National Study Guide: Engineering. See page 325 for order details of individual texts

9

advertising that turned it into the 'must have' item as early as Christmas 2003. It was also praised more by reviewers than other digital players. The Apple iPod stores music on a moving hard disk whereas some players store it on computer chips. Hard disk players have better sound quality and greater storage capacity. The Apple is also easy to use. Apple then developed the brand by adding accessories and introducing the mini iPod which comes in five different colours. Apple is also popular because it was the first to develop a portable MP3 player and supports its customers with its iTunes music store online. Downloads from the site aren't compatible with other players and so iPod users are tied to the iTunes site. Many people have criticised this. Apple, however, is the brand that is cool to own – so much so that over 10 million Apple iPods were sold in 2004 out of total sales worldwide of between 20 and 25 million portable music players.

To obtain a distinction grade you must prove you can make a reasoned judgement based on evidence.

If it says:	This means you should:
Appraise	Consider the plus and minus points and give a reasoned judgement
Assess	Must make a judgement on the importance of something. It is similar to 'evaluate' (see below).
Comment critically	Give your view after you have considered all the evidence. In particular decide the importance of all the relevant positive *and* negative aspects.
Criticise	Review a topic or issue objectively and weigh up both plus and minus points before making a decision. It is similar to 'comment critically'.
Draw conclusions	Use the evidence you have provided to reach a reasoned judgement.
Evaluate	Review the information and then bring it together to form a conclusion. Give evidence for each of your views or statements.
Evaluate critically	Decide the degree to which a statement is true or the importance or value of something by reviewing the information. Include precise and detailed information and assess possible alternatives, bearing in mind their strengths and weaknesses if they were applied instead.

Q   Evaluate the effect of Apple iPods on the music industry.

An example answer that would achieve a distinction grade:

A   Apple iPods – together with other digital music players – have helped to give the music industry a new lease of life. In the late 1990s music companies were alarmed that the Internet could ruin their business because of illegal file sharing and they forced the Napster website to close down. This site had allowed music fans to log on and exchange songs free of charge. Music companies also took legal action against private individuals. A famous case was of an American girl of 12 whose mother had to pay $2,000 in fines, which frightened other parents. However, the development of portable digital music players has boosted the popularity of legal download sites such as Apple iTunes, MyCokeMusic and the new Napster subscription service, which sell tracks for about 80p each. These enable music fans to select and store only the tracks they want to hear, rather than have to spend money on a CD album that may contain many tracks they don't want. In Britain in 2004, 5.7 million download tracks were sold compared with virtually none in 2003 and sales are predicted to double in 2005. This growth is being fuelled by global sales of portable music players – the most popular of which is the Apple iPod. The music industry is taking advantage of the trend by pre-releasing tracks online and there is now an official download chart. By 2009, experts predict that the digital market could be worth 25% of total music sales, compared to a mere 1.5% in late 2004. There is no doubt that the Apple iPod, and other portable digital music players, have been a major factor in this huge growth rate.

BTEC National Study Guide: Engineering. See page 325 for order details of individual texts

10

In a nutshell

The assessment criteria grid for each unit states what you must know to get a pass, merit or distinction grade. It is vital that you understand the command words used and obey them or you will not achieve the best grade possible.

Be smart about your grades

On the Edexcel website you can download a form called *Recording Your Achievement.* This enables you to record the grade for each unit you complete. The form also tells you how many points you achieve for gaining a Pass, Merit or Distinction for each unit and how these are added together to obtain your final grade(s). You obtain *one* final grade if you are taking a BTEC National Award, *two* final grades if you are taking a BTEC National Certificate and *three* final grades if you are taking a BTEC National Diploma.

This is very important information, because it helps you to plan where to target your efforts, particularly later in the course.

- Remember that you will obtain more overall points if you divide up your time so that you put the most effort and work into areas where you are weak, rather than spending the most time on assignments you enjoy or find easy! Although it is tempting to keep working on something you like doing, even when you have already done a good job, the danger is that you then don't do so well in other assignments that you have neglected or where you have cut corners. The secret is to put in the right amount of effort in *every* assignment to get the grade you need. For topics you find easy, this may mean you need to spend less time on the assignment than for work you find difficult – despite the fact that you may be tempted to do exactly the opposite! If you do consistently well in all your assignments you will find that this results in higher overall grades than if you do very well in some but poorly in others.

- Keeping your grade profile up-to-date and discussing it with your tutor at regular intervals is an excellent way of keeping yourself on track throughout the course.

In a nutshell

If you are smart you will plan to manage your grades and your overall profile. Do this by recording your grades, spending more time on important or difficult assessments and discussing your profile, as you go, with your tutor.

Be smart at work or on work experience

On some BTEC National courses there is a vocational element and you will need evidence from work or work experience to prove your skills and abilities. In this case your tutor will give you a logbook to keep. On other courses, workplace evidence is not essential but the knowledge and practical experience you gain is still extremely useful, if not invaluable. This only applies, of course, if you are smart enough to recognise the opportunities that occur. Relevant events are likely to include:

- your induction and any subsequent training courses you are asked to attend – even if these are only very short, work-based sessions

- any performance reviews or appraisals you have with your supervisor or boss

- your dealings with customers of the organisation – particularly if you had to respond to a difficult enquiry or solve a problem.

BTEC National Study Guide: Engineering. See page 325 for order details of individual texts

11

FREE COACHING
TODAY

Your tutor will tell you how to get a witness statement

- the rules, regulations or guidelines that you must follow. You should think about why these have been put in place as well as the consequences of not abiding by them
- your own duties and specific areas of responsibility
- your relationships with your colleagues and how you resolve any problems or difficulties that occur
- skills you have learned or developed by being at work – from time keeping to achieving targets.

If you have to provide formal evidence then one method is to ask your manager, supervisor or colleagues for a **witness statement**. This is a formal document that confirms something you have done and when you did it. Your tutor will give you a form for this. It is also useful to keep your own work diary and to jot down important things that happen that you could use as evidence in current or future assignments to support your arguments for a merit or distinction grade question.

In a nutshell

Work experience may be an essential part of your BTEC National course. Even if it is not, you will gain many useful skills at work that can help you to achieve your award. Make a note of all key events and activities you are involved in. If you need formal evidence, ask your boss for a witness statement.

BTEC National Study Guide: Engineering. See page 325 for order details of individual texts

12

Be smart about key skills

Key skills are so-called because they are considered invaluable to everyone at work. Most BTEC National students study for a key skills award and in this case the majority of key skills will often be integrated into your main programme of study. This not only helps you to improve your skills, it also means you have the potential to achieve additional points when you submit your UCAS application. Unfortunately not all students complete their key skills awards and so fail to achieve their maximum points score. This is less likely to happen if you are smart and get key skills to work for you, and don't simply see them as more work to do!

- Always check the tracking sheet you are given with your assignments to see which key skills are covered by that particular piece of work.

- Take advantage of any specific classes for key skills, particularly Application of Number, unless you have passed a GCSE Maths examination that exempts you. Otherwise use the classes to improve your abilities.

- There are dozens of benefits if you can communicate effectively and there are almost endless opportunities for practice. You communicate every day – with your friends, family, tutor, boss and colleagues at work – in a variety of different ways. You spend time writing notes in class and writing up researched information. You prepare written documents for your assignments. You work with your classmates when you are doing role-plays or preparing a presentation. If you communicate effectively you will be able to make better presentations, ask the right questions when you are interviewing and write clearer answers to your assignments. You will then gain better grades for your BTEC National as well as your key skills award!

- Information technology is a crucial tool for completing work related tasks. If you develop your word processing skills and your Internet research skills you will produce better, more professional assignments more quickly and more easily. If you intend to continue studying you will find that good IT skills are invaluable at university. If you hope to start working in business when you leave your course then you can expect your future employer to take a keen interest in your IT abilities.

Make key skills work for you

BTEC National Study Guide: Engineering. See page 325 for order details of individual texts

- The 'wider' key skills are Improving own learning and performance, Working with others and Problem solving. These are likely to be required in many of your assignments. You will also demonstrate these skills if you go to work or are on work experience. Talk to your tutor about how you can use evidence from the workplace to help you to achieve your key skills award.

In a nutshell

There are many advantages to developing your key skills and achieving your key skills award. You will find this easier if you take advantage of all the opportunities you can to develop your key skills and use naturally occurring situations to provide much of the evidence.

Be smart if you have a problem

Many students have personal problems when they are studying. Knowing what to do in this situation makes all the difference. It also means you have one less thing to worry about when life is going wrong.

- Check your college induction information carefully. This should give you detailed information about the people you can talk to if you have a problem. Normally your personal tutor will be the first person on your list but there will be other people available, too, in case your tutor is absent or if you would prefer to talk to someone else in confidence.

- If you cannot find the information you want, ask a tutor you like and trust for advice – or visit the central student support area instead and ask there.

- All colleges have sets of procedures to cover different events. These include the following.

  - **The appeals procedure**   This tells you what to do if you feel that an assignment has been unfairly marked. The obvious first step in this situation is to ask your tutor to explain the grade you have been given, and how this links with the assessment grid. Do this before you think of taking formal action. If you are unhappy with the tutor's explanation then talk to your personal tutor. If you are still unhappy then you have the right to make a formal appeal.
  - **Student complaint procedures**   This is normally the 'last resort' for a student and is only used when a major worry or concern can't be resolved informally. You therefore have the right to make an official complaint but should only do so when you have exhausted all the other avenues open to you. It is not normally used for trivial matters.
  - **Student disciplinary procedures**   This tells you what to expect if you are disciplined for any reason. Although it is wise to avoid trouble, if you do break a rule then it is sensible to read these procedures carefully. Always remember that an honest confession and an apology will normally count in your favour, so if you do have this type of problem, don't be tempted to make matters worse by being devious.

- All colleges will arrange confidential counselling for you if you have a serious personal problem. The counsellor is a trained expert, not a member of the teaching staff. Without giving away any personal details, your counsellor can ensure that you receive the additional support you need from the teaching team – such as more time for an assignment or time off for personal commitments.

- *Never* be tempted to keep a serious worry or problem to yourself. In this situation your concentration is affected, your time is more precious and allowance must be made for this. Being smart about the way you handle problems will enable you to stay on the course and means the problems will have far less impact on your final grades.

In a nutshell

All colleges have a wide range of support mechanisms and procedures in place that are invoked when problems occur. Take advantage of all the help you can get if you have serious personal difficulties. This can be used to support you on the course until the problem passes and your life is nearer to normal again.

BTEC National Study Guide: Engineering. See page 325 for order details of individual texts

14

Unit 3 Science for technicians

This unit aims to provide you with a foundation in scientific principles, which will enable you to tackle and solve a variety of unique engineering problems at the technician level. After successfully working your way through the subject matter presented in this unit, you will also find that you are adequately prepared for further study of your chosen specialist engineering science units, in addition to having the necessary scientific base for progression onto higher education engineering programmes.

You will be introduced to the *outcomes* that make up the unit, that is: elementary mechanics, the nature of energy, electrical principles and a brief introduction to engineering systems. In the first outcome on mechanics, we consider the way in which *forces* act on rigid bodies, this area of mechanics is known as *statics*. We then study bodies in motion or *dynamics*, where in particular we look at the *nature of the forces* that cause such motion.

The concept of *energy* is fundamental to our understanding of all science. We therefore, consider the major forms of energy, work and power which are particularly applicable to our study of engineering. We look in particular at the various forms of mechanical energy and then at heat energy, leaving electrical energy until we study the outcome on electrical principles.

In the outcome on electrical principles, as already mentioned, we start by considering the nature of *electrical energy.* We then look at *DC circuits* and *magnetism* where, in the latter topic, we investigate the principles of electrical machines.

In the final outcome of the unit we will briefly study engineering systems, in particular we look at the nature of *closed-loop engineering systems* and their engineering uses. We then apply what we have learnt to three simple examples involving *electrical, hydraulic* and *pneumatic engineering systems.*

No study of science would be complete without considering the units of measurement that underpin the subject. For this reason a brief introduction to the *Système International d'unités* (SI) is included as part of the following section on fundamentals.

Fundamentals

Before embarking on our study of the unit outcomes, we first consider some fundamental scientific properties such as mass, matter, weight, etc., in addition to an initial look at the SI system of units. This section may be treated as revision for those who have already successfully studied Physics or Engineering Science at GCSE or First Diploma level. For those new to the subject, this section will

BTEC National Study Guide: Engineering. See page 325 for order details of individual texts

15

provide a useful glossary of essential fundamental concepts, which underpin all that follows.

Units

The SI system of units is now the accepted international standard for all units of scientific measure. It has been legally accepted in America even though it has not been fully adopted – the American preference still being for the old English or imperial system of measurement. All scientific concepts and science teaching in the UK, as well as throughout Europe and many other areas of the world, has legally adopted the SI system and so these units will be used throughout this book for scientific and technological applications.

The International System of Units (SI) consists of three main groups: seven base units, two supplementary units and a number of derived units. Table 3.1 shows the seven base units by *dimension*, *SI name* and *symbol*. Do not worry too much at this stage about *dimension*, you will meet this concept in your later studies. Suffice to say at this stage that, for example: *length* has the *dimension L, no matter what units of length are being considered*. So it does not matter whether we measure the length in miles, metres, kilometres or knots, they all have the same dimension, that of length. The full scientific definitions of these units, as defined by the International Committee for Weights and Measures (CIPM), are given below. You might find these definitions rather strange. They are, however, true and accurate definitions of these quantities we know so well! Do not worry too much if you cannot understand these definitions at this time. Treat this section on units, *as a source of reference*, that is always here for you when needed.

Table 3.1 *SI base units*

Basic quantity/dimension		SI unit name	SI unit symbol
Mass	M	Kilogram	kg
Length	L	Metre	m
Time	T	Second	s
Electric current	I	Ampere	A
Temperature	Θ	Kelvin	K
Amount of substance	N	Mole	mol
Luminous intensity	J	Candela	cd

Kilogram

The kilogram or kilogramme is the unit of mass; it is equal to the mass of the international prototype of the kilogram, as defined by CIPM.

Metre

The metre is the length of the path travelled by light in a vacuum during the time interval of 1/299 792 458 seconds.

BTEC National Study Guide: Engineering. See page 325 for order details of individual texts

16

Second

The second is the duration of 9 192 631 770 periods of radiation corresponding to the transition between the two hyperfine levels of the ground state of the cesium 133 atom.

Ampere

The ampere is that constant current which if maintained in two straight parallel conductors of infinite length, of negligible circular cross-section, and placed 1 metre apart in a vacuum, would produce between these conductors a force equal to 2×10^{-7} newton per metre length.

Kelvin

The kelvin, unit of thermodynamic temperature, is the fraction 1/273.16 of the thermodynamic temperature of the triple point of water.

Mole

The mole is the amount of substance of a system which contains as many elementary particles as there are atoms in 0.012 kg of carbon 12. When the mole is used, the elementary entities must be specified and may be atoms, molecules, ions, electrons, or other particles, or specified groups of such particles.

Candela

The candela is the luminious intensity, in a given direction, of a source that emits monochromatic radiation of frequency 540×10^{12} Hz and that has a radiant intensity in that direction of 1/683 watt per steradian (see below).

In addition to the seven base units given above, as mentioned before there are two supplementary units, the radian for plane angles (which you will meet later) and the steradian for solid three-dimensional angles (Table 3.2). Both of these units are non-dimensional, that is they are ratios and have a dimension of unity (1). In fact *all ratios are non-dimensional*, for example if we divide a distance with dimension L by another distant with dimension L, we have dimension $L/L = 1$. *Ratios* also *have no units*, for the same reason as above, e.g. metres/metres = 1. Again, do not worry too much at this stage, it may become clearer later, when we look at radian measures in our study of dynamics.

Table 3.2 *SI supplementary units*

Supplementary unit	SI unit name	SI unit symbol
Plane angle	Radian	rad
Solid angle	Steradian	srad

The SI derived units are defined by simple equations relating two or more base units. The names and symbols of some of the

BTEC National Study Guide: Engineering. See page 325 for order details of individual texts

17

derived units may be substituted by special names and symbols. Some of the derived units, which you may be familiar with, are listed in Table 3.3 with their special names as appropriate.

Table 3.3 *SI derived units*

Name	Symbol	Physical quantity	Dimension	Equivalent in SI base units
Coulomb	C	Quantity of electricity, electric charge	IT	$1\ C = 1\ A.s$
Farad	F	Electric capacitance	$M^{-1}L^{-2}T^4I^2$	$1\ F = 1\ kg^{-1}.m^{-2}.s^4.A^2$
Henry	H	Electrical inductance	$ML^2T^{-2}I^{-2}$	$1\ H = 1\ kg.m^2.s^2.A^{-2}$
Hertz	Hz	Frequency	T^{-1}	$1\ H = 1\ s^{-1}$
Joule	J	Energy, work, heat	ML^2T^{-2}	$1\ J = 1\ kg.m^2.s^{-2}$
Lux	Lx	Illuminance	$J\Omega L^{-2}$	$1\ lx = 1\ cd.sr.m^{-2}$
Newton	N	Force, weight	MLT^{-2}	$1\ N = 1\ kg.ms^{-2}$
Ohm	Ω	Electrical resistance	$ML^2T^{-3}I^{-2}$	$1\ \Omega = 1\ kg.m^2.s^{-3}.A^{-2}$
Pascal	Pa	Pressure, stress	$ML^{-1}T^{-2}$	$1\ Pa = 1\ kg.m^{-1}.s^{-2}$
Siemen	S	Electrical conductance	$M^{-1}L^{-2}T^3I^2$	$1\ S = 1\ kg^{-1}.m^{-2}.s^3.A^2$
Tesla	T	Induction field, magnetic flux density	$MT^{-2}I^{-1}$	$1\ T = 1\ kg.A^{-1}.s^{-2}$
Volt	V	Electric potential, electromotive force	$ML^2T^{-3}I^{-1}$	$1\ V = 1\ kg.m^2.s^{-3}.A^{-1}$
Watt	W	Power, radiant flux	ML^2T^{-3}	$1\ W = 1\ kg.m^2.s^{-3}$
Weber	Wb	Induction magnetic flux	$ML^2T^{-2}I^{-1}$	$1\ Wb = 1\ kg.m^2.s^{-2}.A^{-1}$

You will be introduced to many of these units as you progress through this chapter and you will be asked to use them when solving problems. The SI is a decimal system of units where fractions have been eliminated, so multiples and submultiples are formed from a series of prefixes. That is, we multiple the original unit by powers of ten for units greater than one and by decimal fractions of ten for numbers less than one. Some of these multiples (with which I am sure you are familiar) are detailed in Table 3.4.

Table 3.4 *SI prefixes*

Prefix	Symbol	Multiply by
peta	P	10^{15}
tera	T	10^{12}
giga	G	10^9
mega	M	10^6
kilo	k	10^3
hecto	h	10^2
deca	da	10^1
deci	d	10^{-1}
centi	c	10^{-2}
milli	m	10^{-3}
micro	μ	10^{-6}
nano	n	10^{-9}
pico	p	10^{-12}
femto	f	10^{-15}

So, for example: 1 millimetre = 1 mm = 10^{-3} m, 1 cm^3 = $(10^{-2}$ m$)^3$ = 10^{-6} m^3 and 1 mm = 10^{-6} m. Note the way in which powers of ten are used. The above examples show us the correct way for representing multiples and submultiples of units.

BTEC National Study Guide: Engineering. See page 325 for order details of individual texts

18

Finally, before we leave our short study on units you should be aware of some commonly used, legally accepted, *non-SI units*. These are detailed in Table 3.5.

Table 3.5 *Non-SI units*

Name	Symbol	Physical quantity	Dimension	Equivalent in SI base units
Ampere-hour	Ah	Electric charge	IT	1 Ah = 3600 C
Day	d	Time, period	T	1 d = 86 400 s
Degree	°	Plane angle	α	1° = π/180 rad
Electronvolt	eV	Electric potential	$ML^2T^{-3}I^{-1}$	1 eV = (e/C) J
Kilometre per hour	kph	Velocity	LT^{-1}	1 kph = (1/3.6) m s^{-1}
Hour	h	Time, period	T	1 h = 3600 s
Litre	L, l	Capacity, volume	L^3	1 L = 10^{-3} m^3
Minute	Min	Time, period	T	1 min = 60 s
Metric tonne	t	Mass	M	1 t = 10^3 kg

Note that velocity in kilometres per hour is a *derived unit*, that is, made up from the units of length (distance) and time.

Having briefly introduced the idea of units of measurement, we are now going to consider some fundamental quantities such as mass, force, weight, density, pressure, temperature, the nature of matter and the concept of energy, which plays a vital role in our understanding of science in general. Knowledge of these fundamental physical parameters will be required when we look in detail at the outcomes of the unit.

Mass, weight and gravity

Mass

The *mass* of a body is a measure of the *quantity of matter* in the body. The amount of matter in a body does not change when the position of the body changes so, *the mass of a body does not change with position*.

As can be seen from Table 3.1, the SI unit of mass is the kilogram (kg). The standard kilogram is the mass of a block of platinum alloy kept at the Office of Weights and Measures in Sèvres near Paris.

Weight

The weight of a body is the gravitational *force* of attraction between the mass of the earth and the mass of a body. The weight of a body decreases as the body is moved away from the earth's centre. It obeys the inverse square law, which states that if the distance of the body is doubled, the weight is reduced to a quarter of its previous value. The SI unit of weight is the newton (N).

Using mathematical symbols this law may be written as:

weight $(W) \propto 1/d^2$

where d = distance and $\propto$ is the symbol for proportionality.

BTEC National Study Guide: Engineering. See page 325 for order details of individual texts

19

Key point

The mass of a body is un-affected by its position.

Key point

In the SI system, weight is measured in newtons (N).

Key point

At sea level, the acceleration due to gravity, g, is approximately 9.81 m/s^2.

So, for example, consider a body of weight (W) at an initial distance of 50 m from the gravitational source, then: $W \propto (1/50)^2 = 4 \times 10^{-4}$.

Now if we double this distance then the weight (W) $\propto (1/100)^2 = 1 \times 10^{-4}$, which clearly shows that if the distance is doubled the weight is reduced to a quarter of its original value.

Gravitational acceleration

When a body is allowed to fall it moves towards the earth's centre with an acceleration caused by the weight of the body. If air resistance is ignored, then at the same altitude all bodies fall with the same gravitational acceleration. Although heavier bodies have more weight, at the same altitude they fall with the same gravitational acceleration because of their greater resistance to acceleration. The concept of resistance to acceleration will be explained more fully when we deal with Newton's laws of motion.

Like weight, gravitational acceleration depends on distance from the earth's centre. At sea level *gravitational acceleration* (g) has an accepted standard value of **9.80665 m s^{-2}**. For the purpose of calculations in this unit, we will use the approximation $g = 9.81$ m s^{-2}.

The mass–weight relationship

From what has already been said, we may define the weight of a body as the product of its mass and the value of gravitational acceleration at the position of the body. This is expressed in symbols as:

$$W = mg$$

where in the SI system the weight (W) is in newtons (N) the mass is in kilograms (kg) and the acceleration due to gravity is taken as 9.81 m s^{-2} unless specified differently.

We now know that the mass of a body does not change with changes in altitude but its weight and gravitational acceleration do. However, for bodies that do not move outside the earth's atmosphere, the changes in gravitational acceleration (and therefore weight) are small enough to be ignored for most practical purposes. We may therefore assume our approximation for $g = 9.81$ m s^{-2} to be reasonably accurate, unless told otherwise.

To clarify the mass–weight relationship let us consider an example calculation, using standard SI units.

Example 3.1

A missile having a mass of 25 000 kg is launched from sea level on a course for the moon. If the gravitational acceleration of the moon is one-sixth that on earth, determine:

(a) the weight of the rocket at launch
(b) the mass of the rocket on reaching the moon
(c) the weight of the rocket on reaching the moon.

BTEC National Study Guide: Engineering. See page 325 for order details of individual texts

20

Test your knowledge 3.1

1. Complete the entries in the table of SI base units shown below:

Base quantity	SI unit name	SI unit symbol
Mass		kg
	Metre	m
Time	Second	
	Ampere	A
Temperature	Kelvin	
Amount of substance		mol
	Candela	cd

2. What is the SI unit for plane angles?
3. What happens to the weight of a body as it is moved away from the centre of the earth?
4. What is the SI unit of weight?
5. What is the approximate value for the acceleration due to gravity at sea level?

Key point

The density of pure water at 4°C is taken as 1000 kg/m³.

Test your knowledge 3.2

1. What is the SI unit of density?
2. Use Table 3.6 to determine the weight of 2 m³ of sodium.
3. What is likely to happen to the density of pure water as its temperature increases?
4. Why does relative density have no units?
5. Approximately how much would a cubic metre of lead weigh on the moon?

(a) Using the relationship $W = mg$, then the weight on earth:

$W = (25\,000 \times 9.81) = 245\,250$ N or **245.25 kN**

(b) We know from our definition of mass, that it does not change with change in position therefore the mass on the moon remains the same as on earth, i.e. **25 000 kg**.

(c) We know that the gravitational acceleration on the moon is approximately one-sixth that on earth.

So $g_m = 9.81/6$ m s^{-2} = 1.635 m s^{-2} and again from $W = mg_m$ then weight of rocket on the moon = $(25\,000 \times 1.635)$ = 40\,875 N = **40.875 kN**

Note that a much easier method of solution for part (c) would have been to divide the weight on earth by 6.

Density and relative density

Density

The density (ρ) of a body is defined as its mass per unit volume. Combining the SI units for mass and volume gives the unit of density as kg m^{-3}. Using symbols the formula for density is given as:

$$\rho = \frac{m}{V}$$

where again the mass is in kilograms (kg) and the volume is in m³.

Relative density

The relative density of a body is the *ratio* of the density of the body with that of the density of pure water measured at 4°C. The density of water under these conditions is 1000 kg m^{-3}. Since relative density is a ratio it has *no units*. The old name for relative density was *specific gravity* (SG) and this is something you need to be aware of in case you meet this terminology in the future.

The density of some of the more common engineering elements and materials is laid out in Table 3.6. To find the relative density of any element or material divide its density by 1000 kg m^{-3}.

Example 3.2

A mild steel component has a mass of 240 grams. Using the density of mild steel given in Table 3.6, calculate the volume of the component in cm³.

From the table mild steel has a density of 7850 kg m^{-3}, therefore using our definition for density:

Since $\rho = \frac{m}{V}$, then $V = \frac{m}{\rho} = \frac{240 \times 10^{-3}}{7850} = 3.057 \times 10^{-3}\ m^3$

Thus, volume of component = **30.57 cm³**

BTEC National Study Guide: Engineering. See page 325 for order details of individual texts

21

Table 3.6 *Density of some engineering elements/materials*

Element/Material	Density (kg/m^3)	Element/Material	Density (kg/m^3)
Acrylic	1200	Nickel	8900
Aluminium	2700	Nitrogen	0.125
Boron	2340	Nylon	1150
Brass	8400–8600	Oxygen	0.143
Cadmium	8650	Platinum	21450
Cast iron	7350	Polycarbonate	914–960
Chromium	7190	Polyethylene	1300–1500
Concrete	2400	Rubber	860–2000
Copper	8960	Sodium	971
Glass	2400–2800	Stainless steel	7905
Gold	19 320	Tin	7300
Hydrogen	0.09	Titanium	4507
Iron	7870	Tungsten	1900
Lead	11 340	UPVC	19 300
Magnesium	1740	Vanadium	6100
Manganese	7430	Wood (Douglas fir)	608
Mercury	13 600	Wood (oak)	690
Mild steel	7850	Zinc	7130

Note that to obtain the standard unit for mass, the 240 grams was converted to kilograms using the multiplier 10^{-3} and, multiplying m^3 by 10^6 converts them into cm^3, as required. Be careful with your conversion factors when dealing with squared or cubic measure!

Example 3.3

An engineering component made from an aluminium alloy weighs 16 N and has a volume of 600 cm^3, determine the relative density of the alloy.

We need to use the mass–weight relationship $m = \dfrac{W}{g}$ to find the mass of the component,

i.e. mass, $m = \dfrac{16}{9.81} = 1.631$ kg

Then, density $= \dfrac{m}{V} = \dfrac{1.631}{600 \times 10^{-6}} = 2.718$ kg m^{-3}

The relative density (RD) is then given by RD $= \dfrac{2718 \text{ kg m}^{-3}}{1000 \text{ kg m}^{-3}}$

= 2.718

Force

In its simplest sense a force is a push or pull exerted by one object on another. In a member in a static structure, a push causes

BTEC National Study Guide: Engineering. See page 325 for order details of individual texts

22

compression and a pull causes tension. Members subject to compressive and tensile forces have special names. A member of a structure that is in *compression* is known as a *strut* and a member in *tension* is called a *tie*.

Only rigid members of a structure have the capacity to act as both a strut and tie. Flexible members, such as ropes, wires or chains, can act only as ties.

Force cannot exist without opposition, as you will see later when you study Newton's laws. An applied force is called an *action* and the opposing force it produces is called *reaction*.

The effects of any force depend on its three characteristics, illustrated in Figure 3.1.

> **Key point**
>
> The *action* of a force always produces an *opposite reaction*.

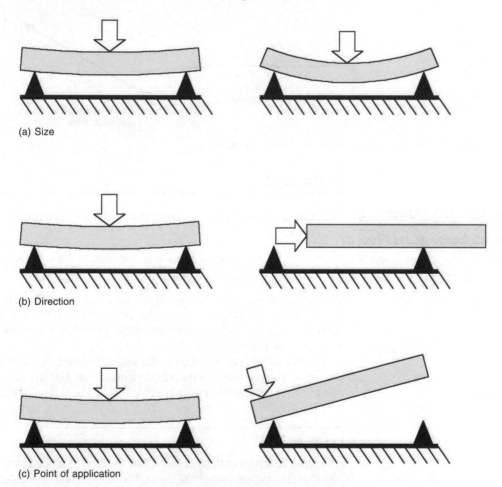

(a) Size

(b) Direction

(c) Point of application

Figure 3.1 *Characteristics of a force*

In general force (F) = mass (m) × acceleration (a) is used as the measure of force.

$$F = ma$$

The SI unit of force is the newton (N). Note that weight force mentioned earlier is a special case where the acceleration acting on the mass is that due to gravity, so *weight force* may be defined as $F = mg$, as mentioned earlier. The newton is thus defined as follows:

BTEC National Study Guide: Engineering. See page 325 for order details of individual texts

23

1 newton is the force that gives a mass of 1 kg an acceleration of 1 m s^{-2}.

It can be seen from Figure 3.1 that a force has size (magnitude), direction and a point of application. A force is thus a *vector quantity*, that is, it has magnitude and direction. A *scalar* quantity has only magnitude, for example mass. A force may therefore be represented graphically in two dimensions by drawing an arrow to scale with its length representing the magnitude of a force and the head of the arrow indicating the direction in relation to a set of previously defined axes. Figure 3.2 illustrates the graphical representation of a force.

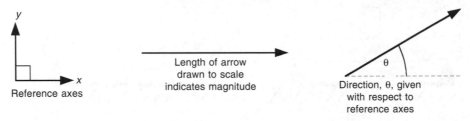

Figure 3.2 *Graphical representation of a force*

Pressure

Pressure, due to the application of force or load, is defined as force per unit area.

$$pressure = \frac{force \text{ or load applied perpendicular to a surface}}{area \text{ over which the force or thrust acts}}$$

The units of pressure in the SI system are normally given as: N m^{-2}, N mm^{-2}, MN m^{-2} or pascal (Pa) where 1 Pa = 1 N m^{-2}. Also pressures in fluid systems are often quoted in bar, where 1 bar = 10^5 Pa, or 100 000 N m^{-2}.

The bar should not be taken as the value for standard atmospheric pressure at sea level. The value quoted in bar for *standard atmospheric pressure* is 1.0132 bar or 101 320 N m^{-2} or 101.32 kPa.

Example 3.4

The area of ground surface contained by the skirt of a hovercraft is 240 m^2. The unladen weight of the craft is 480 kN and total laden weight is 840 kN. Determine the minimum air pressure needed in the skirt to support the craft when unladen and when fully loaded.

When unloaded: pressure = force area = $\dfrac{480 \text{ kN}}{240 \text{ m}^2}$ = **2 kN m^{-2}**

When fully loaded: pressure = $\dfrac{840 \text{ kN}}{240 \text{ m}^2}$ = **3.5 kN m^{-2}**

In practice the skirt would be inflated to the higher of these two pressures and the craft (when static) would rest in the water, at the appropriate level.

BTEC National Study Guide: Engineering. See page 325 for order details of individual texts

24

Temperature

Temperature is a measure of the quantity of energy possessed by a body or substance, it is a measure of the molecular vibrations within the body. The more energetic these vibrations become, the hotter will be the body or substance. For this reason, in its simplest sense, temperature may be regarded as the 'degree of hotness of a body'. We will look more closely at the concept of temperature when we study heat energy.

Problems 3.1

1. A rocket launched into the earth's atmosphere is subject to an acceleration due to gravity of 5.2 m s^{-2}. If the rocket has a mass of 120000 kg, determine:

   (a) the weight of the rocket on earth
   (b) the weight of the rocket in orbit.

2. A solid rectangular body measures 1.5 m × 20 cm × 3 cm and has a mass of 54 kg. Calculate:

   (a) its volume in m^3
   (b) its density in Pa
   (c) its relative density.

3. A fuel storage depot consists of four fuel tanks. Two tanks each have a volume of 20 m^3 and the other two tanks each have a volume of 30 m^3. The fuel used in the depot has a relative density (RD) of 0.85. Determine the weight of fuel when all the tanks are full.

4. A body has a weight of 550 N on the surface of the earth.

   (a) What force is required to give it an acceleration of 6 m s^{-2}?
   (b) What will be the inertia reaction of the body when given this acceleration?

Matter

We have already defined *mass* as the amount of matter in a body but what is the nature of this matter?

All *matter* or *material* is made up from elementary building blocks that we know as atoms and molecules. The *atom* may be further subdivided into *protons*, *neutrons* and *electrons*. Physicists have discovered many more elementary subatomic particles that, for the purposes of this discussion, we do not need to consider.

A *molecule* consists of a collection of two or more atoms, which are joined chemically, in a certain way, to give the material its macroscopic properties. The act of joining atoms and/or joining molecules to form parent material is known as *chemical bonding*.

BTEC National Study Guide: Engineering. See page 325 for order details of individual texts

25

The driving force that encourages atoms and molecules to combine in certain ways is *energy*. Like everything else in nature, matter or material is formed as a consequence of the atoms and/or molecules combining in such a way that, once formed, attain their lowest energy state. We may define *energy* as the capacity to do work. Like nature, we measure our efficiency with respect to work, in terms of the least amount of energy we expend.

The states of matter

Matter exists in *three states*; each state is due to the struggle between the interatomic or intermolecular binding forces and the motion that these atoms and/or molecules have because of their own *internal energy*.

Solids

When matter is chemically bonded together there are *forces of attraction* which bind the atoms and molecules together. Also at very short distances from the centre of the adjacent atoms there are *repulsion forces*. Now, whether or not the force of attraction or repulsion dominates, depends on the atomic distance between the atoms/molecules when combined. It has been shown that at distances greater than one atomic diameter the forces of attraction dominate, while at very small separation distances, the reverse is true. In solids the forces of attraction and repulsion tend to balance each other out. Thus in a solid, if the atoms are brought closer by compression, they will repel each other and if pulled further apart they attract.

Liquids

As temperature increases the *amplitude* (size) of the internal vibration energy of the atoms increases, until they are able to partly overcome the interatomic bonding forces of their immediate neighbours. For short spells they are within range of forces exerted by other atoms which are not quite so near. There is less order and so the solid liquefies. Although the atoms and molecules of a liquid are not much further apart than in a solid, they have greater speeds due to increased temperature and so move randomly in the liquid, while continuing to vibrate. However, the primary differences between liquids and solids may be attributed to *differences in structure*, rather than distance between the atoms. It is these differences in the forces between the molecules which give the liquid its flow characteristics while at the same time holding it sufficiently together, to exhibit shape, within a containing vessel.

Gases

In a gas the atoms and molecules move randomly with high speeds and take up all the space in the containing vessel. Gas molecules are therefore relatively far apart when compared with solids and liquids. Because of the relatively large distances involved, molecular interaction occurs only for those brief spells when molecules collide and large repulsive forces operate between them.

The idea of a gas filling the vessel in which it is contained has its origins in Newton's first law of motion. Each molecule will, in

---

Key point

Matter is generally considered to exist in solid, liquid and gaseous forms.

Key point

The atoms within solids tend to combine in such a manner that the interatomic binding forces are balanced by the very short range repulsion forces.

Key point

Gases always fill the available space of the vessel into which they are introduced.

Test your knowledge 3.4

1. Explain the essential difference between solids and liquids.
2. Over what sort of distances do the atomic repulsion forces act?
3. How is the *internal energy* within matter defined?

BTEC National Study Guide: Engineering. See page 325 for order details of individual texts

26

accordance with this law, travel in a straight line until it collides with another molecule or with the sides of the containing vessel. Therefore, a gas has no particular shape or volume but expands until it fills any vessel into which it is introduced.

MECHANICS

Mechanics is the physical science concerned with the state of rest or motion of bodies under the action of forces. This subject has played a major role in the development of engineering throughout history and up to the present day. Modern research and development in the fields of vibration analysis, structures, machines, spacecraft, automatic control, engine performance, fluid flow, electrical apparatus and subatomic, atomic and molecular behaviour are all reliant on the basic principles of mechanics.

The subject of mechanics is conveniently divided into two major areas: *statics*, which is concerned with the equilibrium of rigid bodies under the action of forces, and *dynamics*, which is concerned with the motion of bodies under the action of forces. Dynamics may be further subdivided into the motion of rigid bodies and the motion of fluids.

Statics

Vector representation of forces

You have already met the concept of *force* when we looked at some important fundamentals. You will remember that the effect of a force was dependent on its magnitude, direction and point of application (Figure 3.1), and that a force may be represented on paper as a *vector* quantity (Figure 3.2).

We will now study the vector representation of a force or combination of forces in more detail, noting that all vector quantities throughout this book will be identified using emboldened text.

In addition to possessing the properties of magnitude and direction from a given reference (Figure 3.2), vectors must obey the *parallelogram law* of combination. This law requires that two vectors v_1 and v_2 may be replaced by their equivalent vector v_T which is the diagonal of the parallelogram formed by v_1 and v_2 as shown in Figure 3.3(a). This vector sum is represented by the vector equation:

$$v_T = v_1 + v_2$$

Note that the plus sign in this equation refers to the addition of two vectors, and should not be confused with ordinary scalar addition, which is simply the sum of the magnitudes of these two vectors and is written as $v_T = v_1 + v_2$, in the normal way without emboldening.

Vectors may also be added head-to-tail using the *triangle law* as shown in Figure 3.3(b). It can also be seen from Figure 3.3(c) that the order in which vectors are added does not affect their sum.

The vector difference $v_1 - v_2$ is obtained by *adding* $-v_2$ to v_1. The effect of the minus sign is to reverse the direction of the vector v_2 (Figure 3.3(d)). The vectors v_1 and v_2 are known as the components of the vector v_T.

Key point

Two vectors may be added using the parallelogram rule or triangle rule.

BTEC National Study Guide: Engineering. See page 325 for order details of individual texts

27

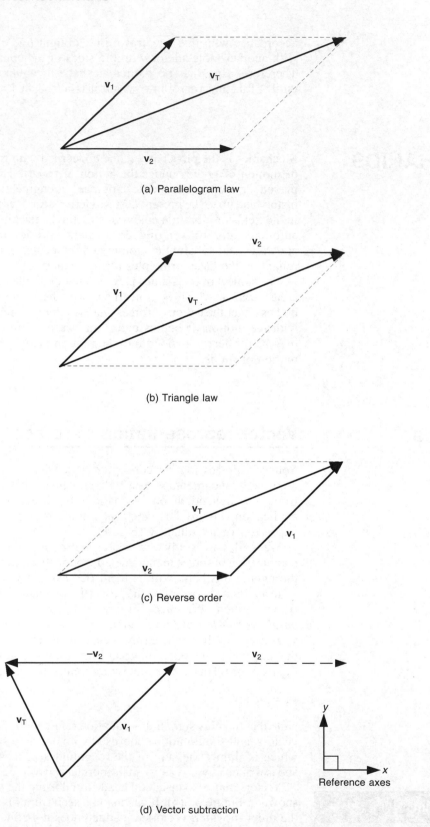

(a) Parallelogram law

(b) Triangle law

(c) Reverse order

(d) Vector subtraction

Figure 3.3 *Vector addition and subtraction*

BTEC National Study Guide: Engineering. See page 325 for order details of individual texts

28

Example 3.5

Two forces act at a point as shown in Figure 3.4. Find by vector addition their *resultant* (their single equivalent force).

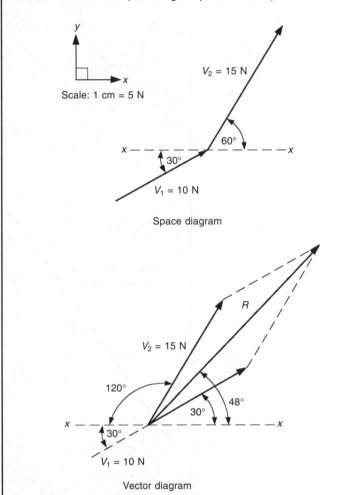

Space diagram

Vector diagram

Figure 3.4 *Vector addition using the parallelogram law*

From the vector diagram the resultant vector **R** is 4.8 cm in magnitude which (from the scale) is equivalent to 24 N. So the resultant vector **R** has a magnitude of 24 N at an angle of 48°.

Note that a *space diagram* is first drawn to indicate the orientation of the forces with respect to the reference axes; these axes should always be shown. Also note that the *line of action* of vector **v₁** passing through the point 0, is shown in the space diagram and may lie anywhere on this line, as indicated on the vector diagram.

Example 3.6

Find the resultant of the system of forces shown in Figure 3.5, using vector addition.

BTEC National Study Guide: Engineering. See page 325 for order details of individual texts

29

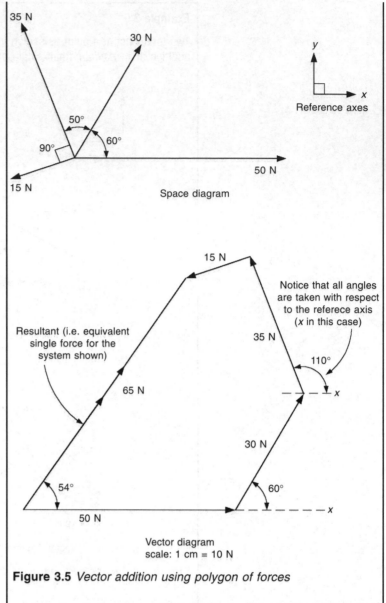

Figure 3.5 *Vector addition using polygon of forces*

From the diagram the resultant = 6.5 cm = 6.5 × 10 N = 65 N. Acting at an angle of 54° from the *x*-reference axis. This result may be written mathematically as resultant = 65 N ∠54°.

Note that for the force system in Example 3.6 vector addition has produced a polygon. Any number of forces may be added vectorially in any order, providing the *head-to-tail rule* is observed. In this example, if we were to add the vectors in reverse order, the same result would be achieved.

If a force, or system of forces, is acting on a body and is balanced by some other force, or system of forces, then the body is said to be in *equilibrium*, so, for example, a stationary body is in equilibrium.

The *equilibrant* of a system of forces is that force which, when added to a system, produces equilibrium. It has been shown in Examples 3.5 and 3.6 that the resultant is the single force which

BTEC National Study Guide: Engineering. See page 325 for order details of individual texts

30

will replace an existing system of forces and produce the same effect. It therefore follows that if the equilibrant is to produce equilibrium it must be equal in magnitude and direction, but opposite in sense to the resultant, Figure 3.6 illustrates this point.

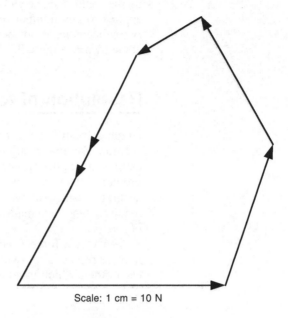

Scale: 1 cm = 10 N

Figure 3.6   *Equilibrant for Example 3.6*

Bow's notation is a convenient system of labelling the forces for ease of reference, when there are three or more forces to be considered. Capital letters are placed in the space between forces in a clockwise direction, as shown in Figure 3.7.

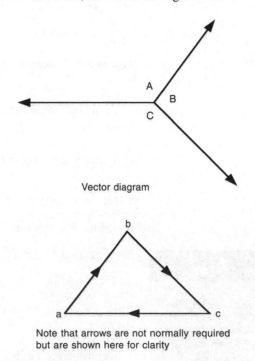

Vector diagram

Note that arrows are not normally required
but are shown here for clarity

Figure 3.7   *Bow's notation*

BTEC National Study Guide: Engineering. See page 325 for order details of individual texts

31

Any force is then referred to by the letters that lie in the adjacent spaces either side of the vector arrow representing that force. The vectors representing the forces are then given the corresponding *lower case* letters. Thus the forces AB, BC and CA are represented by the vectors ab, bc and ca, respectively. This method of labelling applies to any number of forces and their corresponding vectors. Arrowheads need not be used when this notation is adopted, but are shown in Figure 3.7 for clarity.

Resolution of forces

Graphical solutions to problems involving forces are sufficiently accurate for many engineering problems and are invaluable for estimating approximate solutions to more complicated force problems. However, it is sometimes necessary to provide more accurate results, in which case a mathematical method will be required. One such mathematical method is known as the *resolution of forces*.

Consider a force F acting on a bolt (Figure 3.8). The force F may be replaced by two forces P and Q, acting at right angles to each other, which together have the same effect on the bolt.

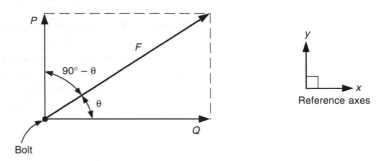

Figure 3.8 *Resolving force F into its components*

From our knowledge of the trigonometric ratios (Unit 4) we know that:

$$\frac{Q}{F} = \cos \theta \text{ and so } Q = F \cos \theta$$

Also, $\frac{P}{F} = \cos(90 - \theta)$ and we know that $\cos(90 - \theta) = \sin \theta$

therefore $P = F \sin \theta$

So from Figure 3.8, $P = F \sin \theta$ and $Q = F \cos \theta$

So the single force F has been resolved or split into two equivalent forces of magnitude $F \cos \theta$ and $F \sin \theta$, which act at right angles (they are said to be *orthogonal* to each other). $F \cos \theta$ is known as the *horizontal component of F* and $F \sin \theta$ is known as the *vertical component of F*.

Determination of the resultant or equilibrant using the resolution method is best illustrated by example.

Key point

The resultant of two or more forces is that force which, acting alone, would produce the same effect as the other forces acting together.

BTEC National Study Guide: Engineering. See page 325 for order details of individual texts

32

Example 3.7

Three *coplanar forces* (forces that act within the same plane), *A*, *B* and *C*, are all applied to a pin joint (Figure 3.9(a)). Determine the magnitude and direction of the equilibrant for the system.

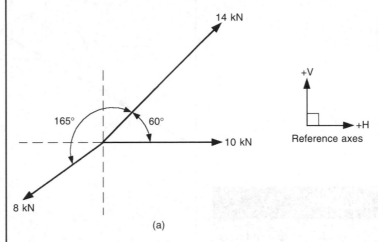

(a)

Figure 3.9(a) *Space diagram*

Each force needs to be resolved into its two orthogonal components, which act along the vertical and horizontal axes respectively. Using the normal algebraic sign convention with our axes then, above the origin, *V* is positive and below it is negative. Similarly, *H* is positive to the right of the origin and negative to the left. Using this convention we need only consider acute angles for the sine and cosine functions; these are tabulated below.

Magnitude of force	Horizontal component	Vertical component
10 kN	+10 kN ($\rightarrow$)	0
14 kN	+14 cos 60 kN ($\rightarrow$)	+14 sin 60 kN ($\uparrow$)
8 kN	− 8 cos 45 kN ($\leftarrow$)	−8 sin 45 kN ($\downarrow$)

Then total horizontal component = 10 + 7 − 5.66 kN = 11.34 kN ($\rightarrow$)

and total vertical component = 0 + 12.22 − 5.66 kN = 6.46 kN ($\uparrow$)

Since both the horizontal and vertical components are positive the resultant force will act upwards to the right of the origin. The three original forces have now been reduced to two which act orthogonally. The magnitude of the resultant *R*, or the equilibrant, may now be obtained using Pythagoras' theorem on the right angle triangle obtained from the orthogonal vectors, as shown in Figure 3.9(b).

From Pythagoras we get $R^2 = 6.46^2 + 11.34^2 = 170.33$ and so resultant *R* = 13.05 kN, so the magnitude of the *equilibrant* also = 13.05 kN.

From the right angled triangle shown in Figure 3.9(b), the angle θ that the resultant *R* makes with the given axes may be calculated using the trigonometric ratios.

Then $\tan \theta = \dfrac{6.46}{11.34} = 0.5697$ and θ = 29.67°

BTEC National Study Guide: Engineering. See page 325 for order details of individual texts

33

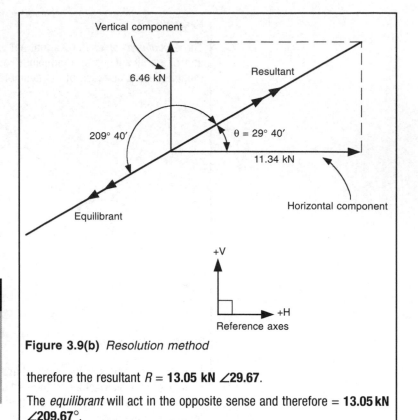

Figure 3.9(b) *Resolution method*

therefore the resultant R = **13.05 kN** $\angle$**29.67**.

The *equilibrant* will act in the opposite sense and therefore = **13.05 kN** $\angle$**209.67°**.

To complete our initial study on the resolution of forces, we consider one final example concerned with *equilibrium on a smooth plane*. Smooth in this case implies that the effects of friction may be ignored. When we study dynamics latter on in this unit, friction and its effects will be covered in some detail.

A body is kept in equilibrium on a plane by the action of three forces as shown in Figure 3.10, these are:

1. the *weight W* of the body acting vertically down
2. *reaction R* of the plane to the weight of the body. *R* is known as the *normal reaction*, normal in this sense means at right angles to, the plane in this case
3. *force P* acting in some suitable direction to prevent the body sliding down the plane.

Forces *P* and *R* are dependent on:

*   the angle of inclination of the plane
*   the magnitude of *W*
*   the inclination of the force *P* to the plane.

It is therefore possible to express the magnitude of both *P* and *R* in terms of *W* and the trigonometric ratios connecting the angle θ.

In the example that follows we consider the case when the body remains in equilibrium as a result of the force *P* being applied parallel to the plane.

BTEC National Study Guide: Engineering. See page 325 for order details of individual texts

34

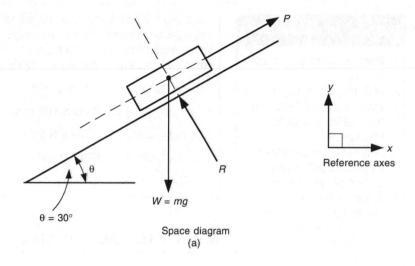

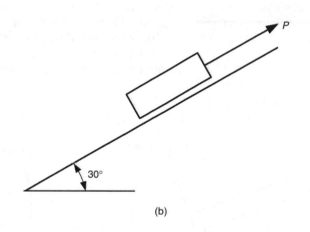

Space diagram
(a)

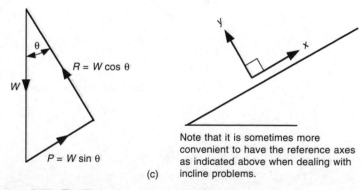

(b)

$R = W\cos\theta$

W

$P = W\sin\theta$

(c)

Note that it is sometimes more convenient to have the reference axes as indicated above when dealing with incline problems.

Figure 3.10 *Equilibrium on a smooth plane*

Example 3.8

A crate of mass 80 kg is held in equilibrium by a force *P* acting parallel to the plane as indicated in Figure 3.10(a). Determine, using the resolution method, the magnitude of the force *P* and the normal reaction *R*, ignoring the effects of friction.

Figure 3.10(b) shows the space diagram for the problem clearly

BTEC National Study Guide: Engineering. See page 325 for order details of individual texts

35

Test your knowledge 3.5

1. What is meant by *coplanar* forces?
2. With respect to a system of coplanar forces define: (a) the equilibrant and (b) the resultant.
3. Determine the conditions for static equilibrium of a system of coplanar forces.
4. A body is held in static equilibrium on an inclined plane, ignoring friction, name and show the direction of the forces required to maintain the body in this state.

indicating the nature of the forces acting on the body. W may therefore be resolved into the two forces P and R. Since the force component at right angles to the plane = $W\cos\theta$ and the force component parallel to the plane = $W\sin\theta$ (Figure 3.10(c)).

Equating forces gives, $W\cos\theta = R$ and $W\sin\theta = P$

So, remembering the mass/weight relationship, we have:

$W = mg = (80)(9.81) = 784.8$ N then,

$R = 784.8\cos 30° = \mathbf{679.7\ N}$ and

$P = 784.8\sin 30° = \mathbf{392.4\ N}$

Moments and couples

A moment is a turning force producing a turning effect. The magnitude of this turning force depends on the size of the *force* applied and the *perpendicular distance* from the pivot or axis to the line of action of the force (Figure 3.11(a)).

Examples of a turning force are numerous: opening a door, using a spanner, turning the steering wheel of a motor vehicle, an

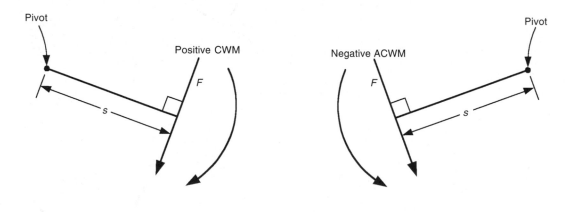

(a) Definition of a moment

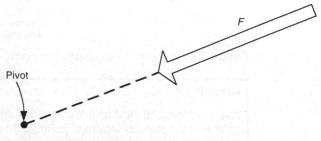

(b) Line of action passing through pivot point

Figure 3.11 *Moment of a force*

BTEC National Study Guide: Engineering. See page 325 for order details of individual texts

36

aircraft tailplane creating a nose-up and nose-down moment are just four examples.

The moment of a force M is defined as:

the product of the magnitude of force F and its perpendicular distance s from the pivot or axis to the line of action of the force.

This may be written mathematically as:

$M = Fs$

The SI unit for a moment is the *newton-metre* (N m).

Moments are always concerned with perpendicular distances.

From Figure 3.11(a), you should note that moments can be clockwise *CWM* or anticlockwise *ACWM*. Conventionally we consider clockwise moments to be positive and anticlockwise moments to be negative.

If the line of action of the force passes through the turning point it has no turning effect and so no moment, Figure 3.11(b) illustrates this point.

Key point

If the line of action passes through the turning point, it has no effect because the effective distance of the moment is zero.

Example 3.9

Figure 3.12 shows a spanner being used to loosen a nut. Determine the turning effect on the nut.

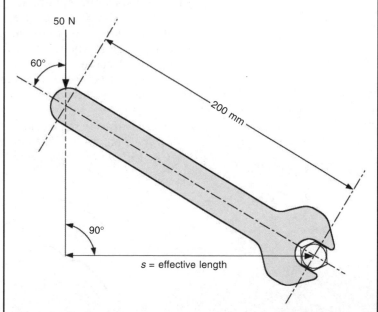

Figure 3.12 *Spanner and nut*

The turning effect on the nut is equal to the moment of the 50 N force about the nut, i.e.

$M = Fs$

Remembering that moments are always concerned with perpendicular distances, the distance s is the perpendicular distance or effective length of the spanner. This length is found using trigonometric ratios:

BTEC National Study Guide: Engineering. See page 325 for order details of individual texts

37

$s = 200 \sin 60°$, therefore $s = (200)(0.866) = 173.2$ mm

Then ACWM = $(50)(173.2) = 8660$ Nmm or 8.66 Nm

So the *turning effect* of the 50 N force acting on a 200 mm spanner at 60° to the centre line of the spanner = **8.66 N m**.

In engineering problems concerning moments you will meet terminology that is frequently used. You are already familiar with the terms CWM and ACWM. Set out below are three more frequently used terms that you are likely to encounter.

Fulcrum: the *fulcrum* is the point or axis about which rotation takes place. In Example 3.9 above, the geometrical centre of the nut is considered to be the fulcrum.

Moment arm: the perpendicular distance from the line of action of the force to the fulcrum is known as the *moment arm*.

Resulting moment: the *resulting moment* is the difference in magnitude between the total clockwise moment and the total anticlockwise moment. Note that if the body is in *static equilibrium* this *resultant will be zero*.

> **Key point**
>
> For static equilibrium the algebraic sum of the moments is zero.

When a body is in equilibrium there can be no resultant *force* acting on it. However, reference to Figure 3.13 shows that a body is not necessarily in equilibrium even when there is no resultant force acting on it. The resultant force on the body is zero but two forces would cause the body to rotate, as indicated. A second condition must be stated to ensure that a body is in equilibrium. This is known as the *principle of moments*, which states:

When a body is in static equilibrium under the action of a number of forces, the total CWM about any point is equal to the total ACWM about the same point.

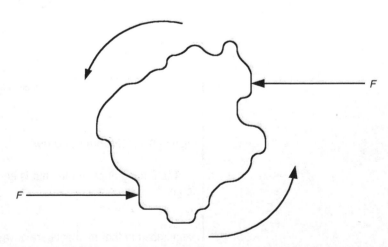

Figure 3.13 *Non-equilibrium condition for equal and opposite forces acting on a body*

BTEC National Study Guide: Engineering. See page 325 for order details of individual texts

38

This means that for static equilibrium the *algebraic sum of the moments must be zero*.

One other important fact needs to be remembered about bodies in static equilibrium, consider the uniform beam (uniform here means an equal cross-section along its total length) shown in Figure 3.14. We already know from the principle of moments that the sum of the CWM must equal the sum of ACWM. It is also true that the beam would sink into the ground or rise if the upward forces did not equal the downward forces. So a further necessary condition for static equilibrium is that:

upward forces = downward forces

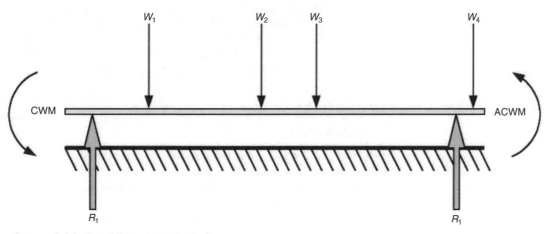

Figure 3.14 *Conditions for equilibrium*

We now have sufficient information to readily solve further problems concerning moments.

Example 3.10

A uniform horizontal beam is supported on a fulcrum (Figure 3.15). Calculate the force F necessary to ensure the beam remains in equilibrium.

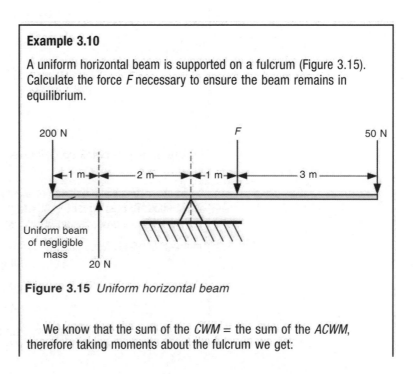

Figure 3.15 *Uniform horizontal beam*

We know that the sum of the CWM = the sum of the $ACWM$, therefore taking moments about the fulcrum we get:

BTEC National Study Guide: Engineering. See page 325 for order details of individual texts

39

$(F \times 1) + (50 \times 4) + (20 \times 2) = (200 \times 3)$ Nm

then, $(F \times 1) + 200 + 40 = 600$ Nm or,

$(F \times 1) = 600 - 200 - 40$ Nm so,

$$F = \frac{360 \text{ Nm}}{1 \text{ m}} = \textbf{360 N}$$

Notes: (a) The 20 N force acting at a distance of 2 m from the fulcrum, tends to turn the beam *clockwise* so is *added* to the sum of the CWM.

(b) The units of F are as required, i.e. they are in newtons, because the RHS is in Nm and is divided by 1 m.

(c) In this example the weight of the beam has been ignored. If the beam is of uniform cross-section, then its mass is deemed to act at its geometrical centre.

Example 3.11

Figure 3.16 shows a motion control system crank lever ABC pivoted at B. AB is 20 cm and BC is 30 cm. Calculate the magnitude of the vertical rod force at C required to balance the horizontal control rod force of magnitude 10 kN applied at A.

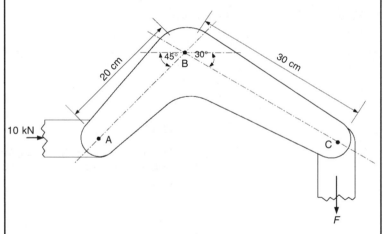

Figure 3.16 *Bell crank control lever*

In order to achieve balance of the forces acting on the lever the CWM about B must equal the ACWM about B. It can also be seen that the 10 kN force produces an ACWM about the fulcrum B. Therefore:

moment of 10 kN force about B = $(10 \times 0.2 \sin 45°)$ kN m (note the manipulation of units)

$= (10)(0.2)(0.7071)$ kN m

$= \textbf{1.414 kN m}$

If we now let the vertical force at C be of magnitude F then F produces a clockwise moment about fulcrum B. Therefore:

BTEC National Study Guide: Engineering. See page 325 for order details of individual texts

40

moment of force of magnitude F about B $= F \times (0.3 \cos 30°) = 0.26F$

Applying the principle of moments for equilibrium, we get:

$$1.414 = 0.26F$$

therefore $\quad F = \dfrac{1.414 \text{ kN}}{0.26 \text{ m}} = \textbf{5.44 kN}$

Our final example on moments introduces the idea of the *uniformly distributed load* (UDL). In addition to being subject to point loads, beams can be subjected to loads that are distributed for all, or part, of the beam's length. For UDLs the whole mass of the load is assumed to act as a point load through the centre of the distribution.

Example 3.12

For the beam system shown in Figure 3.17, determine the reactions at the supports R_A and R_B, taking into consideration the weight of the beam.

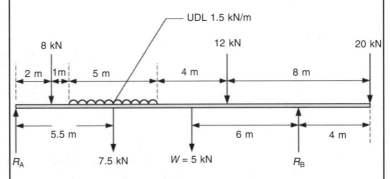

Figure 3.17 *Beam system taking account of weight of beam*

So from what has been said, the UDL acts as a point load of magnitude (1.5 kN × 5 = 7.5 kN) at the centre of the distribution, which is 5.5 m from R_A.

In problems involved with reaction it is essential to eliminate one reaction from the calculations because only one equation is formed and only one unknown can be solved at any one time. This is achieved by taking moments about one of the reactions and then, since the distance from that reaction is zero, its moment is zero and it is eliminated from the calculations.

So taking moments about A (thus eliminating A from the calculations), we get:

$$(2 \times 8) + (5.5 \times 7.5) + (10 \times 5) + (12 \times 12) + (20 \times 20) = 16R_B$$

or

$$651.25 = 16R_B$$

so the reaction at $B = \textbf{40.7 kN}$

We could now take moments about B in order to find the reaction at A. However, at this stage, it is easier to use the fact that for static equilibrium:

BTEC National Study Guide: Engineering. See page 325 for order details of individual texts

41

upward forces = downward forces

so $R_A + R_B = 8 + 7.5 + 5 + 12 + 20$

  $R_A + 40.7 = 52.5$

and so the reaction at A = **11.8 kN**

Couples

So far we have restricted our problems on moments to the turning effect of forces taken one at a time. A *couple occurs when two equal forces acting in opposite directions have their lines of action parallel.*

Example 3.13

Figure 3.18 shows the turning effect of a couple on a beam of regular cross-section.

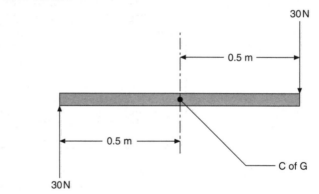

Figure 3.18 *Turning effect of a couple with regular cross section*

  Taking moments about the *centre of gravity* (C of G) (the point at which all the weight of the beam is deemed to act), then we get:

$(30 \times 0.5) + (30 \times 0.5) = $ moment

So moment of couple = **30 Nm**

Example 3.14

Figure 3.19 shows the turning effect of a couple on a beam of irregular

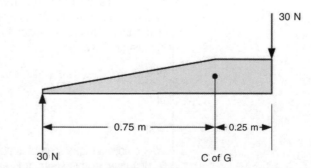

Figure 3.19 *Turning effect of couple, with irregular cross-section beam*

BTEC National Study Guide: Engineering. See page 325 for order details of individual texts

42

Stress and strain

cross-section, which we will again try to revolve about its centre of gravity.
Again taking moments about the C of G gives:

$(30 \times 0.75) = (30 \times 0.25) =$ moment

So the moment of couple = **30 Nm**

It can be seen from the above two examples that the moment is the same in both cases and is independent of the position of the fulcrum. Therefore if the fulcrum is assumed to be located at the point of application of one of the forces the *moment of a couple* is equal to one of the forces multiplied by the perpendicular distance between them. Thus in both cases shown in Examples 3.13 and 3.14 the *moment of the couple = (30 N × 1 m) = 30 Nm*, as before.

Another important application of the couple is its *turning moment* or *torque*. The definition of torque is as follows:

Torque is the turning moment of a couple and is measured in newton-metres (Nm): torque T = force F × radius r.

The *turning moment* of the couple given above in Example 3.14 is $= F \times r = (30\ N \times 0.5\ m) = 15\ Nm$.

Example 3.15

A nut is to be torque loaded to a maximum of 100 Nm. What is the maximum force that may be applied, perpendicular to the end of the spanner, if the spanner is of length 30 cm.

Since $T = F \times r$ then $F = T/r = 100/30$ therefore $F =$ **333.3 N**

Stress

If a solid, such as a metal bar, is subjected to an external force (or load), a resisting force is set up within the bar and the material is said to be in a state of stress. There are three basic types of stress:

- *tensile stress* – which is set up by forces tending to pull the material apart
- *compressive stress* – produced by forces tending to crush the material
- *shear stress* – resulting from forces tending to cut through the material, i.e. tending to make one part of the material slide over the other.

Figure 3.20 illustrates these three types of stress.

Definition of stress

Stress is defined as force per unit area, i.e.

$$\text{stress, } \sigma = \frac{\text{force, } F}{\text{area, } A}$$

BTEC National Study Guide: Engineering. See page 325 for order details of individual texts

43

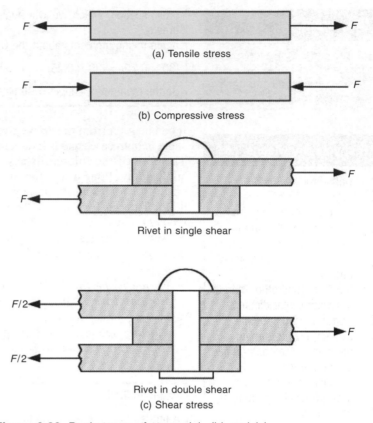

Figure 3.20 *Basic types of stress (a), (b) and (c)*

Note that the Greek letter σ is pronounced sigma.

The basic SI unit of stress is the N m^{-2}; other commonly used units include MN m^{-2}, N mm^{-2} and the pascal (Pa).

In engineering structures components that are designed to carry tensile loads are known as *ties*, while components design to carry compressive loads are known as *struts*.

Strain

A material that is altered in shape due to the action of a force acting on it is said to be *strained*. This may also mean that a body is strained internally even though there may be little measurable difference in its dimensions, just a stretching of the bonds at the atomic level. Figure 3.21 illustrates three common types of strain resulting from the application of external forces (loads).

Definition of strain

Direct strain may be defined as: *the ratio of change in dimension (deformation) over the original dimension*, i.e.

$$\textbf{direct strain, } \varepsilon = \frac{\textbf{deformation, } x}{\textbf{original length, } l}$$

(both x and l are in metres).

The symbol ε is the Greek lower case letter *epsilon*. Note also that the deformation for tensile strain will be an extension and for compressive strain it will be a reduction.

BTEC National Study Guide: Engineering. See page 325 for order details of individual texts

44

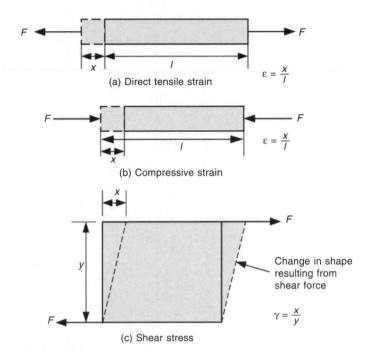

Figure 3.21 *Types of strain (a), (b) and (c)*

Hooke's law

Hooke's law states that: *within the elastic limit of a material the change in shape is directly proportional to the applied force producing it.*

A good example of the application of Hooke's law is the *spring*. A spring balance is used for measuring weight force, where an increase in weight will cause a corresponding extension (see Figure 3.22).

The stiffness (k) of a spring is the force required to cause a certain (unit deflection).

$$\text{stiffness } (k) = \frac{\text{force}}{\text{deflection}}$$

SI units are N m^{-1}.

The concept of elasticity will be looked at in a moment, in the mean time here is a question to consider. What does the slope of the graph in Figure 3.22 indicate?

Modulus

Modulus of elasticity

By considering Hooke's law, it follows that stress is directly proportional to strain, while the material remains *elastic*. That is, while the external forces acting on the material are only sufficient to stretch the atomic bonds, without fracture, so that the material may return to its original shape after the external forces have been removed.

BTEC National Study Guide: Engineering. See page 325 for order details of individual texts

45

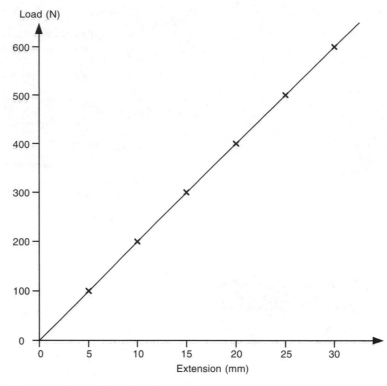

Figure 3.22 *Load–extension graph*

Then from Hooke's law and our definition of stress and strain, we know that *stress is directly proportional to strain in the elastic range*, i.e.

stress ∝ strain   or   stress = (strain × a constant)

so: $\dfrac{\text{stress}}{\text{strain}}$ = a constant, then $E = \dfrac{\textbf{stress}}{\textbf{strain}}$ (where E is the constant)

This constant of proportionality will depend on the material and is given the symbol E. It is known as the *modulus of elasticity* and because strain has no units it has the same units as stress. Modulus values tend to be very high, for this reason GN m^{-2} or GPa are the preferred SI units.

> **Key point**
>
> The *elastic modulus* of a material may be taken as a measure of the *stiffness* of that material.

Modulus of rigidity

The relationship between the shear stress (τ) and shear strain (γ) is known as the modulus of rigidity (G), i.e.

$$\textbf{modulus of rigidity } (\textbf{\textit{G}}) = \frac{\textbf{shear stress } (\boldsymbol{\tau})}{\textbf{shear strain } (\boldsymbol{\gamma})} \text{ (units GPa or GN m}^{-2})$$

Note that the symbol τ is the lower case Greek letter tau and the symbol γ is the lower case Greek letter gamma.

Example 3.16

A rectangular steel bar 10 mm × 16 mm × 200 mm long extends by 0.12 mm under a tensile force of 20 kN. Find:

(a) the stress

BTEC National Study Guide: Engineering. See page 325 for order details of individual texts

46

(b)   the strain
(c)   the elastic modulus of the bar material.

(a)   Now, tensile stress $= \dfrac{\text{tensile force}}{\text{cross-sectional area}}$

Also tensile force = 20 kN = 20×10^3 N and cross-sectional area
$= 10 \times 16 = 160$ mm^2. Remember tensile loads act against the
cross-sectional area of the material.

Then substituting in the above formula we have, tensile stress

$(\sigma) = \dfrac{20\,000 \text{ N}}{160 \text{ mm}^2}$

$\sigma = \textbf{125 N mm}^{-2}$

(b) Now, strain $\varepsilon = \dfrac{\text{deformation (extension)}}{\text{original length}}$

Also extension = 0.12 mm and the original length = 200 mm.

Then substituting gives $\varepsilon = \dfrac{0.12 \text{ mm}}{200 \text{ mm}} = 0.0006$

(c) $E = \dfrac{\text{stress}}{\text{strain}} = \dfrac{125 \text{ N mm}^{-2}}{0.0006} = 208\,000$ N mm^{-2} or **208 GN m**$^{-2}$

Test your knowledge 3.7

1. Define:
   (a) tensile stress;
   (b) shear stress;
   (c) compressive stress.
2. State Hooke's law and explain its relationship to the elastic modulus.
3. Define spring stiffness and quote its SI unit.
4. Define in detail the terms:
   (a) elastic modulus;
   (b) shear modulus;
   (c) bulk modulus.
5. Convert the following into N/m^2:
   (a) 240 kN m^{-2};
   (b) 0.228 gap;
   (c) 600 N mm^{-2};
   (d) 0.0033 N mm^{-2};
   (e) 10 kN m^{-2}.
6. Explain the use of:
   (a) a strut;
   (b) a tie.

Example 3.17

A 10 mm diameter rivet holds three sheets of metal together and is loaded as shown in Figure 3.23. Find the shear stress in the bar.

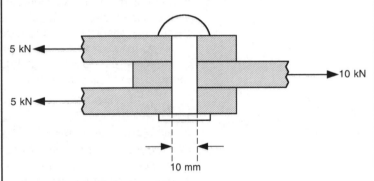

Figure 3.23 *Rivet in double-shear*

We know that each rivet is in double shear.

So the area resisting shear $= 2 \times$ the cross-sectional area

$= 2\pi r^2 = 2\pi 5^2 = 157$ mm^2

So shear stress $(\tau) = \dfrac{10\,000}{157} = 63.7$ N mm^{-2} = **63.7 MN m**$^{-2}$

Note that when a rivet is in double shear, the area under shear is multiplied by 2. With respect to the load we know from Newton's laws that to every action there is an equal and opposite reaction, thus *we only use the action or reaction* of a force in our calculations, *not both*.

BTEC National Study Guide: Engineering. See page 325 for order details of individual texts

Some definitions of mechanical properties

The mechanical properties of a material are concerned with its behaviour under the action of external forces. This is of particular importance to us when considering materials for engineering applications. Here, we will concentrate on a few *simple* definitions of the more important mechanical properties of materials that are needed for our study of statics.

These properties include strength, stiffness, specific strength and stiffness, ductility, toughness, malleability and elasticity, in addition to others given below. We have already considered *stiffness*, which is measured by the *elastic modulus*. Indirectly, we have also defined strength when we considered the various forms of stress that result from the loads applied on a material. However, a more formal definition of strength follows.

Strength

Strength may be defined simply as the applied force a material can withstand prior to fracture. In fact strength is measured by the *yield stress* σ_y or *proof stress* σ_p (see below) of a material. This stress is measured at a known percentage yield for the material under test. Yielding occurs when the material is subject to loads that cause it to extend by a known fraction of its original length. For metals the measure of strength is often taken at the 0.2% yield or 0.2% proof stress.

Working stress

Following on from the argument given above, we now need to define one or two additional types of stress, since these measure the strength characteristics of materials, under varying circumstances.

Working stress is the stress imposed on the material as a result of the worst possible loads that the material is likely to sustain in service. These loads must be within the elastic range of the material.

Proof stress

Proof stress may be formally defined as: *the tensile stress which when applied for a period of 15 seconds and removed, produces a permanent set of a specified amount, usually 0.2 per cent, that is 0.002 or one-five hundredth of the original dimension.*

Ultimate tensile stress (UTS)

The *UTS* of a material is given by the relationship, *maximum load/ original cross-sectional area*. Note that the UTS is a measure of the ultimate tensile strength of the material. The point U on the load–extension graph (Figure 3.24) shows maximum load, this must be divided by the original cross-sectional area (csa), not that directly under the point U where the extension may have altered the original csa.

Specific strength

In many engineering applications such as aircraft and high performance motor vehicles, materials need to be as light and strong

BTEC National Study Guide: Engineering. See page 325 for order details of individual texts

48

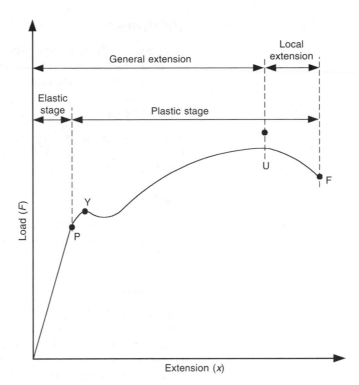

Figure 3.24 *Load–extension curve for a mild steel test piece*

as possible, in order to maximize their performance, while at the same time meeting the stringent safety requirements laid down for their load bearing structures. Thus to be *structurally efficient* aircraft and racing cars need to be made of low density materials, which have the greatest strength. The ratio of the strength of a material (measured by its yield stress) to that of its density is known as *specific strength*, i.e.

$$\text{specific strength} = \frac{\text{yield strength } (\sigma_y)}{\text{density } (\rho)}$$

SI units are joules per kilogram (J kg^{-1}).

Specific stiffness

In a similar manner to the argument given above, the *specific stiffness* of a material is the ratio of its stiffness (measured by its elastic modulus) to that of its density, i.e.

$$\text{specific modulus} = \frac{\text{elastic modulus } (E)}{\text{density } (\rho)}$$

SI units are again joules per kilogram (J kg^{-1}).

Ductility

Ductility is the ability to be drawn out into threads or wire. Wrought iron, aluminum, titanium and low carbon steels are examples of ductile materials.

BTEC National Study Guide: Engineering. See page 325 for order details of individual texts

49

Brittleness

Brittleness is the tendency to break easily or suddenly with little or no prior extension. Cast iron, high carbon steels and glass are examples of brittle materials.

Toughness

Toughness is the ability to withstand suddenly applied shock loads. Certain alloy steels, some plastics and rubber are examples of tough materials.

Malleability

Malleability is the ability to be rolled into sheets or shaped under pressure. Examples of malleable materials include, gold, copper and lead.

Elasticity

Elasticity is the ability of a material to return to its original shape once external forces have been removed. Internal atomic binding forces are stretched but not broken and act like minute springs to return the material to normal, once force has been removed. Rubber, mild and medium carbon steels are good examples of elastic materials.

Safety factors

The *safety factor* is used in the design of materials subject to service loads, to give a margin of safety and take account of a *certain factor of ignorance*. Factors of safety vary in engineering design, dependent on the structural sensitivity of the member under consideration. They are often around 1.5, but can be considerably higher for joints, fittings, castings and primary load bearing structures in general.

Load–extension graphs

These show the results of mechanical tests used to determine certain properties of a material. For instance as a check to see if heat treatment or processing has been successful, a sample from a batch would be used for such tests.

Load–extension graphs show certain phases. When a material is tested to destruction these include: elastic range, limit of proportionality, yield point, plastic stage and final fracture.

Figure 3.24 shows a typical load–extension curve for a specimen of mild steel which is a ductile material.

The point P at the end of the straight line OP is called the *limit of proportionality*. Between the origin O and P the extension x is directly proportional to the applied force and in this range the material obeys Hooke's law. The *elastic limit* is at or very near the limit of proportionality. When this limit has been passed the extension ceases to be proportional to the load, and at the *yield point* Y the extension suddenly increases and the material enters its *plastic*

BTEC National Study Guide: Engineering. See page 325 for order details of individual texts

50

phase. At point U (the ultimate tensile strength) the load is greatest. The extension of the test piece has been general up to point U, after which waisting or necking occurs and the subsequent extension is local (Figure 3.25).

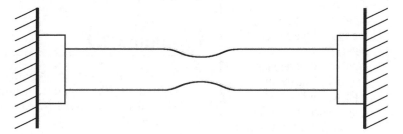

Figure 3.25 *Necking or waisting with local extension*

Since the area at the waist is considerably reduced then from *stress* = *force/area*, the stress will increase, resulting in a reduced load for a given stress and so fracture occurs at point F, that is at a lower load value than at U.

Remember the elastic limit is at the end of the phase that obeys Hooke's law, after this Hooke's relationship is no longer valid, and full recovery of the material is not possible after removal of the load.

Figure 3.26 shows some typical load–extension curves for some common metals. Where:

HDB = hard drawn 70/30 brass
CI = cast iron
HDC = hard drawn copper
AA = aluminium alloy
AC = annealed copper.

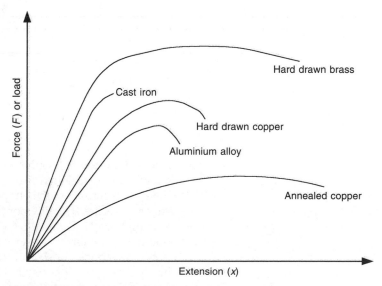

Figure 3.26 *Some typical load–extension graphs*

The above curves show that annealed copper is very ductile, while hard drawn copper is stronger but less ductile. Hard drawn 70/30 brass is both strong and ductile. Cast iron can clearly be seen

Test your knowledge 3.8

1. Explain how the strength of solid materials is determined.
2. What is the engineering purpose of the *factor of safety*?
3. What is the difference between ductility and malleability?
4. With respect to tensile testing and the resultant load–extension graph, define: (a) limit of proportionality; (b) UTS; (c) yield point; (d) plastic range.

as brittle and it is for this reason that cast iron is rarely used under tensile load. Aluminium alloy can be seen to be fairly strong yet ductile, it has excellent *structural efficiency* and it is for this reason that it is still used as one of the premier materials for aircraft construction.

Problems 3.2

1. For the force system shown below (Figure 3.27) determine *graphically* the magnitude and direction of the equilibrant. Then use a *mathematical method* to check the accuracy of your result.

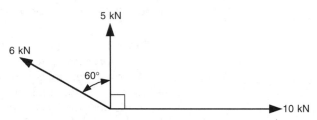

Figure 3.27 *System of forces space diagram*

2. Determine the reactions at the supports for the beam system shown below (Figure 3.28). Assume the beam has negligible mass.

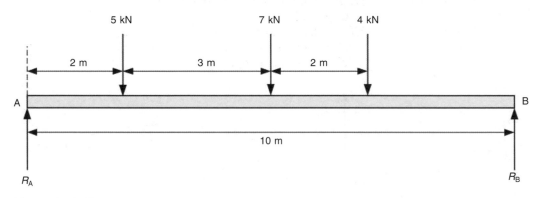

Figure 3.28 *Beam system*

3. A uniform beam of length 5 m and weight 10 kN has to support a uniformly distributed load (UDL) of 1.5 kN m^{-1}. Find the reactions at the supported.
4. An engineering structure contains a steel tie rod that carries a load of 100 kN. If the allowable tensile stress is 75 MN m^{-2}, find the minimum diameter of the tie rod.
5. A hollow copper tube 30 mm outside diameter and 18 mm inside diameter supports an axial compressive load of 60 kN. The axial compression of the cylinder is 0.2 mm and the value of the elastic modulus E for copper is 110 GN m^{-2}. Determine:

   (a) the stress in the copper
   (b) the original length of the tube.

BTEC National Study Guide: Engineering. See page 325 for order details of individual texts

52

Dynamics

We start our study of dynamics by considering Newton's laws of motion. In order to do this we need to briefly introduce the concepts of speed, velocity, acceleration and momentum, which are fundamental to a proper understanding of these laws.

Speed, velocity and acceleration

Speed may be defined as *distance per unit time*. Speed takes no account of direction and is therefore a *scalar* quantity.

The common SI units of speed are:

kilometres per hour   (kph)
metres per second   (m s^{-1})

Example 3.18

Convert:

(a)   150 kph into m s^{-1}
(b)   120 m s^{-1} into kph.

We will derive the conversion factors for the above speeds by considering the *basic* units.

(a)   We know that there are 10^3 metres in a kilometre so 150 kph = 150 $\times 10^3$ metres per hour. Also there are 3600 seconds in an hour (see Table 3.5). So our required conversion factor is $10^3/3600 = 1/3.6$. So:

150 kph = (150)(1/3.6) = **41.67 m s^{-1}**

Note that we did not change our conversion factor (1/3.6) into a decimal fraction, because this cannot be done exactly as 1/3.6 = 0.277777 recurring.

(b)   I hope you can see that all we need do is use the inverse of the conversion factor we have found above to convert m s^{-1} into kph, we are simply converting in reverse. Then the conversion factor becomes (3.6/1) = 3.6. So:

120 m s^{-1} = (120)(3.6) = **432.0 kph**

It will aid your understanding of unit conversion if you attempt to derive your own *conversion factors* from basic units.

Key point

Speed is a scalar quantity whereas velocity is a vector quantity.

Velocity is defined as: *distance per unit time in a specified direction*. Therefore, velocity is a *vector quantity* and the SI units for the magnitude of velocity are the SI units for speed, i.e. m s^{-1}.

The direction of a velocity is not always quoted but it should be understood that the velocity is in some defined direction, even though this direction is unstated.

Acceleration is defined as: *change in velocity per unit time or rate of change of velocity*. Acceleration is also a *vector quantity* and the SI unit of acceleration is m s^{-1}/s or m s^{-2}.

BTEC National Study Guide: Engineering. See page 325 for order details of individual texts

53

Equilibrium, momentum and inertia

A body is said to be in *equilibrium* when *its acceleration continues to be zero*, that is, when *it remains at rest or when it continues to move in a straight line with constant velocity*.

Momentum may be described as the quantity of motion of a body. *Momentum is the product of the mass of a body and its velocity*. Any change in momentum requires a change in velocity, that is an acceleration. It may be said that for a fixed quantity of matter to be in equilibrium, it must have constant momentum. A more rigorous definition of momentum is given next, when we consider Newton's second law.

All matter resists change. The force resisting change in momentum (that is, acceleration) is called *inertia*. The inertia of a body depends on its mass, the greater the mass, the greater the inertia. The inertia of a body is an innate force that only becomes effective when acceleration occurs. An applied force acts against inertia so as to accelerate (or tend to accelerate) a body.

> ### Key point
>
> The momentum of a body is equal to its mass multiplied by its velocity.

Newton's laws of motion

Before we consider Newton's laws we need to revisit the concept of force. We already know that force cannot exist without opposition, i.e. action and reaction. If we apply a 100 N pulling force to a rope, this force cannot exist without opposition.

Force is that which changes, or tends to change, the state of rest or uniform motion of a body. Forces that act on a body may be external (applied from outside the body) such as weight, or internal (such as the internal resistance of a material subject to a compression).

The difference between the forces tending to cause motion and those opposing motion is called the *resultant* or *out-of-balance force*. A body that has no out-of-balance external force acting on it is in equilibrium and will not accelerate. A body that has such an out-of-balance force will accelerate at a rate dependent on the mass of the body and the magnitude of the out-of-balance force. The necessary opposition that permits the existence of the out-of-balance force is provided by the force of inertia (Figure 3.29(a) and (b)).

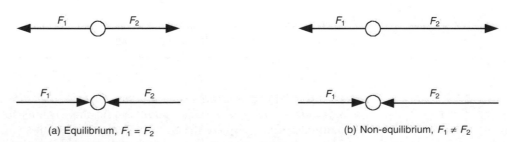

(a) Equilibrium, $F_1 = F_2$ (b) Non-equilibrium, $F_1 \neq F_2$

Figure 3.29 *(a) Equilibrium forces; (b) non-equilibrium forces*

Newton's first law of motion states that: *a body remains in a state of rest, or of uniform motion in a straight line, unless it is acted upon by some external resultant force.*

BTEC National Study Guide: Engineering. See page 325 for order details of individual texts

54

Newton's second law of motion states that: *the rate of change of momentum of a body is directly proportional to the force producing the change, and takes place in the direction in which the force acts.*

We defined force earlier as force = mass × acceleration. We also know that acceleration may be defined as change in velocity per unit time or rate of change in velocity. If we assume that a body has an *initial velocity u* and a *final velocity v*, then the change in velocity is given by $(v - u)$ and so the rate of change of velocity or acceleration may be written as $\dfrac{(v - u)}{t}$ where t is unit time.

So since $F = ma$ then this may be written as:

$$F = \frac{m(v - u)}{t}$$

and multiplying out the brackets gives:

$$F = \frac{mv - mu}{t}$$

Now we also know that momentum was defined earlier as mass × velocity. So the product *mu* gives the initial momentum of the body, prior to the application of the force and *mv* gives the final momentum of the body. Thus the expression $(mv - mu)$ is the change in momentum and so $\dfrac{mv - mu}{t}$ is the rate of change of momentum and so Newton's second law may be expressed as:

$$F = \frac{mv - mu}{t}$$

or

$$F = ma$$

Newton's third law states that: *to every action there is an equal and opposite reaction.*

So, for example, the compressive forces that result from the weight of a building, the *action*, are held in equilibrium by the *reaction* forces that occur inside the materials of the building's foundation. Another example is that of propulsion. An aircraft jet engine produces a stream of high velocity gases at its exhaust, the *action*, these act on the airframe of the aircraft causing a *reaction*, which enables the aircraft to accelerate and increase speed for flight.

Linear equations of motion

You have already been introduced to the concept of force, velocity and acceleration – and now, Newton's laws. All these concepts are further exploited through the use of the *equations of motion*. Look back now and remind yourself of the relationship between mass, force, acceleration and Newton's laws.

The linear equations of motion rely for their derivation on the one very important fact that the *acceleration is assumed to be constant*. We will now consider the derivation of the four standard equations of motion using a graphical method.

Key point

$F = ma$ is a consequence of Newton's second law of motion.

Test your knowledge 3.9

1. Use Table 3.5 to convert the following units:

 (a) 600 km/hr into m/s^1
 (b) 140 km/hr into kph.

2. Define 'inertia' and quote its units.
3. What may we write as the equivalent to the *rate of change of momentum* in Newton's second law.

Key point

For the linear equations of motion to be valid, the acceleration is assumed to be constant.

BTEC National Study Guide: Engineering. See page 325 for order details of individual texts

55

Velocity/time graphs

Even simple linear motion, motion along a straight line, can be difficult to deal with mathematically. However, in the case where acceleration is constant it is possible to solve problems of motion by use of a *velocity/time graph*, without recourse to the calculus. The equations of motion use standard symbols to represent the variables, these are shown below:

s = distance in metres   (m)
u = initial velocity   (m s^{-1})
v = final velocity   (m s^{-1})
a = acceleration in metres/second^2 (m s^{-2})
t = time in seconds   (s)

The *velocity is plotted on the vertical axis and time on the horizontal axis*. Constant velocity is represented by a *horizontal straight line* and acceleration by a *sloping straight line*. Deceleration or *retardation* is also represented by a sloping straight line but with a *negative slope*.

By considering the velocity/time graph shown in Figure 3.30, we can establish the equation for distance.

The distance travelled in a given time is equal to the velocity $m\ s^{-1}$ multiplied by the time s, this is found from the graph by the *area under the sloping line*. In Figure 3.30, a body is accelerating from a velocity u to a velocity v in time t seconds.

> **Key point**
>
> Velocity is speed in a given direction and is a vector quantity.

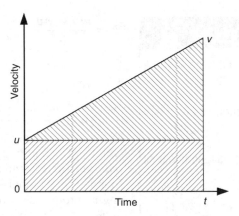

Figure 3.30 *Velocity/time graph for uniform acceleration*

Now the distance travelled s = area under graph

$$s = ut + \frac{(v - u)}{2} \times t$$

$$s = ut + \frac{vt}{2} - \frac{ut}{2}$$

$$s = \frac{(2u + v - u)t}{2}$$

and so: $s = \dfrac{(u + v)t}{2}$

In a similar manner to the above, one of the velocity equations can also be obtained from the velocity/time graph. Since the acceleration

BTEC National Study Guide: Engineering. See page 325 for order details of individual texts

56

is the rate of change of velocity with respect to time, the value of the acceleration will be equal to the gradient of a velocity/time graph. Therefore, from Figure 3.30, we have:

$$\textbf{gradient} = \frac{\textbf{acceleration}}{\textbf{time taken}} = \textbf{velocity}$$

therefore acceleration is given by

$$a = \frac{(v - u)}{t}$$

or $v = u + at$

The remaining equations of motion may be derived from the two equations found above. As an exercise in manipulating formulae try to obtain:

(a) the equation $t = \dfrac{(v - u)}{a}$

(b) $s = ut + \dfrac{1}{2}at^2$

using the above equations.

Example 3.19

A body starts from rest and accelerates with constant acceleration of 2.0 m s^{-2} up to a speed of 9 m s^{-1}. It then travels at 9 m s^{-1} for 15 seconds after which time it is retarded to a speed of 1 m s^{-1}. If the complete motion takes 24.5 seconds, find:

(a) the time taken to reach 9 m s^{-1}.
(b) the retardation
(c) the total distance travelled.

The solution is made easier if we sketch a graph of the motion, as shown in Figure 3.31.

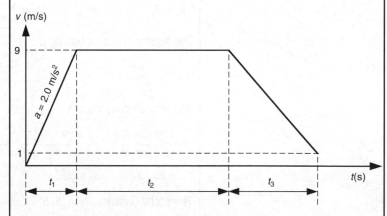

Figure 3.31 *Velocity/time graph of the motion*

(a) We first tabulate the known values:

$u = 0$ m s^{-1} (we start from rest)
$v = 9$ m s^{-1}
$a = 2.0$ m s^{-2}
$t_1 = ?$

BTEC National Study Guide: Engineering. See page 325 for order details of individual texts

57

All we need now do is select an equation which contains all the variables listed above, i.e.

$v = u + at$

and on transposing for t and substituting the variables we get

$$t = \frac{9 - 0}{2}$$

so

$t_1 = \textbf{4.5 s}$

(b) The retardation is found in a similar manner:

$u = 9 \text{ m s}^{-1}$
$v = 2 \text{ m s}^{-1}$
$t_3 = 5 \text{ s}$
$a = ?$

We again select an equation which contains the variables, i.e.

$v = u + at$

and on transposing for a and substituting the variables we get

$$a = \frac{1 - 9}{5}$$

so

$a = -\textbf{1.6 m s}^{-2}$ (the −ve sign indicates a retardation)

(c) The total distance travelled requires us to sum the component distances travelled for the times t_1, t_2 and t_3. Again we tabulate the variable for each stage:

$u_1 = 0 \text{ m s}^{-1}$	$u_2 = 9 \text{ m s}^{-1}$	$u_3 = 9 \text{ m s}^{-1}$
$v_1 = 9 \text{ m s}^{-1}$	$v_2 = 9 \text{ m s}^{-1}$	$v_3 = 1 \text{ m s}^{-1}$
$t_1 = 4.5 \text{ s}$	$t_2 = 15 \text{ s}$	$t_3 = 5 \text{ s}$
$s_1 = ?$	$s_2 = ?$	$s_3 = ?$

The appropriate equation is:

$$s = \frac{(u + v)t}{2}$$

and in each case we get

$$s_1 = \frac{(0 + 9)4.5}{2}, \quad s_2 = \frac{(9 + 9)15}{2}, \quad s_3 = \frac{(9 + 1)5}{2}$$

$s_1 = 20.25 \qquad s_2 = 135 \qquad s_3 = 25$

Then total distance $S_T = 20.5 + 135 + 25 = \textbf{180.25 m}$

Using Newton's laws

You saw earlier that *Newton's second law* may be defined as:

$F = ma$

BTEC National Study Guide: Engineering. See page 325 for order details of individual texts

58

Key point

The inertia force is equal and opposite to the accelerating force.

Test your knowledge 3.10

With reference to the velocity time graphs shown in Figure 3.32, answer questions 1 to 8.
  Fill in the gaps for questions 1 to 8.

1. The slope of the velocity/ time graph measures

   _____.

2. The area under a velocity/time graph determines

   _____.

3. Average velocity may be determined by dividing the _____ by

   _____.

4. Graph (a) is a graph of constant velocity therefore acceleration is given by

   _____ and the distance travelled is equal to

   _____.

5. Graph (b) shows uniformly accelerated motion therefore the distance travelled is equal to

   _____.

6. Graph (c) shows

   _____

   _____.

7. Graph (d) represents uniformly accelerated motion having initial velocity u, final velocity v and acceleration (a). So distanced travelled is equal to

   _____.

8. Graph (e) represents

   _____ acceleration.

or that

$$F = \frac{mv - mu}{t}$$

In words, we may say that force is equal to the rate of change of momentum of a body. Look back again and make sure you understand the relationship between force, mass and the momentum of a body. Remembering that *momentum* may be defined as *the mass of a body multiplied by its velocity*. Also that *the inertia force is such as to be equal and opposite to the accelerating force that produced it*; this essentially is Newton's third law.

Example 3.20

A racing car of mass 1965 kg accelerates from 160 km/hr to 240 km/hr in 3.5 seconds. If the air resistance is 2000 N per tonne, find the:

(a) average acceleration
(b) force required to produce the acceleration
(c) inertia force on the car.

(a) We first need to convert the velocities to standard units.

$$u = 160 \text{ kph} = \frac{160 \times 1000}{60 \times 60} = 44.4 \text{ m s}^{-1}$$

$$v = 240 \text{ kph} = \frac{240 \times 1000}{60 \times 60} = 66.6 \text{ m s}^{-1}$$

also $t = 3.5$ s, and we are required to find the acceleration a. Then using the equation $v = u + at$ and transposing for a we get:

$$a = \frac{v - u}{t} \text{ and substituting values } a = \frac{66.6 - 44.4}{3.5}$$

$$a = 6.34 \text{ m s}^{-2}$$

(b) The accelerating force is readily found using Newton's second law, where:

$$F = ma = 1965 \text{ kg} \times 6.34 \text{ m s}^{-2}$$

$$= 12.46 \text{ kN}$$

(c) From what has already been said you will be aware that the inertia force = the accelerating force, therefore the **inertia force = 12.46 kN**.

Angular motion

You previously met the equations for linear motion. A similar set of equations exists to solve engineering problems that involve angular motion as experienced, for example, in the rotation of a drive shaft. The linear equations of motion may be transformed to represent angular motion using a set of equations that we will refer to as the *transformation equations*. These are given below, followed by the equations of angular motion, which are compared with their linear equivalents.

BTEC National Study Guide: Engineering. See page 325 for order details of individual texts

59

9. Define the terms:
   (a) inertia force;
   (b) momentum.
10. What is the essential difference between speed and velocity?
11. If a rocket is sent to the moon its mass remains constant but its weight changes, explain this statement.
12. Explain how the expression $F = ma$ is related to the rate of change of momentum with respect to Newton's second law.

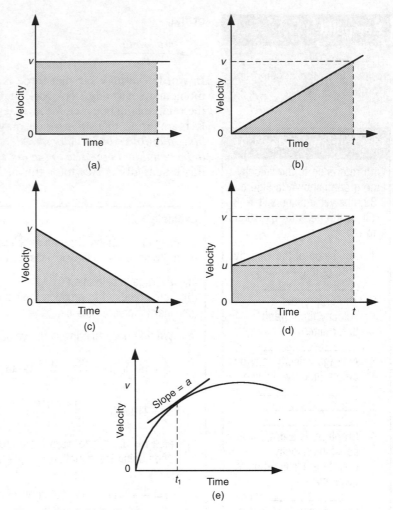

Figure 3.32 *Velocity/time graphs*

Transformation equations

$s = \theta r$

$v = \omega r$

$a = \alpha r$

where r = radius of body from centre of rotation and θ, ω and α are the angular distance, angular velocity and angular acceleration, respectively.

Angular equation of motion	Linear equation of motion
$\theta = \dfrac{(\omega_1 + \omega_2)t}{2}$	$s = \dfrac{(u + v)t}{2}$
$\theta = \omega_1 t + \frac{1}{2}\alpha t^2$	$s = ut + \frac{1}{2}at^2$
$\omega_2^2 = \omega_1^2 + 2\alpha\theta$	$v^2 = u^2 + 2as$
$\alpha = \dfrac{(\omega_2 - \omega_1)}{t}$	$a = \dfrac{(v - u)}{t}$

Angular velocity

Angular velocity refers to a body moving in a circular path and may be defined as:

BTEC National Study Guide: Engineering. See page 325 for order details of individual texts

60

$$\text{angular velocity} = \frac{\text{angular distance moved (radians)}}{\text{time taken (seconds)}}$$

or in symbols $\omega = \theta/s$ (radians per second).

Angular distance is measured in radians, you should refer to 404 if you cannot remember the definition of the radian, or how to convert radians to degrees and vice versa.

We are often given rotational velocity in the non-SI units of *revolutions per minute* (rev/min). It is therefore useful to be able to converts revs/min into radians per second and vice versa.

So, for example, to convert 350 rev/min into radians per second we multiply by $2\pi/360$, i.e.

$$350 \text{ rev/min} = 350 \times 2\pi/60 = 36.65 \text{ rad.s}^{-1}$$

Example 3.21

A 540 mm diameter wheel is rotating at $1500/\pi$ rev/min. Determine the angular velocity of the wheel in rad.s^{-1} and the linear velocity of a point on the rim of the wheel.

All we need do to find the angular velocity is convert from rev/min to rad/sec, i.e.

angular velocity (rad.s^{-1}) = $1500/\pi \times 2\pi/60$ = **50 rad.s^{-1}**

Now from the transformation equations, linear velocity v = angular velocity, $\omega \times$ radius, $r = 50$ rad/sec $\times 0.270$ m

v = **13.5 m s^{-1}**

Angular acceleration

Angular acceleration is defined as the rate of change of angular velocity with respect to time, i.e.

$$\text{angular acceleration, } \alpha = \frac{\text{change in angular velocity (rad.s}^{-1})}{\text{time (s)}}$$

So units for angular acceleration are $\alpha = \theta \text{ s}^{-2}$.

Example 3.22

The pinion shown in Figure 3.33 is required to move with an initial angular velocity of 300 revs/min and final angular velocity of 600 rev/min. If the increase takes place over 15 seconds, determine the linear acceleration of the rack. Assume a pinion radius of 180 mm.

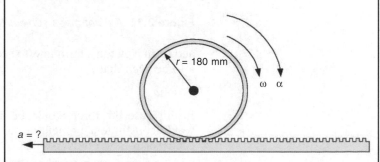

Figure 3.33 *Rack and pinion*

BTEC National Study Guide: Engineering. See page 325 for order details of individual texts

61

In order to solve this problem we first need to convert the velocities into radians per second.

300 rev/min = $300 \times 2\pi/60$ = 31.4 rads^{-1}
600 rev/min = $600 \times 2\pi/60$ = 62.8 rads^{-1}

We can use the equation

$$\alpha = \frac{\omega_1 - \omega_2}{t}$$

to find the angular acceleration.
So

$$\alpha = \frac{62.8 - 31.4}{15} = \textbf{2.09 rads}^{-2}$$

Now we can use the transformation equation $a = \alpha r$ to find the linear acceleration, i.e.

$$\alpha = (2.09 \text{ rad.s}^{-1})(0.18 \text{ m}) = \textbf{0.377 m s}^{-2}$$

Torque and angular acceleration

We can apply Newton's third law of motion to angular motion, if it is realized that the distribution of mass relative to the axis of rotation has some bearing on the calculation. For this reason it is not possible to deal directly with a rotating wheel, but rather with a small element of mass whose radius of rotation can be more easily defined.

Figure 3.34 shows a small element of mass δm rotating at a radius r from the centre O, with uniform angular velocity w (rad.s). We know from the transformation equations that the linear velocity at any instant is given by:

$v = \omega r$

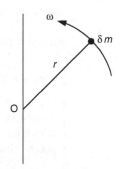

Figure 3.34 *A point mass subject to rotational velocity*

and from Newton's third law, to accelerate this mass would require a force such that:

$F = ma$

In this case the force would be applied at the radius r and thus would constitute a moment or more correctly a torque T about the centre of rotation thus:

$T = Fr$ or $T = mar$

Since the linear acceleration, $a = \alpha r$, then:

$T = m(\alpha r)r$

or

$T = m\alpha r^2$

The quantity mr^2 is a concentrated mass multiplied by its radius of rotation squared and is known as the *moment of inertia I*. The quantity I is an important property of a rotating body, in the SI system it has units $=$ kg m^2. Therefore substituting I for mr^2 in our above equation $T = m\alpha r^2$, gives:

$T = I\alpha$

The last relationship may be compared with $F = ma$ for linear motion.

Key point

Think of the moment of inertia of a rotating body as being equivalent to the mass of a body subject to linear motion.

Example 3.23

A flywheel has a moment of inertia of 130 kg m^2. Its angular velocity drops from 12 000 rpm to 9000 rpm in 6 seconds, determine (a) the retardation; (b) the braking torque.
Then,

$\omega_1 = 12\,000 \times 2\pi/60 = 1256.6$ rads^{-1}
$\omega_2 = 9000 \times 2\pi/60 = 942.5$ rads^{-1}

and from

$$\alpha = \frac{\omega_2 - \omega_1}{t}$$

$$\alpha = \frac{942.5 - 1256.6}{6}$$

$\alpha = -52.35$ or retardation $= \mathbf{52.35\ rads^{-2}}$

Now torque

$T = I\alpha$

$T = (130)(52.35)$

so braking torque

$T = \mathbf{6805.5\ N\ m}$

Centripetal acceleration and force

If we consider Figure 3.35, again we can see that the direction of the mass must be continually changing to produce the circular motion, therefore it is being subject to an acceleration, which is acting towards the centre; this acceleration is known as the *centripetal acceleration* and is equal to $\omega^2 r$. When acting on a mass this acceleration produces a force known as centripetal force, thus:

centripetal force $(F_r) =$ mass $\times$ centripetal acceleration

$F_r = m\omega^2 r$

and since $v = \omega r$

$$F_r = \frac{mv^2}{r}$$

BTEC National Study Guide: Engineering. See page 325 for order details of individual texts

63

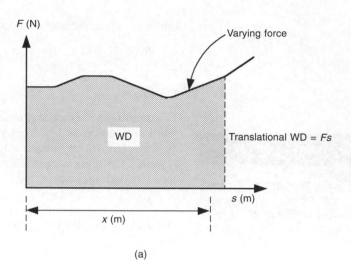

(a)

Test your knowledge 3.11

1. Define the following, stating their SI units:
   (a) angular velocity;
   (b) angular acceleration.
2. A body acting at a radius of 175 mm has a tangential (linear) velocity of 25 m s^{-1}, find its angular velocity.
3. Convert the following angular velocities into standard SI units:
   (a) 250 rev/min;
   (b) 12 500 rev/hr;
   (c) 175 rev/sec.
4. Define:
   (a) torque;
   (b) moment of inertia.
5. Explain why the moment of inertia is used instead of the total mass of the body, when considering objects subject to angular motion?
6. Define the terms:
   (a) centripetal acceleration;
   (b) centrifugal force.
7. If a racing car is in a steady turn on a banked track, explain the nature of the forces acting on the car during the turn. Which one of these forces holds the racing car in the turn?
8. Define the terms:
   (a) momentum;
   (b) inertia.

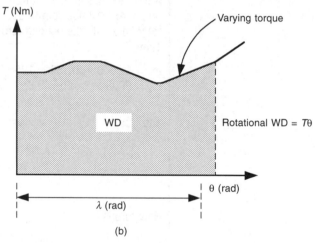

(b)

Figure 3.35 *Work done*

From Newton's third law there must be an *equal and opposite force* opposing the centripetal force; this is known as the *centrifugal force* and *acts outwards* from the centre of rotation.

Example 3.24

An aircraft with a mass of 80 000 kg is in a steady turn of radius 300 m, flying at 800 km/hr. Determine the centripetal force required to hold the aircraft in the turn.

Then the linear velocity of the aircraft = 800 × 1000/3600 m s^{-1}
= 222.2 m s^{-1}

and from $F_r = \dfrac{mv^2}{r}$ we get $F_r = \dfrac{(80\,000)(222.2)^2}{300} =$ **13.166 MN**.

BTEC National Study Guide: Engineering. See page 325 for order details of individual texts

64

Problems 3.3

1. A body weighs 562 N on the surface of the earth:

    (a) What force is required to give an acceleration of 8 m s^{-2}?
    (b) What will be the inertia force of the body when given this acceleration?

2. A car starts from rest and accelerates uniformly at 2 m s^{-2} for 10 seconds. Calculate the distance travelled.

3. A vehicle accelerates at a constant rate from rest to 20 m s^{-1} in a time of 4 seconds. Draw to scale a velocity/time graph and determine the acceleration and distance travelled.

4. Convert 350 rev/min into rad s^{-1}.

5. A Cessna 172 aircraft and a Boeing 747 aircraft are each given an acceleration of 5 m s^{-2}. To achieve this the thrust force produced by the Cessna's engines is 15 kN and the thrust force required by the Boeing 747 is 800 kN. Find the mass of each aircraft.

6. A wheel has a diameter of 0.54 m and is rotating at $\dfrac{1500}{\pi}$ rev/min. Calculate the angular velocity of the wheel in rad s^{-1} and the linear velocity of a point on the rim of the wheel.

7. A flywheel rotating at 20 rad s^{-1} increases its speed uniformly to 40 rad s^{-1} in 1 min. Sketch the angular velocity/time graph and determine:

    (a) the angular acceleration of the flywheel
    (b) the angle turned through by the flywheel in 1 minute and so calculate the number of revolutions made by the flywheel in this time.

8. The flywheel of a cutting machine has a moment of inertia of 130 kg m^2. Its speed drops from 120 rev/min to 90 rev/min in 2 seconds. Determine:

    (a) the deceleration of the flywheel
    (b) the braking torque.

Energy

Introduction

In this section we start our study on energy by considering the interrelationship between mechanical work, energy and power and apply this knowledge to typical engineering problems. We will then look at heat energy considering, in particular: change of state, heat and temperature, expansion of gases and the gas laws. As mentioned previously, electrical energy will be covered separately when we study the outcome on electrical principles.

Energy may exist in many different forms, for example mechanical, electrical, nuclear, chemical, heat, light and sound.

The principle of the conservation of energy states that: energy may neither be created nor destroyed only changed from one form to another.

There are many engineering examples of devices that transform energy, these include the:

BTEC National Study Guide: Engineering. See page 325 for order details of individual texts

65

- loudspeaker which transforms electrical to sound energy
- petrol engine which transforms heat to mechanical energy
- microphone which transforms sound to electrical energy
- dynamo which transforms mechanical to electrical energy
- battery which transforms chemical to electrical energy
- filament bulb which transforms electrical to light energy.

In our study of energy we start by looking at the various forms of mechanical energy and its conservation. Provided no mechanical energy is transferred to or from a body, the total amount of mechanical energy possessed by a body remains constant, unless mechanical work is done; this concept is looked at next.

Mechanical work, energy and power

Work done

The *energy* possessed by a body is its capacity to do work. Mechanical work is done when a force overcomes a resistance and it moves through a distance.

Mechanical work may be defined as:

mechanical work done (J) = force required to overcome the resistance (N) × distance moved against the resistance (m)

The SI unit of work is the newton-metre (N m) or joule where 1 joule = 1 N m.

Note:

(a) No work is done unless there is both resistance and movement.
(b) The resistance and the force needed to overcome it are equal.
(c) The distance moved must be measured in exactly the opposite direction to that of the resistance being overcome.

> **Key point**
>
> Mechanical energy may be defined as the capacity to do work.

The more common resistances to be overcome include: *friction*, *gravity* (the weight of the body itself) and *inertia* (the resistance to acceleration of the body) where:

the work done (WD) against friction = friction force × distance moved

WD against gravity = weight × gain in height

WD against inertia = inertia force × distance moved

Note:

(a) Inertia force is the out-of-balance force multiplied by the distance moved or: the *inertia force = mass × acceleration × distance moved*.
(b) Work done in overcoming friction will be discussed in more detail later.

In any problem involving calculation of work done, the first task should be to identify the type of resistance to overcome. If, and only if, there is motion between surfaces in contact, is work done against friction. Similarly, only where there is a gain in height is

BTEC National Study Guide: Engineering. See page 325 for order details of individual texts

66

the work done against gravity and only if a body is accelerated is work done against inertia (look back at our definition of inertia).

Example 3.25

A body of mass 30 kg is raised from the ground at constant velocity through a vertical distance of 15 m. Calculate the work done (WD).
  If we ignore air resistance, then the only WD is against gravity.

WD against gravity = weight $\times$ gain in height or $WD = mgh$
(and assuming $g = 9.81$ m s^{-2})

then

WD = (30)(9.81)(15)

WD = 4414.5 J or **4.414 kJ**

Work done may be represented graphically and, for linear motion, this is shown in Figure 3.35(a). Where the force needed to overcome the resistance is plotted against the distance moved. The WD is then given by the area under the graph.

Figure 3.35(b) shows the situation for angular motion, where a varying torque T in Nm is plotted against the angle turned through in radians. Again the WD is given by the area under the graph, where the units are Nm $\times$ radian. Then noting that the radian has no dimensions, the unit for work done remains as Nm or joules.

Mechanical energy

Mechanical energy may be subdivided into three different forms of energy: *potential energy*, *strain energy* and *kinetic energy*.

Potential energy

Potential energy (PE) *is energy possessed by a body by virtue of its position*, relative to some datum. The change in PE is equal to its weight multiplied by the change in height. Since the weight of a body = mg, then the change in PE may be written as:

change in PE = mgh

which of course is identical to the work done in overcoming gravity. So the work done in raising a mass to a height is equal to the PE it possesses at that height, assuming no external losses.

Strain energy

Strain energy is a particular form of PE possessed by an elastic body that is deformed within its elastic range, for example a stretched or compressed spring possesses strain energy.

Consider the spring arrangement shown in Figure 3.36. The force required to compress or extend the spring is $F = kx$, where k is the spring constant.

Figure 3.36(a) shows a helical coil spring in the unstrained, compressed and extended positions. The force required to move the spring varies in direct proportion to the distance moved (Figure 3.36(b)). Therefore: *strain energy of spring when compressed or extended = area under graph (force $\times$ distance moved)*

BTEC National Study Guide: Engineering. See page 325 for order details of individual texts

67

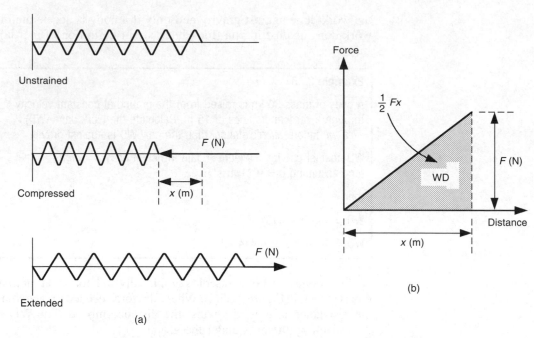

Figure 3.36 *Spring system demonstrating strain energy*

$= \frac{1}{2}Fx$ joules

and since $F = kx$, then substituting for F gives,

strain energy of spring in tension or compression $= \frac{1}{2}kx^2$ *joules*

A similar argument can be given for a spring which is subject to twisting or torsion about its centre (or polar axis). It can be shown that:

strain energy of a spring when twisted $= \frac{1}{2}k_{tor}\theta^2$ *J (where* $\theta =$ *the angle of twist)*

Kinetic energy

Kinetic energy (KE) is energy possessed by a body by virtue of its motion. Translational KE, that is the KE of a body travelling in a linear direction (straight line), is:

$$\text{translational kinetic energy (J)} = \frac{\text{mass (kg)} \times (\text{velocity})^2 \, (\text{m s}^{-1})}{2}$$

translation KE $= \frac{1}{2}\mathbf{mv}^2$

Flywheels are heavy wheel-shaped masses fitted to shafts in order to minimize sudden variations in the rotational speed of the shaft, due to sudden changes in load. A flywheel is therefore a store of rotational KE.

Rotational kinetic energy can be defined in a similar manner to translational KE, i.e.

rotational KE of mass $= \frac{1}{2}I\omega^2$

where $I =$ mass moment of inertia (which was introduced in your earlier work on torque).

Note:
The moment of inertia of a rotating mass I can be defined in

BTEC National Study Guide: Engineering. See page 325 for order details of individual texts

68

general terms by the expression $I = Mk^2$ where M = the *total mass* of the rotating body and k = the *radius of gyration*, that is the radius from the centre of rotation where all of the mass is deemed to act. When we studied torsion earlier we defined I for *concentrated or point masses*, where $I = mr^2$. You should remember that I has different values for different rotating shapes. We will only be considering circular cross-sections, where I is defined as above. One final point, try not to mix up k for the radius of gyration with k for the spring constant!

Example 3.26

Determine the total kinetic energy of a four wheel drive car which has a mass of 800 kg and is travelling at 50 kph. Each wheel of the car has a mass of 15 kg, a diameter of 0.6 m and a radius of gyration of 0.25 m.

The total KE = translational (linear) KE + angular KE

and linear KE = $\frac{1}{2}mv^2$ where v = 50 kph = 13.89 m s^{-1}

= $(\frac{1}{2})(800)(13.89)^2$ = **77.16 kJ**

and angular KE = $\frac{1}{2}I\omega^2$ where $I = Mk^2$

= $(15)(0.25)^2$ = 0.9375 kg m^2 (for each wheel!)

and from v = ωr then $\omega = v / r$ = 13.89/0.3 = 46.3 rad.s

= $(\frac{1}{2})(4 \times 0.9375)(46.3)^2$

= **4.019 kJ**

Therefore total KE of the car = 77.16 + 4.019 = **81.18 kJ**.

Conservation of mechanical energy

From the definition of the conservation of energy we can deduce that the total amount of energy within certain defined boundaries will remain the same. When dealing with mechanical systems, the potential energy possessed by a body is frequently converted into kinetic energy and vice versa. If we ignore air frictional losses, then:

potential energy + kinetic energy = a constant

Thus, if a mass m falls freely from a height h above some datum, then at any height above that datum:

total energy = potential energy + kinetic energy

This important relationship is illustrated in Figure 3.37, where at the highest level above the datum the potential energy is a maximum and is gradually converted into kinetic energy, as the mass falls towards the datum, immediately before impact when height $h = 0$, the potential energy is zero and the kinetic energy is equal to the initial potential energy.

Since the total energy is constant then:

$$mgh_1 = mgh_2 + \tfrac{1}{2}mv_2^2 = mgh_3 + \tfrac{1}{2}mv_3^2 = \tfrac{1}{2}mv_4^2$$

Immediately after impact with the datum surface, the mechanical kinetic energy is converted into other forms such as heat strain and sound.

BTEC National Study Guide: Engineering. See page 325 for order details of individual texts

69

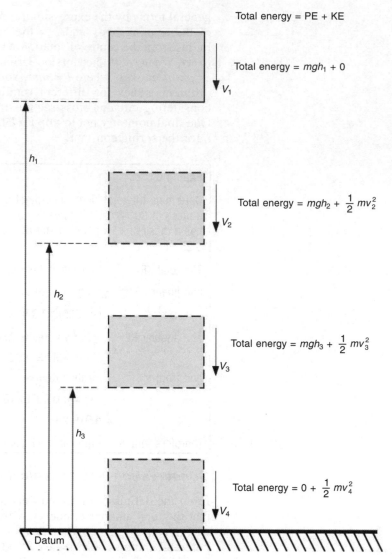

Figure 3.37 *PE + KE = a constant*

If friction is present then work is done overcoming the resistance due to friction and this is dissipated as heat. Then:

initial energy = final energy + work done in overcoming frictional resistance

Note:
Kinetic energy is not always conserved in collisions. Where kinetic energy is conserved in a collision we refer to the collision as *elastic*, when kinetic energy is not conserved we refer to the collision as *inelastic*.

Example 3.27

Cargo weighing 2500 kg breaks free from the top of the cargo ramp (Figure 3.38). Ignoring friction, determine the velocity of the cargo the instant it reaches the bottom of the ramp.

BTEC National Study Guide: Engineering. See page 325 for order details of individual texts

70

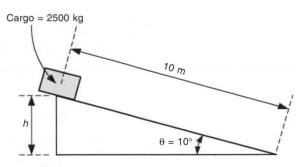

Cargo = 2500 kg

10 m

h

θ = 10°

Figure 3.38 *Cargo ramp*

The vertical height *h* is found using the sine ratio, i.e.

10 sin 10 = *h*   so *h* = 1.736 m

so increase in potential energy = *mgh*

$$= (2500)(9.81)(1.736) \text{ J}$$

$$= 42\,587.2 \text{ J}$$

Now using the relationship PE + KE = total energy. Then immediately prior to the cargo breaking away KE = 0 and so PE = total energy also; immediately prior to the cargo striking the base of slope PE = 0 and KE = total energy (all other energy losses being ignored).

So at base of slope: 42 587.2 J = KE

and $42\,587.2 = \frac{1}{2}mv^2$

so $\dfrac{(20)(42\,587.2)}{2500} = v^2$

and so velocity at bottom of ramp = **18.46 m s⁻¹** (check this working for yourself!).

Power

Power is a measure of the rate at which work is done or the rate of change of energy. Power is therefore defined as: *the rate of doing work*. The SI unit of power is the watt (W), i.e.

$$\textbf{power (W)} = \frac{\textbf{work done (J)}}{\textbf{time taken (s)}} = \frac{\textbf{energy change (J)}}{\textbf{time taken (s)}}$$

or, if the body moves with constant velocity,

power (W) = force used (N) × velocity (m s⁻¹)

Note units are N m s⁻¹ = J s⁻¹ = watt (W).

Key point

Power is the rate of doing work.

Example 3.28

A packing crate weighing 1000 N is loaded onto the back of a lorry by being dragged up an incline of 1 in 5 at a steady speed of 2 m s⁻¹. The frictional resistance to motion is 240 N. Calculate:

BTEC National Study Guide: Engineering. See page 325 for order details of individual texts

71

(a) the power needed to overcome friction
(b) the power needed to overcome gravity
(c) the total power needed.

(a) Power = friction force × velocity along surface

$$= 240 \times 2$$

$$= \textbf{480 W}$$

(b) Power = weight × vertical component of velocity

$$= 1000 \times 2 \times 1/5$$

$$= \textbf{400 W}$$

(c) Since there is no acceleration and therefore no work done against inertia,

Total power = power for friction + power for gravity

$$= 480 + 400$$

$$= \textbf{880 W}$$

Let us now consider power transmitted by a torque. You have already met the concept of torque. Figure 3.39 shows a force F (N) applied at radius r (m) from the centre of a shaft that rotates at n rev/min.

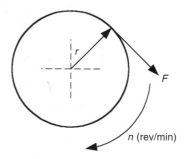

Figure 3.39 *Power transmitted by a torque*

Since the work done is equal to the force multiplied by the distance, then the WD in one revolution is given by:

WD in one revolution = $F \times 2\pi r$ J

but Fr is the torque T applied to the shaft, therefore the work done in one revolution is,

WD in one revolution = $2\pi T$ J

In 1 minute the work done = work done per revolution × number of rev/min (n)

$$= 2\pi n T$$

and WD in 1 second $= 2\pi n T/60$ and since WD per second is equal to power (1 J s^{-1} = 1 W)

then,

Power (W) transmitted by a torque = $2\pi n T/60$

Test your knowledge 3.12

1. Define work done.
2. Write down the equation for work done against gravity, stating SI units.
3. State the principle of the conservation of energy.
4. Detail the forms of energy input and output, for the following devices:
   (a) generator; (b) a reciprocating piston engine; (c) battery; (d) radio.
5. What does the symbol k represent in the formula $F = kx$ and what are its SI units?
6. Write down the formulae for linear and rotational kinetic energy and explain the meaning of each of the symbols within these formulae.
7. Machine A delivers 45 000 joules of energy in 30 seconds, machine B produces 48 kN m of work in 31 seconds, which machine is more powerful and why?

BTEC National Study Guide: Engineering. See page 325 for order details of individual texts

Friction

We have already met *friction*, in terms of the *frictional force that tends to oppose relative motion*, but up till now we have not fully defined the nature of friction.

When a surface is moved over another surface with which it is in contact, a resistance is set up opposing this motion. The value of the resistance will depend on the materials involved, the condition of the two surfaces, and the force holding the surfaces in contact; but the opposition to motion will always be present. This resistance to movement is said to be the result of *friction* between the surfaces.

We require a slightly greater force to start moving the surfaces (*static friction*) than we do to keep them moving (*sliding friction*). As a result of numerous experiments involving different surfaces in contact under different forces, a set of rules or laws has been established which, for all general purposes, materials in contact under the action of forces seem to obey. These rules are detailed below, together with one or two limitations for their use.

Laws of friction

1. The frictional force always opposes the direction of motion, or the direction in which a body is tending to move.
2. The sliding friction force F opposing motion, once motion has started, is proportional to the normal force N that is pressing the two surfaces together, i.e. $F \propto N$.
3. The sliding frictional force is independent of the area of the surfaces in contact. Thus two pairs of surfaces in contact made of the same materials and in the same condition, with the same forces between them, but having different areas, will experience the same frictional forces opposing motion.
4. The frictional resistance is independent of the relative speed of the surfaces. This is not true for very low speeds nor in some cases for fairly high speeds.
5. The frictional resistance at the start of sliding (*static friction*) is slightly greater than that encountered as motion continues (*sliding friction*).
6. The frictional resistance is dependent on the nature of the surfaces in contact. For example, the type of material, surface geometry, surface chemistry, etc.

Key point

Friction always opposes the motion that produces it.

Solving problems involving friction

From the above laws we have established that the sliding frictional force F is proportional to the normal force N pressing the two surfaces together, that is $F \propto N$. You will remember from your mathematical study of proportion that in order to equate these forces we need to insert a constant, the constant of proportionality, i.e. $F = \mu N$. This constant μ is known as the coefficient of friction and in theory it has a maximum value of one. Figure 3.40 shows the space diagram for the arrangement of forces on two horizontal surfaces in contact.

BTEC National Study Guide: Engineering. See page 325 for order details of individual texts

73

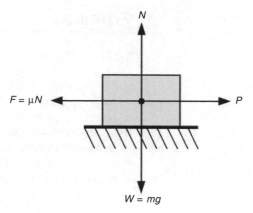

Figure 3.40 *Forces on two horizontal surfaces in contact*

You may find the solution of problems involving friction rather difficult. This is because it is often difficult to visualize the nature and direction of all the forces that act on two bodies in contact, as well as resolving these forces into their component parts. Problems involving friction may be solved by calculation or by drawing. The following generalized example involving the simple case of a block in contact with a horizontal surface should help you understand both methods of solution.

Example 3.29

(a) *Solution by calculation*
Consider again the arrangement of forces shown in Figure 3.40. If the block is in equilibrium, i.e. just on the point of moving, or moving with constant velocity then we can equate the horizontal and vertical forces as follows:

resolving horizontally gives	$P = F$	(1)
resolving vertically	$N = mg$	(2)
but from the laws of dry friction	$F = \mu N$	(3)
substituting (2) into (3) gives	$F = \mu mg$	(4)
substituting (4) into (1) gives	$P = \mu mg$	

(b) *Solution by vector drawing*
You know from your previous work on resolution of coplanar forces (page 188) that two forces can be replaced by a single resultant force in a vector diagram. The space diagram for our horizontal block is shown in Figure 3.41(a), where F and N can be replaced by a resultant R at an angle ϕ to the normal force N.
 From Figure 3.41 it can be seen that:

$$\frac{F}{R} = \sin \phi$$

$$F = R \sin \phi$$

and

$$\frac{N}{R} = \cos \phi$$

$$N = R \cos \phi$$

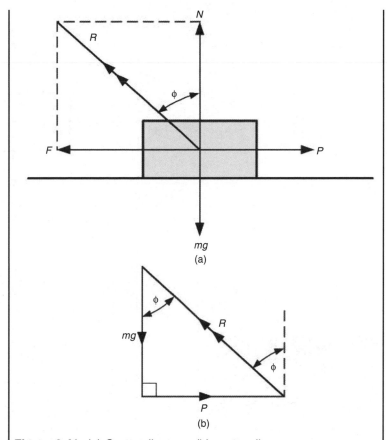

Figure 3.41 *(a) Space diagram, (b) vector diagram*

$$\frac{F}{N} = \frac{R\sin\phi}{R\cos\phi} = \tan\phi$$

however $\qquad \dfrac{F}{N} = \mu$

therefore

$$\mu = \tan\phi$$

ϕ is known as the *angle of friction*.

Once F and N have been replaced by R the problem becomes one of three coplanar forces mg, P and R and can therefore be solved using the triangle of forces you met earlier.

Then choosing a suitable scale the vector diagram is constructed as shown in Figure 3.41(b).

Example 3.30

For the situation illustrated in Figure 3.42(a), find the value of the force P to maintain equilibrium.

We can solve this problem by calculation resolving the forces into their horizontal and vertical components or we can solve by drawing both methods of solution as detailed below.

BTEC National Study Guide: Engineering. See page 325 for order details of individual texts

75

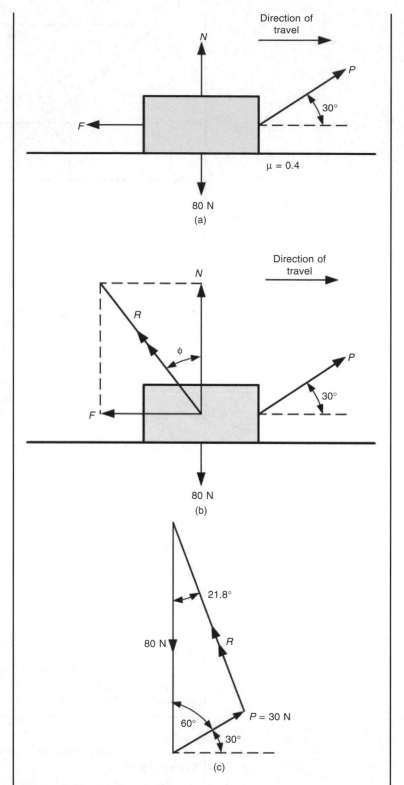

Figure 3.42 *a, b and c*

Key point

The coefficient of friction is given by the tangent of the friction angle.

Test your knowledge 3.13

1. On what variables does the value of frictional resistance depend?
2. 'The frictional resistance is independent of the relative speed of the surfaces, under all circumstances.' Is this statement true or false? You should give reasons for your decision.
3. Define (a) the angle of friction; (b) the coefficient of friction. Explain how they are related.
4. Sketch a space diagram that shows all the forces that act on a body moving with uniform velocity along a horizontal surface.

(a)   *Solution by calculation*

resolving forces horizontally $F = P \cos 30$

BTEC National Study Guide: Engineering. See page 325 for order details of individual texts

76

resolving forces vertically $\qquad N + P \sin 30 = 80$

but $\qquad F = mN$

and substituting for N from above gives $F = m(80 - P \sin 30)$

We are told that $m = 0.4$ and replacing F in the above equation by $P \cos 30$, in a similar manner to the general example, gives:

$P \cos 30 = 0.4(80 - P \sin 30)$

and by multiplying out the brackets and rearrangement we get

$P \cos 30 + 0.4\, P \sin 30 = 0.4 \times 80$

so $P(\cos 30 + 0.4 \sin 30) = 32$

and $P = \mathbf{30.02\ N}$

Make sure you can follow the above trigonometric and algebraic argument.

(b) *Solution by drawing*

The magnitude and direction of all known forces for our block is shown in Figure 3.42(b).

Remembering that $\mu = \tan \phi$ then

$\tan \phi = \mu = 0.4$ so $\phi = \tan^{-1} 0.4$ (the angle whose tangent is) and $\phi = 21.8°$

From the resulting vector diagram Figure 3.42(c), we find that $P = \mathbf{30\ N}$.

Problems 3.4

1. Find the kinetic energy of a mass of 2000 kg moving with a velocity of 40 kph.
2. The scale of a spring balance which indicates weights up to 20 N extends over a length of 10 cm. Calculate the work done in pulling the balance out until it indicates 12 N.
3. A crane raises a load of 1640 N to a height of 10 m in 8 seconds. Calculate the average power developed.
4. A wooden packing case weighing 560 N rests on a concrete floor. The coefficient of friction is 0.3. Calculate the least horizontal force required to move the case.
5. A drilling machine of mass 300 kg is pulled along a horizontal floor by means of a rope inclined at 20° to the horizontal. If a tension in the rope of 600 N is just sufficient to move the machine, determine the coefficient of friction between the machine and the floor.
6. A motor vehicle starting from rest freewheels down a slope whose gradient is 1 in 8. Neglecting all resistances to motion, find its velocity after travelling a distance of 200 m down the slope.
7. A train having a mass of 15 tonnes is brought to rest when striking the buffers of a terminus. The buffers consist of two springs in parallel, each having a spring constant of 120 kN m^{-1} and able to be compressed to a maximum of 0.75 m. Find:

   (a) the strain energy gained by the buffers
   (b) the velocity of the train at the instant it strikes the buffers.

BTEC National Study Guide: Engineering. See page 325 for order details of individual texts

77

HEAT ENERGY

Heat

The study of *heat energy* is a necessary foundation for an understanding of the area of science known as *thermodynamics*. Engineering thermodynamics is concerned with the relationship between heat, work and the properties of systems. As engineers we are concerned with the machines (engines) that convert heat energy from fuels into useful mechanical work. It is therefore appropriate to start our study of heat energy by considering the concept of *heat* itself.

Energy is the most important and fundamental physical property of the universe. We have already defined energy as *the capacity to do work*. A more accurate definition is *the capacity to produce an effect*. These effects are apparent during the process of energy transfer.

A modern idea of heat is that it is energy in transition and cannot be stored by matter. *Heat* (*Q*) may be defined as: *transient energy brought about by the interaction of bodies by virtue of their temperature difference when they communicate*. Matter possesses stored energy but not transient (moving) energy such as heat or work. Heat energy can only travel or *transfer* from a hot body to a cold body, it cannot travel up hill. Figure 3.43 illustrates this fact.

Key point

Heat and work is energy in transit and cannot be stored by matter.

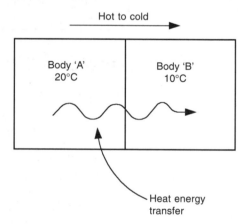

Figure 3.43 *Heat energy transfer*

Within matter the amount of molecular vibration determines the amount of *kinetic energy* a substance possesses. For incompressible fluids (liquids) the amount of molecular vibration is relatively small and can be neglected. For compressible fluids and gases the degree of vibration is so large that it has to be accounted for in thermodynamics. This kinetic energy is classified as *internal energy* (*U*) and is a form of stored energy.

The gas laws

In the study of gases we have to consider the interactions between temperature, pressure and volume (remembering that density is mass per unit volume). A change in one of these characteristics always produces a corresponding change in at least one of the other two.

BTEC National Study Guide: Engineering. See page 325 for order details of individual texts

78

Unlike liquids and solids, gases have the characteristics of being easily compressible and of expanding or contracting readily in response to changes in temperature. Although the characteristics themselves vary in degree for different gases, certain basic laws can be applied to what we call a perfect gas. A *perfect* or *ideal gas* is simply one which has been shown, through experiment, to follow or adhere very closely to these gas laws. In these experiments one factor, for example volume, is kept constant while the relationship between the other two is investigated. In this way it can be shown that:

1. *The pressure of a fixed mass of gas is directly proportional to its absolute temperature, providing the volume of the gas is kept constant.*

In symbols:

$$\frac{P}{T} = \text{constant} \quad \text{(providing } V \text{ remains constant)}$$

The above relationship is known as the *pressure law*.

Gas molecules are in a state of perpetual motion, constantly bombarding the sides of the gas containing vessel. Each molecule produces a minute force as it strikes the walls of the container, since many billion molecules hit the container every second, this produces a steady outward pressure.

Figure 3.44 shows how the pressure of the gas varies with temperature.

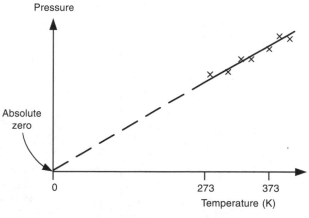

Figure 3.44 *Pressure/temperature relationship of gas*

Key point

When dealing with the gas equations or any thermodynamic relationship we always use absolute temperature (*T*) in degrees kelvin.

If the graph is 'extrapolated' downwards, in theory we will reach a temperature where the pressure is zero. This temperature is known as *absolute zero* and is approximately equal to *–273 kelvin*. Each one degree kelvin *K* is equivalent to one degree celsius *C*. The relationship between the kelvin scale and the celsius scale is shown in Figure 3.45.

Returning to the gas laws, it can also be shown experimentally that:

2. *The volume of a fixed mass of gas is directly proportional to its absolute temperature providing the pressure of the gas remains constant.*

BTEC National Study Guide: Engineering. See page 325 for order details of individual texts

79

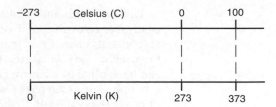

Figure 3.45 *Kelvin/Celsius scales*

So for a fixed mass of gas:

$$\frac{V}{T} = \textbf{constant} \quad \textbf{(providing } M \textbf{ is fixed and } P \textbf{ remains constant)}$$

This relationship is known as *Charles' law.*

A further relationship exists when we keep the temperature of the gas constant, this states that:

The volume of a fixed mass of gas is inversely proportional to its pressure providing the temperature of the gas is kept constant.

In symbols:

$$p \propto \frac{1}{V}$$

or, for a fixed mass of gas:

pV = constant

This relationship is better known as *Boyle's law*, it is illustrated in Figure 3.46.

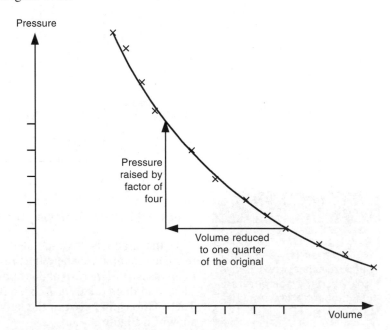

Figure 3.46 *Boyle's pressure/volume relationship*

In dealing with problems associated with the gas laws, remember that we assume that all gases are *ideal*; in reality no gas is ideal but at low and medium pressures and temperatures, most gases behave in an ideal way.

BTEC National Study Guide: Engineering. See page 325 for order details of individual texts

80

The pressure law, Charles' law and Boyle's law can all be expressed in terms of one single equation known as the *combined gas equation*, this is for a fixed mass of gas:

$$\frac{pV}{T} = \textbf{constant}$$

If we consider a fixed mass of gas before and after changes have taken place, then from the combined gas equation, it follows that:

$$\frac{p_1 V_1}{T_1} = \frac{p_2 V_2}{T_2}$$

where subscript 1 is used for the initial state and subscript 2 for the final state of the gas.

The above relationship is very useful when solving problems concerned with the gas laws.

Key point

A perfect gas is one that is assumed to obey the ideal gas laws.

Example 3.31

A quantity of gas occupies a volume of 0.5 m^3. The pressure of the gas is 300 kPa, when its temperature is 30°C. What will be the pressure of the gas if it is compressed to half its volume and heated to a temperature of 140°C?

When solving problems involving several variables, always tabulate the information given, in appropriate units:

p_1 = 300 kPa p_2 = ?
V_1 = 0.5 m^2 V_2 = 0.25 m^2
T_1 = 303 K T_2 = 413 K

Remember to convert temperature to kelvin by adding 273°C.
Using the combined gas equation and after rearrangement:

$$p_2 = \frac{p_1 V_1 T_2}{T_1 V_1} = \frac{(300)(0.5)(413)}{(303)(0.25)} = \textbf{817 kPa}$$

Temperature and its measurement

We have already met the idea of temperature when we considered the pressure law, but as yet, we have not fully defined it. A more formal definition of temperature is as follows:

Temperature is a measure of the quantity of energy possessed by a body or substance. It measures the vibration of the molecules which form the substance.

These molecular vibrations only cease when the temperature of the substance reaches *absolute zero*, that is −273.15°C.

You have already met the celsius temperature scale and the way in which we convert degrees centigrade into kelvin and vice versa.

Key point

Temperature measures the energy possessed by the vibration of the molecules that go to make up a substance.

Example 3.32

Convert 60°C into kelvin

You already know that 1°C = 1 K and that to convert degrees celsius into kelvin, we simple add 273. Therefore 60°C + 273 = **333 K**.

Note that to be strictly accurate we should add 273.15, but for all practical purposes the approximate value of 273 is adequate.

BTEC National Study Guide: Engineering. See page 325 for order details of individual texts

81

The method used to measure temperature depends on the degree of hotness of the body or substance being measured. Measurement apparatus includes liquid-in-glass thermometers, resistance thermometers, thermistor thermometers and thermocouples.

All *thermometers* are based on some property of a material that changes when the material becomes colder or hotter. Liquid-in-glass thermometers use the fact that most liquids expand slightly when they are heated. Two common types of liquid-in-glass thermometer are the mercury thermometer and alcohol thermometer, both have relative advantages and disadvantages.

Alcohol thermometers are suitable for measuring temperatures down to −115°C and have a higher expansion rate than mercury, so a larger containing tube may be used. They have the disadvantage of requiring the addition of a colouring in order to be seen easily. Also, the alcohol tends to cling to the side of the glass tube and may separate.

Mercury thermometers conduct heat well and respond quickly to temperature change. They do not wet the sides of the tube and so flow well in addition to being easily seen. Mercury has the disadvantage of freezing at −39°C and so is not suitable for measuring low temperatures. Mercury is also poisonous and special procedures must be followed in the event of spillage.

Resistance thermometers are based on the principle that current flow becomes increasingly more difficult with increase in temperature. They are used where a large temperature range is being measured, approximately −200°C to 1200°C. *Thermistor thermometers* work along similar lines, except in this case they offer less and less resistance to the flow of electric current as temperature increases.

Thermocouple thermometers are based on the principle that when two different metal wires are joined at two junctions and each junction is subjected to a different temperature, a small current will flow. This current is amplified and used to power an analogue or digital temperature display. Thermocouple temperature sensors are often used to measure the temperatures inside engines, they can operate over a temperature range from about −200°C to 1600°C.

Thermal expansion

We have mentioned in our discussion on thermometers that certain liquids expand with increase in temperature, this is also the case with *solids*. Thermal expansion is dependent on the nature of the material and the magnitude of the temperature increase. We normally measure the linear expansion of solids, such as the increase in length of a bar of the material; with gases (as you have already seen) we measure volumetric or cubic expansion.

Every solid has a *linear expansivity value, that is the amount the material will expand in metres per kelvin or per degree celsius.* This expansivity value is often referred to as the *coefficient of linear expansion* (α), some typical values of α are given below.

Given the length of a material (l), its linear expansion coefficient (α) and the temperature rise (Δt), the *increase in its length* can be calculated using:

increase in length = $\alpha l(t_2 - t_1)$

BTEC National Study Guide: Engineering. See page 325 for order details of individual texts

82

Material	Linear expansion coefficient α/°C
Invar	1.5×10^{-6}
Glass	9×10^{-6}
Cast iron	10×10^{-6}
Concrete	11×10^{-6}
Steel	12×10^{-6}
Copper	17×10^{-6}
Brass	19×10^{-6}
Aluminium	24×10^{-6}

Note that we are using lower case t to indicate temperature because when we find a *temperature difference* (Δt) we do not need to convert to kelvin.

For solids an estimate of the cubic or volumetric expansion may be found using:

change in volume $= 3\alpha V(t_2 - t_1)$

where V is the original volume.

A similar relationship exists for surface expansion, where a body experiences a change in area. In this case the linear expansion coefficient is multiplied by 2, therefore:

change in area $= 2\alpha A(t_2 - t_1)$ where A is the original area.

Example 3.33

A steel bar has a length of 4.0 m at 10°C. What will be the length of the bar when it is heated to 350°C? If a sphere of diameter 15 cm is made from the same material what will be the percentage increase in surface area, if the sphere is subject to the same initial and final temperatures?

Using $\alpha = 12 \times 10^{-6}$ from the above table, then increase in length of the bar is given by:

$x = \alpha l(t_2 - t_1) = (12 \times 10^{-6})(4.0)(350 - 10) = 0.0163$ m

This can now be added to the original length, so

final length $= 4.0 + 0.0163 = $ **4.0163 m**

Increase in surface area of the sphere $= 2\alpha A (t_2 - t_1)$.
We first need to find the original surface area which is given by:

$A = 4\pi r^2 = 4\pi \times (0.075)^2 = 0.0707$ m^2

and from above the increase in surface area
$= (2)(12 \times 10^{-6})(0.0707)(340) = 5.769 \times 10^{-4}$ m.

Therefore, percentage increase in area $= \left(\dfrac{\text{increase in area}}{\text{original area}} \right) \times 100$

$= \dfrac{(300)(0.5)(413)}{0.0707} = $ **0.82%**.

Heat energy transfer

Literature on heat transfer generally recognizes three distinct modes of heat transmission, the names of which will be familiar to you,

BTEC National Study Guide: Engineering. See page 325 for order details of individual texts

83

i.e. *conduction*, *convection* and *radiation*. Technically only conduction and radiation are true heat transfer processes, because both of these depend totally and utterly on a temperature difference being present. Convection also depends on the transportation of a mechanical mass. Nevertheless, since convection also accomplishes transmission of energy from high to low temperature regions, it is conventionally regarded as a heat transfer mechanism.

Thermal conduction in solids and liquids seems to involve two processes; the first is concerned with atoms and molecules (Figure 3.47), the second with free electrons.

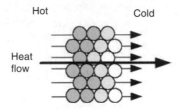

Solid molecules/atoms– direct conduction

(a) Conduction by molecular transfer in solids and gases

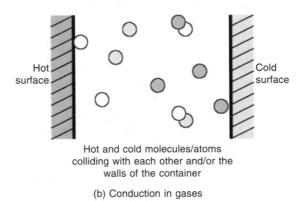

Hot and cold molecules/atoms colliding with each other and/or the walls of the container

(b) Conduction in gases

Figure 3.47 *Conduction by molecular transfer in solids and gases*

Atoms at high temperatures vibrate more vigorously about their equilibrium positions than their cooler neighbours. Since atoms and molecules are bonded to one another, they pass on some of their vibrational energy. This energy transfer occurs from atoms of high vibrational energy to those of low vibrational energy, without appreciable displacement. This energy transfer has a knock-on effect, since high vibrational energy atoms increase the energy in adjacent low vibrational energy atoms, which in turn causes them to vibrate more energetically, causing thermal conduction to occur. In solids (Figure 3.47(a)) the energy transfer is by direct contact between one molecule and another. In gases the conduction process occurs as a result of collisions between hot and cold molecules and the surface of the containing vessel.

The second process involves material with a ready supply of free electrons. Since electrons are considerably lighter than atoms, then any gain in energy by electrons results in an increase in the

BTEC National Study Guide: Engineering. See page 325 for order details of individual texts

84

electron's velocity and it is able to pass this energy on quickly to cooler parts of the material. This phenomenon is one of the reasons why electrical conductors that have many free electrons are also good thermal conductors, Do remember that metals are not the only good thermal conductors; the first mechanism described above which does not rely on free electrons is a very effective method of thermal conduction, especially at low temperatures.

Heat transfer by convection consists of two mechanisms. In addition to energy transfer by random molecular motion (diffusion), there is also energy being transferred by the bulk motion of the fluid.

So in the presence of a temperature difference large numbers of molecules are moving together in bulk (Figure 3.48), at the same time as the individual motion of the molecules takes place. The cumulative effect of both of these energy transfer methods is referred to as heat transfer by convection.

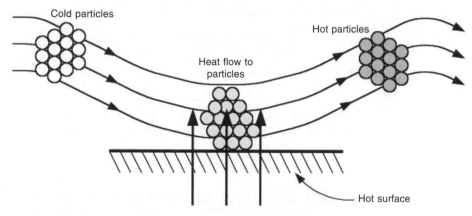

Figure 3.48 *Heat transfer by convection*

Radiation may be defined as the transfer of energy *not requiring* a medium through which the energy must pass, thus radiation can be transferred through empty space. Thermal radiation is attributed to the electron energy changes within atoms or molecules. As electron energy levels change energy is released which travels in the form of electromagnetic waves of varying wavelength. You will meet electromagnetic waves again when you study light. When striking a body the emitted radiation is either absorbed by, reflected by, or transmitted through the body.

Specific heat

From what has been said about heat transfer above, it will be apparent that different materials have different capacities for absorbing and transferring thermal energy. The thermal energy needed to produce a temperature rise depends on the mass of the material, the type of material and the temperature rise to which the material is subjected.

Thus the inherent ability of a material to absorb heat for a given mass and temperature rise is dependent on the material itself. This property of the material is known as its *specific heat capacity*. In the SI system, *the specific heat capacity of a material is the same as the thermal energy required to produce a 1 K rise in temperature*

BTEC National Study Guide: Engineering. See page 325 for order details of individual texts

85

in a mass of 1 kg. Therefore knowing the mass of a substance and its specific heat capacity, it is possible to calculate the thermal energy required to produce any given temperature rise, from:

thermal energy, $Q = mc\Delta t$

where c = specific heat capacity of the material (J/kg K) and ΔT is the temperature change.

Example 3.34

How much thermal energy is required to raise the temperature of 5 kg of aluminium from 20°C to 40°C? Take the specific heat capacity for aluminium as 900 J/kg K.

All that is required is to substitute the appropriate values directly into the equation:

$Q = mc\Delta t = (5)(900)(40 - 20) = 90\,000$ J = **90 kJ**

Another way of defining the specific heat capacity of any substance is: *the amount of heat energy required to raise the temperature of unit mass of the substance through one degree, under specific conditions.*

In *thermodynamics*, two specified conditions are used, those of constant volume and constant pressure. With *gases* the two specific heats do not have the same value and it is essential that we distinguish between them.

Specific heat at constant volume (c_v)

If 1 kg of a gas is supplied with an amount of heat energy sufficient to raise the temperature by 1 degree centigrade or kelvin while the volume of the gas remains constant, then the amount of heat energy supplied is known as the *specific heat capacity at constant volume and is denoted by c_v*.

Note that under these circumstances (Figure 3.49(a)) no work is done, but the gas has received an increase in internal energy (U). The specific heat at constant volume for air is *c_v air = 718 J/kg K*, this value is well worth memorizing!

> **Key point**
>
> Specific heat capacity at constant pressure for air is 1005 J/kg K.

> **Key point**
>
> Specific heat at constant pressure will be greater than specific heat at constant volume, since work is done.

Specific heat at constant pressure (c_p)

If 1 kg of a gas is supplied with a quantity of heat energy sufficient to raise the temperature of the gas by 1 degree centigrade or kelvin while the pressure is held constant, then the amount of heat energy supplied is known as the *specific heat capacity at constant pressure and is denoted by c_p*.

This implies that when the gas has been heated it will expand a distance h (Figure 3.49(b)), so work has been done. Thus for the same amount of heat energy there has been an increase in internal energy (U), plus work. The value of c_p is, therefore, greater than the corresponding value of c_v.

BTEC National Study Guide: Engineering. See page 325 for order details of individual texts

86

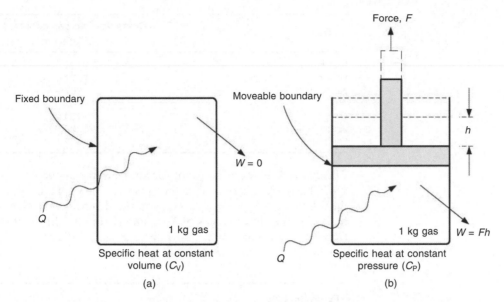

Figure 3.49 *Comparison of constant pressure and constant volume specific heats*

The specific heat capacity at constant pressure for air is c_p *air* = *1005 J/kg K*, again this is a value worth remembering.

The characteristic gas equation

The combined gas law, which you met earlier, stated that for a perfect gas with unit mass:

$$\frac{pV}{T} = \text{a constant}$$

This relationship is of course true for any fixed mass of gas and so we can write that

$$\frac{pV}{T} = \text{mass} \times \text{a constant}$$

Now for any perfect gas which obeys the ideal gas laws this constant *R* is specific to that particular gas, i.e. *R is the characteristic gas constant* or specific gas constant for the individual gas concerned. Therefore, the characteristic gas equation may be written as:

$$\frac{pV}{T} = mR$$

or

$$pV = mRT$$

The unit for the characteristic gas constant is the joule per kilogram kelvin (J/kg K).

Note, that when the above equation is used both *absolute pressure and absolute temperature must be used*.

The characteristic gas constant for a number of gases is given in the table below.

BTEC National Study Guide: Engineering. See page 325 for order details of individual texts

87

Gas	Characteristic gas constant (J/kg K)
Hydrogen	4124
Helium	2077
Nitrogen	297
Air	287
Oxygen	260
Argon	208
Carbon dioxide	189

The characteristic gas constant for air, from the above table, is $R = 287$ J/kg K. This is related to the specific heat capacities for air in the following way, i.e. $R = c_p - c_v$, you should check this relationship by noting the above values of R, c_p and c_v for air. This relationship ($R = c_p - c_v$) is not only valid for air, *it is also valid for any perfect gas that follows the gas laws.*

Example 3.35

0.22 kg of gas at a temperature of 20°C and pressure of 103 kN/m^2 occupies a volume of 0.18 m^3. If the c_v for the gas = 720 J/kg K, find:

(a) the characteristic gas constant
(b) the specific heat capacity at constant pressure.

(a) Using $pV = mRT$
then on rearrangement,

$$R = pV/mT = \frac{(103 \times 10^3)(0.18)}{(0.22)(293)} = \textbf{288 J/kg K}$$

(b) from $R = c_p - c_v$ then $c_p = R + C_v = 288 + 720 = \textbf{1008 J/kg K}$

Latent heat

When a substance changes state, that is when heat is applied to a solid and it turns into a liquid and with further heating the liquid turns into a gas, we say the substance has undergone a *change in state*. The three states of matter are *solid*, *liquid* and *gas*. Therefore, the heat energy added to a substance does not necessarily give rise to a measurable change in temperature, it may be used to change the state of a substance; under these circumstances we refer to the heat energy as *latent* or *hidden heat*.

We refer to the thermal energy required to change a solid material into a liquid as the latent heat of fusion. For water, 334 kJ of thermal energy are required to change 1 kg of ice at 0°C into water at the same temperature. Thus *the specific latent heat of fusion for water is 334 kJ*. In the case of latent heat, *specific* refers to unit mass of the material, i.e. per kilogram. So we define the specific latent heat of fusion of a substance as: *the thermal energy required to turn 1 kg of a substance from a liquid into a solid without change in temperature.*

If we wish to find the thermal energy required to change any amount of a substance from a solid into a liquid, then we use the relationship:

BTEC National Study Guide: Engineering. See page 325 for order details of individual texts

88

$$Q = mL$$

where L is the *specific latent heat* of the substance.

In a similar manner to the above argument: *the thermal energy required to change 1 kg of a substance from a liquid into a gas without change in temperature, is known as the specific latent heat of vaporization.* Again, if we wish to find the thermal energy required to change any amount of a substance from a liquid into a gas we use the relationship $Q = mL$, but in this case L = the specific latent heat of vaporization.

The specific latent heat of vaporization for water = 2.26 MJ/kg K.

Example 3.36

(a) How much heat energy is required to change 3 kg of ice at 0°C into water at 30°C?
(b) What thermal energy is required to condense 0.2 kg of steam into water at 100°C?

(a) The thermal energy required to convert ice at 0°C into water at 0°C is calculated using the equation:

$Q = mL$ and substituting values we get

$Q = (3)(334 \times 10^3) = 1.002$ MJ

The 3 kg of water formed has to be heated from 0°C to 30°C. The thermal energy required for this is calculated using the equation
$Q = mc\Delta t$, you have already met this equation when we studied specific heat earlier.

So in this case $Q = (3)(4200)(30) = 378\,000$ J

Then total thermal energy required = 1.002 + 0.378 = **1.38 MJ**

(b) In this case we simply use $Q = mL$, since we are converting steam to water at 100°C which is the vaporization temperature for water into steam.

Then $Q = (0.2)(2.226 \times 10^6) = $ **445.2 kJ**

Note the large amounts of thermal energy required to change the state of a substance.

Test your knowledge 3.14

1. Convert (a) −20°C into kelvin; (b) 320 K into °C; (c) −50°F into kelvin.
2. We are required to measure the temperature of an oven used to heat-treat metals; under normal operating conditions the oven operating temperature will not exceed 1200°C. Suggest the most suitable temperature measuring device, giving reasons.
3. Define the linear expansion coefficient for solids *and* explain how it may be used for approximating surface expansion and volumetric expansion.
4. Define heat energy and explain the difference between heat energy and internal energy of a substance.
5. Explain the essential differences between heat transfer by conduction and heat transfer by convection.
6. Why, for a gas, is the specific heat capacity at constant pressure greater than the specific heat capacity at constant volume?
7. State the formula for calculating the thermal energy needed to produce a temperature rise *and* explain how this formula varies when calculating latent thermal energy (that is heat energy input without temperature rise).
8. If the characteristic gas constant for a gas is 260 J/kg K and the specific heat capacity at constant volume is 680 J/kg K, what is the value of c_p?
9. Detail three ways in which a liquid can be made to evaporate more readily.

A liquid does not have to boil in order for it to change state; the nearer the temperature is to the boiling point of the liquid, the quicker the liquid will turn into a gas. At much lower temperatures the change may take place by a process of *evaporation*. The steam rising from a puddle, when the sun comes out after a rainstorm, is an example of evaporation. Where water vapour forms as steam, well below the boiling point of the water.

There are several ways that a liquid can be made to evaporate more readily. These include, an *increase in temperature* that increases the molecular energy of the liquid sufficient for the more energetic molecules to escape from the liquid. *Reducing the pressure above the liquid* in order to allow less energetic molecules to escape as a gas. *Increasing the surface area*, thus providing more opportunity for the more energetic molecules to escape or *by passing a gas over the surface* of the liquid to assist molecular escape.

BTEC National Study Guide: Engineering. See page 325 for order details of individual texts

89

Problems 3.5

1. A quantity of gas occupies a volume of 4 m^3. The pressure of the gas is 350 kPa when its temperature is 30°C. What will be its pressure if it is compressed into half its volume and heated to 130°C?

2. A metal bar is heated from 20°C to 120°C and as a result its length increases from 1500 mm to 1503 mm. Determine the linear expansion coefficient of the metal.

3. (a) Write down the formula for the thermal energy input into a solid and explain the meaning of each term.

   (b) If 3 kg of aluminium requires 54 kJ of energy to raise its temperature from 10°C to 30°C, find the specific heat capacity for aluminium.

4. 0.5 kg of a gas at a temperature of 20°C and at standard atmospheric pressure occupies a volume of 0.4 m^3. If the c_p for the gas = 1000 J/kg K find:

   (a) the characteristic gas constant
   (b) the specific heat capacity at constant volume.

5. How much heat energy is required to change 2 kg of ice at 0°C into water at 40°C?

ELECTRICAL PRINCIPLES

Introduction

Throughout our study of electrical principles the concept of *electrical energy* will be apparent. Electrical energy, like heat energy, requires a difference in potential for transfer. For heat energy transfer, this difference in potential was generated by a difference in temperature between two bodies. When electrical energy is transferred this difference in potential can be compared to that of a waterfall, where the water at the top of a waterfall is at a higher potential than that at the bottom. Exactly how this difference in electrical potential is created will be discussed shortly.

In order to discover the nature of this potential difference (pd), we first investigate the fundamental ideas of charge, potential, resistance, current and power. To do this, we need to be familiar with the ideas you first met when we made a brief study of matter at the beginning of this unit.

Therefore, we start our study of electricity by looking at the fundamental properties identified above. This section will include a brief discussion on the ways in which electricity can be produced by chemical means using batteries. We then look at the production of electrical energy in simple circuits where voltage, current, resistance, electrical work and power within these circuits is considered. In the final topic of the outcome the concept of magnetism is studied. The principle of electromagnetic induction is then applied

BTEC National Study Guide: Engineering. See page 325 for order details of individual texts

90

to electrical machines that produce and use electrical energy for many engineering applications.

Electrical fundamentals

Atomic structure and conduction

As you already know, all matter is made up of atoms or groups of atoms (molecules) bonded together in a particular way. In order to understand something about the nature of electrical charge we need to consider a simple model of the atom. This model, known as the Bohr model, shows a single atom (Figure 3.50) consisting of a central nucleus with orbiting electrons.

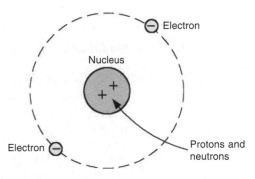

Figure 3.50 *Bohr's model of the atom*

Within the nucleus there are *protons* which are *positively charged* and *neutrons* which, as their name implies, are electrically neutral and *have no charge*. Orbiting the nucleus are *electrons that have a negative charge, equal in magnitude (size) to the charge on the proton*. These electrons are approximately two thousands times lighter than the protons and neutrons in the nucleus.

In a stable atom the number of protons and electrons is equal, so that overall, the atom is neutral and has no charge. However, if we rub two particular materials together, electrons may be transferred from one to another. This alters the stability of the atom, leaving it with a net positive or negative charge. When an atom within a material *loses electrons* it becomes positively charged and is known as a positive ion, when an atom *gains an electron* it has a surplus negative charge and so is known as a *negative ion*. These differences in charge can cause *electrostatic* effects. For example, combing your hair with a nylon comb may result in a difference in charge between your hair and the rest of your body, resulting in your hair standing on end when your hand or some other differently charged body is brought close to it.

The number of electrons occupying a given orbit within an atom is predictable and is based on the position of the element within the periodic table. The electrons in all atoms sit in a particular position (shell) dependent on their energy level. Each of these shells within the atom is filled with electrons from the nucleus outwards (Figure 3.51). The first, inner most, of these shells can have up to two electrons, the second shell can have up to eight and the third up to 18.

BTEC National Study Guide: Engineering. See page 325 for order details of individual texts

91

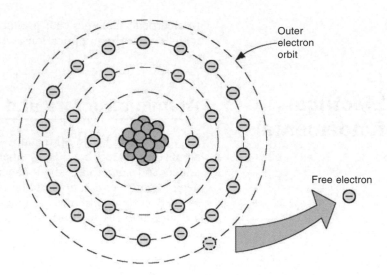

Figure 3.51 *The copper electron with a loosely bound outer electron*

Figure 3.51 shows the copper atom with one outer electron that can become easily detached from the parent atom. It requires a small amount of external energy to overcome the attraction of the nucleus. Sources of such energy may include heat, light or electrostatic fields. The electron once detached from the atom is able to move freely around the structure of the material and is called a *free electron*. It is these free electrons that become the *charge carriers* within a material. Materials that have large numbers of free electrons make good *conductors* of electrical energy and heat.

In a material containing free electrons their direction of motion is random, as shown in Figure 3.52(a), but if an external force is applied that causes the free electrons to move in a uniform manner (Figure 3.52(b)) an electric *current* is said to flow.

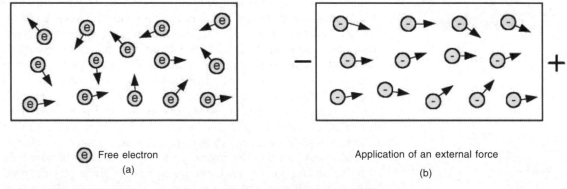

Figure 3.52 *Free electrons and the application of an external force*

Metals are the best conductors, since they have a very large number of free electrons available to act as charge carriers. Materials which do not conduct charge are called *insulators*; their electrons are tightly bound to the nuclei of their atoms.

The effects of electric current flow can be detected by the presence of one or more of the following effects: light, heat, magnetism, chemical, pressure and friction. Thus, for example, if a *piezo-*

BTEC National Study Guide: Engineering. See page 325 for order details of individual texts

92

electric crystal is subject to an electrical current it can change its shape and exert pressure. Heat is another, more obvious, effect, from electric heating elements. Therefore, as free electrons are the mechanism by which electric current flows, the electrical properties of a material are determined by the number of free electrons present.

Electrical terminology

1. Charge

All electrons and protons have an electrostatic *charge*; its value is so small that a more convenient unit of charge is needed for practical use, which we call the *coulomb*. One coulomb C is the total charge Q of 6.21×10^{18} electrons. Thus a single electron has a charge of 1.61×10^{-19} C.

2. Current

You have already met a definition for the *unit of current* at the beginning of this unit when we considered the SI system of units, it stated that: *the ampere* is that *constant current* which, if maintained between two straight parallel conductors of infinite length, of negligible circular cross-section, and placed 1 metre apart in a vacuum, would produce between these conductors a force equal to 2×10^{-7} newton per metre of length. Figure 3.53 illustrates the physical set-up for this definition.

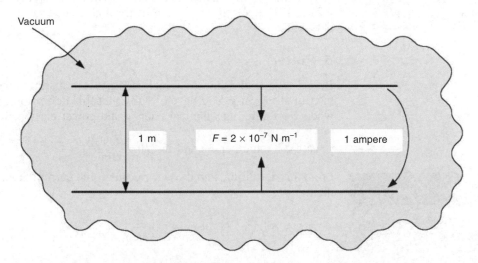

Figure 3.53 *Illustration of the SI definition for the unit of current*

Current I itself is defined as *the rate of flow of charge* and its unit is the ampere (A). One ampere is equal to one coulomb C per second, or:

one ampere of current $I = \dfrac{Q}{t}$ where t = time in seconds

So, for example: if a steady current of 3 A flows for two minutes, then the amount of charge transferred will be:

$Q = I \times t = 3 \text{ A} \times 120 \text{ s} = 360 \text{ coulombs}$

BTEC National Study Guide: Engineering. See page 325 for order details of individual texts

93

If the same 3 A of current was flowing in the conductors then the force set-up between them would be 6×10^{-7} newton per unit length.

3. Voltage

The *force which creates the flow of current* or rate of flow of charge carriers in a circuit is known as the *electromotive force* (emf) and it is measured in volts. The *potential difference* (pd) is the voltage difference, or voltage drop between two points.

One volt is the potential difference between two points if one joule of energy is required to move one coulomb of charge between them.

$V = \dfrac{J}{Q}$ where J = energy and Q = charge, as before. Energy is defined later.

4. Resistance

All materials at normal temperatures oppose the movement of electric charge through them. This opposition to the flow of the charge carriers is known as the *resistance* (R) of the material. This resistance is due to collisions between the charge carriers (electrons) and the atoms of the material. The unit of resistance is the *ohm*, with symbol Ω.

Note that 1 volt is equal to the amount of force required to move 6.21×10^{18} electrons (1 coulomb) through a resistance of 1 Ω in 1 second.

5. Power

Power (P), is the rate at which energy is transferred and it is measured in *watts*. You have already met this definition of power when we studied mechanical energy and power earlier. So:

1 watt = 1 joule per second or, $P = \dfrac{\text{energy}}{\text{time}} = \dfrac{J}{s}$

From this definition, and those for voltage and current given above, then:

$$\text{power} = \text{voltage}\left(\frac{J}{Q}\right) \times \text{current}\left(\frac{Q}{t}\right)$$

$$= \text{voltage}(v) \times \text{current}(I) \text{ with units of } \left(\frac{J}{s}\right) \text{ or watts}$$

6. Electrical energy

Electrical energy is like all other forms of energy you have met before. Energy is the capacity to do work and is always in transit. This means that it can only be transferred when a difference in energy levels exists. As before the unit of energy is the joule. Then, from our definition of power, where 1 watt = 1 joule/second we know that the energy in *joules* = watts × *seconds* or *watt-seconds*.

Key point

Electromotive force (emf) is that electrical force which is initially available for moving electrons round a circuit.

Key point

The difference in *electrical pressure* between any two points in a circuit is called the *potential difference* (pd) between those points.

Key point

Resistance (R) is opposition to current flow.

Key point

1 watt of power = 1 joule per second.

BTEC National Study Guide: Engineering. See page 325 for order details of individual texts

94

Key point

1 kilowatt-hour = 3.6 million joules.

If the power were to be measured in kilowatts and the time in hours, then the unit of electrical energy would be the *kilowatt-hour* (kWh), often known as the *unit of electricity*. The electricity meter in your home records the number of kilowatt-hours and is therefore an *energy* meter.

Example 3.37

An electric fire, when switched to its highest setting, consumes 3 kilowatts of power. If the fire is left on this setting for 2 hours, how much energy is transferred in joules?

We know that our electric fire will consume 3 kilowatts × 2 hour or 6 kWh of electrical energy.

1 kWh = 1000 watt-hours = 1000 × 3600 watt-seconds or joules. Therefore, the number of joules of energy transferred is 6 kWh = 6 × 1000 × 3600 = 2.16×10^7 joules or 21.6 MJ. Quite a lot of electrical energy!

---

7. Conductors, semiconductors and insulators

A material which has many free electrons available to act as charge carriers and thus allows current to flow freely is known as a *conductor*. Examples of good conductors include silver, copper, aluminium and iron.

Conversely, a material with few free electrons that cannot pass a significant current is known as an *insulator*. Examples of insulators include ceramics, glass, plastics and rubber.

In a *semiconductor* there may be a number of electrons, sufficient to allow a small current to flow. It is possible to add foreign atoms to the semiconductor material which modify the properties of the semiconductor. Varying combinations of these additional atoms are used to produce various electrical devices such as diodes and transistors. Typical semiconductors are silicon and germanium.

8. Conductance

The reciprocal of resistance R is called conductance, with symbol G. Conductance is a measure of the ease with which electricity flows. The greater the conductance of a material the easier it conducts electric current. The unit of conductance is the *siemen* (S). When considering resistors in parallel, it is sometimes more convenient to work in terms of conductance rather than resistance where $G = 1/R$ *siemen*.

9. Variation in conduction properties with temperature

All materials, as stated earlier, offer some kind of resistance to current flow. In *conductors* the free electrons, rather than passing unobstructed through the material, collide with the relatively large and solid nuclei of the atoms. As the temperature increases, the nuclei vibrate more energetically further obstructing the path of the free electrons, causing more frequent collisions. The result is that the *resistance of conductors increases with temperature*.

Due to the nature of the bonding in *insulators*, there are no free

BTEC National Study Guide: Engineering. See page 325 for order details of individual texts

95

electrons, except that when thermal energy increases as a result of a temperature increase, a few outer electrons manage to break free from their fixed positions and act as charge carriers. The result is that the *resistance of insulators decreases as temperature increases.*

Semiconductors behave in a similar manner to insulators. Where at absolute zero (–273°C) the insulator and semiconductor insulate in a near perfect manner. However, unlike the insulator, as temperature increases in a semiconductor *large numbers* of electrons break free to act as charge carriers. Therefore *in a semiconductor as temperature increases the resistance decreases rapidly.*

By producing special alloys, such as Eureka and Manganin which combine the effects of insulators and conductors, it is possible to produce a material where the resistance remains constant with increase in temperature. Figure 3.54 illustrates the resistance behaviour of insulators, semiconductors, conductors and special alloys, with change in temperature.

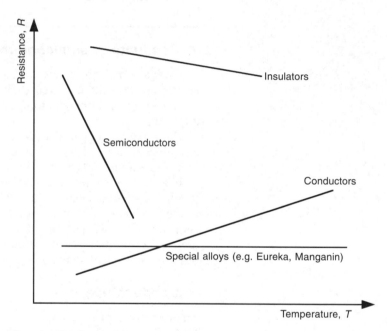

Figure 3.54 *Variation in the resistance of materials with change in temperature*

10. Capacitance

When a conductor is given *more charge*, its positive or negative *potential rises* in value. This happens because the increased charge repels any incoming charge more strongly than before, so large quantities of work have to be done to increase the charge on the conductors still further. Thus the larger the charge on a conductor the larger the potential difference required to get it there. The amount of charge deposited on a conductor is known as its *capacitance.* The capacitance of a conductor is defined as follows:

$$\text{capacitance} = \frac{\text{charge on conductor}}{\text{potential on conductor}} \quad \text{or in symbols } C = \frac{Q}{V}$$

If charge is measured in coulombs C and the potential in volts V, capacitance is measured in coulombs/volt or *farads* (F).

BTEC National Study Guide: Engineering. See page 325 for order details of individual texts

96

For example, if a potential of 350 000 V is required to deposit a charge of 5×10^{-6} C on a conductor then the capacitance in farads is:

$$\text{capacitance} = \frac{\text{charge}}{\text{potential}} = \frac{5 \times 10^{-6}\,\text{C}}{350\,000} = 1.42 \times 10^{-11}\,\text{F}$$

We will use some of the definitions given above when we consider electric circuits in the next section.

Load

Key point

A load converts electrical energy into mechanical movement, light or sound.

A load is simply an electrical component which converts electrical energy into either mechanical movement, light or heat. For example, motors, lamps and heaters are all loads. In all cases, the load will offer resistance to current flow and without resistance there would be no work done.

The factors that govern the value of the load resistance are: the material from which they are made, their cross-sectional area, their length and their temperature. So, for example, copper has a far lower resistance to current flow than, say, glass. A thin wire has greater resistance than a thick wire, a long wire has greater resistance than a short wire and a hot wire has greater resistance than a cold wire. The inherent resistance of the material is known as its resistivity and it is given the symbol ρ. The units of resistivity are Ω m or $\mu\Omega$ mm. Ignoring the change in resistance with temperature, the above relationships may be combined to give a definition of resistance as:

$$R = \rho \frac{l}{A}$$

where ρ = resistivity of the material (Ω m), l = length of material in metres and A = area of cross-section of the material (m^2).

Values of resistivity for some materials are given in the table below.

Material	Resistivity Ω m
Conductors	
Silver	1.6×10^{-8}
Copper	1.7×10^{-8}
Aluminium	2.8×10^{-8}
Iron	10.7×10^{-8}
Manganin	46×10^{-8}
Eureka	49×10^{-8}
Nichrome (Ni, Cr)	109×10^{-8}
Carbon	4000×10^{-8}
Semiconductors	
Germanium	6.0×10^{-1}
Silicon	2300
Insulators	
Glass	10^{10}–10^{14}
Polystyrene	10^{15}

BTEC National Study Guide: Engineering. See page 325 for order details of individual texts

97

Key point

The resistivity of a material is an inherent property of that material and is measured in ohm-metres.

Example 3.38

The element of an immersion heater is to be made from nichrome wire of diameter 0.25 mm. Calculate the length of wire required in order that its resistance is 90 Ω.

Then using the relationship:

$$R = \rho \frac{l}{A}$$

we have

$$R = \rho \frac{l}{A}, \quad \text{then } l = \frac{RA}{\rho} \quad \text{where } R = 90 \text{ and } A = \frac{\pi (0.25)^2}{4} \text{ mm}^2$$

So:

$$l = \frac{90\pi(0.00025)^2}{(109 \times 10^{-8})(4)} \text{ metres}$$

and the required length $l = $ **4.053 m**.

Production of electrical energy by chemical means

Key point

Connected cells form a battery.

Key point

Primary cells use up the chemicals from which they are made.

A *cell* is a device that pushes out charge when a chemical reaction takes place, it is thus a source of electromotive force (emf). When several of these cells are connected together they form a *battery*. We will now look briefly at the nature of cells and batteries. Cells are divided into two main groups known as primary and secondary cells.

Primary cells produce electrical energy at the expense of the chemicals from which they are made and once these chemicals are used up, no more electricity can be obtained from the cell. All cells consist of two *electrodes* which are dissimilar metals, or carbon and a metal, which are placed into an *electrolyte*.

One of the simplest examples of a primary cell is the *voltaic* type. This cell (Figure 3.55) consists of a plate of zinc forming the negative electrode, a plate of copper forming the positive electrode and dilute sulphuric acid as the electrolyte. The negative electrode is known as the *cathode* and the positive electrode is known as the *anode*.

When the electrodes are connected outside the cell, a current flows from the copper electrode, through the external circuit to the zinc and from the zinc to the copper, through the electrolyte in the cell.

One of the problems with the voltaic cell is that it only works for a short time before a layer of hydrogen bubbles builds up on the positive copper electrode, drastically reducing the emf of the cell and increasing its internal resistance. This effect is called *polarization*. The removal of this hydrogen layer from the copper electrode may be achieved by mechanical brushing or adding a depolarizer such as potassium dichromate to the acid solution. The removal of this hydrogen layer is known as *depolarization*.

BTEC National Study Guide: Engineering. See page 325 for order details of individual texts

98

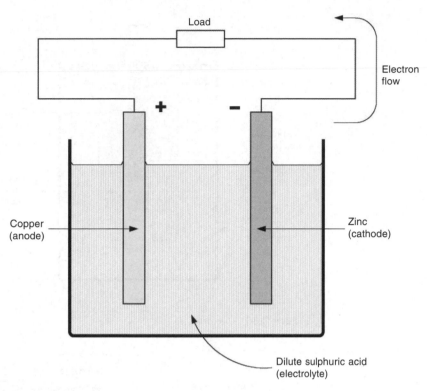

Load

Electron
flow

Copper
(anode)

Zinc
(cathode)

Dilute sulphuric acid
(electrolyte)

Figure 3.55 *The voltaic cell*

Test your knowledge 3.15

1. Does a negative ion have a surplus or shortage of electrons, when compared with the protons in the nucleus?
2. A conductor will have many free electrons, what is required to make these electrons flow?
3. A material is charged with 186.3×10^{18} electrons. How many coulombs of charge is this?
4. 180 joules of energy is required to move 15 coulombs of charge between two conductors. What is the potential

If the zinc electrode is not 100 per cent pure, which for cost reasons is often the case. Then the impurities react with the zinc and the sulphuric acid to produce miniature cells on the surface of the zinc electrode. This reaction takes place in the voltaic cell, irrespective of whether a current is being taken from the cell or not. This *local action*, as it is known, is obviously wasteful and may be eliminated by coating the zinc plate with mercury, or by using the more expensive pure zinc. The emf of a cell of this type is approximately equal to 1.0 V.

A second type of *primary* cell is the *dry* cell. In this type of cell instead of using a dilute acid electrolyte we use ammonium chloride in thick paste form. In one variant of this cell the positive electrode is a centrally positioned carbon rod (Figure 3.56) while the negative electrode is the zinc outer casing of the cell. Carbon and manganese dioxide act as the depolarizing agent that surrounds the carbon electrode.

This type of cell is often used to power torches, each cell has an emf of approximately 1.5 V.

The lead–acid cell is one of the most common secondary cells. In this type of cell, the electrical energy is initially supplied from an external source and converted and stored in the cell as chemical energy. This conversion of energy is reversible and when required this stored chemical energy can be released as a direct electric current. This process of storage leads to the alternative name for this type of cell, the lead–acid accumulator.

The manufacture of this cell is quite complex. The positive plate consists of a grid of lead and antimony filled with lead peroxide (Figure 3.57). The negative plate uses a similar grid, but its open spaces are filled with spongy lead. Thus the cells are made up of a

BTEC National Study Guide: Engineering. See page 325 for order details of individual texts

99

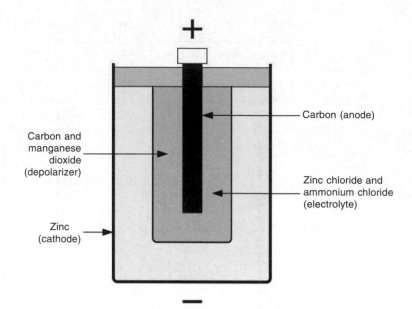

Figure 3.56 *The dry cell*

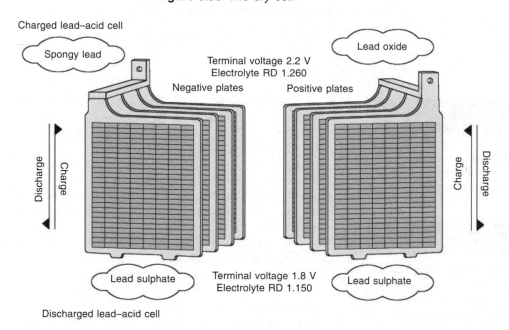

Figure 3.57 *The lead–acid cell*

difference (pd) in volts set up between them?

5. Convert 80 kilowatt-hours into joules.

6. The total conductance of two equal resistors in parallel is 0.125 seimens. What is the resistance in ohms of each resistor?

7. What happens to the resistance of

group of positive plates, joined together and interlaced between a stack of negative plates. Porous separators keep the plates apart and hold a supply of electrolyte in contact with the active materials. The electrolyte consists of a mixture of sulphuric acid and water, which covers the plates and takes an active part in the charging and discharging of the cell.

A fully charged lead–acid cell has an emf of approximately 2.2 V, but when in use this value falls rapidly to about 2.0 V. In the fully charged condition the negative plate is spongy lead and the positive plate is lead peroxide. In the discharged condition, where the emf is about 1.8 V, the chemical action of the cell converts both positive and negative plates into a lead sulphate mix. When

BTEC National Study Guide: Engineering. See page 325 for order details of individual texts

100

8. Define the resistivity of a material.
9. How do primary cells differ from secondary cells?
10. What is polarization and what effect does it have on the performance of a cell?

semiconductors with decrease in temperature?
8. Define the resistivity of a material.
9. How do primary cells differ from secondary cells?
10. What is polarization and what effect does it have on the performance of a cell?

Electrical circuits

The basic circuit

discharged, the cell may then be recharged from an external source and made ready for further use. The condition of this type of cell may be checked by measuring the relative density of the electrolyte. In the fully charged condition this will be around 1.26, while in the discharged condition it drops to around 1.15. This type of cell, when joined together as a battery, has many commercial uses, the most familiar of which is as a motor vehicle battery.

A basic electrical circuit transfers electrical energy from a source to a load, in order to do work. Every electrical circuit has some form of device to control the transfer of this energy. As you have already seen the transfer of energy occurs by the flow of electric current, which in turn requires an emf to force it around the circuit. The emf necessary to produce current flow is provided by the source which is usually a battery or generator. If the current flow is unidirectional (flows in one direction only), then it is referred to as direct current (DC), if the current flows alternatively from one direction to the other, it is referred to as alternating current (AC). These two types of current flow may be illustrated graphically, as shown in Figure 3.58. *During this unit only DC circuits will be considered.*

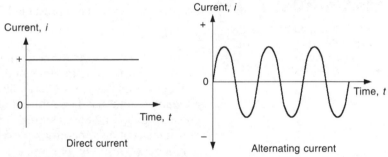

Figure 3.58 *Types of current flow*

Whether current flow is DC or AC it will, by *convention*, always flow from the positive terminal of the source back to the negative terminal of the source (Figure 3.59). You should note that electrons

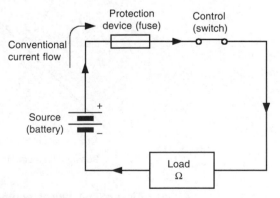

Figure 3.59 *Basic circuit showing current flow*

BTEC National Study Guide: Engineering. See page 325 for order details of individual texts

101

actually flow in the opposite direction. However, when considering current flow in circuits, *we will* stick to this *convention*.

The *control* for the circuit can simply be a switch, which completes the circuit when in the closed position, to enable current to flow. The components of the circuit are joined by conductors, that is the electrical wiring. Circuit components are represented by symbols which must adhere to British Standard 3939. You met these symbols when you studied the unit on Engineering communications.

Ohm's law

George Simon Ohm, a German physicist, introduced a law which provided a very important relationship between *potential difference* in volts (*V*), *resistance* (*R*) in ohms and *current* (*I*) in amperes.

In words, *Ohm's law* states that: *the potential difference (pd) between the ends of a conductor is directly proportional to the current flowing through it, providing that the temperature remains constant.*

Mathematically Ohm's law may be expressed as $V \propto I$, where *V* is the potential difference and *I* is the current. All that we need do to turn this inequality into an equation is to insert a *constant of proportionality k*, such that

$$V = kI$$

The *constant k is defined as the resistance R* of the circuit. Ohm's law may therefore be represented by the equation

$$V = IR$$

where, as stated above, the potential difference *V* must be expressed in volts, resistance *R* in ohms and current *I* in amperes.

Conductors that obey Ohm's law are known as *ohmic* or *linear conductors* and may be represented by a straight-line graph, since constant temperature is assumed. The resistance of non-ohmic or non-linear conductors varies with the potential difference, in the manner shown in Figure 3.60.

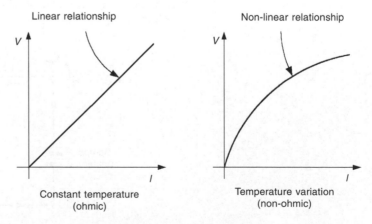

Figure 3.60 *Ohmic and non-ohmic conductors*

BTEC National Study Guide: Engineering. See page 325 for order details of individual texts

102

Example 3.39

A 12 V car battery provides the potential difference to light a car head lamp that offers a resistance of 8 Ω. What current is drawn from the battery?

The solution to this problem simply requires us to find current *I* using Ohm's law. Therefore from $V = IR$ we get

$$I = \frac{V}{R} \quad \text{and so} \quad I = \frac{12}{8} = 1.5 \text{ amperes}$$

The current drawn from the battery = **1.5 amperes**.

Measurement of circuit resistance

In order to understand the behaviour of resistors in electric circuits, we can take electrical measurements to determine their values. One method of measuring resistance involves the use of an *ammeter* and a *voltmeter*, which may be combined into an instrument known as a *multimeter*. These instruments may be *analogue* (continually variable signal values) or *digital* (discrete single point values).

The *ammeter* is used to measure *current* flowing in a circuit. To do this *the ammeter is connected into the circuit*, so as to measure the current flowing through it (Figure 3.61). The *voltmeter* is used for measuring the *potential difference* between any two points in a circuit. The voltmeter is connected *across* a load, with one terminal either side of the load, as shown in Figure 3.61 and the potential difference is measured between these points.

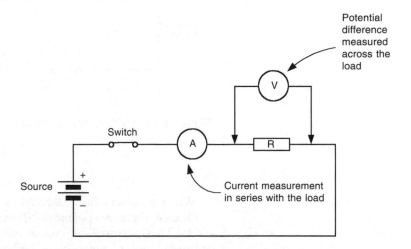

Figure 3.61 *Measurement of current and potential difference in a circuit*

So, to find the resistance of a load all we need do is take measurements of the current flowing through the resistor and the potential difference across the resistor. We then apply Ohm's law,

BTEC National Study Guide: Engineering. See page 325 for order details of individual texts

103

where

$$R = \frac{V}{I}$$

and on substitution of the measured values of potential difference V and current I, we determine the value of the resistive load.

This method of determining resistance values is only suitable when an *approximation* of resistance values is acceptable. This is because the resistance of the measuring instruments themselves alters the readings obtained. Nevertheless, for practical measurements of the resistance of loads such as lamps and heating elements, the above method is sufficiently accurate.

Resistors in series circuits

The various components forming a circuit may be connected in two ways, *series* or *parallel*. The components are said to be in *series* when they are connected end to end providing only one path for the current to flow. The same current must, therefore, pass through all components, including the power supply, as illustrated in Figure 3.62.

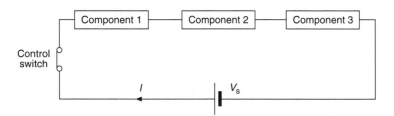

Figure 3.62 *A simple series circuit*

When a current flows through a resistor, or component with resistance, there is a potential difference between its ends (Figure 3.63). This potential difference may be measured by placing a voltmeter *across* the resistor. When more than one resistor is connected in series, the total potential difference produced by the source can be measured, as shown in Figure 3.63, by placing the voltmeter across all the resistors in the circuit. We assume that the current carrying conductors in the circuit offer negligible resistance when compared with the circuit components and, therefore, we see that the sum of the volts drops across each of the individual resistors is equal to the voltage at the source.

BTEC National Study Guide: Engineering. See page 325 for order details of individual texts

104

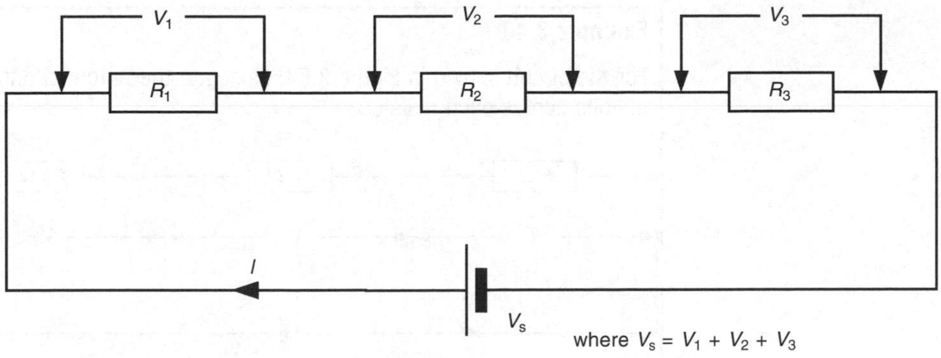

where $V_s = V_1 + V_2 + V_3$

Figure 3.63 *Potential difference across resistors in series*

So, for the above situation we may write:

$V_s = V_1 + V_2 + V_3$ (where V_s = the voltage at source)

Now from Ohm's law we know that $V = IR$. So applying Ohm's law to each of the resistors in turn, we get:

$V_1 = IR_1$, $V_2 = IR_2$ and $V_3 = IR_3$ since the current is common to all resistors.

Therefore:

$V_T = V_1 + V_2 + V_3 = IR_T = IR_1 + IR_2 + IR_3$ (where V_T = total resistance)

or

$IR_T = I(R_1 + R_2 + R_3)$ current I being a common factor

and

$R_T = R_1 + R_2 + R_3$

Key point

For resistors connected in series the total resistance is equal to the sum of the individual resistors.

So, *for resistors in series*:

1.   the total resistance is equal to the sum of the individual resistors
2.   the current is common to all resistors
3.   the sum of the individual volts drops is equal to the applied voltage (voltage at source).

In any series circuit Ohm's law applies to each component and so remembering that $V_1 = IR_1$, $V_2 = IR_2$ ... etc. for any source voltage we can produce any smaller voltage we wish, in the circuit, by inserting resistors of the appropriate value, in series. This arrangement is known as *voltage division*.

BTEC National Study Guide: Engineering. See page 325 for order details of individual texts

105

Example 3.40

For the circuit shown in Figure 3.64, calculate the potential difference in volts across each resistor.

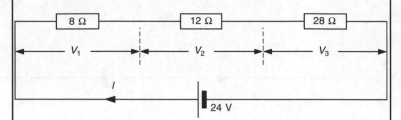

Figure 3.64 *Resistors in series circuit*

Then from Ohm's law $I_T = \dfrac{V_s}{R_T} = \dfrac{24}{48} = 0.5$ amperes

where $R_T = R_1 + R_2 + R_3$.

So $V_1 = IR_1 = (0.5)(8) =$ **4 V**,　　　$V_2 = IR_2 = (0.5)(12) =$ **6 V**,

$V_3 = IR_3 = (0.5)(28) =$ **14 V**

We may check this result by remembering that $V_s = V_1 + V_2 + V_3$ $= 4 + 6 + 14 = 24$ V.

Resistors in parallel circuits

Resistances are said to be connected in *parallel* when they provide *separate pathways* for the *current flow*, the total current being divided between the individual resistors in each pathway or branch.

Consider the circuit shown in Figure 3.65, in which three resistors R_1, R_2 and R_3 are connected in parallel.

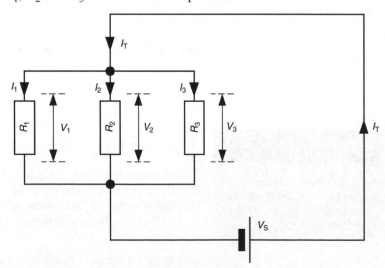

Figure 3.65 *Resistors connected in parallel*

Now the total current I_T is separated as it passes through each resistor into currents I_1, I_2 and I_3. Now:

BTEC National Study Guide: Engineering. See page 325 for order details of individual texts

106

$$I_T = I_1 + I_2 + I_3$$

Also remembering how we measure voltage across resistors, it can be seen that the voltage drop V across each resistor is the same. Then, applying Ohm's law to the resistors in each individual pathway, we have:

$$I_1 = \frac{V}{R_1}, \quad I_2 = \frac{V}{R_2}, \quad I_3 = \frac{V}{R_3}$$

and on adding the equations,

$$I_T = I_1 + I_2 + I_3 = \frac{V}{R_1} + \frac{V}{R_2} + \frac{V}{R_3} = \frac{V_s}{R_T}$$

Now we know from above that the voltage at source is equal to the volts drop across each of the resistors. So we may divide the right-hand side of the above equation by V to give:

$$\frac{1}{R_T} = \frac{1}{R_1} + \frac{1}{R_2} + \frac{1}{R_3}$$

Then, *for resistors or resistive components in parallel:*

1. the voltage across each resistor is the same
2. the reciprocal of the total equivalent resistance is equal to the sum of the reciprocals of the individual resistors
3. Ohm's law applies to each individual resistor or resistive component.

Effective resistance

Now, remembering that for two or more resistors connected in parallel the voltage drop or potential difference across each is the same. Also, that each additional resistor added will draw current, so the *total current* being draw *increases with the addition of further resistors.* Therefore the effective total resistance R_T must decrease ($V = IR$), with V always being the same. The net effect is that the *supply current* drawn, *increases* with each additional resistor added. So the *effective resistance* of the circuit *decreases*, with the addition of each individual resistor. This *effective resistance* will, therefore, *always be less* than that of any individual resistor paralleled into the circuit. An important point to note is that *the supply current increases, as each additional resistor is added.* If not carefully monitored, this supply current could well reach a value where possible wiring damage might occur!

Key point

For resistors in parallel the total resistance is equal to the sum of the reciprocals of the individual resistors.

Key point

For two or more resistors connected in parallel, the total effective resistance is always smaller than any one individual resistor.

Example 3.41

Three resistors of 10 Ω, 20 Ω and 30 Ω are connected into a circuit in parallel, where the supply voltage is 120 V. Find the circuit total equivalent resistance and the total current drawn from the source.

Then total resistance may be found using the formula

$$\frac{1}{R_T} = \frac{1}{R_1} + \frac{1}{R_2} + \frac{1}{R_3}$$

where

$$\frac{1}{R_T} = \frac{1}{10} + \frac{1}{20} + \frac{1}{30} = \frac{3+2+1}{30} = \frac{6}{30} \text{ or } \frac{1}{5} \text{ so } R_T = 5\,\Omega, \text{ with a}$$

total circuit resistance = **5 Ω**

BTEC National Study Guide: Engineering. See page 325 for order details of individual texts

107

Now to find total current we use

$$I = \frac{V_s}{R_T} = \frac{120}{5} = \textbf{24 A}$$

This is a fairly large current!

We may combine the way in which we connect resistive components, so that in many circuits, some components may be in series and others in parallel with the supply. The techniques we have developed for the individual circuits can be combined to solve problems involving *series/parallel circuits*.

Example 3.42

Three resistors of 4 Ω, 6 Ω and 12 Ω are connected in parallel with each other, then in series with the remaining resistor of 4 Ω across a supply of 24 V. Determine:

(a) the total current taken from the supply
(b) the potential difference across the single 4 Ω resistor
(c) the current flowing in each of the paralleled resistors.

The resistor combination is shown in Figure 3.66.

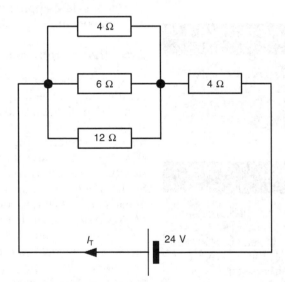

Figure 3.66 *Resistors in parallel circuit*

(a) To establish the *total circuit current* we need first to find the total equivalent resistance R_T. To do this we find the equivalent resistance of the parallel combination and add this equivalent resistance to the one remaining resistor which is in series with the supply. Then:

$$\frac{1}{R_E} = \frac{1}{4} + \frac{1}{6} + \frac{1}{12} = \frac{3+2+1}{12} = \frac{6}{12} = \frac{1}{2} \quad \text{therefore } R_E = 2\,\Omega$$

and so $R_T = 2\,\Omega + 4\,\Omega = 6\,\Omega$ and again using Ohm's law as before:

$$I_T = \frac{V_s}{R_T} = \frac{24}{6} = \textbf{4 A}$$

BTEC National Study Guide: Engineering. See page 325 for order details of individual texts

108

(b) From our analysis above, we now have the equivalent of two resistors in series; one is 2 Ω, which is the single equivalent resistance of the three in parallel and the other is the remaining 4 Ω resistor in series. We have also established the current passing through both of them as 4 A. Therefore the potential difference across the 4 Ω resistor is found from Ohm's law as:

$$V_4 = IR_4 = (4)(4) = \textbf{16 V}$$

(c) Now to find the current flowing in each of the paralleled resistors, all we need do is establish the potential difference across the combination and then apply Ohm's law to each.

Then the potential difference (volts drop) across the single equivalent resistance of 2 Ω is given by Ohm's law as $V_2 = IR_2 = (4)(2) = 8$ V. This volts drop will be the same across each of the original resistors in parallel. Note also that the sum of the volts drops across these two resistors is equal to the supply voltage; this is no coincidence as you will see later.

All we need do now is to reapply Ohm's law to each of the parallel resistors in order to find the current in each pathway. Then:

Current flowing through the 4 Ω resistor $= \dfrac{V_E}{R_4} = \dfrac{8}{4} = \textbf{2 A}$

Similarly the current flowing in the 6 Ω resistor

$$= \dfrac{V_E}{R_6} = \dfrac{8}{6} = \dfrac{\textbf{4}}{\textbf{3}}\ \textbf{A}$$

And in the 8 Ω resistor $= \dfrac{V_E}{R_8} = \dfrac{8}{12} = \dfrac{\textbf{2}}{\textbf{3}}\ \textbf{A}$

It is also no coincidence that the sum of these individual currents is equal to the total current flowing into the parallel combination, i.e.

$$2A + \dfrac{4}{3}A + \dfrac{2}{3}A = 4A$$

notice also, the advantage of leaving these currents in fractions!

Kirchhoff's laws

Although you may not have realized it, you have already meet the consequences of Kirchhoff's laws, when looking at the solution to the problems given in Example 3.42. Kirchhoff identified two important relationships, which have developed into useful laws when solving circuit problems.

Kirchhoff's first law states that: *the total current entering any point (junction) in a circuit must equal the sum of the currents leaving that junction.* Figure 3.67(a) illustrates this law for three pathways leaving the junction. The law is valid no matter what number of pathways are used.

Figure 3.67(b) shows the use of Kirchhoff's law when considering Example 3.42 above. The sum of the individual currents in the parallel pathways equals the input current, as we found.

Kirchhoff's second law states that: *the algebraic sum of the individual voltage drops (potential differences) must equal the applied*

BTEC National Study Guide: Engineering. See page 325 for order details of individual texts

109

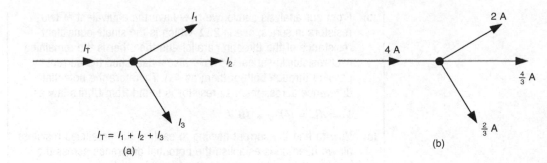

$$I_T = I_1 + I_2 + I_3$$
(a)

(b)

Figure 3.67 *Kirchhoff's current law*

voltage, from the source. Figure 3.68 illustrates this law in general terms.

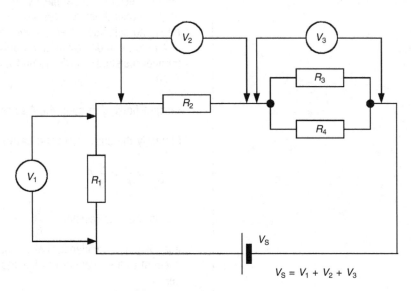

$$V_S = V_1 + V_2 + V_3$$

Figure 3.68 *Kirchhoff's voltage law*

Both of Kirchhoff's laws, apart from simplifying some of the calculations, also provide a useful means of checking the accuracy of your working.

Power in series/parallel circuits

You have already met the definitions of electrical power and electrical energy. Here we are going to apply these definitions.

When current flows through a component offering resistance, electrical energy is converted into heat. You know that the rate at which electrical energy is converted into heat is power. Electrical components such as resistors and bulbs have a *power rating*. In the case of the bulb, this power rating may be sustained for long periods of time, without failure. In the case of a resistor, this power rating is the absolute maximum that the resistor can sustain, therefore we must always ensure that we keep *below this stated value* when considering the use of resistors in circuits.

The surface area and therefore the size of a component determines the rate at which heat is dissipated from the component to its

BTEC National Study Guide: Engineering. See page 325 for order details of individual texts

110

surroundings. So, in general, the larger the component the larger its power rating. Carbon resistors with the same resistance values are commonly available in ratings between 0.25 W and 2 W. For a higher power requirement, different types of resistor may be used.

In order to calculate the power dissipated in circuit components we may use the following formula:

power (in watts) P = (voltage V)(current I)   that is $P = IV$ watts

Now dependent on the variables we are using we may use Ohm's law to express power in terms of resistance and voltage or resistance and current, as well as in terms of current and voltage, shown above. Then using Ohm's law we have:

$V = IR$

so substituting IR for V in $P = IV$ gives

$P = IIR$ or $P = I^2R$

Also from

$$I = \frac{V}{R}$$

then again substituting $\frac{V}{R}$ for I in $P = IV$ gives

$$P = \frac{VV}{R} \quad \text{or} \quad \frac{V^2}{R}$$

These power relationships are summarized below.

$$P = IV \quad \text{or} \quad P = I^2R \quad \text{or} \quad P = \frac{V^2}{R}$$

where power P is in watts, current is in amperes and potential difference or electromotive force is in volts.

Key point

Electrical power in watts is equal to the current in amperes multiplied by the potential difference in volts.

Example 3.43

Calculate the total power dissipated in the circuit shown in Figure 3.69 *and* given that the power rating for resistor R_1 = 10 watts, check the rating of this resistor.

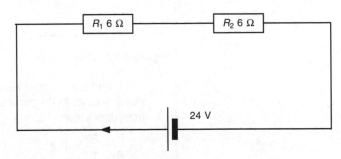

Figure 3.69 *Resistor current rating*

This is a simple series circuit where the total equivalent resistance,

$R_T = R_1 + R_2 = 6 + 6 = 12\ \Omega$

Also from Ohm's law the total current drawn from the supply is

---

BTEC National Study Guide: Engineering. See page 325 for order details of individual texts

111

$$I = \frac{24}{12} = 2 \text{ A}$$

Then we have all three variables for the circuit, so we may use any of our power relationships. Using $P = IV$, then **P = (2)(24) = 48 W**.

Now the power dissipated by R_1 may be found using $P = I^2R =$ (22)(6) = 24 watts. We are told that the maximum allowable power dissipation is 10 watts, thus the power rating is exceeded. This will most likely lead to premature resistor failure.

Example 3.44

A DC motor with a series resistor of 10 Ω is connected in series with a 240 V supply. When the motor is running the pd across the series resistor is found to be 60 V:

(a)   determine the pd across the motor and the current passing through it
(b)   find the power drawn from the supply
(c)   find the power dissipated by the resistor as heat.

(a)   The potential difference across the motor is easily found by remembering Kirchhoff's voltage law. Where the pd across the supply (240 V) is equal to the sum of the pds, i.e.

240 V = 60 V + X, where X, the pd across the motor, is = **180 V**

The set-up is illustrated in Figure 3.70.

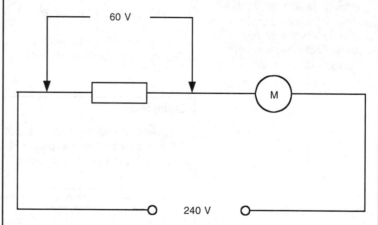

Figure 3.70 *Motor circuit*

Since we have a simple series circuit, the current through the motor is equal to the current through the series resistor and, from Ohm's law:

$$I = \frac{V}{R} = \frac{60}{10} = \textbf{6 A}$$

(b)   The power drawn from the mains supply may be found using $P = IV$, then

(6)(240) = 1440 W

(c)   The power dissipated by the resistor $P_R = IV_R$, where V_R = volts drop across resistor, then $P_R =$ **(6)(60) = 360 W**.

BTEC National Study Guide: Engineering. See page 325 for order details of individual texts

112

Cells and batteries

You are already familiar with the nature of chemical cells that produce an electromotive force (emf) and the fact that when cells are connected together they form a battery.

Cells are said to be connected in *series when the positive plate of one cell is connected to the negative plate of the other*; several cells connected in this way form a battery of cells in series (Figure 3.71).

Figure 3.71 *Battery of cells in series*

This arrangement of cells has the following characteristics:

1. The battery emf equals the sum of the emfs of the individual cells.
2. The maximum current from the battery is the same as that from one individual cell.
3. The internal resistance of the battery equals the sum of the individual cell resistances.

When all the positive terminals of a group of cells are connected together and all the negative terminals are connected together, the cells are said to be connected in parallel (Figure 3.72).

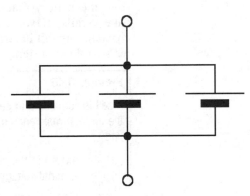

Figure 3.72 *Battery of cells in parallel*

The characteristics of this arrangement are:

1. The emf of several cells in parallel equals the emf of one individual cell.
2. The reciprocal of the total internal resistance equals the sum of the reciprocals of each internal resistance.
3. The total current equals the sum of the individual currents.

The above characteristics need a little explanation. All electrical supplies have internal resistance; in batteries this is mainly due to the resistance of the electrolyte. The circuit in Figure 3.73 shows a single cell battery with emf E, internal resistance r, connected in series with a circuit load resistance R.

BTEC National Study Guide: Engineering. See page 325 for order details of individual texts

113

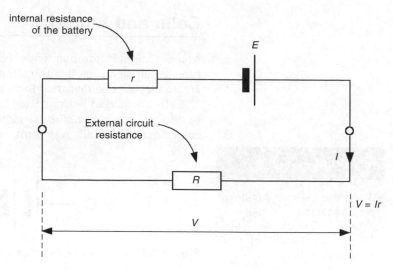

Figure 3.73 *Circuit showing internal resistance of battery*

Now if we measure the voltage V across the battery, when the battery is disconnected from the circuit it will equal the emf in a circuit with *no* resistive load applied. When a resistive load R is connected to the battery, the load current I flows through the internal resistance r of the battery and causes an internal resistance volts drop. So that the *on-load* terminal voltage V, is equal to the emf E, minus the internal resistance volts drop Ir. Or in symbols:

$$V = E - Ir$$

It can be seen from the above formula that as the current drawn from the battery (supply) increases, the terminal voltage at the battery falls. If we assume that the internal resistance remains constant, the fall in terminal voltage is directly proportional to the resistive load current.

Example 3.45

A cell is connected in series with an external resistance $R = 0.1\ \Omega$. If the internal resistance of the battery $r = 0.025\ \Omega$ and the emf = 2 V, find:

(a) the current in the circuit
(b) the terminal voltage of the cell.

(a) The total circuit resistance is $R + r = 0.1 + 0.025 = 0.125\ \Omega$
Now from $V = E - Ir$ and from Ohm's law $V = E - Ir = IR$, then $E = IR + Ir$, and transposing for I, then:

$$\text{circuit current} = I = \frac{E}{R + r} = \frac{2}{0.125} = \textbf{16 A}$$

(b) The terminal voltage V may be found from $V = E - Ir$, and so $V = 2 - (16)(0.025) = 1.6$ V.

So terminal voltage = **1.6 V**.

Capacitance and capacitors

We have already defined the unit of capacitance as the *farad*, which we redefine here.

BTEC National Study Guide: Engineering. See page 325 for order details of individual texts

114

A capacitor has a capacitance of 1 farad when a charging current of one ampere flowing for one second causes a change of one volt across the plates of the capacitor. Or in symbols:

$$C = \frac{Q}{V}$$

where Q is in coulombs (remembering that one ampere is equal to one coulomb per second) and C is the capacitance in farads.

The farad is a very large and impractical unit and in practice capacitors have much smaller values, normally measured in microfarads μF or picofarads pF. Where, from your study of units, you will know that:

$1~\mu F = 10^{-6}$ farads   and $1~pF = 10^{-12}$ farads

In practice, a *capacitor* is an electronic component that can store electrical energy in the form of an electric field. In its simplest form, a capacitor consists of two conducting plates separated by an insulator called the *dielectric*.

You have already seen how by applying a voltage to the capacitor it is *charged*. A battery may be used as the voltage source to charge the capacitor, as shown in Figure 3.74.

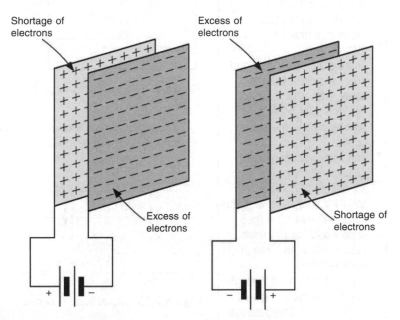

Figure 3.74 *Charging a capacitor with a battery*

Once charged, the capacitor has a large difference in potential energy, which may be *discharged* by connecting (shorting) the two plates together.

Capacitors in circuits

Capacitors, like resistors, may be connected in parallel or in series with a supply. *When capacitors are connected in parallel the total charge Q drawn from the supply is the sum of the individual charges in the capacitor.* Figure 3.75 shows three capacitors connected in parallel with a supply.

Then, from what has been said, in symbols:

Key point

For capacitors in parallel the voltage across each capacitor is the same.

Key point

For capacitors in parallel the charge on each capacitor is directly proportional to the value of its capacitance.

BTEC National Study Guide: Engineering. See page 325 for order details of individual texts

115

Test your knowledge 3.16

1. How does *conventional* current flow differ from *real* current flow?
2. Under what circumstances is Ohm's law valid?
3. Describe how circuit resistance may be measured.
4. Three resistors of 4, 6 and 10 Ω are connected in series with a 24 V supply. Find the total equivalent resistance and the circuit current.
5. The same resistors as in question 4 are now connected in parallel with the 24 V supply. What is the current drawn from the supply *and* the individual currents flowing through each resistor?
6. A circuit with a 12 V supply has four loads connected in series with it. The potential difference across the first three loads is 2 V, 3 V and 4 V, respectively. If the current drawn from the supply is 6 A, what is the resistance of *each* load in the circuit?
7. An electric motor offers a resistance of 10 Ω when operating at full power from a 240 V supply. What is the power rating of this motor in kW?

$$Q_T = Q_1 + Q_2 + Q_3$$

and since supply voltage is the same across each paralleled capacitor then:

$$C_T V = C_1 V + C_2 V + C_3 V$$

and so,

$$C_T = C_1 + C_2 + C_3$$

Thus the combined capacitance of capacitors connected in parallel is found in the same way as that of resistors connected in series. Note also that the charge on each capacitor is directly proportional to the value of its capacitance.

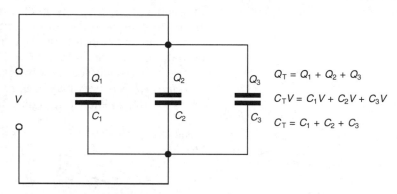

Figure 3.75 *Capacitors in parallel*

Now when *capacitors are connected in series* (Figure 3.76) *the charge on each capacitor is the same as drawn by the supply.*

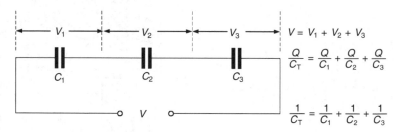

Figure 3.76 *Capacitors in series*

So from Kirchhoff's voltage law, $V = V_1 + V_2 + V_3$ and from our definition of capacitance and what has been said above:

$$\frac{Q}{C_T} = \frac{Q}{C_1} + \frac{Q}{C_2} + \frac{Q}{C_3}$$

and so,

$$\frac{1}{C_T} = \frac{1}{C_1} + \frac{1}{C_2} + \frac{1}{C_3}$$

A consequence of the above argument is that the total capacitance of capacitors connected in series is found in the same way as resistors connected in parallel.

BTEC National Study Guide: Engineering. See page 325 for order details of individual texts

116

Magnetism

Elementary theory of magnetism

Magnetism is an effect created by moving the elementary atomic particles in certain materials such as iron, nickel and cobalt. Iron has outstanding magnetic properties and materials that behave magnetically, in a similar manner to iron, are known as *ferromagnetic* materials. These materials experience forces which act on them when placed near a magnet.

The atoms within these materials group in such a way that they produce tiny individual magnets with their own *North and South poles*. When subject to the influence of a magnet or when an electric current is passed through a coil surrounding them, these individual tiny magnets line up and the material as a whole exhibits magnetic properties.

Figure 3.77(a) shows a ferromagnetic material that has not been influenced by the forces generated from another magnet. In this case, the miniature magnets are oriented in a random manner. Once the material is subject to the influence of another magnet, then these miniature magnets line up (Figure 3.77(b)) and the material itself becomes magnetic with its own North and South poles.

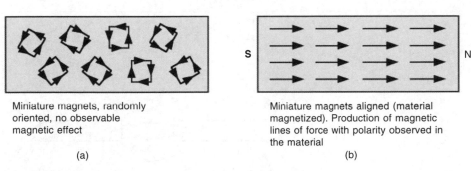

Miniature magnets, randomly oriented, no observable magnetic effect

(a)

Miniature magnets aligned (material magnetized). Production of magnetic lines of force with polarity observed in the material

(b)

Figure 3.77 *The behaviour of ferromagnetic materials*

A magnetic *field of flux* is the region in which the forces created by the magnet have influence. This field surrounds a magnet in all directions, being strongest at the end extremities of the magnet, known as the *poles*. Magnetic fields are mapped by an arrangement of lines that give an indication of strength and direction of the flux as illustrated in Figure 3.78. When freely suspended horizontally a magnet aligns itself North–South parallel with the earth's magnetic field. Now because unlike poles attract, the North of the magnet aligns itself with the South magnetic pole of the earth and the South pole of the magnet aligns itself with the earth's North pole. This is why the extremities of the magnet are known as poles.

Whenever an electric current flows in a conductor a magnetic field is set up around the conductor in the form of concentric circles. The field is present along the whole length of the conductor and is strongest nearest to the conductor. Now like permanent magnets, this field also has direction. The direction of the magnetic field is dependent on the direction of the current passing through the conductor and may be established using the right-hand grip or right-hand screw rule, as shown in Figure 3.79.

If the right-hand thumb is pointing in the direction of current flow in the conductor, then when gripping the conductor in the

BTEC National Study Guide: Engineering. See page 325 for order details of individual texts

117

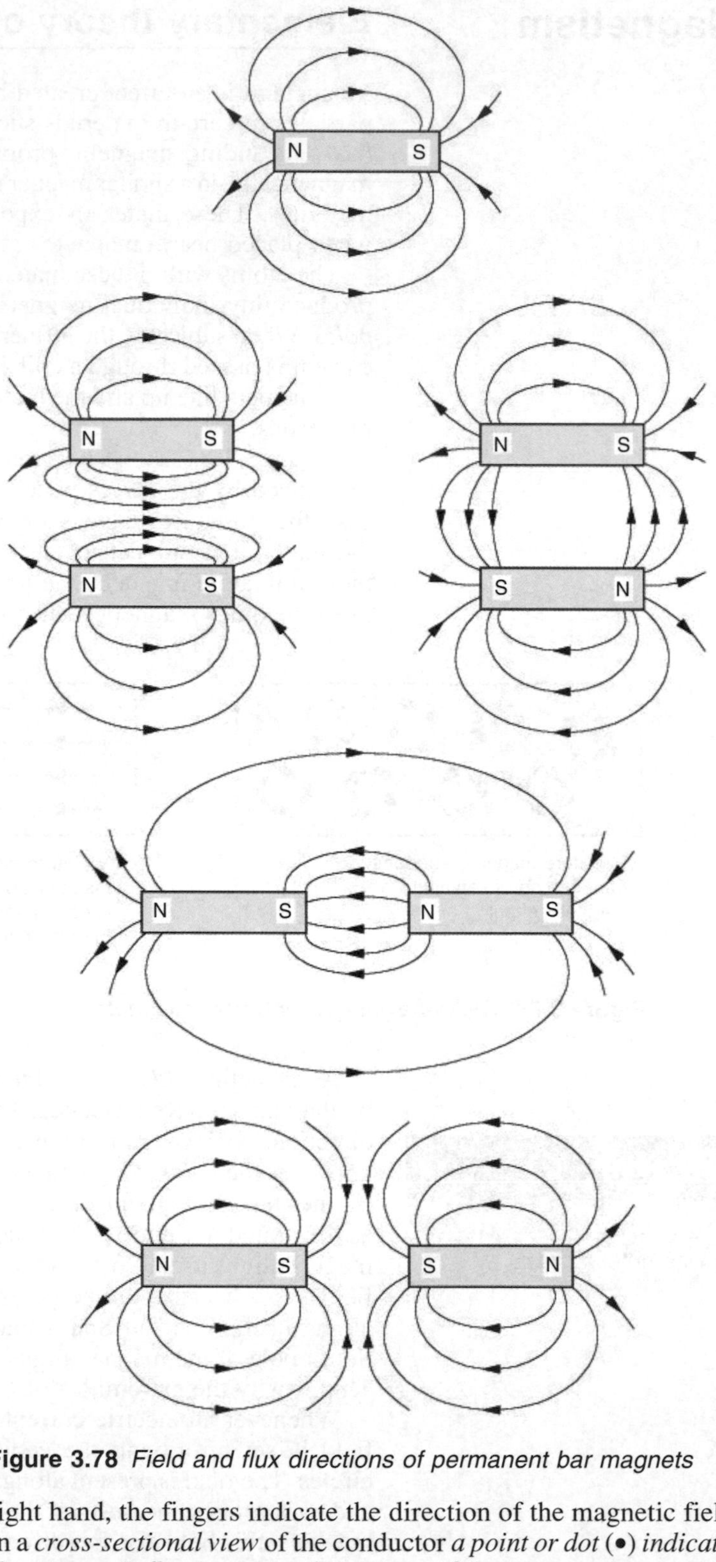

Figure 3.78 *Field and flux directions of permanent bar magnets*

right hand, the fingers indicate the direction of the magnetic field. In a *cross-sectional view* of the conductor *a point or dot (•) indicates the current is flowing towards you*, out of the page, and *a cross (×) indicates the current is flowing away from you*. This convention mirrors arrow flight, where the dot is the tip of the arrow and the cross is the feathers at the tail of the arrow, as the arrow leaves the bow.

BTEC National Study Guide: Engineering. See page 325 for order details of individual texts

118

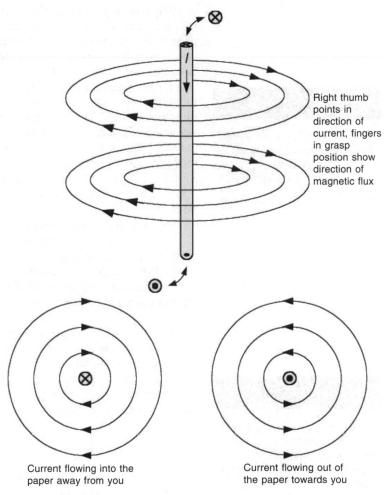

Right thumb points in direction of current, fingers in grasp position show direction of magnetic flux

Current flowing into the paper away from you

Current flowing out of the paper towards you

Figure 3.79 *Right-hand screw rule*

The conductor in a magnetic field

If we place a current carrying conductor in a magnetic field, the conductor has a force exerted on it.

Consider the set-up shown in Figure 3.80, in which a current

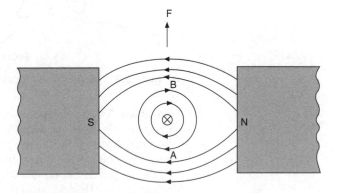

Figure 3.80 *Current carrying conductor in a magnetic field*

BTEC National Study Guide: Engineering. See page 325 for order details of individual texts

119

carrying conductor is placed between the N–S poles of two permanent magnets. The direction of the current passing through it is into the page going away from us. Then by the *right-hand grip rule*, the direction of the magnetic field, created by the current in the conductor, is clockwise, as shown. We also know that the *flux lines* from the permanent magnet *exit at a North pole* and *enter at a South pole*, in other words, they travel from North to South, as indicated by the direction arrows. The net effect of the coming together of these two magnetic force fields is that *at position A*, they both travel in the same direction and *reinforce one another*. While *at position B*, they travel in the opposite direction and tend to *cancel one another*. So with a *stronger force field at position A* and *a weaker force at position B* the conductor is *forced upwards* out of the magnetic field.

If the direction of the current was reversed, i.e. it travelled towards us out of the page, then the direction of the magnetic field in the current carrying conductor would be reversed and therefore so would the direction of motion of the conductor.

A convenient way of establishing the *direction of motion* of the current carrying conductor is to use *Fleming's left-hand (motor) rule*.

This rule is illustrated in Figure 3.81, where the left hand is extended with the thumb, first finger and second finger pointing at right angles to one another. From the figure it can be seen that the *first finger* represents the magnetic *field*, the *second finger* represents the direction of the *current* in the conductor and the *thumb* represents the *motion* of the conductor, due to the forces acting on it. As an *aide-mémoire*, we say:

First finger　　= *Field*

SeCond finger = *Current*

ThuMb　　　　= *Motion*

> **Key point**
>
> The direction of the magnetic field surrounding a current carrying conductor can be found using the right-hand grip rule.

> **Key point**
>
> The direction of motion of a current carrying conductor in a magnetic field is given by Fleming's *left-hand motor* rule.

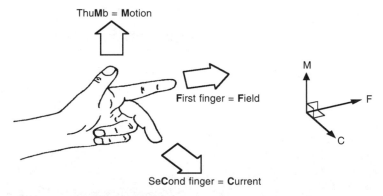

Figure 3.81 *Fleming's left-hand rule*

So much for the direction of a current carrying conductor in a magnetic field. What about the *magnitude of the force* acting on the conductor? Well, the magnitude of the force trying to move the conductor out of the field depends on: the current passing through it, the length of the conductor in the field and the amount of flux per unit area (flux density) that is created by the magnet. Then the force depends upon:

BTEC National Study Guide: Engineering. See page 325 for order details of individual texts

120

- the flux density β in tesla
- the current I in amperes
- the length of the conductor in the field L.

Or in symbols

$$F = \beta I L$$

The term flux density needs just a little more explanation. The total flux in a magnetic field is really a measure of the total magnetic intensity present in the field and it is measured in webers (Wb) and represented by the symbol Φ (phi). Therefore:

$$\text{flux density} = \frac{\text{total flux}}{\text{area of field}} \ (\text{tesla}), \quad \text{or } \beta \ (T) = \frac{\Phi \ (\text{Wb})}{A \ (m^2)}$$

In practice, values of flux density are generally small and millitesla (mT) and microtesla (μT) are often used.

Example 3.46

In Figure 3.82, a straight current carrying conductor lies at right angles to a magnetic field of flux density 1.2 T such that 250 mm of its length lies within the field. If the current passing through the conductor is 15 A, determine the force on the conductor and the direction of its motion.

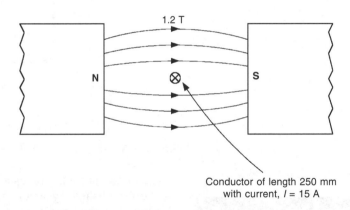

Figure 3.82

In order to find the magnitude of the force we use the relationship $F = \beta I L$ ensuring the correct use of units. Then:

$$F = (1.2)(15)(250 \times 10^{-3}) = \textbf{4.5 N}$$

Now the direction of motion is easily found using *Fleming's left-hand rule*, where we know that the first finger points in the direction of the magnetic field *N–S*, the second finger points inwards into the page in the direction of the current, which leaves your thumb pointing *downwards* in the direction of *motion*.

The DC motor principle

If we wrap our current carrying conductor around a rectangular former (Figure 3.83), pivoted at its centre, and place the conductor

BTEC National Study Guide: Engineering. See page 325 for order details of individual texts

121

in the magnetic field, at right angles to the flux, then when an electric current is passed through the conductor as shown, we set up two equal and opposite forces which act on the conductor in the directions indicated.

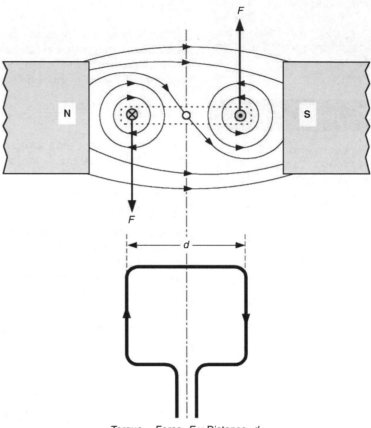

Torque = Force, F × Distance, d

Figure 3.83 *Torque on a coil*

The direction of the forces acting on each arm of the conductor can be established by again using the right-hand grip rule and Fleming's left-hand rule. Now because the conductors are equidistant from their pivot point and the forces acting on them are *equal and opposite*, then they form a couple. You have already met the idea of a couple when you studied *forces* during your study of statics. The important point to remember here is that *the moment of a couple is equal to the magnitude of a single force multiplied by the distance between them* and that this moment is known as *torque*. In symbols:

torque $T = Fd$

We already know that the magnitude of the force F is given by $F = \beta IL$, therefore the torque produced by the current carrying conductor is:

torque $T = \beta ILd$

Now one of the most useful applications for this torque (turning moment) is in the electric motor. In an electric motor the input is electrical energy and the output is motion. A simple direct current

BTEC National Study Guide: Engineering. See page 325 for order details of individual texts

122

motor consists of a rectangular coil of wire mounted on a former and free to rotate about a spindle in a magnetic field, in a similar manner to that illustrated in Figure 3.84.

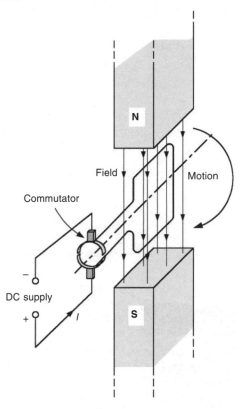

Figure 3.84 *Simple electric motor with commutator*

In real motors, this rotating coil is know as the *armature* and consists of many hundreds of turns of conducting wire. This arrangement is needed in order to maximize the force imposed on the conductor by introducing the *longest possible conductor* into the magnetic field. Also from the relationship $F = \beta IL$ it can be seen that the force used to provide the torque in a motor is directly proportional to the size of the *magnetic flux* β. Instead of using a permanent magnet to produced this flux, in a real motor, an *electromagnet* is used. An electromagnetic field can be set up by utilizing the *solenoid* principle (Figure 3.85). A long length of conductor is wound into a coil consisting of many turns and a current passed through it. Now each of the turns in the conductor assists each other to produce a strong magnetic field, as shown in Figure 3.85.

This field may be intensified by inserting a ferromagnetic core inside the coil. Once the current is applied to the conducting coil, the core is magnetized and all the time the current is on it acts in combination with the coil to produce a permanent magnet, having its own N–S poles.

Now returning to the simple motor illustrated in Figure 3.84. We know that when current is supplied to the *armature* (rotor) a *torque* is produced. In order to produce continuous rotary motion, this torque (turning moment) must always act in the same direction.

BTEC National Study Guide: Engineering. See page 325 for order details of individual texts

123

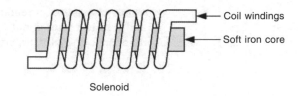

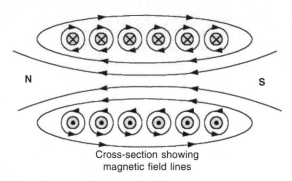

Figure 3.85 *Magnetic field produced by a solenoid*

Therefore, the current in each of the armature conductors must be reversed as the conductor passes between the North and South magnetic field poles. The *commutator* acts like a rotating switch, reversing the current in each armature conductor at the appropriate time to achieve this continuous rotary motion. Without the presence of a commutator in a DC motor, only a half turn of movement is possible!

In Figure 3.86(a) the rotation of the armature conductor is given by Fleming's left-hand rule. When the coil reaches a position mid-

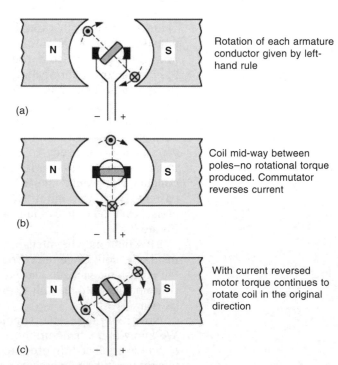

Figure 3.86 *Action of the commutator*

BTEC National Study Guide: Engineering. See page 325 for order details of individual texts

124

way between the poles (Figure 3.86(b)), no rotational torque is produced in the coil. At this stage the commutator reverses the current in the coil. Finally (Figure 3.86(c)) with the current reversed, the motor torque now continues to rotate the coil in its original direction.

Example 3.47

The rectangular armature shown in Figure 3.87 is wound with 500 turns of wire. When situated in a uniform magnetic field of flux density 300 mT, the current in the coil is 20 mA.

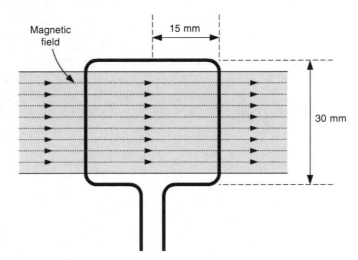

Figure 3.87

Calculate the force acting on the side of the coil *and* the maximum torque acting on the armature.

With this arrangement the ends of the conductor are not within the influence of the magnetic field and therefore have no force exerted on them. Therefore the force acting on one length of conductor is given from $F = \beta I L$ as:

$$F = (300 \times 10^{-3})(20 \times 10^{-3})(30 \times 10^{-3}) = \mathbf{1.8 \times 10^{-4}\ N}$$

Then the force on one side of the coil

$$= (500)(1.8 \times 10^{-4}) = 0.09\ N = 9 \times 10^{-2}\ N$$

Now from our definition of torque $T = Fd$, the torque acting on the armature windings is,

$$T = (9 \times 10^{-2})(30 \times 10^{-3}) = \mathbf{2.7 \times 10^{-3}\ Nm}$$

This is a relatively small amount of torque. Practical motors can be made to produce output torques with very small values as demonstrated here, up to several hundred newton-metres!

One other application of the motor principle may be used in simple *analogue* measuring instruments.

Some meters, including multimeters used to measure current, voltage and resistance, operate on the principle of a coil rotating in a magnetic field. The basic construction is shown in Figure 3.88, where the current I passes through a pivoted coil and the resultant

BTEC National Study Guide: Engineering. See page 325 for order details of individual texts

125

motor force, the deflecting force, is directly proportional to the current flowing in the coil windings which of course is the current being measured. The magnetic flux is concentrated within the coil by a solid cylindrical ferromagnetic core, in exactly the same manner as the flux is concentrated within a solenoid.

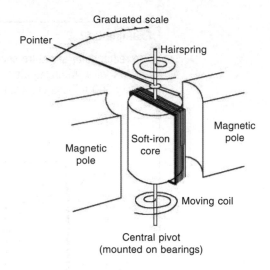

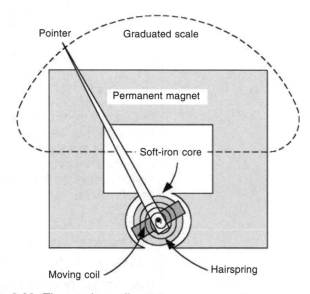

Figure 3.88 *The moving-coil meter*

Electromagnetic induction and electrical generation

The way in which electricity is generated in a conductor may be viewed as being the exact opposite to that which produces the motor force. In order to generate electricity we require *movement in to get electricity out*. In fact we need the same components to generate electricity as those needed for the electric motor, namely a closed conductor, a magnetic field and movement.

Whenever relative motion occurs between a magnetic field and

BTEC National Study Guide: Engineering. See page 325 for order details of individual texts

126

a conductor acting at right angles to the field, an *emf is induced, or generated* in the conductor. The manner in which this emf is generated is based on the *principle of electromagnetic induction.*

Consider Figure 3.89, which shows relative movement between a magnet and a closed coil of wire.

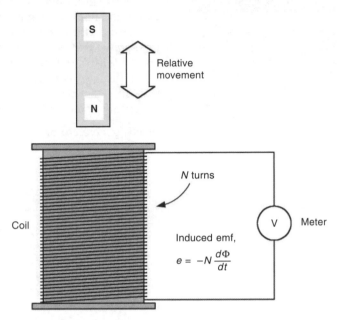

Figure 3.89 *Demonstration of electromagnetic induction*

An emf will be induced in the coil whenever the magnet is moved in or out of the coil (or the magnet is held stationary and the coil moved). The *magnitude* of the induced emf depends on the number of turns N and the rate at which the flux changes in the coil $\dfrac{d\Phi}{dt}$. Do not be concerned about this expression, it is simply a mathematical way of expressing *the rate of change* of flux with respect to time. You will meet similar expressions when you study the differential calculus in your mathematics!

In general this relationship is written as

$$E = -N\frac{d\Phi}{dt} \text{ volts}$$

The minus sign is a consequence of the way the induced emf acts, which we will discuss later.

Put another way, the *magnitude of the induced emf depends on*:

- the velocity of the conductor v in m s^{-2}
- the strength of the magnetic field β in tesla
- the length of the conductor L in metres.

This is so if we realize that the number of turns N is *directly related to the length of the conductor L*, moving through the magnetic field, with flux density β. Also *the velocity with which the conductor moves through the field* determines the *rate at which the flux changes in the coil* as it cuts the flux field. Thus the magnitude of the induced (generated) emf E is proportional to the flux density, length

Key point

The emf induced in a coil is equal to the product of the number of turns on the coil and the rate of change of flux through the coil.

BTEC National Study Guide: Engineering. See page 325 for order details of individual texts

127

of conductor and relative velocity between the field and the conductor, or in symbols:

$E \propto \beta L v$ volts

Now you are probably wondering why the above relationship has the *proportionality* sign. In order to generator an emf the conductor must cut the lines of magnetic flux.

If they cut the lines of flux at a right angle (Figure 3.90(a)) then the *maximum* emf is generated; cutting them at any other angle θ (Figure 3.90(b)), reduces this value until θ = 0, at which point the *lines of flux are not being cut at all and no emf is induced* or generated in the conductor. So the magnitude of the induced emf is also dependent on sin θ. So we may write:

induced (generated) emf $E = \beta L v \sin \theta$

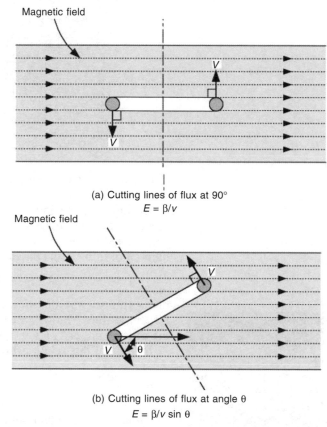

(a) Cutting lines of flux at 90°
$E = \beta / v$

(b) Cutting lines of flux at angle θ
$E = \beta / v \sin \theta$

Figure 3.90 *Cutting lines of flux and the generated emf*

So much for the magnitude of the generated emf, what about its direction in the conductor? Since the conductor offers some resistance, the generated emf will initiate current flow as a result of the potential difference and the *direction of this current* can be found using *Fleming's right-hand rule*.

Note that for *generators* we use the *right*-hand rule (Figure 3.91), for motors we used the left-hand rule.

The first finger, second finger and thumb represent the field, current and motion, respectively, as they did when we looked at the motor rule.

BTEC National Study Guide: Engineering. See page 325 for order details of individual texts

128

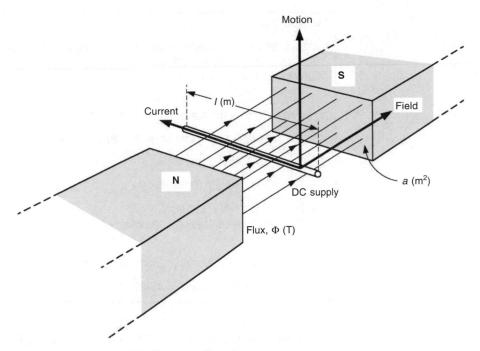

Figure 3.91 *Fleming's right-hand generator rule*

To finish our theory on induced emf, we need to consider two important laws which describe the nature of *electromagnetic induction*.

Faraday's law:

> *When a magnetic flux through a coil is made to vary, an emf is induced. The magnitude of this emf is proportional to the rate of change of flux.*

What this law is saying in effect is that *relative movement* between the magnetic flux and the conductor is essential to generate an emf. The voltmeter shown in Figure 3.89 reads the induced (generated) emf and *if the direction of motion changes the polarity of the induced emf in the conductor changes*. Faraday's law also tells us that the magnitude of the induced emf is dependent on the *relative velocity* with which the conductor cuts the lines of magnetic flux.

Lenz's law:

> *The induced current always acts in such a direction so as to oppose the change in flux producing the current.*

This is the reason for the minus sign in the formula

$$E = -\frac{d\Phi}{dt}$$

because E tends to oppose any change in the current I, in other words it is a *back* emf.

BTEC National Study Guide: Engineering. See page 325 for order details of individual texts

129

Example 3.48

A closed conductor of length 15 cm cuts the magnetic flux field of 1.25 T, at an angle of 60°, with a velocity of 25 m s^{-1}. If the conductor current is 13 A:

(a) what is the induced emf?
(b) what would be the maximum induced emf?

(a) The induced emf is found using $E = \beta L v \sin \theta$ so

$E = (1.25)(0.15)(25)(\sin 60)$

$E = (1.25)(0.15)(25)\,(0.866)$

The induced emf $E = 4.06$ V

(b) The maximum induced emf occurs when the lines of flux are cut at 90°. Then:

$E = \beta L v \sin 90 = \beta L v = (1.25)(0.15)(25)$ and

maximum generated emf = **4.6875 V**

Mutual inductance and the transformer

We know that the relative movement between a closed coil of wire and a magnetic field induces an emf in the coil. The same effect occurs if *two coils* are in close proximity and a current in one of the coils is varied, as shown in Figure 3.92.

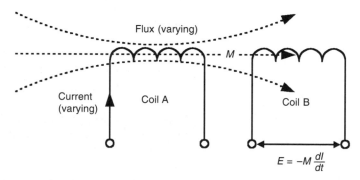

Figure 3.92 *Mutual inductance*

The polarity of E depends upon whether I is increasing or decreasing. It is called a *back emf* because by Lenz's law, E tends to oppose any change in I. In practice this means that if the coil B circuit is closed, the current due to E flows in such a direction as to produce a flux which opposes any change in the coil A flux.

The magnitude of E depends partly upon factors such as the angle and distance between the coils and the *reluctance* (magnetic resistance) of the flux path but, for a given pair of coils, E is directly proportional to the rate of change of I, which we represent as $\dfrac{dI}{dt}$.

The ratio between E and $\dfrac{dI}{dt}$ is the mutual inductance of the two coils, which has the symbol M. Then

BTEC National Study Guide: Engineering. See page 325 for order details of individual texts

130

$$E = -M\frac{dI}{dt} \text{ volts}$$

The negative sign has the same meaning as with the induced emf generated by a coil and a magnetic field. The negative sign indicating the back emf, in accordance with Lenz's law. The unit of mutual inductance M is the *henry H. A circuit has a mutual inductance M of one henry if one volt is induced by a rate of change of current $\frac{dI}{dt}$ of one ampere per second.*

Notice that mutual inductance is proportional to the rate of change of current in one of the coils. Therefore, no induction will take place mutually unless there is a continually changing current. This can be alternating polarity DC current activated by continuous switching or, more usually, alternating current (AC) that continually changes polarity at its frequency of generation.

Transformers

The main application of mutual inductance is in voltage transformers for *alternating current* (AC) power supply circuits. The basic construction of such a transformer is illustrated in Figure 3.93.

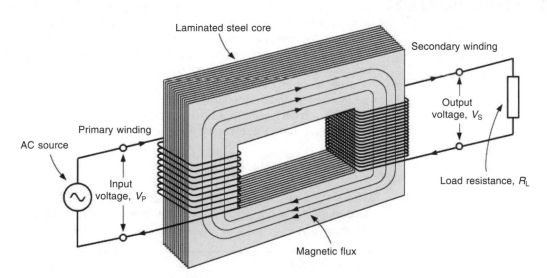

Figure 3.93 *The voltage transformer*

The *input* and *output windings* are called the *primary* and *secondary*, respectively. The ferromagnetic core provides a low reluctance (think of reluctance at this stage as AC resistance) flux path. Our mutual inductance formula for transformers may be written as:

$$V_s = -M\frac{dI_p}{dt}$$

where V_s = voltage induced in the secondary coil in volts, M = the mutual inductance in henries H, I_p = current in the primary coil in amperes A and t = time in seconds, s.

BTEC National Study Guide: Engineering. See page 325 for order details of individual texts

131

Example 3.49

Two coils of a transformer have a mutual inductance of 0.3 H. If the current in the primary coil is varied uniformly from 5 A to 2 A in 0.4 s, calculate the emf induced into the secondary coil.

The solution to this problem simply requires us to substitute the given values into our equation, ensuring that we use the correct value of $\dfrac{dI_p}{dt}$ which is 3 A/0.4 s or 7.5 A/s, then:

$$V_s = -M\frac{dI_p}{dt} = -(0.3)\frac{3}{0.4} = -(0.3)(7.5) = -2.25 \text{ V}$$

remembering that the minus sign indicates a back emf.
So emf in the secondary coil = **2.25 V**.

Transformers are easily the most efficient machines built by man, 98% or better! So it is reasonable to say that the *power input = power output*. Then, remembering our power formulae, we may write:

$$I_pV_p = I_sV_s$$

where V_p = rms voltage across the primary, I_p = rms current through the primary, V_s = rms voltage across the secondary and I_s = rms current through the secondary, all with the normal units.

Note that the *rms (root mean squared) values* of current and voltage *give their direct current equivalent* for the purpose of power calculations. For example, the rms equivalent voltage for our domestic household supply is *240 V (rms)*.

Another important transformer formula recognizes that the same flux through each coil, that is the voltage across each coil, must be proportional to the number of turns, or:

$$\frac{V_p}{V_s} = \frac{N_p}{N_s}$$

where V_p = rms voltage across primary, V_s = rms voltage across secondary, N_p = number of turns on primary, N_s = number of turns on secondary.

Key point

For mutual inductance to occur between two coils one coil must be subject to a continually changing current.

Example 3.50

240 V is applied to the primary windings of a transformer that has 1280 windings and draws a current of 13 A. Given that the required output voltage from the transformer is to be 12 V, determine:

(a)   the number of windings on the secondary
(b)   the output power from the transformer, given that the transformer is 98% efficient.

(a)   This is simply found using the volts-to-turns ratio formula, where:

$$N_s = \frac{N_pV_s}{V_p} = \frac{(1280)(12)}{240} = \mathbf{64}$$

(b)   To find the output power, that is the power available from the secondary windings, we need first to find the input power

---

BTEC National Study Guide: Engineering. See page 325 for order details of individual texts

132

because we are given the current flowing in the primary windings of the transformer.

Then from our power formula where $P = IV$ watts, the power at the primary windings, $I_pV_p = (13)(240) = 3120$ watts. We are told that the transformer is 98% efficient, so the power at the secondary will be 0.98 times the power at the primary or,

power at the secondary (output power) = **(0.98)(3120) = 3057.6 W**

Self-inductance

Up till now, we have concentrated on mutual inductance involving two coils; however, a back emf E is also produced by a flux change in a *single* coil. The back emf is proportional to the rate of change of current I (from Lenz's law), as illustrated in Figure 3.94.

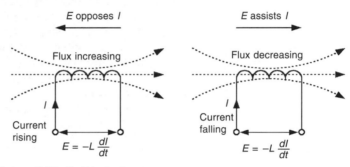

Figure 3.94 *Self-Inductance*

This effect is called *self-inductance*, which has the symbol L. Self-inductance L is measured in *henries* and is calculated in the same way as for mutual inductance M. In symbols:

$$E = -L\frac{dI}{dt}$$

A circuit is said to have an inductance L of one henry if one volt is induced by a rate of change of current

$$\frac{dI}{dt}$$

of one ampere per second.

Example 3.51

A coil has a self-inductance of 15 mH and is subject to a rate of change of current of 450 A s^{-1}. What is the back emf?

All we need do is place the appropriate values in the formula, then:

$$E = -L\frac{dI}{dt} = -\frac{(15 \times 10^{-3})(450)}{1} = -6.75\text{ V}$$

So the back emf = **6.75 V**.

Problems 3.6

1. (a) Define the unit of electrical energy.
   (b) An electric heater consumes 1 kJ of energy every second. If the heating element has a resistance of 57.6 Ω:

---

1. Give three examples of magnetic materials.
2. From which pole do the magnetic flux lines come from?
3. If, when using Fleming's left-hand motor rule, your thumb is pointing upwards, sketch the direction of the magnetic field and current flow.
4. What are the units of flux *and* flux density?
5. How may the torque produced on the coil of an electric motor be found?
6. What is a commutator used for?
7. What does the deflecting force in a moving coil meter depend upon?
8. Explain the requirements necessary to produce electricity.
9. State Lenz's law and explain what it tells us.
10. What does Faraday's law tell us about induced emf?
11. What is mutual inductance and how is it produced?
12. Define the henry.

BTEC National Study Guide: Engineering. See page 325 for order details of individual texts

133

(i)   How much current is taken from the supply?

(ii)   What is the supply voltage?

2. The heating element in question 1(b) above, with resistance of 57.6 Ω, is made from copper wire of diameter 0.25 mm, calculate its length in metres.

3. (a) State Ohm's law and explain the circumstances under which it may be used.

   (b) Three resistors of 5 Ω, 10 Ω and 30 Ω are connected in parallel with one another, then in series with the remaining 17 Ω resistor across a 120 V supply. Determine:

      (i)   the total current taken from the supply

      (ii)   the potential difference across the 17 Ω resistor

      (iii) the current flowing in each of the paralleled resistors

      (iv)   the power dissipated as heat through the 17 Ω resistor.

4. A current of 13 A enters a junction where it splits four ways. The current drawn by three of these pathways is 2 A, 4 A and 2.6 A, respectively. Find the current in the fourth pathway.

5. (a) Four cells each of 1.5 V are connected in parallel as a battery. What is the total emf of the battery?

   (b) The internal resistance of each cell in the battery identified in (a) is 0.01 Ω. What is the total internal resistance of the battery?

   (c) Each cell of this same battery draws a current of 0.2 A. What is the total current drawn by the battery?

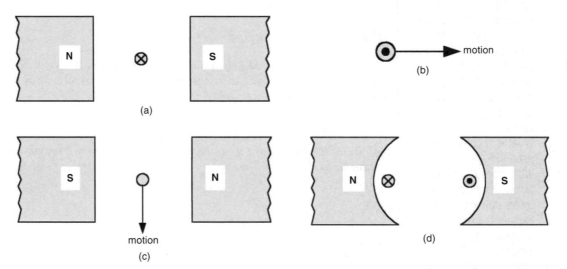

Figure 3.95 *Force on a conductor (a to d)*

6. Study the four diagrams shown in Figure 3.95(a) to (d) and mark on them the direction of motion, field or current as appropriate.

7. Study the six diagrams shown in Figure 3.96(a) to (f) and mark on them the direction of the induced emf.

8. A motor armature conductor of length 10 cm carries 50 A. The flux is at right angles to the conductor and has a flux density of 1.5 T. What is the motor force on the conductor.

9. If an emf of 5 V is induced in a coil when the current in an adjacent coil varies uniformly at the rate of 80 A s^{-1}, what is the value of the mutual inductance of the coil?

10. If the current through a coil of inductance 0.5 H is reduced

BTEC National Study Guide: Engineering. See page 325 for order details of individual texts

134

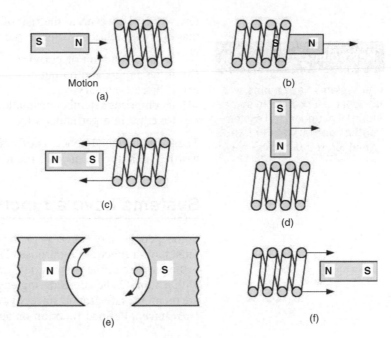

Figure 3.96 *Electromagnetic induction (a to f)*

from 5 A to 2 A in 0.05 seconds, calculate the value of the back emf induced in the coil

ENGINEERING SYSTEMS

Introduction

In this final outcome we look briefly at some of the underlying principles concerned with engineering systems and then apply these principles, in particular, to the study of servo systems.

We start by considering the concept of the *system*, looking in general at the idea of system boundaries, system inputs and outputs and system functions. We then adapt these rather abtract ideas to closed-loop systems and their engineering applications. We also consider the simple analysis of block diagrams for open- and closed-loop systems. Looking in particular at the way we calculate overall system gain through use of transfer functions. We then look at system response and identify the reasons for system damping.

In the final part of our study we will look at the application of closed-loop control to the operation of remote position servo systems and a typical analogue speed control system for a DC electric motor.

What is a system?

Systems are all around us. Indeed, we ourselves are examples of a complex system that in turn contains its own nervous, respiratory and muscular subsystems.

We use the word system so liberally and in such a wide range of contexts that it is difficult to explain what the term means in just a

BTEC National Study Guide: Engineering. See page 325 for order details of individual texts

135

few words. However, at the risk of oversimplification, we can say that every system conforms to the following main points:

(a) it has a function or purpose
(b) it has inputs and outputs
(c) it has a boundary
(d) it comprises a number of smaller components or elements linked together in a particular way.

These fundamental concepts of systems are so important that it is worth expanding on each of them in turn.

Systems have a function or purpose

Some people may argue with the assumption that *every* system must have a function or purpose. They may, for example, ask what is the purpose of the solar system other than, perhaps, providing us with a home! When considering engineering systems, however, we are on pretty safe ground since, by definition, an engineered system *must* have a defined function or purpose.

Systems have a number of inputs and outputs

A system without inputs and outputs cannot interact with its environment and is thus useless! It is worth noting, however, that not all inputs and outputs may be desirable. An example of an undesirable input to a telecommunication system would be noise picked up by the cables and wires along which the signals travel. In effect, this noise presents itself as an unwanted signal superimposed on top of the wanted signal. An example of an undesirable output from a system would be the exhaust gases produced by an internal combustion engine.

Systems have a boundary

Because all systems have a boundary, it is possible to say what is inside the system and what is outside it. This sometimes becomes important when there are a number of systems (and/or subsystems) and they interact with one another.

Sometimes the boundary of a system is not very clearly defined. That said, it is usually possible to construct a diagram for a system showing all of the components and elements within the system and then place this inside a box that contains the system as a whole. We sometimes refer to this as a 'black box', see Figure 3.97.

System components are linked in a particular way

The elements, parts, components or subsystems that make up a system are connected together (i.e. linked) in a particular way.

BTEC National Study Guide: Engineering. See page 325 for order details of individual texts

136

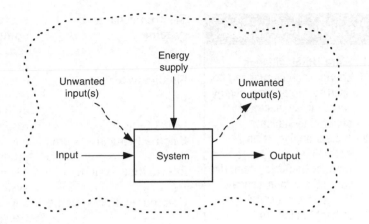

Figure 3.97 *A black box system*

This may sound obvious but it is quite an important point. Consider a box of bicycle parts that can be assembled to produce a fully working bicycle. The box of bicycle parts *does not* constitute a system whereas the fully assembled bicycle *does* constitute a system. Exactly the same physical parts are present in both cases – what *is* important is the way in which the parts are connected together so that they can interact with one another. Figure 3.98 illustrates this point.

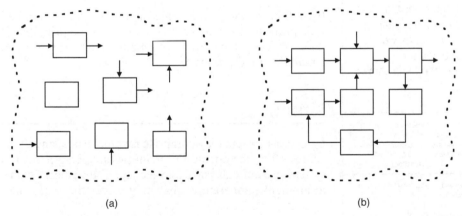

(a)   (b)

Figure 3.98 *(a) Not a system, (b) a system*

Definition of a system

Systems comprise a number of elements, components or subsystems that are connected together in a particular way. The individual elements of an engineering system interact together to satisfy a particular functional requirement.

Types of system

Various types of system are used in engineering. Listed below are some of the most common types of system. You will already be familiar with some of them but others may be completely new to you.

BTEC National Study Guide: Engineering. See page 325 for order details of individual texts

137

1. State THREE different energy sources that can be used as the primary energy source in an electrical generating station.
2. A 'heat engine' is an example of a thermodynamic system. Use your library to investigate the operation of ONE type of heat engine. Write a brief report explaining how the system operates and include relevant diagrams.
3. Identify the inputs to, and outputs from, each of the following systems:
a traffic lights system
a domestic central heating system
a engineering lathe system
a motor vehicle hydraulic brake system.
(Hint: Remember that there can be unwanted outputs from a system as well as wanted outputs!)
4. Complete the table shown below:

System	Main functional components (the 'doer')	Performance checking component (the 'monitor')	Controlling component (the 'decision maker')
Central heating	Boiler and radiators	Thermostat	Gas valve
Car	Engine and transmission	Driver's eyes and ears	_____
Computer	Micro-processor and memory	_____	Application program

5. A domestic central heating system has the following components, inputs and outputs:

Inputs
Cold water supply (via expansion tank in loft)
Thermostat setting (set point)

Energy sources
Domestic gas supply

Electromechanical systems	e.g. a vehicle electrical system comprising battery, starter motor, ignition coil, contact breaker, distributor, etc.
Fluidic systems	e.g. a vehicle braking system comprising foot operated lever, master cylinder, slave cylinder, piping, fluid reservoir, etc.
Electrochemical systems	e.g. a cell that uses gas as a fuel to produce electricity, pure water and heat.
Information systems	e.g. a computerized airport flight arrival system.
Communication systems	e.g. a local area network comprising file server, coaxial cable, network adapters, several computers and a laser printer
Control systems	e.g. a microcomputer-based controller that regulates the flow and temperature of material used in a diecasting process.
Transport systems	e.g. an overhead conveyor for transporting gravel from a quarry to a nearby processing site.

Function and purpose

By definition, an engineering system must have a defined purpose. This purpose is normally associated with the principal function of the system (e.g. the purpose of a manufacturing system is to produce a manufactured product).

Inputs

Inputs to a system may comprise raw materials, energy and control values set by the operator or manufacturer. In practical, real-world systems we must also take into account disturbances (such as changes in ambient temperature) that may affect the performance of the system.

Outputs

Outputs from a system can comprise finished products, processed materials, converted energy, etc. We also need to give some consideration to the by-products produced by the system, such as waste heat, toxic materials, inert materials, chemically active materials, radiation, etc.

System components

Most systems comprise several different types of component. Some components provide the main function of a system (e.g. a boiler in

BTEC National Study Guide: Engineering. See page 325 for order details of individual texts

138

240 V AC mains electricity to operate the gas ignition system and water pump

Outputs
Heat from radiators
Waste heat and combustion products

Functional components
Gas fired boiler
Gas ignition system
Room thermostat (adjustable)
Water pump
Water tank
Radiators
Gas valve (on/off)
Water valve (on/off)
Control panel

Sketch a diagram showing how the system components are connected together. Label your diagram clearly. (Hint: Take a look at your central heating system at home if you are not sure about how the system components are linked together.)

a central heating system) while others monitor the output of the system (e.g. a room thermostat in a central heating system). Other components are used to set or determine the required output of the system (e.g. the human operator who interacts with the system through a programmable controller).

The following categories can be applied to system components:

Functional components	Essentially, these are the components that do the work of the system.
Performance checking components	These components ascertain the level of performance of the system. As such, they measure or in some way respond to the output produced by the system.
Controlling components	These components are responsible for determining the level of performance of the system. They establish the desired output from the system and, in complex systems, manage the overall operation of the system.

As an example, a satellite positioning system might comprise the following:

Directional thrusters (functional components)
Fuel tank (functional component)
Control valve (functional component)
Earth-link antenna (functional component)
Command receiver/decoder (functional component)
Position computer (performance checking component)
Ground command station (controlling component).

Controlling engineering systems

Now that you have some idea about the general make-up of systems, it is time to consider how they are controlled. All modern engineering systems include a certain aspect of control, at some point. When we *control systems*, we are ensuring that they *behave in a desired way*. So, for example, if you drive a car you need to ensure that the car engine produces the right amount of *torque* to overcome variations in the terrain, such as going up hill. The torque needs to be varied not only to meet changing loads, but also to maintain the appropriate speed of rotation of the driving wheels.

Control systems may be simple as in the case of a light being controlled by a switch, or complex such as an automatic instrument landing system for a modern passenger aircraft. In the simple case, the fact that the light did or did not illuminate would have been observed by the operator and if a fault had been detected then it would need to be remedied by the operator. In the case of the complex system the tendency of the aircraft to move off the correct glide path, as the aircraft is landing, is automatically corrected by the system and requires no operator intervention. The simple system

BTEC National Study Guide: Engineering. See page 325 for order details of individual texts

139

requiring operator intervention is often referred to as *open loop*; the complex system, which automatically corrects for errors, is commonly known as *closed loop*.

The *type of system control method* used is dependent on the type of control strategy being employed, as well as the output being controlled. Thus different control methods are appropriate to different types of system and the overall control strategy can be based on *analogue or digital techniques* and may also be classed as either *sequential* or *combinational*.

Analogue control

Analogue control involves the use of *signals* and quantities that are *continuously variable*. Within analogue control systems, signals may, for example, be represented by voltage, current, pressure, temperature, etc. that can take any value between two set limits. Figure 3.99 shows how the output of a typical analogue system varies with time.

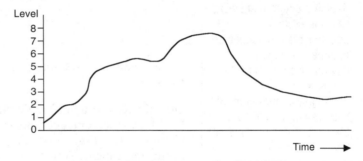

Figure 3.99 *Output of analogue system shown against time*

The majority of analogue control systems use *electrical signalling*, where the signals are *modified or conditioned* using *operational amplifiers* (see Figure 3.100). These devices are capable of performing *mathematical operations* such as addition, subtraction, multiplication, division, integration and differentiation!

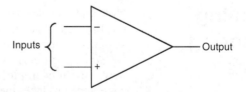

Figure 3.100 *An operational amplifier*

The exact way in which operational amplifiers perform these mathematical operations is not required at this stage in your learning. However, you will see how we use them when we consider closed-loop control, a little later.

Digital control

Digital control involves the use of signals and quantities that vary in *discrete steps*. Values that fall between two adjacent steps must

BTEC National Study Guide: Engineering. See page 325 for order details of individual texts

140

take one or other value as intermediate values are disallowed! Figure 3.101 shows how the output of a typical digital system varies with time.

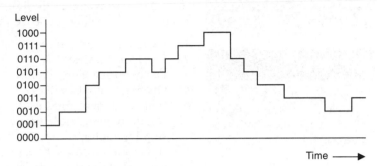

Figure 3.101 *Output of a digital system shown against time*

Digital control systems are usually based on electronic digital logic devices (see Figure 3.102) or microprocessor-based computer systems.

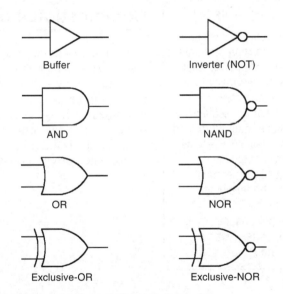

Figure 3.102 *A selection of digital logic devices*

Values represented within a digital system are expressed in *binary coded form* using a number of signal lines. The voltage on each line can be either 'high' (representing logic 1) or 'low' (representing logic 0). The more signal lines, the greater the resolution of the system. For example, with just two signal lines it is possible to represent a number using only two binary digits (or 'bits'). Since each bit can be either 0 or 1 it is possible to represent only four different values (00, 01, 10 and 11) using this system. With three signal lines we can represent numbers using three bits and eight different values are possible (000, 001, 010, 011, 100, 101, 110 and 111).

The relationship between the number of bits, n, and the number of different values possible, m, is given by $m = 2^n$. So, in an 8-bit system the number of different discrete states is given by $m = 2^8 = 256$.

BTEC National Study Guide: Engineering. See page 325 for order details of individual texts

141

Sequential control systems

Many systems are required to perform a series of operations in a set order. For example, the ignition system of a gas boiler may require the following sequence of operations:

1. Operator's start button pressed.
2. Fan motor operates.
3. Delay 60 seconds.
4. Open gas supply valve.
5. Igniter operates for 2 seconds.
6. If ignition fails, close gas supply valve, delay 60 seconds, then stop fan motor.
7. If ignition succeeds, boiler will continue to operate until either stop switch operates or flame fails.

The components of simple sequential systems often include timers, relays, counters, etc.; however, digital logic and microprocessor-based controllers are used on more complex systems.

Combinational control systems

Combinational control systems take several inputs and perform comparisons on a continuous basis. In effect, everything happens at the same time – there are no delays or predetermined sequences that would be associated with sequential controllers. The aircraft instrument landing system (ILS) we considered earlier, for example, makes continuous comparisons of an aircraft's position relative to the ILS radio beam (Figure 3.103). Where any deviation is detected, appropriate correction is applied to the aircraft's flight controls.

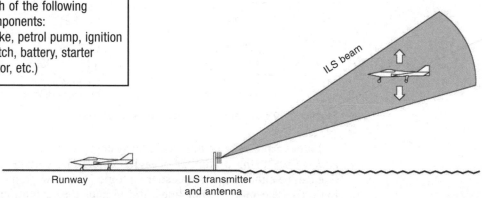

Figure 3.103 *An aircraft instrument landing system (ILS)*

Closed-loop control

We looked earlier at a simple control system, the light switch, and a complex system, the aircraft ILS system, indicating that the former was open loop and the latter closed loop. We need to define and compare open-loop and closed-loop control systems before considering the closed-loop system in detail.

BTEC National Study Guide: Engineering. See page 325 for order details of individual texts

142

Open-loop control

In a system that employs open-loop control, the value of the input variable is set to a given value in the expectation that the output will reach this desired value. In such a system there is no *automatic* comparison of the actual output value with the desired output value in order to compensate for any differences. Thus *open-loop control may be regarded as: a system that needs human operator intervention to monitor performance and to modify matters if the outcome is not correct.*

A simple example of an open-loop control method is the manual adjustment of the regulator that controls the flow of gas to a burner on the hob of a gas cooker. This adjustment is carried out in the expectation that food will be raised to the correct temperature in a given time and without burning. Other than the occasional watchful eye of the chef, there is no means of automatically regulating the gas flow in response to the actual temperature of the food.

Consider another example, the control of the motor vehicle (Figure 3.104), we mentioned earlier.

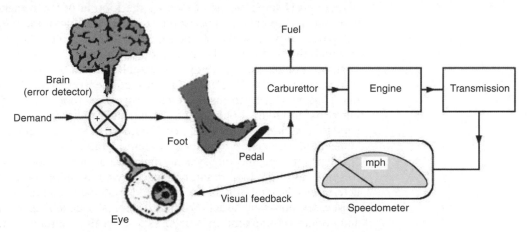

Figure 3.104 *Control of motor vehicle speed, using human operator*

Let us assume that we wish to drive the vehicle at 30 mph. Starting from rest, with the engine running, we need to press down on the accelerator pedal to open the throttle, this in turn increases the amount of fuel charge entering the carburettor and so increases the available power being delivered by the engine. Now, against a given load (weight of the car, terrain, etc.) this increase in power increases the torque to the driving wheels which, acting against frictional resistance, provide the driving force necessary to accelerate the vehicle up to the desired speed. We, as the driver, are now required to monitor the speed of the vehicle and correct matters accordingly, to ensure that we travel at the desired speed of 30 mph. The way in which we correct matters is to continually monitor our speed using the speedometer, while at the same time adjusting the throttle setting, in order to keep us at 30 mph.

The finesse with which the speed may be controlled depends on two main factors. One is the accuracy of reading the speedometer and the other the accuracy of setting the throttle. There is always bound to be a time delay between the observed effect on the speed

BTEC National Study Guide: Engineering. See page 325 for order details of individual texts

143

and the measures taken to remedy the disturbance. Our average thinking time is around 0.2 of a second, this is why we always need to allow a thinking distance as well as a stopping distance between vehicles!

Now, on motor vehicles, this is the normal way of watching and controlling our speed. What if we adopt the same system for controlling the flight speed of, say, a supersonic jet fighter? Imagine two such aircraft approaching each other at, say, 1600 km/hr, that is a relative closing speed of 3200 km/hr or approximately 890 m s^{-1}. By the time we have thought about avoiding action, we have closed by another 200 m, never mind the time it takes for the aircrafts' flight controls to react! We therefore need another form of control, which is faster and more accurate and does not necessarily depend on human operator intervention. For this function and many other engineering functions, we use *closed-loop* control.

Nature of closed-loop control

Clearly, open-loop control has some significant disadvantages. What is required is some means of closing the loop in order to make a continuous automatic comparison of the actual value of the output compared with the setting of the input control variable. The speed at which this is done is also of some importance.

In our cooker example, the chef actually closes the loop on an intermittent basis. In effect, the gas cooker relies on human intervention in order to ensure consistency of the food produced. If our cooking requires only boiling water, this intervention can be kept to a minimum; however, for 'haute cuisine' we require the constant supervision of a skilled human operator!

All practical engineering systems make use of closed-loop control. In some cases, the loop might be closed by a human operator who determines the deviation between the desired and actual output. In most cases, however, the action of the system is made *fully automatic* and no human intervention is necessary other than initially setting the desired value of the output.

If we again consider the example of controlling the speed of the car, this could be done *automatically* by controlling the engine rpm, for varying load conditions, thus producing the correct amount of torque at the driving wheels to maintain the *desired* speed. In this case our automatic closed-loop control system for the car will need to be modified so that we are able to *sense* and *control* engine rpm (Figure 3.105).

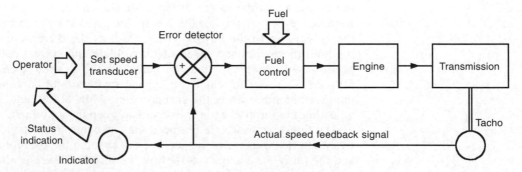

Figure 3.105 *Closed-loop control of engine rpm*

BTEC National Study Guide: Engineering. See page 325 for order details of individual texts

144

So the demanded speed signal for the car in this system is set using an *input transducer*, such as a potentiometer (transducers and other system components are explained next, when we generalize our closed-loop system). The actual speed achieved by the car (the load) is monitored by a *feedback transducer*. In this case, a tachogenerator is used that converts engine rpm into a corresponding voltage output. The *error detector* is a device which produces a difference or error signal to the throttle (a summing operational amplifier could achieve this). The *error signal* is equal to the demand signal minus the feedback signal. As the speed of the car (the actual speed) approaches the demand speed (set by the input transducer) the signal to the throttle becomes smaller and to provide greater sensitivity and accuracy of the set speed an amplifier is included in the system (the *error signal amplifier*). Remember it is the error between the desired and actual values that continues to drive the system (*error actuated*). Once the desired value is equal to the actual value (of speed in this case), there is no error and the system remains at this value, unless subject to an external disturbance.

From the outline described above, we may deduce the general schematic (Figure 3.106) required for any closed-loop control system.

Key point

The system is driven by the error from the comparator or error detecting device.

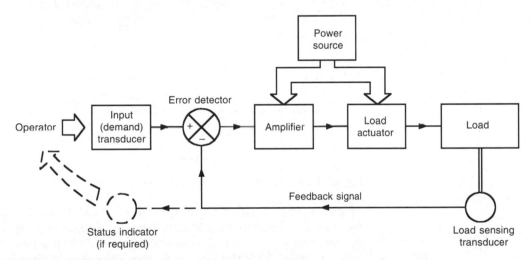

Figure 3.106 *Generalized schematic diagram of a closed-loop control system*

Any variation in the performance of the load, not called for by the operator, produces an automatic change in the error signal which attempts to counteract the load performance variation. How quickly corrections are made to counteract the load performance depends to a large extent on the system *gain*. In order to appreciate control systems more fully we need to consider the nature and function of transducers, amplifiers (signal conditioners), error detectors and power actuation components that go to make up closed-loop control systems.

Transducers

In its simplest sense, a *transducer* is essentially an *energy converter*. Although you might not realize it, transducers are all around us! For example, the light switch we mentioned earlier converts position into a voltage. The tachogenerator mentioned earlier, as a type of transducer, converts rotational velocity into a voltage. Thus

BTEC National Study Guide: Engineering. See page 325 for order details of individual texts

145

transducers may be simple or complex but essentially they all perform the same function, that of energy conversion. More complex transducers may be composed of two components: the primary component or *sensor* and the secondary component or *conversion/ control element*. In this sense, any but the simplest of transducers are really *systems* in their own right.

Consider Figure 3.107, which shows a Bourdon pressure gauge.

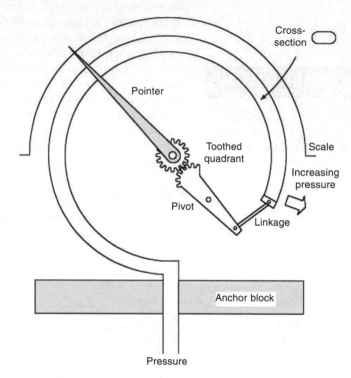

Figure 3.107 *Bourdon pressure gauge*

This instrument is essentially a *transducer system*. It consists of a flattened oval cross-section hollow tube, bent round in a circular manner; this is the *sensing element* that senses fluid pressure, the *primary signal*. This fluid pressure causes the tube to straighten, thus the Bourdon tube converts fluid pressure into movement, so it is in its own right, a transducer; in this system it is used as the *sensing element*. The *secondary signal* (linear movement) from the tube is converted by the *gearing* into rotary movement at the *pointer*. Thus the gearing acts as the *conversion/control element* of the overall transducer system. The final output is the movement of the pointer across a scale, which enables us to read off the pressure.

We can represent any transducer (Figure 3.108) by a generalized flow diagram of the transduction process described above for our Bourdon pressure gauge example.

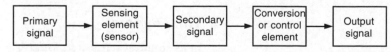

Figure 3.108 *Transducer flow diagram*

Transducers may be grouped according to the type of signal received by the sensing element and given out by the conversion or

BTEC National Study Guide: Engineering. See page 325 for order details of individual texts

146

control element. The most frequently used transducers are those that convert any physical, mechanical, thermal, chemical or radiation input to a voltage or current output. That is, any transducer that measures force, pressure, displacement, vibration, light, concentration, temperature, etc., then converts these input signals into an electrical voltage output. A few examples of these transducers, together with others that do not have a voltage output, are tabulated below.

Devices	Input quantity sensed	output signal
Switch	Position	Voltage
Potentiometer	Position	Voltage
Linear variable differential transformer (LVDT)	Position	Voltage
Tachogenerator	Rotational speed	Voltage
Thermistor	Temperature	Voltage
Thermocouple	Temperature	Voltage
Accelerometer	Acceleration	Voltage
Photodiode	Light	Voltage
Photoelectric cell	Light	Voltage
Electric motor	Voltage	Rotational movement
Voltmeter	Voltage	Movement of needle
Lamp	Voltage	Light
Bourdon gauge	Fluid pressure	Movement of needle
Hydraulic motor	Fluid flow	Rotational movement
Hydraulic pump	Rotational movement	Fluid flow
Bimetallic strip	Heat	Angular movement
Radiation pyrometer	Radiated heat	Voltage
Strain gauge	Displacement	Voltage

As can be seen from the above table, some transducers are relatively simple, others are really systems in their own right, for instance the electric motor and hydraulic pump are *energy conversion devices* and therefore *transducers*, but physically they are made from many parts, in such a way as to be a *system*.

A *transducer is a device which essentially converts one form of energy into another*. Alternatively a *transducer* may be defined as: *a sensing device that converts physical phenomena and chemical composition into electric, mechanical, pneumatic or hydraulic output signals*.

Key point

Transducers are essentially energy conversion devices.

Error detector or comparison element

An *error detector* or *comparison element monitors output performance against a stored model of what it should be. Deviations from the desired output create an error signal, which drives the system*.

This may sound a little complicated. Look back at our closed-loop version of speed control for the car. The operator (driver) sets the desired output speed of the vehicle by setting the engine rpm, as explained earlier. It is this engine rpm that we are controlling for varying loads at the driving wheels. The engine, in turn, provides the necessary torque to maintain the selected driving speed of the car. So with respect to the *error detector*, our stored model may be set using a *potentiometer* (look back at the input/output we get from this device). By altering our potentiometer setting using, say, a dial, a certain engine rpm and therefore a certain car speed are set

BTEC National Study Guide: Engineering. See page 325 for order details of individual texts

147

by the dial. This produces a corresponding voltage output from the potentiometer that becomes the *set input to the error detector*. At this stage it is worth mentioning that the error detector is often a type of *operational amplifier* that *compares* this set imput (the desired output) with the actual output measured by some form of transducer at the output. In the case of our car, this transducer is likely to be positioned on the gearbox, so that drive speed can be measured using a tachogenerator. The tachogenerator, you will remember, converts rotational velocity into a corresponding voltage output. This voltage signal (*feedback signal*) is *compared in the error detector* with our desired signal and the net difference is the *error* which continues to drive the load (in our case supplying the necessary fuel charge to maintain the desired engine rpm and road speed).

Signal conditioning

In reality the electrical output signal from the error detector is very small and in order to provide sufficient power to drive the load actuator (fuel control unit in our car example), we need to amplify the output from the error detector. This amplification modifies (increases) the signal, so we say that it has been *conditioned* and the general name for this is *signal conditioning*. Any modification of the output signal from the error detector is referred to as signal conditioning. So, for example, converting a DC voltage output signal to an AC voltage output signal is also known as signal conditioning. Also, the signal need not necessarily be electrical. Figure 3.109 shows two forms of mechanical amplifiers, which act as signal conditioners.

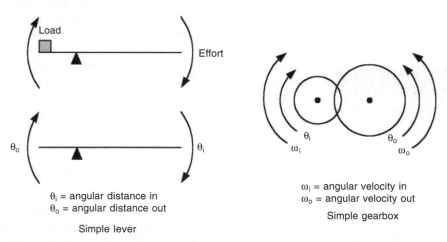

Figure 3.109 *Mechanical amplifiers (signal conditioners)*

In the case of the simple lever, this can be used to amplify distance (displacement) or amplify load. In the case of the gearbox, this can reduce/increase speed and displacement, as well as increase/reduce the torque available at the drive from the gearbox. In the case of our Bourdon pressure gauge (see Figure 3.107), the gearing is used to amplify the displacement of the pointer across a pressure scale (not shown).

BTEC National Study Guide: Engineering. See page 325 for order details of individual texts

148

Load actuation

The load may be driven by electrical, mechanical, hydraulic or pneumatic motors and associated gearing. These machines are collectively known as the *load actuators* or *power source*; they are the muscle of the system and provide the driving power to the *load*. In the case of our car, the power source was an internal combustion engine, where the input is a chemical charge and the output is driving torque, which is *signal conditioned* via a gearbox and drive shafts to the road wheels.

System block diagrams

We have already represented a closed-loop control system in block diagram form (Figure 3.106). However, this particular representation tells us little about the relationship between system inputs, outputs and feedback. The simplest type of open-loop system may be represented diagrammatically using an input, an output and a block to represent the system process. For example, Figure 3.110 illustrates a simple block diagram of a thermocouple open-loop system.

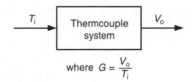

Figure 3.110 *Thermocouple system*

Now we know that for this type of transducer, the input signal is temperature, which is a measure of heat; the output signal is a corresponding voltage. The relationship,

$$\frac{V_{\mathrm{o}}}{T_{\mathrm{i}}}$$

is known as the *gain (G)* of the system or as the system *transfer function* (TF). In general terms for any input signal θ_{i} and output signal θ_{o}, then:

open-loop system gain $G = \dfrac{\text{output}}{\text{input}} = \dfrac{\theta_{\mathrm{o}}}{\theta_{\mathrm{i}}}$

or the system transfer function

$$\mathrm{TF} = \frac{\theta_{\mathrm{o}}}{\theta_{\mathrm{i}}}$$

So, for example, if in the case of our thermocouple for every 1°C rise in temperature we get a 2 mV increase at the output, then the system gain or transfer function is

$$G = \frac{\theta_{\mathrm{o}}}{\theta_{\mathrm{i}}} = \frac{2\,\mathrm{mV}}{1°\mathrm{C}} = 2\,\mathrm{mV}/°\mathrm{C}$$

Now we can extend our open-loop system to contain any number of components between the system input and output. When this happens, we simply multiply the individual component values (gains) together (Figure 3.111) to produce the overall system output.

BTEC National Study Guide: Engineering. See page 325 for order details of individual texts

149

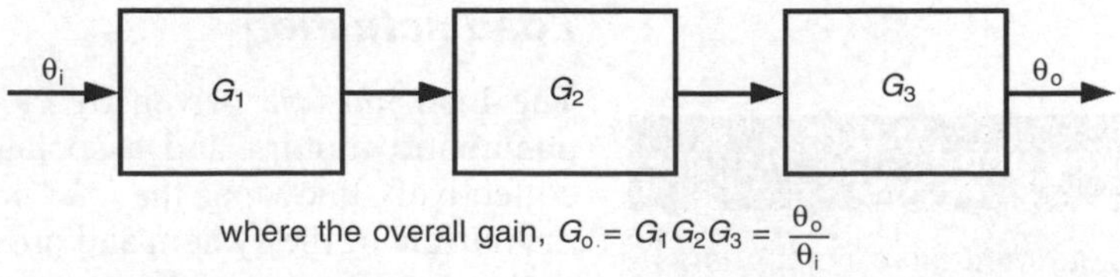

where the overall gain, $G_o = G_1 G_2 G_3 = \dfrac{\theta_o}{\theta_i}$

Figure 3.111 *Overall system gain for components in cascade*

In this particular configuration, where individual system components are connected in series, we refer to them as being connected in *cascade* and, as shown, in this case:

$$G_o = G_1 G_2 G_3 = \frac{\theta_o}{\theta_i}$$

Also these components are said to be in the *feed-forward path* of the system. Symbolically, we may represent feed-forward components by the letter G on system block diagrams. If we were to convert this system to *closed loop*, then we require some percentage of the output to be *monitored* and *fed back* to the error detector for comparison.

> ## Key point
>
> When components are connected in series, they are said to be in cascade.

Example 3.52

An open-loop system consists of an input potentiometer, an amplifier and a motor. If the gain of these components 2 mV/degree, 1 V/mV and 1 Nm/V, respectively, determine the system transfer function and the value of the output for a given input of 30°. Then the overall system gain G_o or transfer function

$$TF = \left(\frac{2\ mV}{degree} \right)\left(\frac{1\ V}{mV} \right)\left(\frac{0.1\ Nm}{V} \right) = \frac{\mathbf{0.2\ Nm}}{\mathbf{degree}}$$

and so for 30° of input,

$$\theta_0 = \left(\frac{0.2\ Nm}{degree} \right) 30° = \mathbf{6\ Nm}$$

In other words, the motor produces 6 Nm of torque at the output shaft when the input transducer dial is turned through 30°.

We can represent a closed-loop system in its simplest form by the block diagram shown in Figure 3.112.

In this diagram the *feed-forward path components* are represented by G, as before. The additional components shown are required to convert the system from open loop to *closed loop*. They include the essential *error detector* or comparison element, with output ε, which is the sum of the input signal θ_i (desired output) and a proportion of the output signal $-\gamma_o$, being fed back to the error detector, the negative sign indicating *negative feedback*. In reality, if the feedback signal is a voltage, the *negative symbol* represents an *inverse in polarity* of the voltage, when compared with the input signal to the error detector. Thus the error signal (which drives the system) may be represented symbolically as:

BTEC National Study Guide: Engineering. See page 325 for order details of individual texts

150

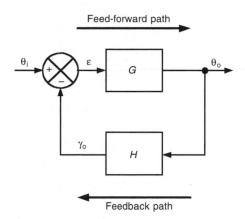

Figure 3.112 *Closed-loop system block diagram*

$$\varepsilon = \theta_i - \gamma_o \tag{1}$$

Also, in the feed-forward path, the system output θ_o is the product of the error signal ε and the overall gain of the feed-forward components G, that is:

$$\theta_o = G\varepsilon \tag{2}$$

Now, if we substitute the expression for ε from equation (1) into equation (2), we get:

$$\theta_o = G(\theta_i - \gamma_o)$$

or

$$\theta_o = G\theta_i - G\gamma_o \tag{3}$$

Now in the *feedback line* we have the component H, which represents the feedback transducer, used to modify (signal condition) the signal from the output of the system, prior to entry into the error detector. For example, a transducer that converts, say, rpm into a corresponding voltage. Then, this modified feedback signal:

$$\gamma_o = H\theta_o$$

and on substitution of this expression for γ_o into equation (3) we get:

$$\theta_o = G\theta_i - GH\theta_o$$

or

$$\theta_o + GH\theta_o = G\theta_i$$

$$(1 + GH)\theta_o = G\theta_i$$

therefore the closed-loop transfer function (CLTF) for a *negative feedback* system is:

$$\frac{\theta_o}{\theta_i} = \frac{G}{1 + GH}$$

Note that in our block diagram of a closed-loop system, the feedback components are represented conventionally by the letter H. The expression for the CLTF also represents the *overall system gain* for this particular type of system.

BTEC National Study Guide: Engineering. See page 325 for order details of individual texts

151

Example 3.53

In a particular system the forward path gain is 56. Determine the gain if negative feedback is used to convert the system to closed loop, where the feedback component has a gain of 8.

This is a simple example of the use of our CLTF for a negative feedback system, i.e.:

$$\frac{\theta_o}{\theta_i} = \text{closed loop gain} = \frac{G}{1 + GH} = \frac{56}{1 + (56)(8)} = \frac{56}{449} \simeq \mathbf{0.125}$$

Now if *positive feedback* is used, it can be easily shown that

$$\text{CLTF} = \frac{\theta_o}{\theta_i} = \frac{G}{1 - GH}$$

simply by replacing the negative sign in the error detector (hot-cross bun) by a positive sign and following through the analysis, shown above!

Also, if there is no necessity to include a component in the feedback line, then we say that we have a *unity feedback* (because we replace the H component(s) by the number one) system.

Thus with unity feedback the CLTF for a negative feedback system is given by:

$$\frac{\theta_o}{\theta_i} = \frac{G}{1 + G}$$

Strictly speaking, we should differentiate between the overall gain of a system and the system transfer function. The TF is the generalized version of the system gain. In other words we tend to use the words 'system gain G' when we are finding numerical values. The TF is often an algebraic expression that is found when analysing relatively complex systems.

Test your knowledge 3.20

1. Detail three advantages of fully automatic closed-loop control systems over their open-loop counterparts.
2. Explain the function of transducers in a typical closed-loop control system.
3. What is the function of the error detector or comparator in a closed-loop control system?
4. In a closed-loop control system, explain how the load is always driven towards its demanded output value.
5. What is the function of the feedback transducer when fitted into a closed-loop control system?
6. Write down the CLTF for a unity positive feedback, closed-loop control system.
7. How may we differentiate between the overall gain of a closed-loop system and the system transfer function?

Example 3.54

1. Determine an expression for the overall transfer function, for the system shown in Figure 3.113.

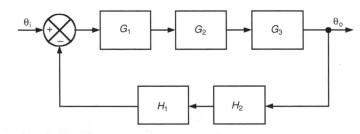

Figure 3.113

2. Determine the overall gain of the system if $G_1 = 20$, $G_2 = 15$, $G_3 = 10$, $H_1 = 0.05$ and $H_2 = 0.05$.

1. From the system block diagram it can be seen that the system is closed loop with negative feedback. Therefore we can use,

$$\frac{\theta_o}{\theta_i} = \frac{G}{1 + GH}$$

BTEC National Study Guide: Engineering. See page 325 for order details of individual texts

152

where $G = G_1G_2G_3$ and $H = H_1H_2$.
Then:

$$\frac{\theta_0}{\theta_i} = \frac{G_1G_2G_3}{1 + G_1G_2G_3H_1H_2}$$

2. To find the *overall system gain*, it is just a question of substituting the appropriate values and completing the arithmetic. Then:

overall system gain

$$= \frac{(20)(15)(10)}{1 + (20)(15)(10)(0.05)(0.05)} = \frac{3000}{1 + 7.5} = \mathbf{400}$$

Closed-loop system response

In a perfect system, the output value, θ_o, will respond instantaneously to a change in the input, θ_i. There will be no delay when changing from one value to another and no time required for the output to 'settle' to its final value. This ideal state of affairs is illustrated in Figure 3.114(b). In practice, real-world systems take time to reach their final state. Indeed, a very sudden change in output may, in some cases, be undesirable.

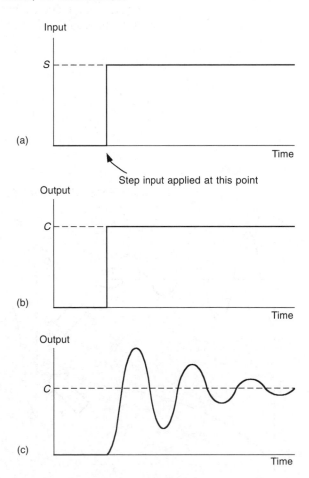

Figure 3.114 *(a) Step input, (b) ideal response to step input, (c) response of real system to step input*

BTEC National Study Guide: Engineering. See page 325 for order details of individual texts

153

Furthermore, *inertia* is present in many systems. Consider the case of the motor speed control system shown in Figure 3.115 (we study this system in detail later) where the output shaft is connected to a substantial flywheel. The flywheel effectively limits the acceleration of the motor speed when the set point (S) is increased. Furthermore, as the output speed reaches the desired value, the inertia present will keep the speed increasing despite the reduction in voltage (V) applied to the motor. Thus the output shaft speed *overshoots* the desired value before eventually falling back to the required value.

Increasing the *gain* present in the system will have the effect of increasing the acceleration but this, in turn, will also produce a correspondingly greater value of overshoot. Conversely, decreasing the gain will reduce the overshoot but at the expense of slowing down the response. The actual response of the system represents a compromise between speed and an acceptable value of overshoot. Figure 3.114(c) shows the typical response of a system to the step input shown in Figure 3.114(a).

Key point

Increasing the gain of a system reduces response time but increases overshoot.

Second order response

The graph shown in Figure 3.114(c) is known as a '*second order*' *response*. This response has two basic components, a logarithmic growth curve and a damped oscillation (see Figure 3.116).

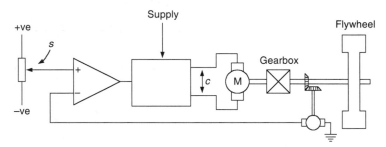

Figure 3.115 *Motor speed control system with inertia*

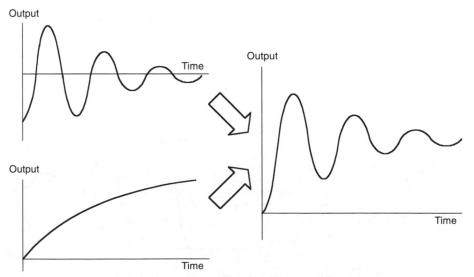

Figure 3.116 *System response resulting from added damped oscillation to a logarithmic growth curve*

BTEC National Study Guide: Engineering. See page 325 for order details of individual texts

154

The oscillatory component can be reduced (or eliminated) by artificially slowing down the response of the system. This is known as *damping*. The optimum value of damping is that which *just* prevents overshoot. When a system is 'underdamped', some overshoot is still present. Conversely, an 'overdamped' system may take a significantly greater time to respond to a sudden change in input (see Figure 3.117).

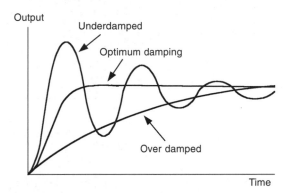

Figure 3.117 *System response with different amounts of damping*

Delay time, settling time and damping factor

The delay time for a system is the time taken for the output to reach 50 per cent of its final (steady-state) value after the application of a step input (see Figure 3.118(a)). The settling time for a system is the time taken for the system to enter and remain within defined tolerance limits for its output. Typical values for tolerance limits are 5 per cent or 10 per cent. In relation to the steady-state step value, the size of the first overshoot is an indicator of the *damping factor*. The smaller the damping factor, the larger the overshoot. Optimum damping is associated with a damping factor of unity.

Natural frequency

The natural frequency f_n of a system is the reciprocal of the time taken t for one cycle of the damped oscillation (see Figure 3.118(b)). Natural frequency is normally specified in Hertz (Hz) or in terms of angular velocity, ω_n, where:

$$\omega_n = 2\pi f_n \quad \text{and} \quad f_n = 1/t$$

Decrement

From Figure 3.118 you should note that each successive cycle of damped oscillation has a smaller amplitude than its predecessor. However, the amount of reduction in amplitude is constant from each peak to the next. This is known as the *decrement* and it can be most easily measured from the ratio of the amplitude of the first undershoot to that of the first overshoot. In each case the amplitudes

BTEC National Study Guide: Engineering. See page 325 for order details of individual texts

155

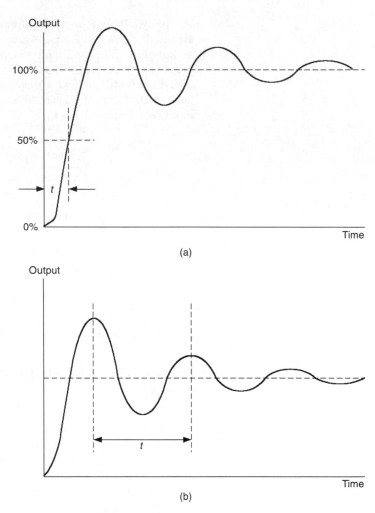

Figure 3.118 *(a) Delay time (b) natural frequency*

are measured either side of the steady-state value. If, for example, the amplitude of the first undershoot is 0.1 while that of the first overshoot is 0.2, the decrement is (0.1/0.2) or 0.5.

Engineering applications of closed-loop control systems

To finish our short study of engineering systems we are going to look at two engineering applications of automatic closed-loop control. Before we do so, let me remind you of some of the reasons for making a system *fully automatic*.

1. Some systems use a very large number of input variables and it may be difficult or impossible for a human operator to keep track of them.
2. Some processes are extremely complex and there may be significant interaction between the input variables.
3. Some systems may have to respond very quickly to changes in variables (human reaction times may just not be fast enough).
4. Some systems require a very high degree of precision (human operators may be unable to work to a sufficiently high degree of accuracy).

BTEC National Study Guide: Engineering. See page 325 for order details of individual texts

156

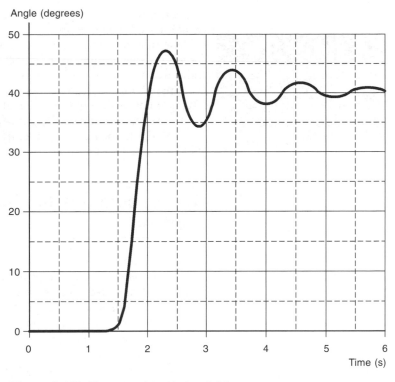

Angle (degrees)

Time (s)

Figure 3.119 *Test your knowledge 3.21*

Thus reasons (1) and (2) could apply to the aircraft independent landing system (ILS), which wc considered earlier. There are simply too many variables for the pilot to contend with during take-off and landing of a complex modern airliner. Reason (4) is particularly applicable to modern manufacturing systems, where a high degree of precision is necessary to produce complex components.

Servo systems

Servo systems are closed-loop automatic control systems that are designed to control the position (linear or angular) and velocity (linear or angular) of a load, remotely. Their major engineering use is to overcome the large torques required to move heavy loads through the application of a relatively small input load or torque. Examples of such systems include:

- controlling torque of gearboxes and other transmission components used with heavy machinery
- controlling the movement of an industrial robot
- the automatic piloting of an aircraft
- control of a ship's steering system
- control of a guided missile
- control of a vehicle transmission system
- industrial precision positioning system
- speed control of a process control system.

These systems can include electronic, electromechanical, pneumatic, hydraulic and mechanical devices. The above examples demonstrate

BTEC National Study Guide: Engineering. See page 325 for order details of individual texts

157

Key point

Servo systems are closed-loop automatic control systems that control displacement and/or velocity parameters, remotely.

the versatility of these systems. We are going to look at two particular examples of such systems.

The first is a remote position control (RPC) system which may be used for such functions as accurately positioning a workpiece prior to a drilling operation or as a powerful gear selector in a large automatic transmission system or even to operate the powered flying controls of a modern aircraft.

The second example is concerned with controlling the speed of an electric motor by automatically controlling the current to the field windings of the motor, under varying torque conditions.

The remote position control (RPC) servo system

For this system we will consider two methods that may be adopted for the remote and accurate positioning of a large workpiece in an automated manufacturing system. The power source for such a system could be electrical, hydraulic or pneumatic. In our system we will be using hydraulic power, which we are able to control both mechanically and electrically.

The first of our systems is illustrated in Figure 3.120 where a *hydromechanical* RPC servo system is shown. The hydraulic fluid flow to the servo valve input is supplied by a constant displacement hydraulic pump and a solenoid operated, closed centre, directional control valve. The displacement of the load is controlled by the operator, via a mechanically operated spool valve. If, for example, the operator moves the spool valve to the right, then fluid is ported into the right-hand chamber via hydraulic line A. This fluid flow reacts against the fixed piston assembly and walls of the cylinder body. At the same time, hydraulic fluid in the left-hand oil chamber is ported back to return, via line B. The whole cylinder body now moves to the right, this movement of the cylinder body, over the now stationary spool valve, gradually shuts off the hydraulic system supply and return lines, creating a hydraulic lock, bringing the cylinder body and thus the load (workpiece) to rest. If the operator mechanically moves the spool valve to the left, the cylinder body moves the workpiece to the left, until follow-up action again causes the movement to cease.

The speed of operation is dependent on the amount of displacement of the spool valve pistons relative to the cylinder body. Thus the workpiece can be moved in both directions, at the required feed rate, dependent on the movement of the spool valve, initiated by the operator, who may be remote from the workstation.

A similar system to that shown in Figure 3.120 could also be used to operate the flying controls of an aircraft where the input to the spool valve is controlled by the pilot.

A rather more sophisticated electrohydraulic servo system could be used for workpiece positioning. Such a system is illustrated in Figure 3.121, where, in this case, the servo valve (spool valve) is electrically actuated using an appropriate motor and the follow-up action is electrically sensed using a pair of electrical potentiometers.

The hydraulic power supply and hydraulic actuator are identical to those shown before in Figure 3.120. The difference lies in the

BTEC National Study Guide: Engineering. See page 325 for order details of individual texts

158

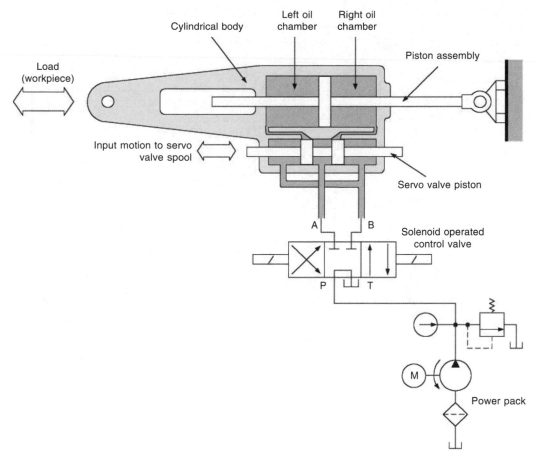

Figure 3.120 *Simplified hydromechanical RPC servo system*

way the servo spool valve is actuated. In this case electrical positioning of the valve spool is set via a rotary potentiometer, which supplies the electrical input voltage via an amplifier to the spool motor. The follow-up signal is provided by the linear potentiometer, which acts as the feedback transducer. There is a separate electrical power supply for the electrical position control system.

There are several alternative ways in which to control the position of a load remotely, including an electric–electric system or electropneumatic system, where the power for the heavy duty position actuator could be supplied by electrical or pneumatic means. The advantages of hydraulic actuation include available actuator power, speed of response, robustness and sensitivity. Disadvantages include possible leakage of hydraulic fluid and associated contamination, component weight and expense.

Electric motor speed control

Figure 3.122 shows a schematic diagram of a motor speed control system, which you met earlier. Here the closed-loop servo system provides speed control for the DC motor M. The actual motor speed is sensed by means of a small DC tachogenerator, G, coupled

BTEC National Study Guide: Engineering. See page 325 for order details of individual texts

159

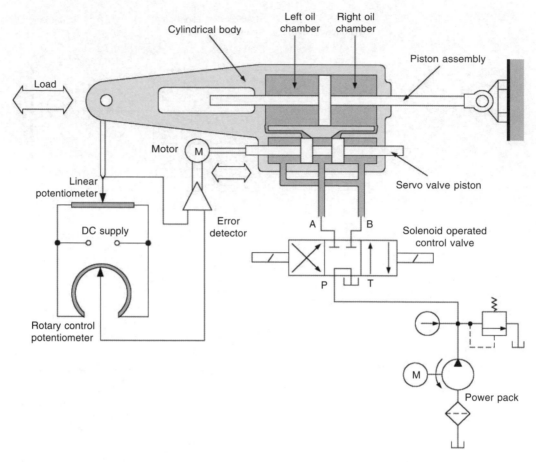

Figure 3.121 *Electrohydraulic RPC servo system*

to the output shaft. The voltage produced by the tachogenerator is compared with that produced at the slider of a potentiometer, R, which is used to set the desired speed. The comparison of the two voltages (i.e. that of the tachogenerator with that corresponding to the desired value or *set point*) is performed by an operational amplifier connected as the error detector or comparator. The output of the comparator stage is applied to a power amplifier that supplies current to the DC motor. Energy is derived from a mains-powered DC power supply comprising transformer, rectifier and smoothing circuits.

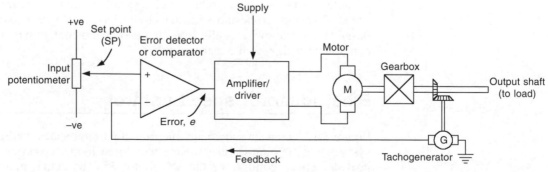

Figure 3.122 *Motor speed control system*

BTEC National Study Guide: Engineering. See page 325 for order details of individual texts

160

How exactly does the variation in voltage to the motor control its speed? When you studied *motor force*, you may well remember that it depends on the electromagnetic field strength β, the current in the armature windings *I* and the length of the conductor *L* in the magnetic field. This force, acting at a distance from the centre of rotation of the armature, produced a *driving torque*, i.e. the *output* from the motor. Therefore, this torque may be varied as the force is varied within the motor. When the motor operates against varying loads, the amount of torque required to sustain a particular speed (rpm) also needs to be varied. This is achieved by varying the voltage and therefore current to the electromagnetic *field* windings. The higher the current in these windings the greater the field strength β and so the greater the motor force and torque, from $F = \beta IL$.

A simplified schematic diagram of this control system is shown in Figure 3.123. Note, once again, that the error signal from the comparator requires amplification (signal conditioning) in order to supply sufficient change in current to alter the field strength.

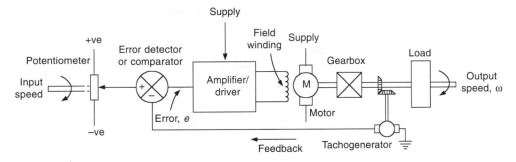

Figure 3.123 *Motor speed control using variation in field strength*

Example 3.55 A digital closed-loop control system

Figure 3.124 shows a microprocessor-based digital, closed-loop control system developed by Lotus. This system provides active ride suspension control for a high-performance road vehicle and it avoids the need for the road springs, dampers and anti-roll bars that are found in a conventional vehicle. The system allows the car to be 'self-levelling' and it can eliminate roll when the vehicle corners at both low and high speed. The overall ride can be set to 'hard' or 'soft' to suit the driver and also to cater for a variety of load conditions. The three principal input signals (all in analogue form) are derived from a load cell (which forms part of the suspension unit), an accelerometer and a linear displacement (position) transducer attached to each wheel. These analogue signals are converted to digital signals that can be processed by the microprocessor by means of analogue to digital converters (ADC). The 8-bit digital signals produced by the ADC are connected directly to the microprocessor's 8-bit data bus.

The two main output signals are used to drive two servo control valves that regulate the supply of hydraulic fluid to the hydraulic ram arrangement. The supply of hydraulic fluid is powered by a small engine-driven pump.

BTEC National Study Guide: Engineering. See page 325 for order details of individual texts

161

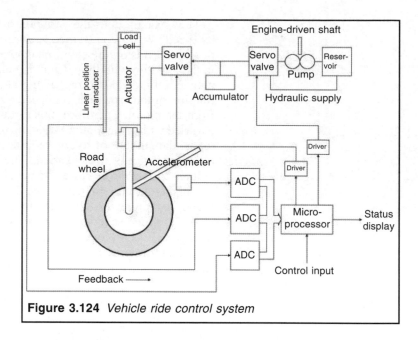

Figure 3.124 *Vehicle ride control system*

Problems

1. Explain the difference between the terms open loop and closed loop, when applied to a system.
2. An automatic telescope, used for tracking and monitoring solar activity, has a large motor which drives the telescope mechanism through a reduction gearbox. The motor is driven by an amplifier, the signal to which is a voltage proportional to the error between the desired and actual positions. Sketch a block diagram to represent the system and explain its operation.
3. Classify the following list of system components under the headings: sensor or transducer, controlling device, signal conditioning device, actuation device or output device:

    a rotary switch
    an actuator
    a gearbox
    a voltage regulator
    a motor
    a pressure relief valve
    a speed governor
    an amplifier
    a visual display unit (VDU).

4. A guided missile direction control system operates as follows. The directions of the missile and the target are measured using the missile's gyroscope. The difference between these two measurements is fed, as an electrical signal, to a comparator. The error signal from the comparator is amplified and used to drive a servo motor which deflects the jet efflux from the rocket, so altering the rocket's trajectory and guiding it towards the target. Sketch a block diagram of this system.
5. Sketch block diagrams of each of the following systems, clearly identify the system's inputs, outputs, signal conditioning and actuation devices:

BTEC National Study Guide: Engineering. See page 325 for order details of individual texts

162

a petrol engine ignition system
a hi-fi system.

6. The following data refer to measurements made on a motor speed control system:

Time (s)	0	1	2	3	4	5
Output (rev/sec)	0	2.1	11.0	19.5	25.0	28.6

	6	7	8	9	10	11
	29.8	28.8	24.5	20.5	17.0	15.5

	12	13	14	15	16	17
	14.8	15.6	16.9	19.1	21.0	21.9

	18	19	20
	22.8	21.9	21.0

Plot the response of this system and use it to determine:

(a) the final (steady-state) value
(b) the delay time
(c) the 15 per cent settling time
(d) the natural frequency.

7. An amplifier has an open-loop gain of 200 and is used in a circuit in which 5 per cent of the output is fed back as negative feedback. Determine the overall voltage gain with negative feedback applied.

8. The forward path gain of an open-loop system is 100. If the system is made into a closed-loop system with negative feedback gain of 2 determine the percentage reduction in the overall gain.

9. Investigate the following systems and in particular determine how these systems are controlled during their operation:

(a) a water-level control system
(b) a milk bottle filling, conveyor system
(c) a fluid flow, measurement and display system
(d) a digital velocity measuring system.

10. Explain the nature of servo system damping, including the need for compromise with respect to the 'degree' of damping.

BTEC National Study Guide: Engineering. See page 325 for order details of individual texts

163

BTEC National Study Guide: Engineering. See page 325 for order details of individual texts

164

Chapter 1 Mechanical principles

Summary

The design, manufacture and servicing of engineered products are important to the nation's economy and well-being. One has only to think of the information technology hardware, aircraft, motor vehicles and domestic appliances we use in everyday life to realise how reliant we have become on engineered products. A product must be fit for its purpose. It must do the job for which it was designed for a reasonable length of time and with a minimum of maintenance. The term 'mechatronics' is often used to describe products which contain mechanical, electrical, electronic and IT systems. It is the aim of this unit to broaden your knowledge of the underpinning mechanical principles which are fundamental to engineering design, manufacturing and servicing.

Engineering structures

Loading systems

Forces whose lines of action lie in a single plane are called *coplanar forces*. If the lines of action pass through a single point, the forces are said to be *concurrent* and the point through which they pass is called the *point of concurrence* (Figure 1.1).

A concurrent system of coplanar forces can be reduced to a single force acting at the point of concurrence. This is called the *resultant force*. If a body is subjected to a system of concurrent coplanar forces and is not constrained, it will move in the direction of the resultant force. To prevent this from happening, a force must be applied which is equal and opposite to the resultant. This

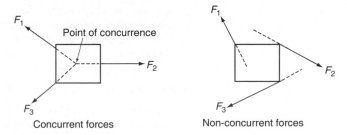

Figure 1.1 *Coplanar force systems*

BTEC National Study Guide: Engineering. See page 325 for order details of individual texts

165

Key point

A system of concurrent co-planar forces can be reduced to a single resultant force.

Key point

A system of non-concurrent coplanar forces can be reduced to a single resultant force and a resultant couple or turning moment.

balancing force, which will hold the body in a state of static equilibrium, is called the *equilibrant* of the system.

When a body is subjected to a system of non-concurrent coplanar forces, there is a tendency for the forces not only to make it move in a particular direction, but also to make it rotate. Such a non-concurrent system can be reduced to a single *resultant force* and a *resultant couple*. If the body is to be held at rest, an equilibrant must again be applied which is equal and opposite to the resultant force. This alone however will not be sufficient. A balancing couple or turning moment, must also be applied which is equal and opposite to the resultant couple.

If you have completed the core unit Science for Technicians, you will know how to find the resultant and equilibrant of a coplanar force system graphically by means of a force vector diagram. We will use this method again shortly but you now need to know how to do the same using mathematics.

Sign convention

When you are using mathematics to solve coplanar force system problems, you need to adopt a method of describing the action of the forces and couples. The following sign convention is that which is most often used (Figure 1.2):

(i) Upward forces are positive and downward forces are negative.
(ii) Horizontal forces acting to the right are positive and those acting to the left are negative.
(iii) Clockwise acting moments and couples are positive and anti-clockwise acting ones are negative.

Figure 1.2 *Sign convention*

Resolution of forces

Forces which act at an angle exert a pull which is part horizontal and part vertical. They can be split into their horizontal and vertical parts or *components*, by the use of trigonometry. When you are doing this, it is a useful rule to always measure angles to the horizontal.

In Figure 1.3(a), the horizontal and vertical components are both acting in the positive directions and will be

$$F_H = +F\cos\theta \quad \text{and} \quad F_V = +F\sin\theta$$

In Figure 1.3(b), the horizontal and vertical components are both acting in the negative directions and will be

$$F_H = -F\cos\theta \quad \text{and} \quad F_V = -F\sin\theta$$

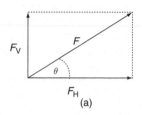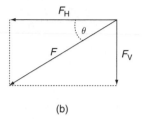

Figure 1.3 *Resolution of forces*

Forces which act upward to the left or downward to the right will have one component which is positive and one which is negative. Having resolved all of the forces in a coplanar system into their horizontal and vertical components, each set can then be added algebraically to determine the resultant horizontal pull, ΣF_H, and the resultant vertical pull, ΣF_V. The Greek letter Σ (sigma) means 'the sum or total' of the components. Pythagoras' theorem can then be used to find the single resultant force R, of the system.

That is,

$$R^2 = (\Sigma F_H)^2 + (\Sigma F_V)^2$$

$$\boldsymbol{R = \sqrt{(\Sigma F_H)^2 + (\Sigma F_V)^2}} \tag{1.1}$$

The angle θ, which the resultant makes with the horizontal can also be found using

$$\boldsymbol{\tan\theta = \frac{\Sigma F_V}{\Sigma F_H}} \tag{1.2}$$

With non-concurrent force systems, the algebraic sum of the moments of the vertical and horizontal components of the forces, taken about some convenient point, gives the resultant couple or turning moment. Its sign, positive or negative, indicates whether its direction is clockwise or anticlockwise. This in turn can be used to find the perpendicular distance of the line of action of the resultant from the chosen point.

Example 1.1

Find the magnitude and direction of the resultant and equilibrant of the concurrent coplanar force system shown in Figure 1.4.

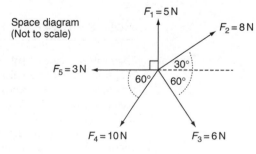

Figure 1.4

BTEC National Study Guide: Engineering. See page 325 for order details of individual texts

167

When you resolve the forces into their horizontal and vertical components it is essential to use the sign convention. A logical way is to draw up a table as follows with the forces, and their horizontal and vertical components, set out in rows and columns.

Force	Horizontal component	Vertical component
$F_1 = \ 5\,\text{N}$	0	$+5.0\,\text{N}$
$F_2 = \ 8\,\text{N}$	$+8\cos 30 = +6.93\,\text{N}$	$+8\sin 30 = +4.0\,\text{N}$
$F_3 = \ 6\,\text{N}$	$+6\cos 60 = +3.0\,\text{N}$	$-6\sin 60 = -5.2\,\text{N}$
$F_4 = 10\,\text{N}$	$-10\cos 60 = -5.0\,\text{N}$	$-10\sin 60 = -8.66\,\text{N}$
$F_5 = \ 3\,\text{N}$	$-3.0\,\text{N}$	0
Totals	$\boldsymbol{\Sigma F_\text{H} = +1.93\,\text{N}}$	$\boldsymbol{\Sigma F_\text{V} = -4.86\,\text{N}}$

The five forces have now been reduced to two forces, ΣF_H and ΣF_V. They can now be drawn as vectors (Figure 1.5).

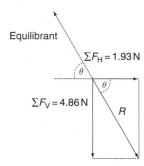

Figure 1.5

The resultant R, is found by Pythagoras as follows:

$$R = \sqrt{1.93^2 + 4.86^2}$$

$$\boldsymbol{R = 5.23\,\text{N}}$$

The angle θ is found from

$$\tan \theta = \frac{\Sigma F_\text{V}}{\Sigma F_\text{H}} = \frac{4.86}{1.93} = 2.52$$

$$\theta = \tan^{-1} 2.52$$

$$\boldsymbol{\theta = 68.3°}$$

The equilibrant, which is required to hold the system in a state of static equilibrium, is equal to the resultant but opposite in sense.

Bow's notation

Example 1.1 can be solved graphically by means of a force vector diagram drawn to a suitable scale. The process is known as *vector addition*. The force vectors are taken in order, preferably working clockwise around the system, and added nose to tail to produce *a polygon of forces*.

Should the final vector be found to end at the start of the first, there will be no resultant and the system will be in equilibrium. If however there is a gap between the two, this when measured from

BTEC National Study Guide: Engineering. See page 325 for order details of individual texts

168

the start of the first vector to the end of the last, represents the magnitude, direction and sense of the resultant. The equilibrant will, of course, be equal and opposite. It must be remembered that when you solve problems graphically, the accuracy of the answers will depend on the accuracy of your measurement and drawing.

Bow's notation is a useful method of identifying the forces on a vector diagram and also the sense in which they act. In the space diagram, which shows the forces acting at the point of concurrence, the spaces between the forces are each given a capital letter. Wherever possible, the letters should follow a clockwise sequence around the diagram. In the solution shown in Figures 1.6 and 1.7, the force F_1 is between the spaces A and B, and when drawn on the vector diagram it is identified by the lower case letters as force *ab*.

The clockwise sequence of letters on the space diagram, i.e. A to B, gives the direction of the force on the vector diagram. The letter *a* is at the start of the vector and the letter *b* is at its end. Although arrows have been drawn to show the directions of the vectors, they are not really necessary and will be omitted in future graphical solutions.

> **Key point**
>
> Use capital letters and work in a clockwise direction when lettering space diagram using Bow's notation.

Example 1.1a Alternative graphical solution for Example 1.1

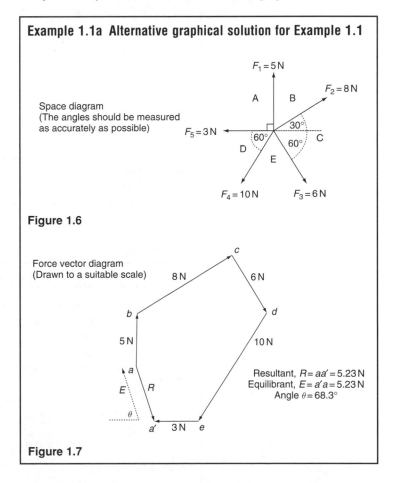

Space diagram
(The angles should be measured as accurately as possible)

Figure 1.6

Force vector diagram
(Drawn to a suitable scale)

Resultant, $R = aa' = 5.23\,\text{N}$
Equilibrant, $E = a'a = 5.23\,\text{N}$
Angle $\theta = 68.3°$

Figure 1.7

You can use the same graphical method to find the magnitude and direction of the resultant of a non-concurrent system of coplanar forces. Generally, however, it is best to use the analytical method as in Example 1.2. In problems, you are also usually asked to find the resultant couple or turning moment and this has to be done by calculation.

BTEC National Study Guide: Engineering. See page 325 for order details of individual texts

169

When drawing up a table for each force and its components, two extra columns are required. These are for the moments of the components, taken about some convenient point, and their total gives the resultant turning moment. With a little intuition, you can then determine the position of the line of action of the resultant.

Example 1.2

Determine the magnitude and direction of the resultant of the coplanar forces acting on the component shown in Figure 1.8. Determine also the perpendicular distance of its line of action from the corner A.

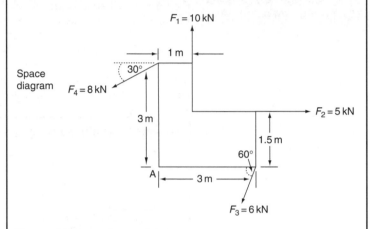

Figure 1.8

Force F (kN)	Horizontal component F_H (kN)	Vertical component F_V (kN)	Moment of F_H about A (kN m)	Moment of F_V about A (kN m)
10	0	+10	0	$-(1 \times 10) = -10$
5	+5	0	$+(5 \times 1.5) = +7.5$	0
6	$-6 \cos 60 = -3$	$-6 \sin 60 = -5.2$	0	$+(5.2 \times 3) = +15.6$
8	$-8 \cos 30 = -6.93$	$-8 \sin 30 = -4.0$	$-(6.93 \times 3) = -20.8$	0
Totals	$\Sigma F_H = -4.93$ kN	$\Sigma F_V = +0.8$ kN	$\Sigma M = -7.7$ kN m	

Note: When taking moments of the components about A, disregard the plus or minus sign in the components' columns. The sign of the moments is determined only by whether they are clockwise or anticlockwise about A.

The resultant of the force system is again found using Pythagoras (Figure 1.9).

Figure 1.9

$$R = \sqrt{\Sigma F_H^2 + \Sigma F_V^2}$$

$$R = \sqrt{4.93^2 + 0.8^2}$$

$$\mathbf{R = \sqrt{4.99}\ kN}$$

BTEC National Study Guide: Engineering. See page 325 for order details of individual texts

170

The angle θ is a again given by

$$\tan \theta = \frac{\Sigma F_V}{\Sigma F_H} = \frac{0.8}{4.93} = 0.162$$

$$\theta = \tan^{-1} 0.162$$

$$\boldsymbol{\theta = 9.22°}$$

Let the perpendicular distance of the line of action of the resultant from the corner A be *a*. Because the resultant turning moment is negative, i.e. anticlockwise about A, the line of action of the resultant must be above A (Figure 1.10).

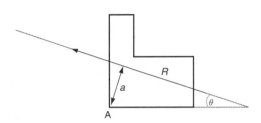

Figure 1.10

Now it must be that,

Resultant moment about A = moment of resultant about A

$$\Sigma M = R \times a$$

$$a = \frac{\Sigma M}{R} = \frac{7.7}{4.99}$$

$$\boldsymbol{a = 1.54\,m}$$

Test your knowledge 1.1

1. What are coplanar forces?
2. What are concurrent forces?
3. What are the conditions necessary for a body to be in static equilibrium under the action of a coplanar force system?
4. What are the resultant and equilibrant of a coplanar force system?
5. What can a non-concurrent coplanar force system be reduced to?

Activity 1.1

A connecting plate, which links the members in an engineering structure, is acted upon by four forces as shown in Figure 1.11. Calculate the magnitude, direction and sense of the resultant force, and the perpendicular distance of its line of action from the point A at which the 1 kN force acts.

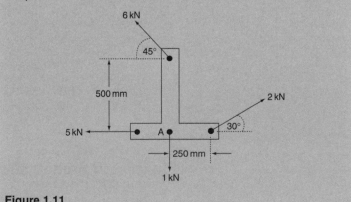

Figure 1.11

BTEC National Study Guide: Engineering. See page 325 for order details of individual texts

171

Problems 1.1

1. Determine the magnitude and direction of the resultant force for the coplanar force system shown in Figure 1.12.

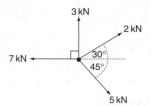

Figure 1.12

[1.79 kN, 15° to horizontal, upward to the left.]

2. Determine the magnitude and direction of the equilibrant required for the coplanar force system shown in Figure 1.13.

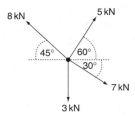

Figure 1.13

[4.54 kN, 50.2° to horizontal, downward to the left.]

3. Determine the magnitude and direction of the resultant force and turning moment for the force system shown in Figure 1.14.

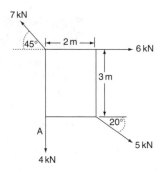

Figure 1.14

Determine also the perpendicular distance of the line of action of the resultant from the corner, A.

[5.8 kN, 7.53° to horizontal, downward to right, 6.57 kN m clockwise about A, 1.13 m.]

Pin-jointed framed structures

Examples of framed structures which you see in everyday life are bicycles, roof trusses, electricity pylons and tower cranes. They are

BTEC National Study Guide: Engineering. See page 325 for order details of individual texts

172

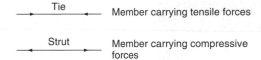

Figure 1.15 *Representation of structural members*

made up of members which are joined at their ends. Some of these are three-dimensional structures whose analysis is complex and it is only the two-dimensional, or coplanar structures, which we shall consider. There are three kinds of member in these structures (Figure 1.15).

1. *Ties*, which are in tension are shown diagrammatically with arrows pointing inwards. You have to imagine yourself in the place of a tie. You would be pulling inwards to stop yourself from being stretched. The arrows describe the force which the tie exerts on its neighbours to keep the structure in position.
2. *Struts*, which are in compression are shown diagrammatically with arrows pointing outwards. Once again, you have to imagine the way you would be pushing if you were in the place of a strut. You would be pushing outwards to keep the structure in position and to stop yourself from being squashed.
3. The third type is *redundant members*. A perfect framed structure is one which has just sufficient members to prevent it from becoming unstable. Any additional members, which may have been added to create a stiffer or stronger frame, are known as redundant members. Redundant members may be struts or ties or they may carry no load in normal circumstances. We shall avoid framed structures with redundant members as very often they cannot be solved by the ordinary methods of statics.

In reality the members are bolted, riveted or welded together at their ends but in our analysis we assume that they are pin-jointed or hinged at their ends, with frictionless pins. We further assume that because of this, the only forces present in the members are tensile and compressive forces. These are called *primary forces*. In practice there might also be bending and twisting forces present but we will leave these for study at a higher level.

When a structure is in a state of static equilibrium, the external active loads which it carries will be balanced by the reactions of its supports. The conditions for external equilibrium are:

1. The vector sum of the horizontal forces or horizontal components of the forces is zero.
2. The vector sum of the vertical forces or vertical components of the forces is zero.
3. The vector sum of the turning moments of the forces taken about any point in the plane of the structure is zero. That is,

$$\Sigma F_H = 0, \qquad \Sigma F_v = 0, \qquad \Sigma M = 0$$

We can also safely assume that if a structure is in a state of static equilibrium, each of its members will also be in equilibrium. It follows that the above three conditions can also be applied to individual members, groups of members and indeed to any internal part or section of a structure.

Key point

When a body or structure is in static equilibrium under the action of three concurrent external forces, the forces must be concurrent.

BTEC National Study Guide: Engineering. See page 325 for order details of individual texts

173

A full analysis of the external and internal forces acting on and within a structure can be carried out using mathematics or graphically by drawing a force vector diagram. We will use the mathematical method first and begin by applying the conditions for equilibrium to the external forces. This will enable us to find the magnitude and direction of the support reactions.

Next, we will apply the conditions for equilibrium to each joint in the structure, starting with one which has only two unknown forces acting on it. This will enable us to find the magnitude and direction of the force in each member.

Example 1.3

Determine the magnitude and direction of the support reactions at X and Y for the pin-jointed cantilever shown in Figure 1.16, together with the magnitude and nature of the force acting in each member.

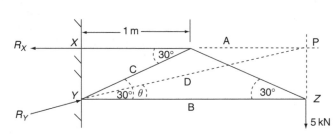

Figure 1.16

The wall support raction R_X must be horizontal because it is equal and opposite to the force carried by the top member CA. Also, the three external forces must be concurrent with lines of action meeting at the point P.

Begin by locating the point P and drawing in the support reactions at X and Y in the sense which you think they are acting. If you guess wrongly, you will obtain a negative answer from your calculations, telling you that your arrow should be pointing in the opposite direction. Letter the diagram using Bow's notation, with capital letters in the spaces between the external forces and inside the structure. Now you can begin the calculations.

Finding distances XY, YZ and the angle θ:

$$XY = 1 \times \tan 30 = 0.577\,\text{m}, \quad YZ = 2.0\,\text{m}$$

$$\tan \theta = \frac{XY}{YZ} = \frac{0.577}{2.0} = 0.289$$

$$\theta = \mathbf{16.1°}$$

Take moments about Y to find R_X. For equilibrium, $\Sigma M_Y = 0$,

$$(5 \times 2) - (R_X \times 0.577) = 0$$
$$10 - 0.577 R_X = 0$$
$$\boldsymbol{R_X = \frac{10}{0.577} = 17.3\,\text{kN}}$$

BTEC National Study Guide: Engineering. See page 325 for order details of individual texts

174

The force in member AC will also be 17.3 kN because it is equal and opposite to R_x. It will be a tensile force, and this member will be a tie.

Take vertical components of external forces to find R_Y. For equilibrium, $\Sigma F_v = 0$,

$$R_Y \sin 16.1° - 5 = 0$$
$$0.277 \, R_Y - 5 = 0$$
$$\boldsymbol{R_Y = \frac{5}{0.277} = 18.0 \, kN}$$

You can now turn your attention to the forces in the individual members. You already know the force F_{AC} acting in member AC because it is equal and opposite to the support reaction R_X. Choose a joint where you know the magnitude and direction of one of the forces and the directions of the other two, i.e. where there are only two unknown forces. Joint ABD will be ideal. It is good practice to assume that the unknown forces are tensile, with arrows pulling away from the joint. A negative answer will tell you that the force is comperessive (Figure 1.17).

Figure 1.17

Take vertical components of the forces to find the force F_{DA} in member DA. For eqilibrium, $\Sigma F_v = 0$,

$$F_{DA} \sin 30 - 5 = 0$$
$$0.5 \, F_{DA} - 5 = 0$$
$$\boldsymbol{F_{DA} = \frac{5}{0.5} = 10 \, kN}$$

The positive answer denotes that the force F_{DA} in member DA is tensile and that the member is a tie. Now take horizontal components of the forces to find F_{BD} in member BD. For equilibrium, $\Sigma F_H = 0$,

$$-F_{DA} \cos 30 - F_{BD} = 0,$$
$$-10 \cos 30 - F_{BD} = 0$$
$$\boldsymbol{F_{BD} = -10 \cos 30 = -8.66 \, kN}$$

The negative sign denotes that the force F_{BD} in member BD is compressive and that the member is a strut. Now go to joint ADC and take vertical components of the forces to find F_{DC}, the force in member DC (Figure 1.18). For equilibrium, $\Sigma F_v = 0$,

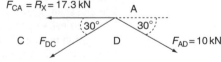

Figure 1.18

BTEC National Study Guide: Engineering. See page 325 for order details of individual texts

175

$$-(10 \sin 30) - (F_{DC} \sin 30) = 0$$

$$-10 - F_{DC} = 0$$

$$\boldsymbol{F_{DC} = -10\,kN}$$

The negative sign denotes that the force F_{DC} in member DC is compressive and that the member is a strut. You have now found the values of all the external and internal forces which can be tabulated and their directions indicated on the structure diagram as shown in Figure 1.19.

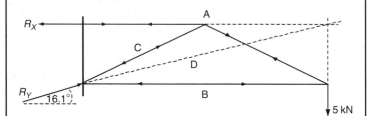

Figure 1.19

Reaction/Member	Force	Nature
R_x	17.3 kN	
R_y	18.0 kN	
AC	17.3 kN	Tie
DA	10.0 kN	Tie
BD	8.66 kN	Strut
DC	10.0 kN	Strut

You may also solve framed structure problems graphically. Sometimes this is quicker but the results may not be so accurate. As before, it depends on the accuracy of your drawing and measurement. An alternative solution to the above framed structure is given in Example 1.3a. Once again, use is made of Bow's notation to identify the members.

Example 1.3a Alternative graphical solution for Example 1.3

Begin by drawing the space diagram shown in Figure 1.20 to some suitable scale. Take care to measure the angles as accurately as possible. The angle of R_x can be measured, giving $\theta = 16.1°$.

Now each of the joints is in equilibrium. Choose one where you know the magnitude and direction of one force and the directions of the other two. The joint ABD is in fact the only one where you know these conditions.

BTEC National Study Guide: Engineering. See page 325 for order details of individual texts

176

Space diagram

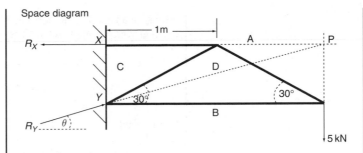

Figure 1.20

Draw the force vector diagram for this joint to a suitable scale, beginning with the 5 kN load. It will be a triangle of forces, which you can quite easily construct because you know the length of one side and the directions of the other two. The force vectors are added together nose to tail but don't put any arrows on the diagram. Bow's notation is sufficient to indicate the directions of the forces (Figure 1.21).

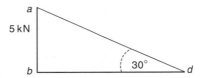

Figure 1.21

Accurate measurement gives
Force in DA = da = 10.0 kN
Force in BD = bd = 8.66 kN

Remember, the clockwise sequence of letters around the joint on the space diagram ABD gives the directions in which the forces act on the joint in the vector diagram, i.e. the force ab acts from a to b, the force bd acts from b to d and the force da acts from d to a.

Now go to another joint where you know the magnitude and direction of one of the forces, and the directions of the other two. Such a joint is ADC where the same 10 kN force da, which acts on joint ADB, also acts in the opposite direction on joint ADC. We now call it force ad, and the triangle of forces is as shown in Figure 1.22.

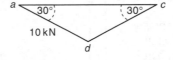

Figure 1.22

Accurate measurement gives
Force in DC = dc = 10.0 kN
Force in CA = ca = 17.3 kN

All of the internal forces have now been found and also the reaction R_X, which is equal and opposite to ca, and can thus be written as ac. A final triangle of forces ABC, can now be drawn, representing the three external forces (see Figure 1.23). Two of these,

BTEC National Study Guide: Engineering. See page 325 for order details of individual texts

177

the 5 kN load and R_X, are now known in both magnitude and direction together with the angle θ which R_Y makes with the horizontal.

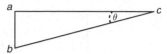

Figure 1.23

Accurate measurement gives
Reaction $R_Y = bc = 18.0\,\text{kN}$
Angle $\theta = 16.10°$

You will note that the above three vector diagram triangles have sides in common and to save time it is usual to draw the second and third diagrams as additions to the first. The combined vector diagram appears as in Figure 1.24.

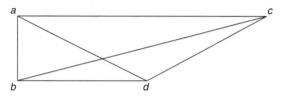

Figure 1.24

The directions of the forces, acting towards or away from the joints on which they act, can be drawn on the space diagram (Figure 1.25). This will immediately tell you which members are struts, and which are ties. The measured values of the support reactions and the forces in the members can then be tabulated.

Reaction/Member	Force	Nature
R_X	17.3 kN	
R_Y	18.0 kN	
AC	17.3 kN	Tie
DA	10.0 kN	Tie
BD	8.66 kN	Strut
DC	10.0 kN	Strut

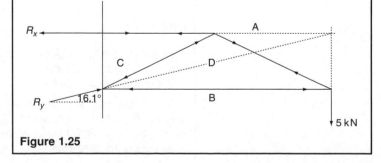

Figure 1.25

Test your knowledge 1.2

1. What are the three different types of member found in framed structures?
2. What are the primary forces which act in structural members?
3. How do you indicate using arrows, which members of a structure are ties and which are struts?
4. How do you letter the space diagram of a coplanar force system using Bow's notation?

BTEC National Study Guide: Engineering. See page 325 for order details of individual texts

178

Activity 1.2

The jib-crane shown in Figure 1.26 carries a load of 10 kN. Making use of Bow's notation find the reactions of the supports at *X* and *Y*, and the magnitude and nature of the force in each member graphically by means of a force vector diagram. Apply the conditions for static equilibrium to the structure and check your results by calculation.

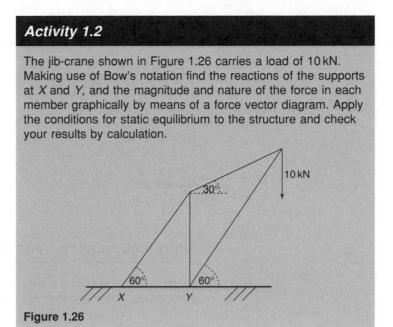

Figure 1.26

Problems 1.2

For each of the following framed structures, determine the support reactions, and the magnitude and nature of the force in each member (Figures 1.27, 1.28, and 1.29).

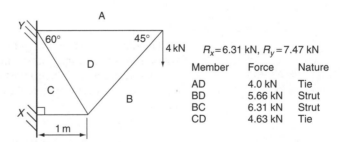

$R_x = 6.31$ kN, $R_y = 7.47$ kN

Member	Force	Nature
AD	4.0 kN	Tie
BD	5.66 kN	Strut
BC	6.31 kN	Strut
CD	4.63 kN	Tie

Figure 1.27

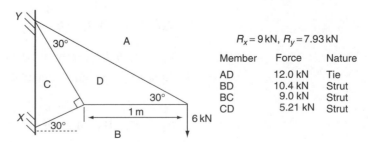

$R_x = 9$ kN, $R_y = 7.93$ kN

Member	Force	Nature
AD	12.0 kN	Tie
BD	10.4 kN	Strut
BC	9.0 kN	Strut
CD	5.21 kN	Strut

Figure 1.28

BTEC National Study Guide: Engineering. See page 325 for order details of individual texts

179

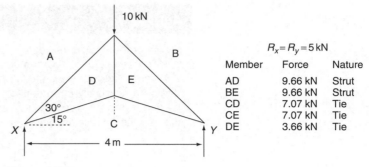

Member	Force	Nature
AD	9.66 kN	Strut
BE	9.66 kN	Strut
CD	7.07 kN	Tie
CE	7.07 kN	Tie
DE	3.66 kN	Tie

Figure 1.29

Simply supported beams

A simply supported beam is supported at two points in such a way that it is allowed to expand and bend freely. In practice the supports are often rollers. The loads on the beam may be concentrated at different points or uniformly distributed along the beam. Figure 1.30 shows concentrated loads only.

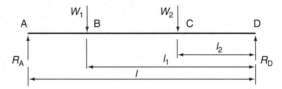

Figure 1.30 *Simply supported beam with concentrated loads*

The downward forces on a beam are said to be active loads, due to the force of gravity, whilst the loads carried by the supports are said to be reactive. When investigating the effects of loading, we often have to begin by calculating the supporting reactions. The beam is in static equilibrium under the action of these external forces, and so we proceed as follows:

1. Equate the sum of the turning moments, taken about the right hand support D, to zero. That is,

$$\Sigma M_{\mathrm{D}} = 0$$
$$R_{\mathrm{A}}l - W_1 l_1 - W_2 l_2 = 0$$

You can find R_{A} from this condition.

2. Equate vector sum of the vertical forces to zero. That is,

$$\Sigma F_{\mathrm{V}} = 0$$
$$R_{\mathrm{A}} + R_{\mathrm{B}} - W_1 - W_2 = 0$$

You can find R_{D} from this condition.

BTEC National Study Guide: Engineering. See page 325 for order details of individual texts

180

Example 1.4

Calculate the support reactions of the simply supported beam shown in Figure 1.31.

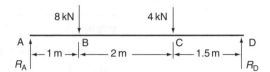

Figure 1.31

Take moments about the point D, remembering to use the sign convention that clockwise moments are positive and anticlockwise moments are negative. For equilibrium, $\Sigma M_D = 0$,

$$(R_A \times 4.5) - (8 \times 3.5) - (4 \times 1.5) = 0$$
$$4.5R_A - 28 - 6 = 0$$
$$R_A = \frac{28 + 6}{4.5} = 7.56 \text{ kN}$$

Equate the vector sum of the vertical forces to zero, remembering the sign convention that upward forces are positive and downward forces are negative. For equilibrium, $\Sigma F_V = 0$.

$$8 + 4 - 7.56 - R_D = 0$$
$$R_D = 8 + 4 - 7.56 = 4.44 \text{ kN}$$

Uniformly distributed loads (UDLs)

Uniformly distributed loads, or UDLs, are evenly spread out along a beam. They might be due to the beam's own weight, paving slabs or an asphalt surface. UDLs are generally expressed in kN per metre length, i.e. kN m^{-1}. This is also known as the 'loading rate'. Uniformly distributed loads are shown diagrammatically as in Figure 1.32.

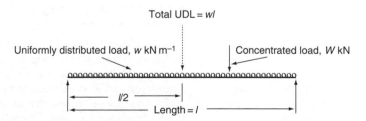

Figure 1.32 *Simply supported beam with concentrated and distributed loads*

The total UDL over a particular length l, of a beam is given by the product of the loading rate and the length. That is,

total UDL $= wl$

BTEC National Study Guide: Engineering. See page 325 for order details of individual texts

181

When you are equating moments to find the beam reactions, the total UDL is assumed to act at its centroid, i.e. at the centre of the length l. You can then treat it as just another concentrated load and calculate the support reactions in the same way as before.

Example 1.5

Calculate the support reactions of the simply supported beam shown in Figure 1.33.

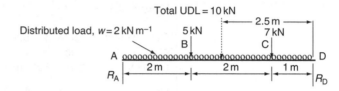

Figure 1.33

Begin by calculating the total UDL. Then, replace it by an equal concentrated load acting at its centroid. This is shown with a dotted line above.

Total UDL $= wl = 5 \times 2 = 10$ kN

You can now apply the conditions for static equilibrium. Begin by talking moments about the point D. For equilibrium, $\Sigma M_D = 0$,

$$(R_A \times 5) - (5 \times 3) - (10 \times 2.5) - (7 \times 1) = 0$$
$$5R_A - 15 - 25 - 7 = 0$$
$$R_A = \frac{15 + 25 + 7}{5} = 9.4 \text{ kN}$$

Now equate the vector sum of the vertical forces to zero. For equilibrium, $\Sigma F_V = 0$,

$$9.4 + R_D - 5 - 10 - 7 = 0$$
$$R_D = 5 + 10 + 7 - 9.4 = 12.6 \text{ kN}$$

Bending of beams

When structural engineers are designing beams to carry given loads, they have to make sure that the maximum allowable stresses will not be exceeded. On any transverse section of a loaded beam or cantilever, shear stress, tensile stress and compressive stress are all usually present.

As you can see in the cantilever in Figure 1.34(a), the load F, has a shearing effect and thus sets up shear stress at section $Y-Y$. The load also has a bending effect and at any section $Y-Y$, this produces tensile stress in the upper layers of the beam and compressive stress in the lower layers.

Generally, the stresses and deflection caused by bending greatly exceed those caused by shear, and the shearing effects of the loading are usually neglected for all but short and stubby cantilevers. Nevertheless, the distribution of shear loading is of importance

BTEC National Study Guide: Engineering. See page 325 for order details of individual texts

182

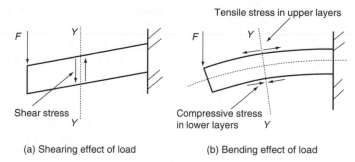

(a) Shearing effect of load   (b) Bending effect of load

Figure 1.34 *Stress in beams*

because it enables the likely positions of maximum bending stress to be pin-pointed, as will be shown.

Somewhere inside a beam there is a layer called the *neutral layer or neutral axis*. Although this becomes bent, like all the other layers, it is in neither tension nor compression and there is no tensile or compressive stress present. For elastic materials which have the same modulus of elasticity in tension and compression, it is found that the neutral axis is located at the centroid of the cross-section.

Shear force distribution

At any transverse section of a loaded horizontal beam the *shear force* is defined as being *the algebraic sum of the forces acting to one side of the section*. You might think of it as the upward or downward breaking force at that section. Usually, it is forces to the left of the section which are considered and the following sign convention is used.

1. Upward forces to the left of a section are positive and downward forces are negative.
2. Downward forces to the right of a section are positive and upward forces are negative.

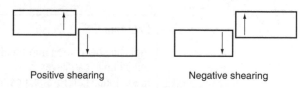

Positive shearing   Negative shearing

Figure 1.35 *Positive and negative shearing*

This gives rise to the idea of positive and negative shearing as shown in Figure 1.35, and the variation of the shear force along a loaded beam can be plotted on a shear force diagram.

Bending moment distribution

At any transverse section of a loaded beam, the *bending moment* is defined as being *the algebraic sum of the moments of the forces acting to one side of the section*. Usually it is moments to the left of

BTEC National Study Guide: Engineering. See page 325 for order details of individual texts

183

a section which are considered and the following sign convention is used.

1. Clockwise moments to the left of a section are positive and anticlockwise moments are negative.
2. Anticlockwise moments to the right of a section are positive and clockwise moments are negative.

This gives rise to the idea of positive and negative bending as shown in Figure 1.36, and the variation of bending moment along a loaded beam can be plotted on a bending moment diagram.

Key point

Clockwise bending moments to the left of a section through a loaded beam are positive and anticlockwise moments are negative.

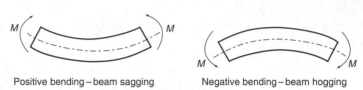

Positive bending – beam sagging   Negative bending – beam hogging

Figure 1.36 *Positive and negative bending*

When you are plotting shear force and bending moment diagrams you will see that

1. The maximum bending moment always occurs where the shear force diagram changes sign.
2. The area of the shear force diagram up to a particular section gives the bending moment at that section.
3. Under certain circumstances, the bending moment changes sign and this is said to occur at a point of contraflexure.

Key point

If a beam is to be made up of joined sections, it is good practice, when practicable, to position the joints at points of contraflexure where there are no bending stresses.

At a point of contraflexure, where the bending moment is zero, the deflected shape of a beam changes from sagging to hogging or vice versa. The location of these points is of importance to structural engineers since it is here that welded, bolted or riveted joints can be made which will be free of bending stress.

Example 1.6

Plot the shear force and bending moment distribution diagrams for the simple cantilever beam shown in Figure 1.37 and state the magnitude, nature and position of the maximum values of shear force, and bending moment.

shear force from A to B $= -5\,\text{kN}$

shear force from B to C $= -5 - 3 = -8\,\text{kN}$

   maximum shear force $= -8\,\text{kN}$ **between B and C**

bending moment at A $= 0$

bending moment at B $= -(5 \times 2) = -10\,\text{kN m}$

bending moment at C $= -(5 \times 3) - (3 \times 1) = -18\,\text{kN m}$

maximum bending moment $= -18\,\text{kN m}$ **at C**

BTEC National Study Guide: Engineering. See page 325 for order details of individual texts

184

As you can see, the shear force is negative over the whole length of the cantilever because there is a downward breaking force to the left of any section, i.e. negative shear.

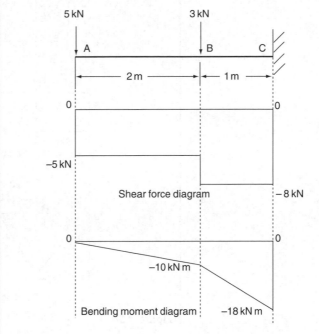

Figure 1.37

The bending moment is always zero at the free end of a simple cantilever and negative over the remainder of its length. You might think of a cantilever as being half of a hogging beam in which the bending moment at any section is anticlockwise, i.e. negative bending.

Example 1.7

Plot the shear force and bending moment distribution diagrams for the simply supported beam shown in Figure 1.38. State the magnitude, nature and position of the maximum values of shear force, and bending moment and the position of a point of contraflexure.

Begin by finding the support reactions:

For equilibrium, $\Sigma M_D = 0$,

$$(R_B \times 2) - (6 \times 3) - (10 \times 1) = 0$$
$$2R_B - 18 - 10 = 0$$
$$R_B = \frac{18 + 10}{2} = 14\ kN$$

Also, for equilibrium, $\Sigma F_V = 0$,
$$14 + R_D + 6 + 10 = 0$$
$$R_D = 6 + 10 - 14 = 2\ kN$$

BTEC National Study Guide: Engineering. See page 325 for order details of individual texts

185

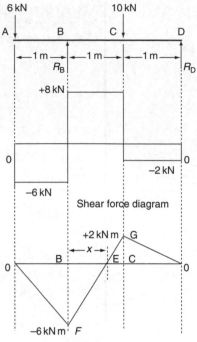

Figure 1.38

Next find the shear force values:

SF from A to B = −6 kN
SF from B to C = −6 + 14 = +8 kN
SF from C to D = −6 + 14 − 10 = −2 kN

maximum shear force = + 8 kN between B and C

Now find the bending moment values:

BM at A = 0
BM at B = −(6 × 1) = −6 kN m
BM at C = −(6 × 2) + (14 × 1) = +2 kN m
BM at D = 0

maximum bending moment = − 6 kN m at B

There is a point of contraflexure at E, where the bending moment is zero. To find its distance x, from B, consider the similar triangles BEF and ECG (Figure 1.39).

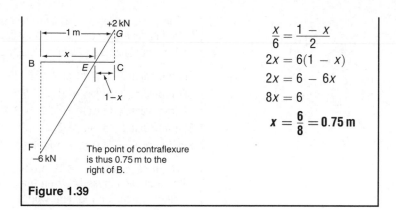

$$\frac{x}{6} = \frac{1-x}{2}$$
$$2x = 6(1-x)$$
$$2x = 6 - 6x$$
$$8x = 6$$
$$x = \frac{6}{8} = 0.75\,\text{m}$$

The point of contraflexure is thus 0.75 m to the right of B.

Figure 1.39

If you examine the shear force and bending moment diagrams in the above examples, you will find that there is a relationship between shear force and bending moment. Calculate the area under the shear force diagram from the left hand end, up to any point along the beam. You will find that this is equal to the bending moment at that point. Try it, but remember to use the sign convention that areas above the zero line are positive and those below are negative.

Example 1.8

Plot the shear force and bending moment distribution diagrams for the cantilever shown in Figure 1.40 and state the magnitude and position of the maximum values of shear force and bending moment.

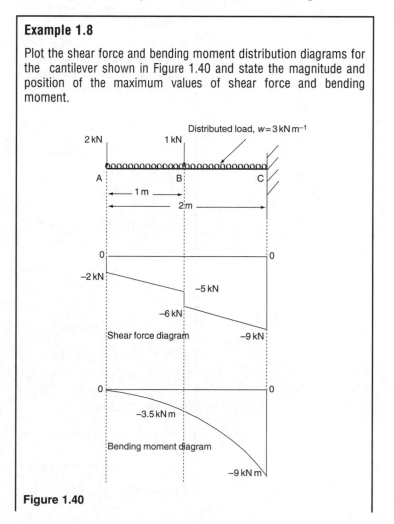

Figure 1.40

BTEC National Study Guide: Engineering. See page 325 for order details of individual texts

187

The presence of the UDL produces a gradually increasing shear force between the concentrated loads.

Finding shear force values:

SF immediately to right of A $= -2$ kN

SF immediately to left of B $= -2 - (3 \times 1) = -5$ kN

SF immediately to right of B $= -2 - 1 - (3 \times 1) = -6$ kN

SF immediately to left of C $= -2 - 1 - (3 \times 2) = -9$ kN

maximum SF $= -9$ kN immediately to left of C

The presence of the UDL produces a bending moment diagram with parabolic curves between the concentrated load positions.

Finding bending moment values:

BM at A $= 0$

BM at B $= -(2 \times 1) - (3 \times 1 \times 0.5) = -3.5$ kN m

BM at C $= -(2 \times 1) - (1 \times 1) - (3 \times 2 \times 1) = -9$ kN m

maximum bending moment $= -9$ kN m at C

Example 1.9

Plot the shear force and bending moment distribution diagrams for the simply supported beam shown in Figure 1.41. State the magnitude, nature and position of the maximum values of shear force and bending moment.

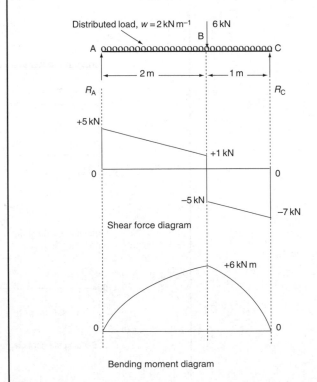

Figure 1.41

BTEC National Study Guide: Engineering. See page 325 for order details of individual texts

188

Finding support reactions:

For equilibrium, $\Sigma M_C = 0$,

$(R_A \times 3) - (6 \times 1) - (2 \times 3 \times 1.5) = 0$

$3R_A - 6 - 9 = 0$

$$R_A = \frac{6+9}{3} = 5\,\text{kN}$$

Also for equilibrium, $\Sigma F_V = 0$,

$5 + R_C - 6 - (2 \times 3) = 0$

$5 + R_C - 6 - 6 = 0$

$R_C = 6 + 6 - 5 = 7\,\text{kN}$

Finding the shear force values:

SF immediately to right of A $= +5\,\text{kN}$
SF immediately to left of B $= 5 - (2 \times 2) = +1\,\text{kN}$
SF immediately to right of B $= 5 - (2 \times 2) - 6 = -5\,\text{kN}$
SF immediately to left of C $= 5 - (2 \times 3) - 6 = -7\,\text{kN}$

maximum SF $= -7\,\text{kN}$ immediately to left of C

Finding bending moment values:

BM at A $= 0$
BM at B $= (5 \times 2) - (2 \times 2 \times 1) = +6\,\text{kN m}$
BM at C $= 0$

maximum BM $= +6\,\text{kN m}$ at B

As you can see from the diagrams in Figure 1.41, the effect of the UDL is to produce a shear force diagram that slopes between the supports and the concentrated load. Its slope $2\,\text{kN m}^{-1}$, which is the uniformly distributed loading rate. The effect on the bending moment diagram is to produce parabolic curves between the supports and the concentrated load.

Test your knowledge 1.3

1. What is the difference between an active and a reactive load?
2. How do you define the shear force at any point on a loaded beam?
3. How do you define the bending moment at any point on a loaded beam?
4. What is a point of contraflexure?

Activity 1.3

The simply supported beam shown in Figure 1.42 is made in two sections which will be joined together at some suitable point between the supports. Draw the shear force and bending moment diagrams for the beam. State the maximum values of shear force and bending moment, and the positions where they occur. Where would be the most suitable point to join the two sections of the beam together?

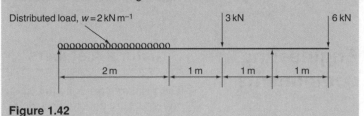

Figure 1.42

BTEC National Study Guide: Engineering. See page 325 for order details of individual texts

189

Problems 1.3

Sketch the shear force and bending moment diagrams for the simply supported beams and cantilevers shown in Figures 1.43–1.47. Indicate the magnitude and nature of the maximum shear force and bending moment and the positions where they occur. Indicate also the position of any point of contraflexure.

1.

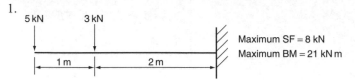

Maximum SF = 8 kN
Maximum BM = 21 kN m

Figure 1.43

2.

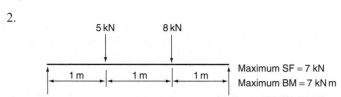

Maximum SF = 7 kN
Maximum BM = 7 kN m

Figure 1.44

3.

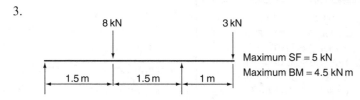

Maximum SF = 5 kN
Maximum BM = 4.5 kN m

Figure 1.45

4.

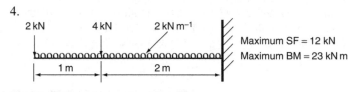

Maximum SF = 12 kN
Maximum BM = 23 kN m

Figure 1.46

5.

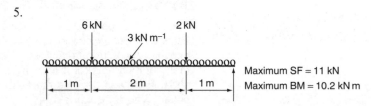

Maximum SF = 11 kN
Maximum BM = 10.2 kN m

Figure 1.47

Engineering components

Structural members

The primary forces acting in structural components such as ties and struts are direct tensile and compressive forces. Direct, or uni-axial loading occurs when equal and opposite tensile or compres-

BTEC National Study Guide: Engineering. See page 325 for order details of individual texts

190

sive forces act on along the same line of action. The intensity of the loading in the component material is quantified as *direct stress*, and the deformation which it produces is quantified as *direct strain*.

Direct stress

Consider a component of original length *l*, and cross-sectional area *A*, which is subjected to a direct tensile load *F* as shown in Figure 1.48. Let the change of length be *x*.

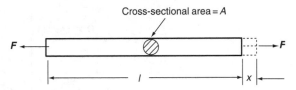

Cross-sectional area = *A*

Figure 1.48 *Direct loading*

It is assumed that the load in the material is distributed evenly over the cross-sectional area *A*, of the component. The direct stress σ in the material is the load carried by each square millimetre or square metre of cross-sectional area.

$$\text{direct stress} = \frac{\text{direct load}}{\text{cross-sectional area}}$$

$$\sigma = \frac{F}{A} \ (\textbf{Pa or N\,m}^{-2}) \tag{1.3}$$

In Figure 1.47, the load and the stress are tensile and these are sometimes given a positive sign. Compressive loads produce compressive stress and these are sometimes given a negative sign. You will recall from the work you did in the core unit Science for Technicians, that the approved SI unit of stress is Pascal although you will often find its value quoted in $N\,m^{-2}$ and $N\,m\,m^{-2}$. These are, in fact, more convenient and because many engineers prefer them, you will still see them used in trade catalogues, British Standards and engineering publications.

Direct strain

Direct strain ε, is a measure of the deformation which the load produces. It is the change in length given as a fraction of the original length.

$$\text{direct strain} = \frac{\text{change in length}}{\text{original length}}$$

$$\varepsilon = \frac{x}{l} \ (\textbf{No units}) \tag{1.4}$$

Modulus of elasticity (Young's Modulus)

An elastic material is one in which the change in length is proportional to the load applied and in which the strain is proportional to the stress. Furthermore, a perfectly elastic material will immediately return to its original length when the load is removed.

BTEC National Study Guide: Engineering. See page 325 for order details of individual texts

191

A graph of stress σ, against strain ε, is a straight line whose gradient is always found to be the same for a given material. Figure 1.49 shows typical graphs for steel, copper and aluminium. The value of the gradient is a measure of the elasticity or 'stiffness' of the material, and is known as its Modulus of Elasticity, E.

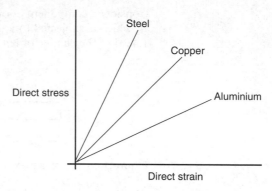

Figure 1.49 *Graph of stress v. strain*

$$\text{modulus of elasticity} = \frac{\text{direct stress}}{\text{direct strain}}$$

$$E = \frac{\sigma}{\varepsilon} \ (\mathbf{Pa} \ \text{or} \ \mathbf{N\,m^{-2}}) \tag{1.5}$$

Substituting the expressions for stress and strain from equations (1.3) and (1.4) gives an alternative formula.

$$E = \frac{\frac{F}{A}}{\frac{x}{l}}$$

$$E = \frac{F}{A} \times \frac{l}{x} \tag{1.6}$$

Key point

The modulus of elasticity of a material is a measure of its stifness, i.e. its resistance to being stretched or compressed.

Factor of safety

Engineering components should be designed so that the working stress which they are likely to encounter is well below the ultimate stress at which failure occurs.

$$\textbf{factor of safety} = \frac{\textbf{ultimate stress}}{\textbf{working stress}} \tag{1.7}$$

A factor of safety of at least 2 is generally applied for static structures. This ensures that the working stress will be no more than half of that at which failure occurs. Much lower factors of safety are applied in aircraft design where weight is at a premium, and with some of the major components it is likely that failure will eventually occur due to metal fatigue. These are rigorously tested at the prototype stage to predict their working life and replaced periodically in service well before this period has elapsed.

BTEC National Study Guide: Engineering. See page 325 for order details of individual texts

192

Example 1.9

A strut of diameter 25 mm and length 2 m carries an axial load of 20 kN. The ultimate compressive stress of the material is 350 MPa and its modulus of elasticity is 150 GPa. Find (a) the compressive stress in the material, (b) the factor of safety in operation, (c) the change in length of the strut.

(a) Finding cross-sectional area of strut:

$$A = \frac{\pi d^2}{4} = \frac{\pi \times 0.025^2}{4}$$

$$A = 491 \times 10^{-6} \, \text{m}^2$$

Finding compressive stress:

$$\sigma = \frac{F}{A} = \frac{20 \times 10^3}{491 \times 10^6}$$

$$\sigma = 40.7 \times 10^6 \, \text{Pa} \quad \text{or} \quad 40.7 \, \text{MPa}$$

(b) Finding factor of safety in operation:

$$\text{factor of safety} = \frac{\text{ultimate stress}}{\text{working stress}} = \frac{350 \times 10^6}{40.7 \times 10^6}$$

$$\textbf{factor of safety} = 8.6$$

(c) Finding compressive strain:

$$E = \frac{\sigma}{\varepsilon}$$

$$\varepsilon = \frac{\sigma}{E} = \frac{40.7 \times 10^6}{150 \times 10^9}$$

$$\varepsilon = 271 \times 10^{-6}$$

Finding change in length:

$$\varepsilon = \frac{x}{l}$$

$$x = \varepsilon l = (271 \times 10^{-6}) \times 2$$

$$x = 0.543 \times 10^{-3} \, \text{m} \quad \text{or} \quad 0.543 \, \text{mm}$$

Test your knowledge 1.4

1. What is meant by uni-axial loading?
2. What is the definition of an elastic material?
3. A tie bar of cross-sectional area 50 mm^2 carries a load of 10 kN. What is the tensile stress in the material measured in Pascals?
4. If the ultimate tensile stress at which failure occurs in a material is 550 MPa and a factor of safety of 4 is to apply, what will be the allowable working stress?

Activity 1.4

A tube of length 1.5 m has an inner diameter 50 mm and a wall thickness of 6 mm. When subjected to a direct tensile load of 75 kN the length is seen to increase by 0.55 mm. Determine (a) the tensile stress in the material, (b) the factor of safety in operation if the ultimate tensile strength of the material is 350 MPa, (c) the modulus of elasticity of the material.

Thermal loading

Most materials expand when their temperature rises. This is certainly true of the more commonly used metals in engineering and the effect is measured as the *linear expansivity* of a material. It is

BTEC National Study Guide: Engineering. See page 325 for order details of individual texts

193

defined as *the change in length per unit of length per degree of temperature change* and its symbol is α. It is also known as the *coefficient of linear expansion* and its units are $°C^{-1}$.

To find the change in length x, of a component of original length l and linear expansivity α, when its temperature changes by $t\,°C$, we use the formula,

$$x = l\alpha t \tag{1.8}$$

Some typical values of linear expansivity α, are shown in Table 1.1.

Table 1.1 *Linear expansivity values*

Material	Linear expansivity ($°C^{-1}$)
Aluminium	24×10^{-6}
Brass and bronze	19×10^{-6}
Copper	17×10^{-6}
Nickel	13×10^{-6}
Carbon steel	12×10^{-6}
Cast iron	10×10^{-6}
Platinum	9×10^{-6}
Invar	1.6×10^{-6}

Invar is an alloy steel containing around 36% nickel. The combination results in a material with a very low expansivity. It is used in applications such as instrumentation systems, where expansion of the components could result in output errors.

Example 1.10

A steel bar of length 2.5 m and linear expansivity $12 \times 10^{-6}\,°C^{-1}$ undergoes a rise in temperature from 15 °C to 250 °C. What will be its change in length?

$x = l\alpha t$

$x = 2.5 \times 12 \times 10^{-6} \times (250 - 15)$

$x = 7.05 \times 10^{-3}\,\text{m}$ or $7.05\,\text{mm}$

Equation (1.8) can be rearranged to give the thermal strain ε, which has resulted from the temperature change. It is measured in just the same way as the strain due to direct loading.

$$\varepsilon = \frac{x}{l} = \alpha t \tag{1.9}$$

If a material is allowed to expand freely, there will be no stress produced by the temperature change. If, however, the material is securely held and the change in length is prevented, thermal stress σ, will be induced. The above equation gives the virtual mechanical strain to which it is proportional and if the modulus of elasticity, E, for the material is known, the value of the stress can be calculated as follows.

$$E = \frac{\sigma}{\varepsilon} = \frac{\sigma}{\alpha t}$$

$$\sigma = E\alpha t \tag{1.10}$$

You will see from the above equation that thermal stress depends only on the material properties and the temperature change.

Key point

Thermal stress is independent of the dimensions of a restrained component. It is dependant only on its modulus of elasticity, its linear expansivity and the temperature change which takes place.

BTEC National Study Guide: Engineering. See page 325 for order details of individual texts

194

Example 1.11

A steam pipe made from steel is fitted at a temperature of 20 °C. If expansion is prevented, what will be the compressive stress in the material when steam at a temperature of 150 °C flows through it? Take $\alpha = 12 \times 10^{-6}\,^{\circ}\text{C}^{-1}$ and $E = 200\,\text{GN}\,\text{m}^{-2}$.

$$\sigma = E\alpha t$$

$$\sigma = 200 \times 10^{9} \times 12 \times 10^{-6} \times (150 - 20)$$

$$\boldsymbol{\sigma = 312 \times 10^{6}\,\text{Pa}} \quad \text{or} \quad \boldsymbol{312\,\text{MPa}}$$

You should note that this is quite a high level of stress which could very easily cause the pipe to buckle. This is why expansion loops and expansion joints are included in steam pipe systems, to reduce the stress to an acceptably low level.

Combined direct and thermal loading

It is of course quite possible to have a loaded component which is rigidly held and which also undergoes temperature change. This often happens with aircraft components and with components in process plant. Depending on whether the temperature rises or falls, the stress in the component may increase or decrease.

When investigating the effects of combined direct and thermal stress, it is useful to adopt the sign convention that tensile stress and strain are positive, and compressive stress and strain are negative. The resultant strain and the resultant stress are the algebraic sum of the direct and thermal values.

resultant strain = direct strain + thermal strain

$$\sigma = \sigma_{\text{D}} + \sigma_{\text{T}}$$

$$\sigma = \frac{F}{A} + E\alpha t \tag{1.11}$$

resultant strain = direct strain + thermal strain

$$\varepsilon = \varepsilon_{\text{D}} + \varepsilon_{\text{T}}$$

$$\varepsilon = \frac{x}{l} + \alpha t \tag{1.12}$$

Having calculated either the resultant stress or the resultant strain, the other can be found from the modulus of elasticity of the material.

$$\text{modulus of elasticity} = \frac{\text{resultant stress}}{\text{resultant strain}}$$

$$E = \frac{\sigma}{\varepsilon} \tag{1.13}$$

> **Key point**
>
> Residual thermal stresses are sometimes present in cast and forged components which have cooled unevenly. They can cause the component to become distorted when material is removed during machining. Residual thermal stresses can be removed by heat treatment and this will be described in Chapter 3.

Example 1.12

A rigidly held tie bar in a heating chamber has a diameter of 15 mm and is tensioned to a load of 150 kN at a temperature of 15 °C. What is the initial stress in the bar and what will be the resultant stress when the temperature in the chamber has risen to 50 °C? Take $E = 200\,\text{GN}\,\text{m}^{-2}$ and $\alpha = 12 \times 10^{-6}\,^{\circ}\text{C}^{-1}$.

BTEC National Study Guide: Engineering. See page 325 for order details of individual texts

195

Note: The initial tensile stress will be positive but the thermal stress will be compressive and negative. It will thus have a cancelling effect.

Finding cross-sectional area:

$$A = \frac{\pi d^2}{4} = \frac{\pi \times 0.015^2}{4}$$

$$A = 2.83 \times 10^{-3}\,\text{m}^2$$

Finding initial direct tensile stress at 15 °C:

$$\sigma_D = \frac{F}{A} = \frac{+150 \times 10^3}{2.83 \times 10^{-3}}$$

$$\sigma_D = +53.0 \times 10^6\,\text{Pa} \quad \text{or} \quad +53.0\,\text{MPa}$$

Finding thermal compressive stress at 50 °C:

$$\sigma_T = E\alpha t = -200 \times 10^9 \times 12 \times 10^{-6} \times (50 - 15)$$

$$\sigma_T = -84.0 \times 10^6\,\text{Pa} \quad \text{or} \quad -84.0\,\text{MPa}$$

Finding resultant stress at 180 °C:

$$\sigma = \sigma_D + \sigma_T = +53.0 + (-84.0)$$

$$\sigma = -31.0\,\text{MPa}$$

That is, the initial tensile stress has been cancelled out during the temperature rise and the final resultant stress is compressive.

Test your knowledge 1.5

1. How do you define the linear expansivity of a material?
2. If identical lengths of steel and aluminium bar undergo the same temperature rise, which one will expand the most?
3. What effect do the dimensions of a rigidly clamped component have on the thermal stress caused by temperature change?

Activity 1.5

A rigidly fixed strut in a refrigeration system carries a compressive load of 50 kN when assembled at a temperature of 20 °C. The initial length of the strut is 0.5 m and its diameter is 30 mm. Determine the initial stress in the strut and the amount of compression under load. At what operating temperature will the stress in the material have fallen to zero? Take $E = 150\,\text{GN}\,\text{m}^{-2}$ and $\alpha = 16 \times 10^{-6}$.

Problems 1.4

1. A steel spacing bar of length 0.5 m is assembled in a structure whilst the temperature is 20 °C. What will be its change in length if the temperature rises to 50 °C? What will be the stress in the bar if free expansion is prevented? Take $E = 200\,\text{GPa}$ and $\alpha = 12 \times 10^{-1}\,°\text{C}^{-1}$.

   [0.18 mm, 72 MPa]

2. A copper bar is rigidly fixed at its ends at a temperature of 15 °C. Determine the magnitude and nature of the stress induced in the material (a) if the temperature falls to −25 °C, (b) if the temperature rises to 95 °C. Take $E = 96\,\text{GPa}$ and $\alpha = 17 \times 10^{-1}\,°\text{C}^{-1}$.

   [66 MPa, 131 MPa]

3. A steel tie bar of length 1 m and diameter of 30 mm is tensioned to carry a load of 180 kN at a temperature of 20 °C. What is the stress in the bar and its change in length when tensioned? What

BTEC National Study Guide: Engineering. See page 325 for order details of individual texts

196

will be the stress in the bar if the temperature rises to $80\,^\circ$C and any change in length is prevented? Take $E = 200\,\text{GN}\,\text{m}^{-2}$ and $\alpha = 12 \times 10^{-6}\,^\circ\text{C}^{-1}$.

[255 MPa, 1.27 mm, 111 MPa]

4. A metal component of initial length 600 mm undergoes an increase in length of 0.05 mm when loaded at a temperature of $18\,^\circ$C. Determine, (a) the tensile stress in the component when first loaded, (b) the temperature at which the stress will be zero if the component is rigidly held at its extended length. Take $E = 120\,\text{GPa}$ and $\alpha = 15 \times 10^{-6}\,^\circ\text{C}^{-1}$ for the component material.

[10 MPa, 73.6 $^\circ$C]

5. A brittle cast iron bar is heated to $140\,^\circ$C and then rigidly clamped so that it cannot contract when cooled. The bar is seen to fracture when the temperature has fallen to $80\,^\circ$C. What is the ultimate tensile strength of the cast iron? Take $E = 120\,\text{GPa}$ and $\alpha = 10 \times 10^{-6}\,^\circ\text{C}^{-1}$.

[72 MPa]

Compound members

Engineering components are sometimes fabricated from two different materials. Materials joined end to end form series compound members. Materials which are sandwiched together or contained one within another form parallel compound members.

With a series compound member as shown on Figure 1.50, the load F is transmitted through both materials.

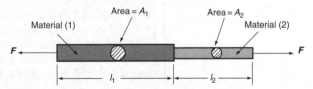

Figure 1.50 *Series compound member*

Let the moduli of elasticity or the materials be E_1 and E_2.
Let the cross-sectional areas be A_1 and A_2.
Let the stresses in the materials be σ_1 and σ_2.
Let the strains in the materials be ε_1 and ε_2.
Let the changes in length be x_1 and x_2.

The stress in each material is given by

$$\sigma_1 = \frac{F}{A_1} \tag{1.14}$$

and

$$\sigma_2 = \frac{F}{A_2} \tag{1.15}$$

If the modulus of elasticity of the material (1) is E_1, the strain in the material will be

$$\varepsilon_1 = \frac{\sigma_1}{E_1}$$

BTEC National Study Guide: Engineering. See page 325 for order details of individual texts

197

and the change in length will be

$$x_1 = \varepsilon_1 l_1$$

$$x_1 = \frac{\sigma_1 l_1}{E_1} \tag{1.16}$$

If the modulus of elasticity of the material (2) is E_2, the strain in the material will be,

$$\varepsilon_2 = \frac{\sigma_2}{E_2}$$

and the change in length will be

$$x_2 = \varepsilon_2 l_2$$

$$x_2 = \frac{\sigma_2 l_2}{E_2} \tag{1.17}$$

The total change in length will thus be

$$x = x_1 + x_2 \tag{1.18}$$

Substituting for x_1 and x_2 from equations (1.16) and (1.17) gives

$$x = \frac{\sigma_1 l_1}{E_1} + \frac{\sigma_2 l_2}{E_2} \tag{1.19}$$

Key point

The load is transmitted through both materials in series compound members, i.e. both materials carry the same load.

Example 1.13

The compound member, shown in Figure 1.51, consists of a steel bar of length 2 m and diameter 30 mm, to which is brazed a copper tube of length 1.5 m, outer diameter 30 mm and inner diameter 15 mm. If the member carries a tensile load of 15 kN, determine the stress in each material and the overall change in length. For steel, $E = 200\,\text{GN m}^{-2}$, for copper $E = 120\,\text{GN m}^{-2}$.

Material (1) – Steel   Material (2) – Copper

F ←   → $F = 15\,\text{kN}$

Figure 1.51

Finding cross-sectional area of steel:

$$A_1 = \frac{\pi D_1^2}{4} = \frac{\pi \times 0.03^2}{4}$$

$$A_1 = 707 \times 10^{-6}\,\text{m}^2$$

Finding cross-sectional area of copper:

$$A_2 = \frac{\pi(D_1^2 - d_2^2)}{4} = \frac{\pi \times (0.03^2 - 0.015^2)}{4}$$

$$A_2 = 530 \times 10^{-6}\,\text{m}^2$$

BTEC National Study Guide: Engineering. See page 325 for order details of individual texts

198

Finding stress in steel:

$$\sigma_1 = \frac{F}{A_1} = \frac{15 \times 10^3}{707 \times 10^{-6}}$$

$$\sigma_1 = 21.2 \times 10^6 \, \text{Pa} \quad \text{or} \quad 21.2 \, \text{MPa}$$

Finding stress in copper:

$$\sigma_2 = \frac{F}{A_2} = \frac{15 \times 10^3}{530 \times 10^{-6}}$$

$$\sigma_2 = 28.3 \times 10^6 \, \text{Pa} \quad \text{or} \quad 28.3 \, \text{MPa}$$

Finding overall change in length using equation (1.19):

$$x = \frac{\sigma_1 l_1}{E_1} + \frac{\sigma_2 l_2}{E_2} = \frac{(21.2 \times 10^6 \times 2)}{200 \times 10^9} + \frac{(28.3 \times 10^6 \times 1.5)}{120 \times 10^9}$$

$$x = (212 \times 10^{-6}) + (354 \times 10^{-6})$$

$$x = 0.566 \times 10^{-3} \, \text{m} \quad \text{or} \quad 0.566 \, \text{mm}$$

With parallel compound members, the loads in each material will most likely be different but when added together, they will equal the external load. The change in length of each material will be the same. When you are required to find the stress in each material, this information enables you to write down two equations, each of which contains the unknown stresses. You can then solve these by substitution and use one of the stress values to find the common change in length.

Consider a member made up of two plates of the same material between which is bonded a plate of another material as shown in Figure 1.52. It is a good idea to let the material with the larger modulus of elasticity be material (1) and that with the lower value be material (2).

Let the moduli of elasticity of the materials be E_1 and E_2.
Let the loads carried be F_1 and F_2.
Let the cross-sectional areas be A_1 and A_2.
Let the stresses in the materials be σ_1 and σ_2.

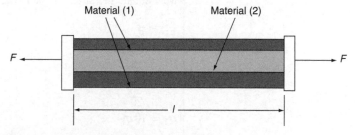

Figure 1.52 *Parallel compound member*

The external load is equal to the sum of the loads carried by the two materials.

$F = F_1 + F_2$

Now, $F_1 = \sigma_1 A_1$ and $F_2 = \sigma_2 A_2$

$$F = \sigma_1 A_1 + \sigma_2 A_2 \tag{1.20}$$

BTEC National Study Guide: Engineering. See page 325 for order details of individual texts

199

Key point

Both materials undergo the same strain in parallel compound members and the sum of the loads carried by each material is equal to the external load.

The strain in each material is the same, and so

$$\varepsilon_1 = \varepsilon_2$$

Now, $\varepsilon_1 = \sigma_1/E_1$ and $\varepsilon_2 = \sigma_2/E_2$

$$\frac{\sigma_1}{E_1} = \frac{\sigma_2}{E_2} \qquad\qquad (1.21)$$

Equations (1.20) and (1.21) can be solved simultaneously to find σ_1 and σ_2. The common strain can then be found from either of the above two expressions for strain, and this can then be used to find the common change in length.

Example 1.14

A concrete column 200 mm square is reinforced by nine steel rods of diameter 20 mm. The length of the column is 3 m and it is required to support an axial compressive load of 500 kN. Find the stress in each material and the change in length of the column under load. For steel $E = 200\,\text{GN m}^{-2}$ and for concrete, $E = 20\,\text{GN m}^{-2}$.

Because the steel has higher modulus of elasticity, let it be material (1) and the concrete be material (2).

Begin by finding the cross-sectional areas of the two materials:

$$A_1 = 9 \times \frac{\pi d^2}{4} = 9 \times \frac{\pi \times 0.02^2}{4}$$

$$\boldsymbol{A_1 = 2.83 \times 10^{-3}\,\text{m}^2}$$

$$A_2 = (0.2 \times 0.2) - A_1 = 0.04 - (2.83 \times 10^{-3})$$

$$\boldsymbol{A_2 = 37.2 \times 10^{-3}\,\text{m}^2}$$

Now equate the external force to the sum of the forces in the two materials using equation (1.20):

$$F = \sigma_1 A_1 + \sigma_2 A_2$$

$$500 \times 10^3 = (2.83 \times 10^{-3})\sigma_1 + (37.2 \times 10^{-3})\sigma_2$$

This can be simplified by dividing both sides by 10^{-3}:

$$\boldsymbol{500 \times 10^6 = 2.83\sigma_1 + 37.2\sigma_2} \qquad (1)$$

Now equate the strains in each material using equation (1.21) :

$$\frac{\sigma_1}{E_1} = \frac{\sigma_2}{E_2}$$

$$\sigma_1 = \frac{E_1 \sigma_2}{E_2}$$

$$\sigma_1 = \frac{200 \times 10^9}{20 \times 10^9} \times \sigma_2$$

$$\boldsymbol{\sigma_1 = 10\,\sigma_2} \qquad (2)$$

Substitute in equation (1) for σ_1:

$$500 \times 10^6 = 2.83(10\sigma_2) + 37.2\sigma_2$$

$$500 \times 10^6 = 28.3\sigma_2 + 37.2\sigma_2 = 65.5\sigma_2$$

$$\sigma_2 = \frac{500 \times 10^6}{65.5}$$

$$\boldsymbol{\sigma_2 = 7.63 \times 10^6\,\text{Pa}} \quad \text{or} \quad \boldsymbol{7.63\,\text{MPa}}$$

BTEC National Study Guide: Engineering. See page 325 for order details of individual texts

200

Test you knowledge 1.6

1. What is the parameter that the two materials in a series compound member have in common when it is under load?
2. What is the parameter that the two materials in a parallel compound member have in common when it is under load?
3. On which material property does the ratio of the stresses in the materials of a parallel compound member depend?

Finding σ_1 from equation (2):

$$\sigma_1 = 10 \times 7.63 = 7.63\,\text{MPa}$$

Now find the common strain using the stress and modulus of elasticity for material (2):

$$\varepsilon = \frac{\sigma_2}{E_2} = \frac{7.63 \times 10^6}{20 \times 10^9}$$

$$\varepsilon = 382 \times 10^{-6}$$

Finally find the common change in length:

$$\varepsilon = \frac{x}{l}$$

$$x = \varepsilon\,l = 382 \times 10^{-6} \times 3$$

$$x = 1.15 \times 10^3\,\text{m} \quad \text{or} \quad 1.15\,\text{mm}$$

Activity 1.6

The tie bar shown in Figure 1.53 consists of a steel core 25 mm in diameter on to which is cast an aluminium outer case of outer diameter 40 mm. The compound section 1.5 m long, carries a tensile load of 30 kN. The load is applied to the protruding steel core as shown below.

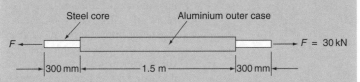

Figure 1.53

Find (a) the stress in the protruding steel which carries the full load, (b) the stress in the two materials in the compound section, (c) the overall change in length. For steel, $E = 200\,\text{GN m}^{-2}$ and for aluminium, $E = 90\,\text{GN m}^{-2}$.

Problems 1.5

1. A duralumin tie bar of diameter 40 mm and length 600 mm carries a tensile load of 180 kN. If the bar contains a 30 mm diameter hole along 100 mm of its length, determine the stress in the two sections and the overall change in length. Take $E = 180\,\text{GPa}$.
   [143 MPa, 327 MPa, 1.24 mm]

2. A compound strut consists of a steel tube of length 1 m, outer diameter 35 mm and inner diameter 25 mm which is brazed to a copper tube of length 1.5 m, outer diameter 35 mm and inner diameter 20 mm. If the member carries a compressive load of 20 kN, determine the stress in each material and the overall change in length.
   For steel, $E = 200\,\text{GN m}^{-2}$, for copper $E = 120\,\text{GN m}^{-2}$.
   [42.4 MPa, 30.9 MPa, 0.6 mm]

BTEC National Study Guide: Engineering. See page 325 for order details of individual texts

201

3. A rectangular timber strut of cross-section $125\,\text{mm} \times 105\,\text{mm}$ is reinforced by two aluminium bars of diameter 60 mm. Determine the stress in each material when the member carries a load of 300 kN. For aluminium, $E = 90\,\text{GN}\,\text{m}^{-2}$, for timber $E = 15\,\text{GN}\,\text{m}^{-2}$.

[103 MPa, 17.2 MPa]

4. A compression member is made up of a mild steel bar, 38 mm in diameter, which is encased in a brass tube of inner diameter 38 mm and outer diameter 65 mm. Determine the stress in the two materials and the reduction in length when the member carries a load of 200 kN. For steel, $E = 200\,\text{GPa}$, for brass $E = 96\,\text{GPa}$.

[92.9 MPa, 43.3 MPa, 0.068 mm]

5. A steel reinforced concrete column of height 3 m has a square cross-section with sides of 375 mm. If the column contains four steel reinforcing rods of diameter 25 mm, determine the stress in each material and the amount of compression when carrying a compressive load of 600 kN. For steel, $E = 200\,\text{GPa}$, for concrete $E = 13.8\,\text{GPa}$.

[53.6 MPa, 3.56 MPa, 0.77 mm]

Fastenings

Engineering fastenings such as rivets, bolts, the different kinds of machine screws and setscrews, self-tapping screws and hinge pins are frequently subjected to shear loading. Shear loading occurs when equal and opposite parallel forces act on a component. Direct loading tends to cause failure perpendicular to the direction of loading whereas shear loading tends to cause failure parallel to the direction of loading. Direct loading and its effects have already been dealt with and we will now examine the effects of shear loading (Figure 1.54).

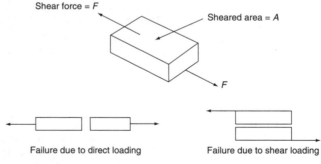

Figure 1.54 *Direct and shear loading*

Shear stress

Shear stress τ, is a measure of the intensity of loading over the sheared area A.

$$\text{shear stress} = \frac{\text{shear force}}{\text{sheared area}}$$

$$\tau = \frac{F}{A} \; (\textbf{Pa or N}\,\textbf{m}^{-2}) \tag{1.22}$$

BTEC National Study Guide: Engineering. See page 325 for order details of individual texts

202

Shear strain

Shearing forces tend to distort the shape of a component as shown in Figure 1.55.

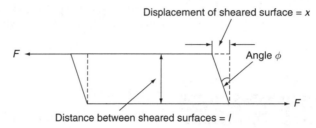

Figure 1.55 *Deformation due to shearing*

Shear strain γ, is a measure of the deformation which the shearing force produces. It is the ratio of the displacement of the sheared surfaces to the distance between them.

$$\text{shear strain} = \frac{\text{displacement of sheared surfaces}}{\text{distance between sheared surfaces}}$$

$$\gamma = \frac{x}{l} \text{ (No units)} \tag{1.23}$$

The angle ϕ, is called the angle of shear. Its tangent is equal to the shear strain.

$$\tan \phi = \frac{x}{l}$$

$$\boldsymbol{\tan \phi = \gamma} \tag{1.24}$$

Shear modulus or (Modulus of rigidity)

When an elastic material is subjected to shear loading, the displacement x of the sheared surfaces is proportional to the load F, which is applied. Also the shear stress τ is proportional to the shear strain γ.

A graph of shear stress against shear strain is a straight line, as shown in Figure 1.56, whose gradient for a given material is always found to be the same. It gives a measure of the elasticity or

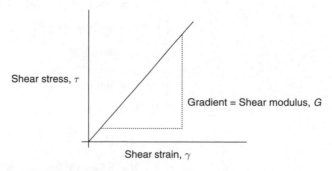

Figure 1.56 *Graph of shear stress v. shear strain*

BTEC National Study Guide: Engineering. See page 325 for order details of individual texts

203

'stiffness' of the material in shear and is known as its *Shear Modulus, G*. In older text books you might find that it is called the *Modulus of Rigidity*.

$$G = \frac{\tau}{\gamma} \text{ (Pa or } \mathbf{N\,m^{-2}}) \tag{1.25}$$

Substituting the expressions for shear stress and shear strain from equations (1.22) and (1.23) gives an alternative formula

$$G = \frac{\frac{F}{A}}{\frac{x}{l}}$$

$$G = \frac{F}{A} \times \frac{l}{x} \tag{1.26}$$

It will be noted that several of the above formulae are similar to those derived for direct stress and strain and the Modulus of Elasticity but they should not be confused. The symbols F, A, l and x have different meanings when used to calculate shear stress, shear strain and shear modulus. Furthermore, the values of Modulus of Elasticity E, and Shear Modulus G, are not the same for any given material. With mild steel, for example, $E = 210\,\text{GN}\,\text{m}^{-2}$ whilst $G = 85\,\text{GN}\,\text{m}^{-2}$.

Key point

Shear modulus is a measure of the shear stiffness of a material, i.e. its resistance to being deformed by shearing forces.

Example 1.15

A block of an elastic material is subjected to a shearing force of 50 kN which deforms its shape as shown in Figure 1.57. Find (a) the shear stress, (b) the shear strain, (c) the shear modulus for the material.

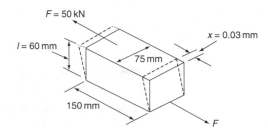

Figure 1.57

(a) Finding shear stress:

$$\tau = \frac{F}{A} = \frac{50 \times 10^3}{0.15 \times 0.075}$$
$$\tau = \mathbf{4.44 \times 10^6 \ Pa} \quad \text{or} \quad \mathbf{4.44\ MPa}$$

(b) Finding shear strain:

$$\gamma = \frac{x}{l} = \frac{0.03}{60}$$
$$\gamma = \mathbf{500 \times 10^{-6}}$$

(c) Finding shear modulus:

$$G = \frac{\tau}{\gamma} = \frac{4.44 \times 10^6}{500 \times 10^{-6}}$$
$$G = \mathbf{8.88 \times 10^9 \ Pa} \quad \text{or} \quad \mathbf{8.88\ GPa}$$

BTEC National Study Guide: Engineering. See page 325 for order details of individual texts

204

Fastenings in single shear

Riveted lap joints and joints employing screwed fastenings are often subjected to shearing forces. Tensile forces may also be present and these are very necessary to hold the joint surfaces tightly together. It is very likely, however, that the external loads will have a shearing effect and it is assumed that this will be carried entirely by the fastenings. The tendency is to shear the fastenings at the joint interface and this is known as *single shear* as shown in Figure 1.58.

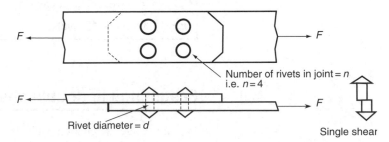

Figure 1.58 *Lap joint with rivets in single shear*

The total sheared cross-sectional area of the fastenings is

$$A = \frac{n\pi d^2}{4}$$

The shear stress in the fastenings will be

$$\tau = \frac{F}{A} = \frac{F}{\frac{n\pi d^2}{4}}$$

$$\tau = \frac{4F}{n\pi d^2} \qquad (1.27)$$

In design problems you will probably know the safe working stress and the recommended rivet or bolt diameter for the thickness of the materials being joined. The task will then be to calculate the number of fastenings required and to decide on their spacing. Transposing the above formula gives

$$n = \frac{4F}{\tau \pi d^2} \qquad (1.28)$$

The fastenings should not be too close together or too near to the edge of the material being joined. You can find the rules for particular applications in British and international standard specifications, and also in design code handbooks which are based on them.

Example 1.16

A lap joint is required to join plates using rivets of diameter 6 mm. The shearing force to be carried by the joint is 12 kN and the shear strength of the rivet material is 300 MPa . If a factor of safety of 8 is to apply, find the number of rivets required for the joint.

BTEC National Study Guide: Engineering. See page 325 for order details of individual texts

205

Finding allowable shear stress in rivets:

$$\tau = \frac{\text{shear strength}}{\text{factor of safety}} = \frac{300}{8}$$

$$\tau = \textbf{37.5 MPa}$$

Finding number of rivets required:

$$n = \frac{4F}{\tau \pi d^2}$$

$$n = \frac{4 \times 12 \times 10^3}{37.5 \times 10^6 \times \pi \times (6 \times 10^{-3})^2}$$

$$n = \textbf{11.3} \text{ i.e. use } \textbf{12 rivets}$$

Fastenings in double shear

In joints where the plates must be butted together, connecting plates are used above and below the joint. There is then a tendency to shear the rivets in two places and they are said to be in *double shear*.

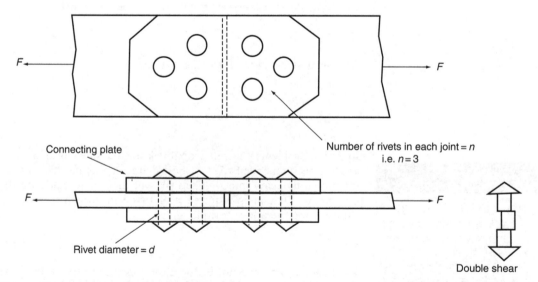

Figure 1.59 *Butt joint with rivets in double shear*

There are in fact two joints in Figure 1.59, where each of the butted plates is riveted to the connecting plates. As a result, the number of rivets per joint is half the total number shown. That is, $n = 3$ rivets in this particular example.

The total sheared cross-sectional area of the fastenings is double that for single shear. That is,

$$A = \frac{2n\pi d^2}{4}$$

BTEC National Study Guide: Engineering. See page 325 for order details of individual texts

206

The shear stress in the fastenings will be

$$\tau = \frac{F}{A} = \frac{F}{\frac{2n\pi d^2}{4}}$$

$$\tau = \frac{2F}{n\pi d^2} \tag{1.29}$$

If you compare this with equation (1.27) you will note that for the same load, diameter and number of rivets, the shear stress for double shear is half the value for single shear. A joint in double shear can therefore carry twice as much load as the equivalent joint in single shear. If it is required to find the number of rivets required, the above equation can be transposed to give

$$n = \frac{2F}{\tau\pi d^2} \tag{1.30}$$

Key point

A rivet in double shear can carry twice as much load as a rivet in single shear before failure occurs.

Test your knowledge 1.7

1. What is the difference between direct loading and shear loading?
2. Define shear stress and shear strain.
3. What is the angle of shear?
4. Define shear modulus.
5. Compare the load carrying capacity for rivets of a given diameter when subjected to single shear and double shear.

Example 1.17

Two aluminium plates are to be joined by means of a double strap riveted butt joint. The joint is required to support a load of 15 kN and the total number of rivets is 12. The rivet material has a shear strength of 200 MPa and a factor of safety of 6 is to apply. Determine the required diameter of the rivets.

Finding allowable shear stress in rivets:

$$\tau = \frac{\text{shear strength}}{\text{factor of safety}} = \frac{200}{6}$$

$$\tau = \textbf{33.3 MPa}$$

Finding required rivet diameter:

$$\tau = \frac{2F}{n\pi d^2}$$

$$d^2 = \frac{2F}{n\pi\tau}$$

$$d = \sqrt{\frac{2F}{n\pi\tau}} \quad \text{where } n = \frac{12}{2} = 6 \text{ rivets}$$

$$d = \sqrt{\frac{2 \times 10 \times 10^3}{6 \times \pi \times 33.3 \times 10^6}}$$

$$d = \textbf{5.64} \times \textbf{10}^{-3} \textbf{ m} \quad \text{or} \quad \textbf{5.64 mm} \quad \text{i.e. use } \textbf{6.0 mm revets}$$

Activity 1.7

Two steel plates are riveted together by means of a lap joint. Ten rivets of diameter 9 mm are used, and the load carried is 20 kN. What is the shear stress in the rivet material and the factor of safety in operation if the shear strength is 300 MPa? If the lap joint were replaced by a double strap butt joint with ten rivets per joint and each carrying the same shear stress as above, what would be the required rivet diameter?

BTEC National Study Guide: Engineering. See page 325 for order details of individual texts

207

Problems 1.6

1.

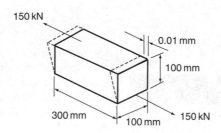

Figure 1.60

A block of elastic material is loaded in shear as shown in Figure 1.60. Determine (a) the shear stress, (b) the shear strain, (c) the shear modulus of the material.

$$[5\,\text{MPa},\ 100 \times 10^{-6},\ 50\,\text{GPa}]$$

2. A mild steel plate of thickness 15 mm has a 50 mm diameter hole punched in it. If the ultimate shear stress of the steel is 275 MPa, determine (a) the punching force required, (b) the compressive stress in the punch.

$$[648\,\text{kN},\ 330\,\text{MPa}]$$

3.

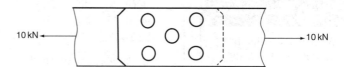

Figure 1.61

Figure 1.61 shows a riveted lap joint. Determine a suitable diameter for the rivets if the ultimate shear strength of the rivet material is 325 MPa and a factor of safety of 6 is to apply.

$$[6.86\,\text{mm},\ \text{i.e. use 7 mm dia rivets}]$$

4.

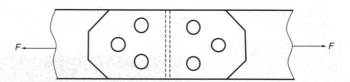

Figure 1.62

Determine the load F which the double strap butt joint shown in Figure 1.62 can carry. The rivets are 6 mm in diameter with an ultimate shear strength of 325 MPa. A factor of safety of 8 is to apply.

$$[6.9\,\text{kN}]$$

BTEC National Study Guide: Engineering. See page 325 for order details of individual texts

208

Centripetal acceleration and centripetal force

Newton's first law of motion states that *a moving body will continue in a straight line unless acted upon by some external force*. It follows that when a body is travelling in a circular path, there must be some sideways force pushing, or pulling it, towards the centre of rotation. This is known as *centripetal* force, which means 'centre seeking'. With a car travelling round a curve, the centripetal force is provided by friction between the tyres and the road surface, and with an orbiting satellite, it is provided by the earth's gravitational pull.

Vector change of velocity

You will recall that velocity is a vector quantity. This means that it has both magnitude and direction. For a body travelling in a straight path we very often only state the magnitude of its velocity, i.e. its speed. We take its direction for granted but strictly speaking, we should state both magnitude and direction when we write down the velocity of a body.

Because velocity is a vector quantity, it can be represented in magnitude direction and sense by a line v_1 drawn to a suitable scale on a vector diagram. If either the speed or the direction of a body should change, then its velocity will change. The new vector v_2 will be drawn from the same starting point but to a different length or in a different direction. There is then said to have been a vector change of velocity which can be measured as the distance between the end of the initial vector to the end of the final vector.

> **Key point**
>
> Velocity is a vector quantity and if either the speed or the direction of a body changes, its velocity will change.

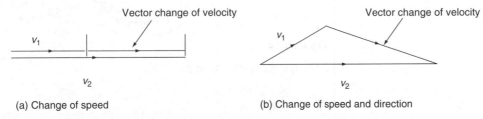

(a) Change of speed   (b) Change of speed and direction

Figure 1.63 *Vector change of velocity*

You will also recall that acceleration is the rate of change of velocity, i.e., the change of velocity per second. This applies not only for changes of speed, as in Figure 1.63(a), but also for vector changes of velocity as in Figure 1.63(b). If the time taken for the vector change is known, the acceleration which has taken place can be calculated. This is also a vector quantity whose direction is the same as the vector change of velocity.

> **Key point**
>
> Acceleration is the rate of change of velocity which can result from a change of speed or a change of direction.

$$\text{acceleration} = \frac{\text{vector change of velocity}}{\text{time taken for change}}$$

$$a = \frac{\Delta v}{t} \tag{1.31}$$

When a body picks up speed or changes direction, there must be some external force acting to cause the change. This force is given by Newton's second law of motion which states that *the rate of*

BTEC National Study Guide: Engineering. See page 325 for order details of individual texts

209

change of momentum of a body is equal to the force which is causing the change. It is from this law that we obtain the formula

force = mass × acceleration

$$\boldsymbol{F = ma} \tag{1.32}$$

Having found the vector change of velocity of a body from a vector diagram, you can then calculate the acceleration which has occurred using expression (1.31). If you know the mass m of the body, you can then calculate the force which has produced the change using expression (1.32). The direction in which the force acts on the body is the same as that of the vector change of velocity and the acceleration it produces.

Example 1.18

A vehicle of mass 750 kg travelling east at a speed of 50 km h^{-1} accelerates around a bend in the road and emerges 10 s later at a speed of 90 km h^{-1} travelling in a north easterly direction. What is its vector change of velocity, the acceleration and the force which produces the change?

The vector change of velocity Δv, is 65.1 km h^{-1} in a direction which is 77.8° north of west as shown in Figure 1.64.

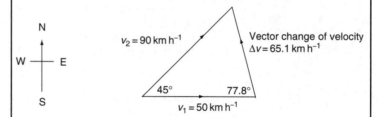

Figure 1.64

Finding velocity change in ms^{-1}:

$$\Delta v = \frac{65.1 \times 1000}{60 \times 60}$$

$$\boldsymbol{\Delta v = 18.1 \, ms^{-1}}$$

Finding acceleration produced:

$$a = \frac{\Delta v}{t} = \frac{18.1}{10}$$

$$\boldsymbol{a = 1.81 \, m \, s^{-2}}$$

Finding force which has produced the change of speed and direction:

$$F = ma = 750 \times 1.81$$

$$\boldsymbol{F = 13.6 \times 10^3 \, N} \quad \text{or} \quad \boldsymbol{13.6 \, kN}$$

This force is the resultant of the force between the driving wheels and the road, which is producing the increase in speed, and the side thrust on the vehicle, which results from turning the steering wheel into the bend. Its direction is the same as the vector change which it produces.

BTEC National Study Guide: Engineering. See page 325 for order details of individual texts

210

If the vehicle in Example 1.18 had been travelling around the bend without increasing its speed, there would still have been a vector change in velocity and a resulting acceleration. It is thus possible to have acceleration at constant speed. This may sound a bit odd, but you must remember that velocity is a vector quantity and if either the speed or the direction of a body changes, there will be a change of velocity and an acceleration.

Centripetal acceleration and force

Consider now what happens when a body is travelling at a constant speed v m s^{-1} and angular velocity ω rad s^{-1} around a circular path of radius r. Its direction, and also its velocity, is continually changing.

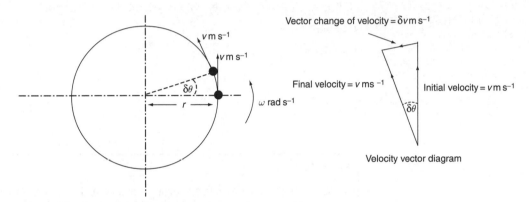

Figure 1.65 *Uniform circular motion*

Let the body move through a small angle $\delta\theta$ radians in time δt s, as shown in Figure 1.65. There will be a vector change in velocity during this period, as shown on the velocity vector diagram. If the angle $\delta\theta$ is very small, the velocity vector diagram will be a long, thin isosceles triangle and the vector change in velocity will be given by

$$\delta v = v\delta\theta$$

The acceleration which occurs will be

$$a = \frac{\delta v}{\delta t} = v\frac{\delta\theta}{\delta t}$$

But $\frac{\delta\theta}{\delta t} = \omega$, the angular velocity of the body,

$$a = v\omega \tag{1.33}$$

This is known as the *centripetal acceleration* of the body and whatever its position, its centripetal acceleration is always directed towards the centre of the circular path.

BTEC National Study Guide: Engineering. See page 325 for order details of individual texts

211

Key point

When a body is travelling in a circular path, its direction is continually changing. The change of velocity gives rise to centripetal acceleration which is directed towards the centre of rotation.

Key point

Centripetal force is an active force which pulls or pushes a body towards the centre of rotation. Centrifugal force is the equal and opposite reaction whose direction is away from the centre of rotation.

Now $v = \omega r$ and $\omega = \dfrac{v}{r}$. Substituting for v and ω in equation (1.33) gives

$$a = \omega^2 r \tag{1.34}$$

and

$$a = \frac{v^2}{r} \tag{1.35}$$

It is more usual to use these expressions when calculating centripetal acceleration than that given by equation (1.33).

Wherever acceleration occurs, there must be a force present. For a body travelling in a circular path, this is the centripetal force, pulling or pushing it towards the centre of the path. If the body shown in Figure 1.65 were attached to the centre of its path by a cord, this would all the time be pulling it inwards and the tension in the cord would be the centripetal force. For a body of mass m kg, the centripetal force is obtained using expression (1.32) which comes from Newton's second law of motion.

$$F = ma$$

$$F = m\omega^2 r \tag{1.36}$$

or

$$F = \frac{mv^2}{r} \tag{1.37}$$

Example 1.19

A body of mass 5 kg travels in a horizontal circular path of radius 2 m at a speed of 100 rpm and is attached to the centre of rotation by a steel rod of diameter 3 mm. Determine (a) the centripetal acceleration of the mass, (b) the centripetal force, (c) the tensile stress in the rod.

(a) Finding angular velocity of rotation:

$$\omega = N(\text{rpm}) \times \frac{2\pi}{60} = 100 \times \frac{2\pi}{60}$$

$$\omega = 10.5 \, \text{rad s}^{-1}$$

Finding centripetal acceleration of mass:

$$a = \omega^2 r = 10.5^2 \times 2$$

$$a = 219 \, \text{m s}^{-2}$$

(b) Finding centripetal force:

$$F = ma = 5 \times 219$$

$$F = 1.10 \times 10^3 \, \text{N} \quad \text{or} \quad 1.10 \, \text{kN}$$

(c) Finding cross-sectional area of rod:

$$A = \frac{\pi d^2}{4} = \frac{\pi \times 0.003^2}{4}$$

$$A = 7.07 \times 10^{-6} \, \text{m}^2$$

BTEC National Study Guide: Engineering. See page 325 for order details of individual texts

212

Finding tensile stress in rod:

$$\sigma = \frac{F}{A} = \frac{1.10 \times 10^3}{7.07 \times 10^{-6}}$$

$$\sigma = 155 \times 10^6 \text{ Pa} \quad \text{or} \quad 155 \text{ kPa}$$

Activity 1.8

A body of mass 0.6 kg rotates on the end of a helical spring of stiffness 1.2 kN m⁻¹ in a horizontal plane. The initial distance from the centre of rotation to the centre of the mass is 200 mm. What will be the radius of rotation of the mass when the rotational speed is 300 rpm?

Centrifugal clutches

Centrifugal clutches are to be found on motor-driven equipment such as lawn mowers, mixers and pumps. They engage automatically when the motor speed reaches a pre-determined level, and do not depend on the skill of the operator.

In its simplest form a centrifugal clutch consists of a drive shaft to which are attached two or more spring loaded masses. These are lined with a friction material on their outer surfaces and rotate inside a drum which is fixed to the output shaft (see Figure 1.66).

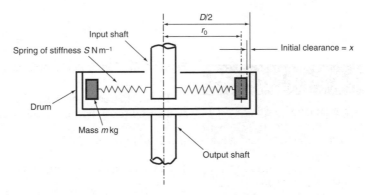

Figure 1.66 *Centrifugal clutch*

The masses, or 'bobs', are free to slide outwards in guides which are rigidly fixed to the input shaft. These are not shown in the above diagram. As the angular velocity of the input shaft increases, the masses slide outwards and eventually make contact with the drum. A further increase in speed causes the drive to be transmitted to the output shaft through friction between the masses and the drum.

Let initial clearance between the masses and the drum be x.
Let the initial radius of rotation from the centre of the shafts to the centre of gravity of the masses be r_0.
Let the diameter of the drum be D.

BTEC National Study Guide: Engineering. See page 325 for order details of individual texts

213

Let the coefficient of friction between the drum and the masses be μ. Let the angular velocity at which the masses just make contact with the drum be ω_0.

When the masses just make contact with the drum, the tension F_0 in the springs is given by

spring tension = spring stiffness × extension

$$F_0 = Sx \tag{1.38}$$

This is also the centripetal force acting on the masses whose radius of rotation is now $r_0 + x$. Equating spring tension and centripetal force enables the angular velocity ω_0, at which the masses engage with the drum, to be found

$$F_0 = m\omega_0^2 (r_0 + x)$$

$$\omega_0 = \sqrt{\frac{F_0}{m(r_0 + x)}} \tag{1.39}$$

Consider now the normal force and the tangential force between the masses and the drum at some higher speed ω, when the drive is being transmitted to the output shaft. These are shown in Figure 1.67.

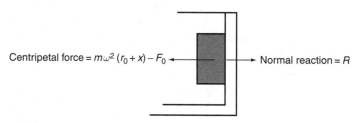

Centripetal force = $m\omega^2 (r_0 + x) - F_0$ ← → Normal reaction = R

Figure 1.67 *Forces acting on clutch drum*

The normal force between each mass and the drum is equal to the centripetal force, part of which is supplied by the spring tension F_0.

$$R = m\omega^2 (r_0 + x) - F_0 \tag{1.40}$$

The tangential friction force between each mass and the drum will be

$$F = \mu R$$
$$F = \mu [m\omega^2 (r_0 + x) - F_0] \tag{1.41}$$

If the number of masses is n, the torque transmitted will be

$$T = nF\frac{D}{2}$$
$$T = n\mu [m\omega^2 (r_0 + x) - F_0]\frac{D}{2} \tag{1.42}$$

Having calculated the torque transmitted, the power transmitted can be calculated.

$$\text{power} = T\omega \tag{1.43}$$

BTEC National Study Guide: Engineering. See page 325 for order details of individual texts

214

Example 1.20

A centrifugal clutch has two rotating contact masses of 0.25 kg each. These are able to move in guides attached to the input shaft and are held by springs of stiffness 8 kN m^{-1}. The initial clearance between the masses and the internal surface of a drum on the output shaft is 5 mm. The inner diameter of the drum is 300 mm and the distance from the centre of rotation to the centre of gravity of the masses is 135 mm. The coefficient of friction between the masses and the drum is 0.35. Determine (a) the rotational speed in revs per minute at which the clutch begins to transmit power, (b) the torque and power transmitted at a speed of 1000 rpm.

(a) Finding tension in springs as masses make contact with drum:

$$F_0 = Sx = 8 \times 10^3 \times 5 \times 10^{-3}$$
$$\boldsymbol{F_0 = 40\,N}$$

Finding angular velocity at which masses just make contact with the drum:

$$\omega_0 = \frac{F_0}{\sqrt{m(r_0 + x)}} = \frac{40}{\sqrt{0.25(0.135 + 0.005)}}$$
$$\omega_0 = 33.8\,\text{rad s}^{-1}$$

Changing to revs per minute,

$$N_0 = \omega_0 \times \frac{60}{2\pi} = 33.8 \times \frac{60}{2\pi}$$
$$\boldsymbol{N_0 = 323\,rpm}$$

(b) Finding angular velocity at rotational speed of 1000 rpm:

$$\omega = N \times \frac{2\pi}{60} = 1000 \times \frac{2\pi}{60}$$
$$\boldsymbol{\omega = 105\,rad\,s^{-1}}$$

Finding torque transmitted at this speed:

$$T = n\mu[m\omega^2(r_0 + x) - F_0]\frac{D}{2}$$
$$T = 2 \times 0.35 \times [\{0.25 \times 105^2 \times (0.135 + 0.005)\} - 40] \times 0.15$$
$$\boldsymbol{T = 36.3\,N\,m}$$

Finding power transmitted at this speed:

Power $= T\omega = 36.3 \times 105$

Power $= 3.81 \times 10^3$ W or **3.81 kW**

Test your knowledge 1.9

1. What are the units in which spring stiffness is measured?
2. If the normal force between two surfaces is 100 N and their coefficient of friction is 0.3, what force will be required to make them slide over each other?
3. What determines the rotational speed at which a centrifugal clutch starts to engage?
4. How do you convert rotational speed in revolutions per minute to angular velocity measured in radians per second?

Activity 1.9

A centrifugal clutch has four bobs of mass 0.25 kg each which can slide outwards in guides and are attached to the input shaft by restraining springs. The drum attached to the output shaft has an inner diameter of 350 mm. The static clearance between the bobs and the drum is 6 mm, and the distance from the centre of

---

BTEC National Study Guide: Engineering. See page 325 for order details of individual texts

215

rotation to the centre of gravity of the bobs is initially 155 mm. The coefficient of friction between the bobs and the drum is 0.3. If the clutch starts to engage at a speed of 500 rpm, what is the stiffness of the restraining springs? What will be the power transmitted by the clutch at a speed of 1200 rpm?

Problems 1.7

1. A body of mass 3 kg is whirled round in a horizontal plane at the end of a steel wire. The distance from the centre of rotation to the centre of the mass is 1.5 m and the diameter of the wire is 2 mm. If the ultimate tensile strength of the steel is 500 MPa, determine the rotational speed at which the wire will break.

    [178 rpm]

2. A body of mass 1 kg is whirled in a horizontal plane at the end of a spring. The spring stiffness is 5 kN m^{-1} and the initial distance from the centre of rotation to the centre of the body is 200 mm. What will be the extension of the spring at a rotational speed of 300 rpm?

    [49.1 mm]

3. A centrifugal clutch has four shoes, each of mass 2 kg which are held on retaining springs of stiffness 10 kN m^{-1}. The internal diameter of the clutch drum is 600 mm and the radius of the centre of gravity of the shoes when in contact with the drum is 250 mm. The stationary clearance between the shoes and the drum is 20 mm, and the coefficient of friction is 0.25. Determine (a) the speed at which the clutch starts to engage, (b) the power transmitted at a speed of 1500 rpm.

    [191 rpm, 2.29 MW]

4. A centrifugal clutch has four shoes, each of mass 0.3 kg. When at rest, the radial clearance between the shoes and the clutch drum is 5 mm and the radius to the centre of gravity of the shoes is 195 mm. The shoes are held on retaining springs of stiffness 8 kN m^{-1} and the internal diameter of the clutch drum is 500 mm. The coefficient of friction between the shoes and the drum is 0.2. Determine for a rotational speed of 1000 rpm (a) the radial force which each shoe exerts on the drum, (b) the torque transmitted, (c) the power transmitted.

    [622 N, 124 N m, 13.1 kW]

Stability of vehicles

When you are travelling around a bend on a motor cycle or in a car the centripetal force is supplied by friction between the wheels and the road surface as you turn into the curve. If you are travelling too fast for the road conditions, or the condition of your vehicle, one of two things may happen.

BTEC National Study Guide: Engineering. See page 325 for order details of individual texts

216

1. The friction force between the wheels and the road surface will be insufficient and you will skid. The direction of your skid will be at a tangent to the curve.
2. If the centre of gravity of your vehicle is high it may overturn before starting to skid.

With a motor cycle only the first option is possible. You may of course skid into the kerb and then overturn but it is skidding which will initiate the problem. Cars, buses and trucks are designed so that even when fully loaded, they should skid before reaching the speed at which overturning would occur. Large heavy items stacked on a roof rack may raise the centre of gravity of a car to such a height that overturning is a possibility and of course this would also increase the possibility of overturning should the vehicle skid into the kerb.

Consider a four wheeled vehicle of mass m, travelling at a speed v, round a level unbanked curve of radius r as shown in Figure 1.68.

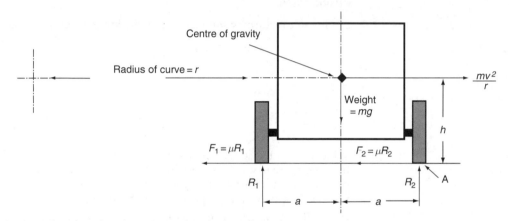

Figure 1.68 *Vehicle on an unbanked horizontal curve*

Although the vehicle is moving, it can be considered to be in a state of dynamic equilibrium. In the vertical direction, the active force is the weight W acting downwards, which is balanced by the upward reactions R_1 and R_2 of the wheels. The active forces in the horizontal direction are the friction forces F_1 and F_2 which provide the centripetal force. The equal and opposite reaction to them is the centrifugal force given by mv^2/r. This method of equating the forces acting on a moving object is known as D'Alembert's principle which will be explained more fully in Chapter 2.

Let the height of the centre of gravity be h.
Let the track width be $2a$.
Let the limiting coefficient of friction between the wheels and the road be μ.

To find the speed at which skidding is likely to occur, equate horizontal forces as the vehicle is about to skid.

centripetal force = centrifugal reaction

$$F_1 + F_2 = \frac{mv^2}{r}$$

BTEC National Study Guide: Engineering. See page 325 for order details of individual texts

217

In the limit as the vehicle is about to skid, $F_1 = \mu R_1$ and $F_2 = \mu R_2$. Substituting for these gives

$$\mu R_1 + \mu R_2 = \frac{mv^2}{r}$$

$$\mu(R_1 + R_2) = \frac{mv^2}{r}$$

But $R_1 + R_2 = m\,g$, the weight of the vehicle

$$\mu \cancel{m}g = \frac{\cancel{m}v^2}{r}$$

$$\mu rg = v^2$$

$$v = \sqrt{\mu rg} \tag{1.44}$$

To find the speed at which overturning is likely to occur, equate moments about the point A in the limit as the vehicle is about to overturn. In this condition, R_1 is zero as the nearside wheels are about to lift off the road and all the weight will be carried on the offside wheels.

clockwise overturning moment = anticlockwise righting moment

$$\frac{\cancel{m}v^2 h}{r} = \cancel{m}ga$$

$$v^2 = \frac{gar}{h}$$

$$v = \sqrt{\frac{arg}{h}} \tag{1.45}$$

Whichever of the equations (1.44) and (1.45) gives the lower value of velocity, that will be the limiting value. You should note that both values of limiting velocity are independent of the mass of the vehicle. Comparison of the two equations shows that

If $\mu < \dfrac{a}{h}$, the vehicle will skid before the overturning speed is reached.

If $\mu > \dfrac{a}{h}$, the vehicle will overturn before the skidding speed is reached.

The reaction of the outer wheels will always be greater than that of the inner wheels. To find these reactions at any speed below that at which overturning is likely, take moments about the point A again but this time include the moment of the reaction R_1.

clockwise overturning = anticlockwise righting
    moments   moment

$$\frac{mv^2}{r}h + R_1 2a = mga$$

$$R_1 2a = mga - \frac{mv^2}{r}h = m\left(ga - \frac{v^2 h}{r}\right)$$

$$R_1 = \frac{m}{2a}\left(ga - \frac{v^2}{r}h\right) \tag{1.46}$$

Now equate vertical forces to find the reaction of the outer wheels:

$$R_1 + R_2 = mg$$

$$R_2 = mg - R_1 \tag{1.47}$$

BTEC National Study Guide: Engineering. See page 325 for order details of individual texts

218

Example 1.21

A car of mass 900 kg travels round an unbanked horizontal curve of radius 30 m. The track width of the car is 1.5 m, and its centre of gravity is central and at a height of 0.9 m above the road surface. The limiting coefficient of friction between the tyres and the road is 0.7. Show that the car is likely to skid rather than overturn if the speed is excessive and calculate the maximum speed in km h^{-1} at which it can travel round the curve. Determine also the reactions of the inner and outer wheels at this speed.

Finding the ratio of half the track width to height of centre of gravity:

$$\frac{a}{h} = \frac{0.75}{0.9} = 0.833$$

Comparing this with the coefficient of friction, whose value is $\mu = 0.7$, shows that,

$$\mu < \frac{a}{h}$$

This indicates that the car will skid before the overturning speed is reached.

Finding speed at which car can travel round the curve, i.e. when skidding is likely to occur:

$$v = \sqrt{\mu r g} = \sqrt{0.7 \times 30 \times 9.81}$$
$$v = \textbf{14.35 m s}^{-1}$$

Changing to km h^{-1}

$$v = \frac{14.4 \times 60 \times 60}{1000}$$
$$v = \textbf{51.7 km h}^{-1}$$

Finding reaction R_1 of inner wheels by taking moments about point of contact of outer wheels and road:

$$R_1 = \frac{m}{2a}\left(ga - \frac{v^2}{r}h\right)$$
$$R_1 = \frac{900}{1.5}\left[(9.81 \times 0.75) - \frac{(14.35^2 \times 0.9)}{30}\right]$$
$$R_1 = \textbf{708 N}$$

Finding R_2 by equating vertical forces:

$$R_2 = mg - R_1 = (900 \times 9.81) - 708$$
$$R_2 = \textbf{8121 N} \quad \text{or} \quad \textbf{8.12 kN}$$

In practice the bends on major roads are banked to reduce the tendency for side-slip. When driving at the speed where there is no side-slip, the forces acting on a vehicle are as shown in Figure 1.69.

BTEC National Study Guide: Engineering. See page 325 for order details of individual texts

219

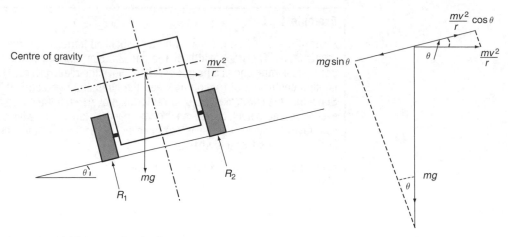

Figure 1.69 *Vehicle on a banked curve*

The speed at which there is no side-slip can be found by resolving forces parallel to the road surface. The two wheel reactions are perpendicular to the road surface, and are not involved. This just leaves the component of the weight down the slope, which is the active centripetal force, and the component of the centrifugal reaction up the slope. For no side-slip, these must be equal and opposite.

$$\frac{\cancel{m}v^2}{r}\cos\theta = \cancel{m}g\sin\theta$$

$$v^2 = rg\frac{\sin\theta}{\cos\theta} = rg\tan\theta$$

$$v = \sqrt{rg\tan\theta} \tag{1.48}$$

Key point

In the condition where there is no tendency for side-slip, the reactions of the inner and outer wheels are equal.

Example 1.22

A vehicle has a track width of 1.4 m and the height of its centre of gravity is 1.2 m above the road surface. The limiting coefficient of friction between the wheels and the road surface is 0.7.

(a) What is the maximum speed at which the vehicle can travel round a curve of radius 75 m?
(b) To what angle would the curve have to be banked for the vehicle to travel round it at a speed of 50 km h^{-1} without any tendency to side-slip?

(a) Finding the ratio of half the track width to height of centre of gravity:

$$\frac{a}{h} = \frac{0.7}{1.2} = 0.583$$

Comparing this with the coefficient of friction whose value is $\mu = 0.7$ shows that

$$\mu > \frac{a}{h}$$

This indicates that the car will overturn before the skidding speed is reached.

BTEC National Study Guide: Engineering. See page 325 for order details of individual texts

220

(b) Finding speed at which car can travel round the curve, i.e. when overturning is likely to occur:

$$v = \sqrt{\frac{arg}{h}} = \sqrt{\frac{0.7}{1.2} \times 75 \times 9.81}$$

$$v = 20.7 \,\text{m s}^{-1}$$

Changing to km h^{-1}

$$v = \frac{20.7 \times 60 \times 60}{1000}$$

$$v = 74.6 \,\text{km h}^{-1}$$

Changing $50\,\text{km h}^{-1}$ to m s^{-2},

$$v = \frac{50 \times 1000}{60 \times 60}$$

$$v = 13.9 \,\text{m s}^{-1}$$

Finding angle to which curve would need to be banked for no side-slip at this speed:

$$v = \sqrt{rg \tan \theta}$$

$$v^2 = rg \tan \theta$$

$$\tan \theta = \frac{v^2}{rg} = \frac{13.9^2}{75 \times 9.81}$$

$$\tan \theta = 0.262$$

$$\theta = 14.7°$$

Test your knowledge 1.10

1. What effect does the mass of a vehicle have on the maximum speed at which it can travel round a curve?
2. If $\mu < \frac{a}{h}$, is a vehicle likely to skid or overturn if its speed is excessive?
3. How is the centripetal force provided when a car travels round an unbanked curve?
4. How is the centripetal force provided when a car travels round a banked curve?

Activity 1.10

A vehicle of mass 1 tonne travels round a horizontal unbanked curve of radius 35 m. The track width of the vehicle is 1.8 m and the height of its centre of gravity above the road surface is 0.95 m. The coefficient of friction between the tyres and the road is 0.65.

(a) Show that if the speed of the vehicle is excessive, it is likely to skid rather than overturn.
(b) Calculate the speed at which skidding is likely to occur.
(c) Calculate the reactions of the inner and outer wheels at this speed.
(d) If the curve were to be banked at an angle of 3.5° what would be the speed at which the vehicle could travel around it without any tendency for side-slip?

Problems 1.8

1. A four-wheeled vehicle has a track width of 1.15 m and a mass of 750 kg. Its centre of gravity is 1.2 m above the road surface and equidistant from each of the wheels. What will be the reactions of the inner and outer wheels when travelling at a speed of $60\,\text{km h}^{-1}$ around a level curve of radius 80 m.

[6.4 kN, 961 N]

BTEC National Study Guide: Engineering. See page 325 for order details of individual texts

221

2. What is the maximum speed at which a car can travel over a hump-backed bridge whose radius of curvature is 18 m?

[47.8 km h^{-1}]

3. A railway wagon has a mass of 12 tonne and the height of its centre of gravity is 1.5 m above the rails. The track width is 1.37 m and the wagon travelling at 70 km h^{-1}. What is the minimum radius of level curve that the wagon can negotiate at this speed without overturning?

[84.4 m]

4. A car of mass 850 kg travels round an unbanked horizontal curve of radius 35 m. The limiting coefficient of friction between the tyres and the road is 0.65. The track width of the car is 1.65 m and its centre of gravity is central at a height of 0.8 m above the road surface. Show that the car is likely to skid rather than overturn if the speed is excessive and calculate the maximum speed in km h^{-1} at which it can travel round the curve. What will be the reactions of the inner and outer wheels at this speed?

[53.8 km h^{-1}, 1541 N, 4149 N]

5. The height of the centre of gravity of a four-wheeled vehicle is 1.1 m above the road surface and equidistant from each of the wheels. The track width is 1.5 m and the limiting coefficient of friction between the wheels and the road surface is 0.7. Determine (a) the maximum speed at which the vehicle can travel round a curve of radius 90 m, (b) the angle to which the curve would have to be banked for the vehicle to travel round it at a speed of 60 km h^{-1} without any tendency to side-slip?

[88.3 km h^{-1}, 17.5°]

Simple machines

A simple machine is an arrangement of moving parts whose purpose is to transmit motion and force. The ones which we will consider are those in which a relatively small input force is used to raise a heavy load. They include lever systems, inclined planes, screw jacks, wheel and axle arrangements, and gear trains.

For all simple machines the *mechanical advantage* or *force ratio* is the ratio of the load W, raised to the input effort E (Figure 1.70).

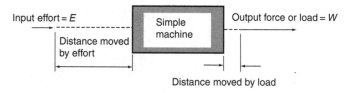

Figure 1.70 *Block diagram of a simple machine*

$$\text{mechanical advantage} = \frac{\text{load}}{\text{effort}}$$

$$MA = \frac{W}{E} \tag{1.49}$$

A characteristic of a simple machine is that the distance moved by the load is much smaller than the distance moved by the input

BTEC National Study Guide: Engineering. See page 325 for order details of individual texts

222

effort. The *velocity ratio* or *movement ratio* is used to measure this effect.

$$\text{velocity ratio} = \frac{\text{distance moved by effort}}{\text{distance moved by load}} \qquad (1.50)$$

or

$$\text{velocity ratio} = \frac{\text{velocity at which effort moves}}{\text{velocity at which load moves}} \qquad (1.51)$$

The efficiency η of a simple machine is the ratio of the work output to the work input. It is usually given as a percentage.

$$\text{efficiency} = \frac{\text{work output}}{\text{work input}}$$

$$\eta = \frac{\text{load} \times \text{distance moved by load}}{\text{effort} \times \text{distance moved by effort}} \times 100\%$$

$$\eta = MA \times \frac{1}{VR} \times 100\%$$

$$\eta = \frac{MA}{VR} \times 100\% \qquad (1.52)$$

> **Key point**
>
> The mechanical advantage is always less than the velocity ratio.
>
> The velocity ratio is a constant which depends on the dimensions of a machine's components.

There is always some friction between the moving parts of a machine. Some of the work input must be used to overcome friction and so the work output is always less than the input. As a result, the efficiency can never be 100% and it is very often a great deal less. If there were no friction present, the mechanical advantage would be equal to the velocity ratio. In practice it is always a lower figure.

Example 1.23

A jack requires an input effort of 25 N to raise a load of 150 kg. If the distance moved by the effort is 500 mm and the load is raised through a height of 6 mm, find (a) the mechanical advantage, (b) the velocity ratio, (c) the efficiency, (d) the work done in overcoming friction.

(a) Finding mechanical advantage:

$$MA = \frac{\text{load}}{\text{effort}} = \frac{150 \times 9.81}{25}$$

$$MA = 58.9$$

(b) Finding velocity ratio:

$$VR = \frac{\text{Distance moved by effort}}{\text{Distance moved by load}} = \frac{500}{6}$$

$$VR = 83.3$$

(c) Finding efficiency:

$$\eta = \frac{MA}{VR} = \frac{58.9}{83.3} \times 100\%$$

$$\eta = 70.7\%$$

BTEC National Study Guide: Engineering. See page 325 for order details of individual texts

223

(d) Finding work done in overcoming friction:

The work output is 70.7% of the work input. The remaining 29.3% of the work input is the work done in overcoming friction.

Friction work = work input $\times \frac{29.3}{100}$

Friction work = effort $\times$ distance effort moves $\times \frac{29.3}{100}$

Friction work = $25 \times 0.5 \times \frac{29.3}{100}$

Friction work = 3.66 J

Velocity ratio formulae

The expressions (1.50) and (1.51) are general formulae for calculating velocity ratio, and these can now be applied to a range of devices. Each will then have its own particular formula for velocity ratio which is dependent upon its dimensions and its mode of operation. For each device let the distance moved by the effort be a, and the corresponding distance moved by the load be b. That is,

$$\text{velocity ratio} = \frac{\text{distance moved by effort}}{\text{distance moved by load}}$$

$$VR = \frac{a}{b} \tag{1.53}$$

Simple lever systems

For both types of lever shown in Figure 1.71, the distances moved by the effort and the load are proportional to the distances x and y from the fulcrum of the lever.

$$VR = \frac{a}{b} = \frac{x}{y} \tag{1.54}$$

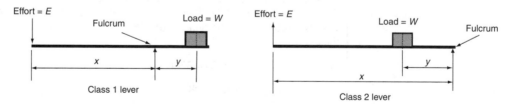

Figure 1.71 *Lever systems*

Inclined plane

In pulling the load up the incline, the effort moves through distance a whilst lifting the load through a vertical height b (Figure 1.72).

$$VR = \frac{a}{b} = \frac{\alpha}{\alpha \sin \theta}$$

$$VR = \frac{1}{\sin \theta} \tag{1.55}$$

BTEC National Study Guide: Engineering. See page 325 for order details of individual texts

224

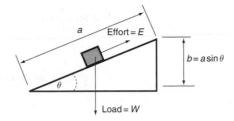

Figure 1.72 *Inclined plane*

Screw jack

The screw jack is a practical form of the inclined plane. The plane is now in the form of a spiral and the effort is applied horizontally to the end of the operating handle. One complete turn of the handle causes the load to rise through a distance equal to the pitch of the screw thread (Figure 1.73).

$$VR = \frac{\text{distance moved by effort in one revolution of screw thread}}{\text{pitch of screw thread}}$$

$$VR = \frac{2\pi r}{p} \tag{1.56}$$

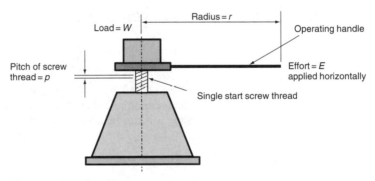

Figure 1.73 *Screw jack*

Pulley blocks

Here the velocity ratio is equal to the number of pulleys in operation or alternatively, the number of rope lengths connecting the pulleys, excluding the effort rope (Figure 1.74).

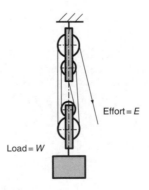

Figure 1.74 *Pulley blocks*

BTEC National Study Guide: Engineering. See page 325 for order details of individual texts

225

$$VR = \textbf{number of pulleys} \qquad (1.57)$$

or

$$VR = \textbf{number of connecting rope lengths} \qquad (1.58)$$

Weston differential pulley block

This comprises a compound pulley with diameters D_1 and D_2, and a snatch block which carries the load. They are connected by an endless chain to which the effort is applied as shown in Figure 1.75.

For one rotation of the compound pulley, the chain is wound onto the larger diameter and off the smaller diameter. That part of the chain passing round the snatch block shortens by a length equal to the difference between the circumferences of the compound pulley. The load is raised by half of this distance.

$$VR = \frac{\text{circumference of larger compound pulley}}{\text{half the difference of the compound pulley circumferences}}$$

$$VR = \frac{\pi D_1}{\frac{\pi D_1 - \pi D_2}{2}} = \frac{\cancel{\pi} D_1}{\frac{\cancel{\pi}(D_1 - D_2)}{2}}$$

$$VR = \frac{2D_1}{(D_1 - D_2)} \qquad (1.59)$$

The links of the chain engage on teeth or 'flats' which are cut on the compound pulley. If the numbers of flats n_1 and n_2, are known, they too can be used to calculate the velocity ratio.

$$VR = \frac{2n_1}{(n_1 - n_2)} \qquad (1.60)$$

You will note that it is the difference between the diameters on the compound pulley which determines the velocity ratio. The closer the two diameters, the higher will be the velocity ratio.

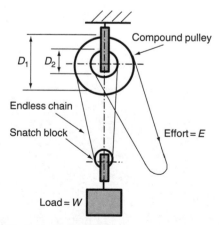

Figure 1.75 *Differential pulley block*

BTEC National Study Guide: Engineering. See page 325 for order details of individual texts

226

Simple wheel and axle

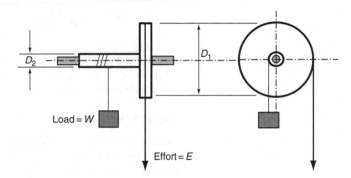

Figure 1.76 *Simple wheel and axle*

For one revolution of the wheel and axle, the effort moves a distance equal to the wheel circumference and the load is raised through a distance equal to the axle circumference (Figure 1.76).

$$VR = \frac{\text{circumference of wheel}}{\text{circumference of axle}} = \frac{\pi D_1}{\pi D_2}$$

$$VR = \frac{D_1}{D_2} \tag{1.61}$$

Differential wheel and axle

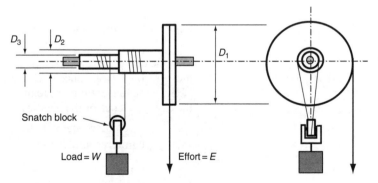

Figure 1.77 *Differential wheel and axle*

Here the wheel, whose diameter is D_1, has a compound axle with two diameters, D_2 and D_3. The two axle diameters are wound in opposite directions with the same cord which also passes round the snatch block. For one revolution of the wheel, the effort moves a distance equal to the wheel's circumference. At the same time the length of cord around the snatch block shortens by a length equal to the difference between the two axle circumferences, and the load is raised by a distance which is half of this difference (Figure 1.77).

$$VR = \frac{\text{circumference of wheel}}{\text{half the difference of the axle circumferences}}$$

BTEC National Study Guide: Engineering. See page 325 for order details of individual texts

227

$$VR = \frac{\pi D_1}{\frac{\pi D_2 - \pi D_3}{2}} = \frac{\not{\pi} D_1}{\frac{\not{\pi}(D_2 - D_3)}{2}}$$

$$VR = \frac{2D_1}{(D_2 - D_3)} \tag{1.62}$$

You will note that it is not only the wheel diameter, but also the difference between the two axle diameters which determines the velocity ratio. The closer the two axle diameters, the higher will be the velocity ratio for a given wheel size.

Simple gear winch

The number of teeth on the gears A and B in the speed reduction gear train are t_A and t_B respectively (Figure 1.78). The gear ratio, or velocity ratio, of the simple gear train alone will be

$$\text{gear ratio} = \frac{t_A}{t_B}$$

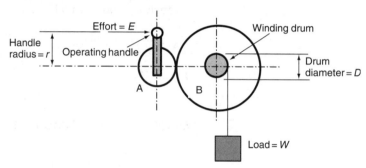

Figure 1.78 *Simple gear winch*

For one complete revolution of the operating handle, the effort will move through a distance equal to the circumference of its turning circle. At the same time, the load will rise through a distance equal to the circumference of the winding drum multiplied by the gear ratio.

$$VR = \frac{\text{circumference of handle turning circle}}{\text{circumference of winding drum} \times \text{gear ratio}}$$

$$VR = \frac{2 \not{\pi} r}{\not{\pi} D \times \left(\dfrac{t_A}{t_B}\right)}$$

$$VR = \frac{2rt_B}{Dt_A} \tag{1.63}$$

Compound gear winch or crab winch

The numbers of teeth on gears A, B, C and D are t_A, t_B, t_C and t_D respectively. Gears B and C are keyed on the same shaft and rotate together to form a compound gear (Figure 1.79). The gear ratio or velocity ratio of the compound reduction gear train alone will be

$$\text{gear ratio} = \frac{t_A}{t_B} \times \frac{t_C}{t_D}$$

BTEC National Study Guide: Engineering. See page 325 for order details of individual texts

228

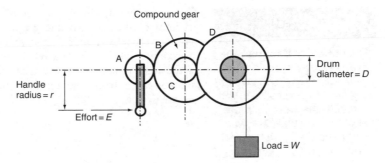

Figure 1.79 *Crab winch*

As with the simple gear winch, one complete revolution of the operating handle will cause the effort to move through a distance equal to the circumference of its turning circle. At the same time the load will rise through a distance equal to the circumference of the winding drum multiplied by the gear ratio.

$$VR = \frac{\text{circumference of handle turning circle}}{\text{circumference of winding drum} \times \text{gear ratio}}$$

$$VR = \frac{2\cancel{\pi}r}{\cancel{\pi}D \times \left(\dfrac{t_A}{t_B} \times \dfrac{t_C}{t_D}\right)}$$

$$VR = \frac{2r}{D}\left(\frac{t_B}{t_A} \times \frac{t_D}{t_C}\right) \tag{1.64}$$

Law of a machine

When a range of load and the corresponding effort values are tabulated for any of the above machines, a graph of effort against load is found to have the straight line form shown in Figure 1.80(a).

The equation of graph in Figure 1.80(a) is

$$E = aW + b \tag{1.65}$$

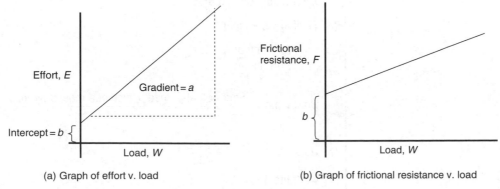

(a) Graph of effort v. load

(b) Graph of frictional resistance v. load

Figure 1.80 *Graphs of effort and frictional resistance v. load*

BTEC National Study Guide: Engineering. See page 325 for order details of individual texts

229

Key point

Frictional resistance increases with load and some of the effort is required to overcome it. As a result, the work output is always less than the work input and the efficiency can never be 100%.

This is known as the *law of the machine*. The constant *a*, is the gradient of the straight line graph. The constant *b*, is the intercept on the effort axis. This is the effort initially required to overcome friction before any load can be lifted. It is found that as the load is increased, the frictional resistance in the mechanism increases from the initial value *b*, in a linear fashion as shown in Figure 1.80(b).

Example 1.24

A differential wheel and axle has a wheel diameter of 275 mm and axle diameters of 50 mm and 100 mm. The law of the machine is $E = 0.11\,W + 4.5$. Determine (a) the velocity ratio of the device, (b) mechanical advantage and efficiency when raising a load of 25 kg, (c) the work input which is required to raise the load through a height of 1.5 m.

(a) Finding velocity ratio:

$$VR = \frac{2D_1}{(D_2 - D_3)} = \frac{2 \times 275}{(100 - 50)}$$

$VR = 11$

(b) Finding effort required to raise a mass of 25 kg:

$$E = 0.15\,W + 4.5 = (0.11 \times 25 \times 9.81) + 4.5$$

$E = 31.5\,N$

Finding mechanical advantage when raising this load:

$$MA = \frac{W}{E} = \frac{25 \times 9.81}{31.5}$$

$MA = 7.79$

Finding efficiency when raising this load:

$$\eta = \frac{MA}{VR} = \frac{7.79}{11}$$

$\eta = 0.708$ or 70.8%

(c) Finding work input:

$$\eta = \frac{\text{work output}}{\text{work input}}$$

$$\text{work input} = \frac{\text{work output}}{\eta} = \frac{\text{load} \times \text{distance moved by load}}{\eta}$$

$$\text{work input} = \frac{25 \times 9.81 \times 1.5}{0.708}$$

work input $= 520\,J$

BTEC National Study Guide: Engineering. See page 325 for order details of individual texts

230

Limiting efficiency and mechanical advantage

It is found that the efficiency of a simple machine increases with load but not in a linear fashion.

As can be seen in Figure 1.81, the efficiency eventually levels off at a limiting value. This is found to depend on the constant a, in the law of the machine, and its velocity ratio.

$$\text{efficiency} = \frac{\text{mechanical advantage}}{\text{velocity ratio}}$$

$$\eta = \frac{MA}{VR} = \frac{W}{E \times VR}$$

Now, from the law of the machine, $E = aW + b$

$$\eta = \frac{W}{(aW + b) \times VR}$$

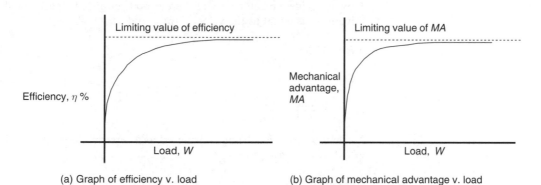

Efficiency, η %

Limiting value of efficiency

Load, W

Mechanical advantage, MA

Limiting value of MA

Load, W

(a) Graph of efficiency v. load

(b) Graph of mechanical advantage v. load

Figure 1.81 *Variation of efficiency and mechanical advantage with load*

Dividing numerator and denominator by W gives

$$\eta = \frac{1}{\left(a + \dfrac{b}{W}\right) \times VR}$$

$$\eta = \frac{1}{a\,VR + \dfrac{b}{W}\,VR} \tag{1.66}$$

Examination of this expression shows that as the load W, increases, the second term in the denominator becomes smaller and smaller. When the load becomes very large, this term tends to zero and the limiting value of efficiency is

$$\eta = \frac{1}{a\,VR} \tag{1.67}$$

In this limiting condition the mechanical advantage levels off to a value given by

$$\eta = \frac{MA}{VR}$$

$$MA = \eta \times VR$$

$$MA = \frac{1}{a} \tag{1.68}$$

The limiting value of mechanical advantage is thus the reciprocal of the gradient of the effort v. load graph.

Key point

The mechanical advantage and the efficiency of a simple machine increase with load but eventually level off at a limiting value.

BTEC National Study Guide: Engineering. See page 325 for order details of individual texts

231

Overhauling

A simple machine is said to *overhaul* if when the effort is removed, the load falls under the effects of gravity. If a machine does not overhaul, then friction alone must be sufficient to support the load. If you have changed a wheel on a car you probably used a screw jack to raise the wheel off the road surface. Friction in the screw thread is then sufficient to support the car. This means, of course that there must be quite a lot of friction present which results in a low value of efficiency. This however is the price that often has to be paid for safety in lifting devices such as car jacks and engine hoists.

Frictional resistance can be considered as an additional load which the effort must overcome.

$$\frac{\text{total}}{\text{effort}} = \frac{\text{effort to overcome}}{\text{friction load, } F} + \frac{\text{effort to overcome}}{\text{actual load, } W}$$

Now in an ideal machine where there is no friction, the mechanical advantage is equal to the velocity ratio and

$$VR = MA = \frac{\text{load}}{\text{effort}}$$

and

$$\text{effort} = \frac{\text{load}}{VR} = \frac{W}{VR}$$

If friction force, F is being considered as a separate load, the total effort can be written as

$$\text{total effort} = \frac{F}{VR} + \frac{W}{VR}$$

$$E = \frac{F + W}{VR} \tag{1.69}$$

Now, the efficiency is given by

$$\eta = \frac{MA}{VR} = \frac{W}{E \times VR}$$

Substituting for E gives

$$\eta = \frac{W}{\left(\dfrac{F + W}{VR}\right) VR}$$

$$\eta = \frac{W}{F + W} \tag{1.70}$$

When the effort is removed there is only the frictional resistance F, to oppose the load W. To stop it overhauling the friction force must be equal or greater than the load. In the limit when $F = W$, the efficiency will be

$$\eta = \frac{W}{2W} = 0.5 \quad \text{or} \quad 50\% \tag{1.71}$$

It follows that a machine will overhaul if its efficiency is greater than 50%.

BTEC National Study Guide: Engineering. See page 325 for order details of individual texts

232

Example 1.25

The law of the gear winch shown in Figure 1.82 is $E = 0.0105\,W + 5.5$ and it is required to raise a load of 150 kg. Determine, (a) its velocity ratio, (b) the effort required at the operating handle, (c) the mechanical advantage and efficiency when raising this load, (d) the limiting mechanical advantage and efficiency and (e) state whether the winch is likely to overhaul when raising the 150 kg load.

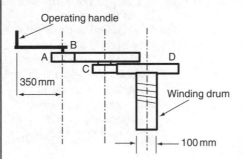

Operating handle

Teeth on gear A = 16
Teeth on gear B = 72
Teeth on gear C = 18
Teeth on gear D = 60

350 mm

Winding drum

100 mm

Figure 1.82

(a) Finding velocity ratio:

$$VR = \frac{2r}{D}\left(\frac{t_B}{t_A} \times \frac{t_D}{t_C}\right) = \frac{2 \times 350}{100}\left(\frac{72 \times 60}{16 \times 18}\right)$$

$$\boldsymbol{VR = 105}$$

(b) Finding effort required:

$$E = 0.0105\,W + 5.5 = (0.0105 \times 150 \times 9.81) + 5.5$$

$$\boldsymbol{E = 21.0\,N}$$

(c) Finding mechanical advantage:

$$MA = \frac{W}{E} = \frac{150 \times 9.81}{21.0}$$

$$\boldsymbol{MA = 70.1}$$

Finding efficiency:

$$\eta = \frac{MA}{VR} = \frac{70.1}{105}$$

$$\boldsymbol{\eta = 0.668} \quad \text{or} \quad \boldsymbol{66.8\%}$$

(d) Finding limiting mechanical advantage:

$$\text{limiting } MA = \frac{1}{a} \quad (\text{where } a = 0.0105, \text{from the law of the machine})$$

$$\text{limiting } \boldsymbol{MA = \frac{1}{0.0105} = 95.2}$$

Finding limiting efficiency:

$$\text{limiting } \eta = \frac{1}{aVR}$$

$$\text{limiting } \boldsymbol{\eta = \frac{1}{0.0105 \times 105} = 0.907} \quad \text{or} \quad \boldsymbol{90.7\%}$$

(e) When raising the 150 kg load the efficiency is greater than 50% and so the winch will overhaul under these conditions.

Test your knowledge 1.11

1. How does the mechanical advantage of a simple machine vary with the load raised?
2. How does the frictional resistance in a simple machine vary with the load raised?
3. How is the efficiency of a simple machine defined?
4. What information does the law of a machine contain?
5. What is meant by overhauling and how can it be predicted?

BTEC National Study Guide: Engineering. See page 325 for order details of individual texts

233

Activity 1.11

A screw jack has a single start thread of pitch 6 mm and an operating handle of radius 450 mm. The following readings of load and effort were taken during a test on the jack.

Load (kN)	0	1	2	3	4	5	6	7	8	9	10
Effort (N)	2.2	6.6	11.8	17.0	22.2	27.2	32.2	36.8	41.4	46.9	52.4

(a) Plot a graph of effort against load and from it, determine the law of the machine.
(b) Plot a graph of mechanical advantage against load.
(c) Plot a graph of efficiency against load and state whether the machine is likely to overhaul.
(d) Calculate the theoretical limiting values of mechanical advantage and efficiency, and state whether your graphs tend towards these values.
(e) Calculate the work input and the work done against friction when raising the 10 kN load through a height of 50 mm.

Problems 1.9

1. A screw jack has a single start thread of pitch 10 mm and is used to raise a load of 900 kg. The required effort is 75 N, applied at the end of an operating handle 600 mm long. For these operating conditions, determine (a) the mechanical advantage, (b) the velocity ratio, (c) the efficiency of the machine.

[118, 377, 31.3%]

2. The top pulleys of a Weston differential pulley block have diameters of 210 mm and 190 mm. Determine the effort required to raise a load of 150 kg if the efficiency of the system is 35%. What is the work done in overcoming friction when the load is raised through a height of 2.5 m?

[200 N, 6.83 kJ]

3. A differential wheel and axle has a wheel diameter of 300 mm and axle diameters of 100 mm and 75 mm. The effort required to raise a load of 50 kg is 55 N and the effort required to raise a load of 200 kg is 180 N. Determine (a) the velocity ratio, (b) the law of the machine, (c) the efficiency of the machine when raising a load of 100 kg.

[24, $E = 0.085\,W + 13.3$, 42.3%]

4.

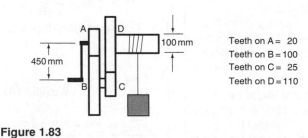

Teeth on A = 20
Teeth on B = 100
Teeth on C = 25
Teeth on D = 110

Figure 1.83

BTEC National Study Guide: Engineering. See page 325 for order details of individual texts

234

The crab winch shown in Figure 1.83 has a law of the form $E = 0.01\,W + 7.5$. Determine (a) its velocity ratio, (b) its mechanical advantage and efficiency when raising a load of 50 kg, (c) the limiting values of its mechanical advantage and efficiency.

[198, 20%, 100, 50.5%]

Belt drives

Power is often transmitted between parallel shafts by means of a belt running on pulleys attached to the shafts. Belt drives are friction drives. They depend on the frictional resistance around the arcs of contact between the belt and the pulleys in order to transmit torque. You will find many examples of belt drives in everyday life. The alternator and water pump on most car engines are driven by a belt from a pulley on the crankshaft. Washing machine drums and tumble dryers are also driven by a belt from an electric motor.

Torque is transmitted from the driving to the driven pulley as a result of the difference in tension which is present on opposite sides of the belt. As more and more torque is transmitted, a point is reached where the frictional resistance has a limiting value. Here the belt begins to slip. Slipping always occurs on the smaller of the two pulleys where the arc of contact, or 'angle of lap' is least. Compared with geared systems, chain drives and shaft drives, belt drives have certain advantages.

- They are automatically protected against overload because slipping occurs if the load exceeds the maximum which can be sustained by friction.
- The initial tension to which the belt is set can be adjusted to determine the load at which slipping occurs.
- The length of the belt can be selected to suit a wide range of shaft centre distances.
- Different sizes of pulley may be used to step up or step down the rotational speed.
- The cost is less than for the equivalent gear train or chain drive.

Consider a typical belt drive in which torque is transmitted from a driving pulley A, to a driven pulley B as in Figure 1.84.

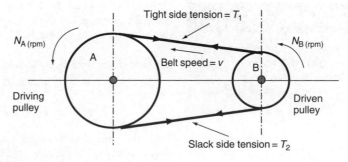

Figure 1.84 *Belt drive*

BTEC National Study Guide: Engineering. See page 325 for order details of individual texts

235

The velocity ratio of the belt drive is given by

$$VR = \frac{\text{input speed}}{\text{output speed}}$$

$$VR = \frac{N_A}{N_B} = \frac{\omega_A}{\omega_B} \tag{1.72}$$

Alternatively, the velocity ratio may be found from the pulley dimensions. Now, pulley speed is inversely proportional to size so if you use the pulley diameters or radii, remember to invert the subscript letters as follows:

$$VR = \frac{D_B}{D_A} = \frac{r_B}{r_A} \tag{1.73}$$

The speed of the belt can be found from either of the pulley speeds. First, change the speed in revolutions per minute to angular velocity in radians per second. Then, multiply by the appropriate pulley radius to change angular velocity to belt speed in metres per second.

For pulley A,

$$\omega_A = N_A \times \frac{2\pi}{60} \quad \text{and} \quad v = \omega_A \, r_A \tag{1.74}$$

For pulley B,

$$\omega_B = N_B \times \frac{2\pi}{60} \quad \text{and} \quad v = \omega_B \, r_B \tag{1.75}$$

The power transmitted from A to B is given by

power = resultant belt tension × belt speed

$$\textbf{power} = (\textbf{\textit{T}}_1 - \textbf{\textit{T}}_2)\, \textbf{\textit{v}} \tag{1.76}$$

Power loss in the shaft bearings is usually negligible compared to the power transmitted and it can be assumed that

input power = output power

input torque × input angular velocity = output torque × output angular velocity

$$T_A \times \omega_A = T_B \times \omega_B$$

$$\frac{T_A}{T_B} = \frac{\omega_B}{\omega_A} = \frac{1}{VR} \tag{1.77}$$

The material from which a belt is made, is assumed to be perfectly elastic so that when the drive is taken up, the increase in tension on the tight side is equal to the decrease in tension on the slack side. If the initial tension setting is T_0, then

increase in tension on tight side = decrease in tension on slack side

$$T_1 - T_0 = T_0 - T_2$$

$$\textbf{\textit{T}}_1 + \textbf{\textit{T}}_2 = 2\textbf{\textit{T}}_0 \tag{1.78}$$

Both flat and V-section belts are used in belt drives. It is found that V-section belts can transmit more power before slipping occurs because of the wedge action between the belt and the

> **Key point**
>
> The maximum power which a belt drive can transmit before slipping occurs depends on its initial tension setting.

BTEC National Study Guide: Engineering. See page 325 for order details of individual texts

236

Key point

V-section belts are able to transmit more power than a flat belt of the same material and tension setting. This is because the wedge action of the belt in the pulley grooves gives increased frictional resistance.

sides of the V-shaped pulley. It is possible to calculate the ratio of the tight and slack side tensions at which slipping takes place. If you continue your studies to a higher level you will derive the formulae used.

For flat belts, slipping typically occurs when $\dfrac{T_1}{T_2} = 2 - 2.5$

For V-section belts, slipping typically occurs when $\dfrac{T_1}{T_2} = 6 - 15$

Example 1.26

In a belt drive, the smaller driving pulley A has a diameter of 110 mm and rotates at a speed of 500 rpm. The larger driven pulley B, has a diameter of 275 mm. The tension in the belt is not to exceed 2 kN and the initial tension setting is 1.2 kN. Find (a) the angular velocity of the driven pulley, (b) the belt speed, (c) the limiting slack side tension, (d) the maximum power that the belt can transmit, (e) the maximum output torque.

(a) Finding velocity ratio:

$$VR = \frac{D_B}{D_A} = \frac{275}{110}$$

$VR = 2.5$

Finding output speed:

$$VR = \frac{N_A}{N_B}$$

$$N_B = \frac{N_A}{VR} = \frac{500}{2.5}$$

$N_B = 200$ rpm

Changing to angular velocity in radss^{-1}

$$\omega_B = N_B \times \frac{2\pi}{60} = 200 \times \frac{2\pi}{60}$$

$\omega_B = 20.9$ rad s^{-1}

(b) Finding belt speed from angular velocity of pulley B:

$$v = \omega_B r_B = 20.9 \times \frac{275 \times 10^{-3}}{2}$$

$v = 2.87$ m s^{-1}

(c) Finding the slack side tension when the tight side tension is 2 kN:

$$2\,T_0 = T_1 + T_2$$

$$2 \times 1200 = 2000 + T_2$$

$$2400 = 2000 = T_2$$

$$T_2 = 2400 - 2000$$

$T_2 = 400$ N

BTEC National Study Guide: Engineering. See page 325 for order details of individual texts

237

1. Where is slipping likely to occur on a belt drive?
2. How can a belt drive be adjusted to alter the load at which slipping occurs?
3. Why is a V-section belt drive able to transmit more power before slipping than a flat belt of the same material and tension setting?
4. What is the relationship between the velocity ratio of a belt drive and the ratio of the input and output torques?

(d) Finding maximum power that the belt can transmit:

$$\text{maximum power} = (T_1 - T_2)v$$
$$\text{maximum power} = (2000 - 400) \times 2.87$$
$$\textbf{maximum power} = \textbf{4.59} \times \textbf{10}^3 \textbf{ W} \quad \text{or} \quad \textbf{4.59 kW}$$

(e) Finding maximum output torque T_B:

$$\text{maximum power} = \text{output torque} \times \text{output angular velocity}$$
$$\text{maximum power} = T_B \omega_B$$
$$T_B = \frac{\text{maximum power}}{\omega_B} = \frac{4.59 \times 10^3}{20.9}$$
$$T_B = \textbf{220 N m}$$

Activity 1.12

A flat belt connects a driving pulley of diameter 350 mm and a driven pulley of diameter 150 mm. The driving pulley rotates at 250 rpm and the belt is given an initial tension of 1 kN. When the belt is on the point of slipping, the ratio of the tight and slack side tensions is 2.5. Find (a) the angular velocity of the driven pulley, (b) the belt speed, (c) the tight and slack side tensions when the belt is on the point of slipping, (d) the maximum power which can be transmitted, (e) the maximum output torque.

Problems 1.10

1. A belt drive for speed reduction has pulley diameters of 180 mm and 320 mm. The tight side tension is to be limited to 500 N and it is required to transmit 1.5 kW with an output speed of 400 rpm. Determine (a) the input torque, (b) belt speed, (c) the limiting slack side tension, (d) the initial tension to which the belt should be set. Friction losses may be neglected.

   [20.1 N m, 6.71 m s^{-1}, 276 N, 388 N]

2. A belt drive is set to an initial tension of 350 N. The driving pulley is 300 mm in diameter and rotates at 500 rpm. The driven pulley is 200 mm in diameter and friction losses may be neglected. If the tight side tension is to be limited to 600 N, determine (a) the limiting slack side tension, (b) the belt speed, (c) the maximum power that the belt can transmit, (d) the maximum values of input and output torque.

   [100 N, 7.85 m s^{-1}, 3.93 kW, 75 Nm, 50 N m]

3. The input pulley of a belt drive is 150 mm in diameter and rotates at a speed of 600 rpm. The output pulley is 350 mm in diameter and it can be assumed that there are no friction losses in the bearings. The belt is initially set to a tension of 200 N

BTEC National Study Guide: Engineering. See page 325 for order details of individual texts

238

and slipping occurs when the tight and slack side tensions are in the ratio 10:1. Determine (a) the limiting tight and slack side tensions, (b) the maximum power which can be transmitted, (c) the output torque.

[36 N, 400 N, 1.71 kW, 81.8 N m]

Plane linkage mechanisms

Machines are devices in which the input work, or energy, is converted into a more useful form in order to do a particular job of work. The screw jacks, pulley systems and gear winches, which we have already examined, are examples of simple machines. Here the input power, which may be manual or from a motor, is converted into a lifting force.

Machines may contain a number of parts. Levers, transmission shafts, pulleys, lead screws, gears, belts and chains are all typical machine components. Machines may also contain rigid links. The crank, connecting rods and pistons in an internal combustion engine are links. Car suspension units are made up of links and they are also to be found in machine tools, photocopiers and printers. A *linkage mechanism* may be defined as a device which transmits or transfers motion from one point to another.

Two of the most common plane linkage mechanisms are the slider-crank and the four-bar chain shown in Figure 1.85.

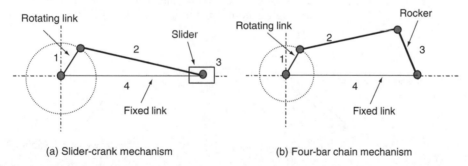

(a) Slider-crank mechanism   (b) Four-bar chain mechanism

Figure 1.85 *Linkage mechanisms*

With the slider-crank mechanism, the crank (1) rotates at a uniform speed and imparts a reciprocating translational motion to the piston (3). It is said to have an input rotation and output translation. The connecting link (2) has both a rotational and translational motion and link (4) is formed by the stationary machine frame or cylinder block.

With the four-bar linkage the crank (1) rotates at a uniform speed and imparts a rocking rotational motion to the output link (3). It has input rotation and output rotation. Here again, the connecting link (2) has both a rotational and translational motion and link (4) is formed by the stationary machine frame.

The nature of the output rotation can be altered by changing the lengths of the links. Different output characteristics can also be obtained by fixing a different link in the chain. Such mechanisms are called *inversions* of the slider crank and four-bar chain. Whatever the arrangement, there are three types of link in the above mechanisms.

Key point

A link may have linear motion, rotational motion, or a combination of the two. Translational motion is another name for linear motion.

BTEC National Study Guide: Engineering. See page 325 for order details of individual texts

239

1. *Links which have translational motion*
   These are links such as the piston (4) in the slider-crank. Here, all points on the link have the same linear velocity. The velocity vector diagram for such a link is shown in Figure 1.86.

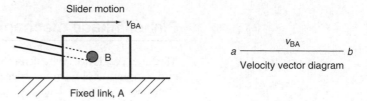

Figure 1.86 *Slider velocity vector*

The velocity vector *ab* gives the magnitude and direction of the piston velocity. No arrow is necessary. The sequence of the letters, *a* to *b*, gives the direction. The notation v_{BA}, indicates that this is the velocity of the piston B, relative to a point A on the fixed link or machine frame. The notation is similar to that which we have already used on force vector diagrams, where upper case letters are used on the space diagram and lower case letters on the vector diagram.

2. *Links with rotational motion*
   These are links where one end rotates about a fixed axis through a point on the link. Link (1) in the slider crank and

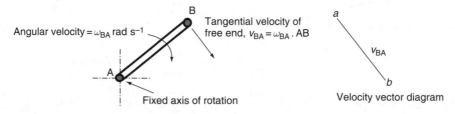

Figure 1.87 *Rotating link velocity vector*

links (1) and (4) in the four-bar chain are of this type. The velocity vector diagram for such a link is shown in Figure 1.87.

Here the velocity vector *ab*, gives the magnitude and direction of the velocity of the free end B, as it rotates about the fixed axis through the end A, i.e. in the direction *a* to *b*. The notation v_{BA} again indicates that this is the velocity of B relative to A.

3. *Links which have a combined translational and rotational motion*
   Links such as the connecting link (2) in both the slider crank and the four-bar chain are of this type. The velocity vector diagram for such a link is shown in Figure 1.88.

Here the two ends of the link BC are moving in different directions at the instant shown. This gives both a rotational and translational motion to the link. The two velocity vectors *ab* and *ac* are drawn from the same point and the vector *bc* is the velocity of C relative to B. In other words, if you sat on the end B, looking at C, that is what its velocity v_{CB}, would appear to be. You should

BTEC National Study Guide: Engineering. See page 325 for order details of individual texts

240

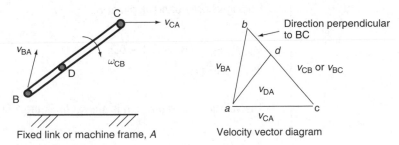

Figure 1.88 *Velocity vector diagram for link with translational and rotational motion*

note that the direction of the vector *bc* is always perpendicular to the link BC.

If you sat on the end B looking at C, it would also appear to be rotating about you with angular velocity ω_{CB}. This angular velocity can be calculated by dividing v_{CB} by the radius of rotation which is the length BC. That is,

$$\omega_{CB} = \frac{v_{CB}}{CB} \qquad (1.79)$$

Alternatively, if you sat on the end C, looking at B, it would appear to be moving with velocity v_{BC} which is given by the vector *cb*. The velocity vector diagram also enables the velocity of any point D, on the link to be measured. Suppose that the point D is one third of the way along the link from the end B. The point *d*, on the vector diagram is similarly located at one third of the distance *bc* measured from *b*. The vector *ad* then gives the velocity v_{DA} of the point D relative to the fixed point A.

Key point

When the two ends of a link are travelling in different directions, the velocity of one end relative to the other is always at right angles to the link.

Example 1.27

In the slider-crank mechanism shown in Figure 1.89, the crank AB is of length 200 mm and the connecting rod BC is of length 800 mm. The crank rotates clockwise at a steady speed of 240 rpm. At the instant shown, determine (a) the velocity of the crank pin at B, (b) the velocity of the piston, (c) the velocity of the point D which is at the centre of the connecting rod, (d) the angular velocity of the connecting rod.

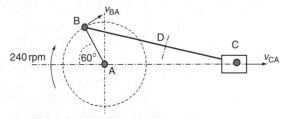

Figure 1.89

(a) Finding angular velocity of crank:

$$\omega_{BA} = N \times \frac{2\pi}{60} = 240 \times \frac{2\pi}{60}$$

$$\omega_{BA} = 25.1 \text{ rad s}^{-1}$$

BTEC National Study Guide: Engineering. See page 325 for order details of individual texts

241

Finding velocity of crank pin at B:

$$v_{BA} = \omega_{BA} \times AB = 25.1 \times 0.2$$
$$v_{BA} = 5.03\,\text{m s}^{-1}$$

The velocity vector diagram is shown in Figure 1.90.

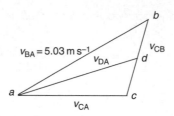

Figure 1.90

1. Draw vector *ab* for v_{BA} to a suitable scale.
2. From the point *a*, draw in a horizontal construction line for the direction of vector *ac*.
3. From the point *b*, draw a construction line perpendicular to the connecting rod BC for the vector *bc*. The intersection of the two construction lines fixes the point *c*.
4. Locate the point *d* which is the mid-point of vector *bc* and draw in the vector *ad*.

(b) Finding velocity of piston v_{CA}:
From diagram,

$$v_{CA} = ac = 3.8\,\text{m s}^{-1}$$

(c) Finding v_{DA}, which is the velocity of D, the mid-point of the connecting rod:
From diagram,

$$v_{DA} = ad = 4.3\,\text{m s}^{-1}$$

(d) Finding v_{CB}, which is the velocity of C relative to B:
From diagram,

$$v_{CB} = bc = 2.6\,\text{m s}^{-1}$$

Finding v_{CB}, which is the velocity of the conecting rod:

$$\omega_{CB} = \frac{v_{CB}}{BC} = \frac{2.6}{0.8}$$
$$\omega_{CB} = 3.25\,\text{m s}^{-1}$$

BTEC National Study Guide: Engineering. See page 325 for order details of individual texts

242

Example 1.28

In the four-bar linkage shown in Figure 1.91, AB = 200 mm, BC = 250 mm, CD = 200 mm and the distance between the axes of rotation at A and D is 500 mm. At the instant shown, the crank AB is rotating clockwise at a speed of 300 rpm. Determine (a) the angular velocity of the crank AB and the velocity of the point B, (b) the velocity of the point C and the angular velocity of the rocker CD, (c) the velocity of the point E on the connecting rod BC which is 100 mm from B, (d) the angular velocity of the connecting rod.

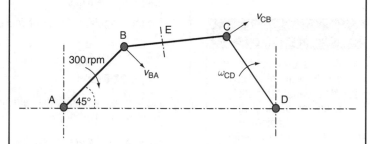

Figure 1.91

(a) Finding angular velocity of crank:

$$\omega_{BA} = N \times \frac{2\pi}{60} = 300 \times \frac{2\pi}{60}$$

$$\omega_{BA} = 31.4 \, \text{rad s}^{-1}$$

Finding velocity of B:

$$v_{BA} = \omega_{BA} \times AB = 31.4 \times 0.2$$

$$\boldsymbol{v_{BA} = 6.28 \, \text{m s}^{-1}}$$

The vector diagram is shown in Figure 1.92.

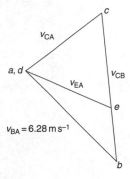

Figure 1.92

1. Draw vector *ab* for v_{BA} to a suitable scale.
2. From the point *a*, draw in a construction line in a direction at right angles to DC for the vector *dc*.

BTEC National Study Guide: Engineering. See page 325 for order details of individual texts

243

3. From the point b, draw a construction line perpendicular to the connecting rod BC for the vector bc. The intersection of the two construction lines fixes the point c.

4. Locate the point e, on vector bc such that

$$\frac{BE}{EC} = \frac{be}{ec} = \frac{100}{150} = \frac{2}{3}$$

5. Draw in the vector ae which gives the velocity of the point E.

(b) Finding velocity v_{CD}, of the point C:
From diagram,

$$v_{AD} = ac = 4.5\,\text{m s}^{-1}$$

Finding angular velocity of rocker CD:

$$\omega_{CD} = \frac{v_{CD}}{CD} = \frac{4.5}{0.2}$$

$$\omega_{CD} = 22.5\,\text{rad s}^{-1}$$

(c) Finding v_{EA}, which is the velocity of E, on the connecting rod:
From diagram,

$$v_{EA} = ae = 4.4\,\text{m s}^{-1}$$

(d) Finding v_{CB}, which is the velocity of C relative of B:
From diagram,

$$v_{CB} = bc = 7.1\,\text{m s}^{-1}$$

Finding ω_{CB}, the angular velocity of the connecting rod:

$$\omega_{CB} = \frac{v_{CB}}{BC} = \frac{7.1}{0.25}$$

$$\omega_{CB} = 28.4\,\text{rad s}^{-1}$$

Test your knowledge 1.13

1. What is the function of a linkage mechanism?
2. What constitutes the fixed link of the slider-crank mechanism in an internal combustion engine?
3. What is meant by an *inversion* of a slider-crank or four-bar chain mechanism?
4. Describe the lettering system used on space diagrams and velocity vector diagrams for plane mechanisms.

Activity 1.13

In the plane mechanism shown in Figure 1.93, the crank AB is rotating clockwise at 250 rpm at the instant shown. The links have the following dimensions:

AB = 165 mm
BC = 240 mm
CD = 200 mm
CE = 350 mm

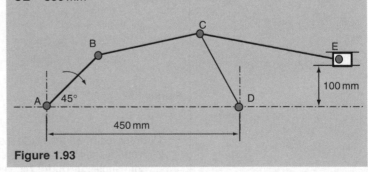

Figure 1.93

BTEC National Study Guide: Engineering. See page 325 for order details of individual texts

244

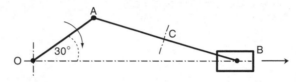

Determine (a) the angular velocity of the crank AB and the velocity of the point B, (b) the velocity of the point C and the angular velocity of the rocker CD, (c) the angular velocity of the connecting rod BC, (d) the velocity of the piston E.

Problems 1.11

1. In the slider-crank mechanism shown in Figure 1.94, the crank OA is 150 mm long and the connecting rod AB is 300 mm long. The crank rotates clockwise at a speed of 3600 rpm, and C is the mid-point of the connecting rod. At the instant shown, determine (a) the velocity of the piston, (b) the velocity of the point C, (c) the angular velocity of the connecting rod.

$$[40.5\,\text{m s}^{-1}, 48.6\,\text{m s}^{-1}, 252\,\text{rad s}^{-1}]$$

Figure 1.94

2. The crank OA of the engine mechanism shown in Figure 1.95 rotates clockwise at a speed of 3000 rpm. The length of the crank is 200 mm and the length of the connecting rod AB is 500 mm. The point C on the connecting rod is 200 mm from the crankpin at A. At the position shown, determine (a) the velocity of the piston, (b) the velocity of the point C, (c) the angular velocity of the connecting rod.

$$[66\,\text{m s}^{-1}, 61.8\,\text{m s}^{-1}, 66\,\text{rad s}^{-1}]$$

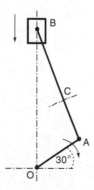

Figure 1.95

3. A four-bar linkage is shown in Figure 1.96. The crank OA, the connecting rod AB and the rocker BC are 20 mm, 120 mm and 60 mm long respectively. The crank rotates at a speed of 60 rpm and the centre distance OC is 90 mm. At the instant shown,

BTEC National Study Guide: Engineering. See page 325 for order details of individual texts

245

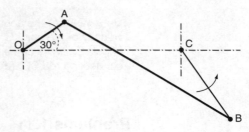

Figure 1.96

determine (a) the velocity of C, (b) the angular velocity of the rocker BC, (c) the angular velocity of the connecting rod AB.

$$[0.22\,\mathrm{m\,s^{-1}},\ 2.12\,\mathrm{rad\,s^{-1}},\ 3.72\,\mathrm{rad\,s^{-1}}]$$

BTEC National Study Guide: Engineering. See page 325 for order details of individual texts

246

1

Units associated with basic electrical quantities

At the end of this chapter you should be able to:

- state the basic SI units

- recognize derived SI units

- understand prefixes denoting multiplication and division

- state the units of charge, force, work and power and perform simple calculations involving these units

- state the units of electrical potential, e.m.f., resistance, conductance, power and energy and perform simple calculations involving these units

1.1 SI units

The system of units used in engineering and science is the Système Internationale d'Unités (International system of units), usually abbreviated to SI units, and is based on the metric system. This was introduced in 1960 and is now adopted by the majority of countries as the official system of measurement.

The basic units in the SI system are listed below with their symbols:

Quantity	Unit
length	metre, m
mass	kilogram, kg
time	second, s
electric current	ampere, A
thermodynamic temperature	kelvin, K
luminous intensity	candela, cd
amount of substance	mole, mol

Derived SI units use combinations of basic units and there are many of them. Two examples are:

Velocity – metres per second (m/s)

Acceleration – metres per second
squared (m/s^2)

SI units may be made larger or smaller by using prefixes which denote multiplication or division by a particular amount. The six most common multiples, with their meaning, are listed below:

Prefix	Name	Meaning
M	mega	multiply by 1 000 000 (i.e. $\times 10^6$)
k	kilo	multiply by 1000 (i.e. $\times 10^3$)
m	milli	divide by 1000 (i.e. $\times 10^{-3}$)
μ	micro	divide by 1 000 000 (i.e. $\times 10^{-6}$)
n	nano	divide by 1 000 000 000 (i.e. $\times 10^{-9}$)
p	pico	divide by 1 000 000 000 000 (i.e. $\times 10^{-12}$)

1.2 Charge

The **unit of charge** is the coulomb (C) where one coulomb is one ampere second. (1 coulomb =

BTEC National Study Guide: Engineering. See page 325 for order details of individual texts

247

6.24×10^{18} electrons). The coulomb is defined as the quantity of electricity which flows past a given point in an electric circuit when a current of one ampere is maintained for one second. Thus,

$$\text{charge, in coulombs } \boxed{Q = It}$$

where I is the current in amperes and t is the time in seconds.

Problem 1. If a current of 5 A flows for 2 minutes, find the quantity of electricity transferred.

Quantity of electricity $Q = It$ coulombs

$$I = 5\,\text{A}, t = 2 \times 60 = 120\,\text{s}$$

Hence $\quad Q = 5 \times 120 = \textbf{600 C}$

1.3 Force

The **unit of force** is the **newton (N)** where one newton is one kilogram metre per second squared. The newton is defined as the force which, when applied to a mass of one kilogram, gives it an acceleration of one metre per second squared. Thus,

$$\text{force, in newtons } \boxed{F = ma}$$

where m is the mass in kilograms and a is the acceleration in metres per second squared. Gravitational force, or weight, is mg, where $g = 9.81\,\text{m/s}^2$

Problem 2. A mass of 5000 g is accelerated at $2\,\text{m/s}^2$ by a force. Determine the force needed.

Force = mass × acceleration

$$= 5\,\text{kg} \times 2\,\text{m/s}^2 = 10\,\text{kg m/s}^2 = \textbf{10 N}$$

Problem 3. Find the force acting vertically downwards on a mass of 200 g attached to a wire.

Mass = 200 g = 0.2 kg and acceleration due to gravity, $g = 9.81\,\text{m/s}^2$

$$\left.\begin{array}{l}\text{Force acting} \\ \text{downwards}\end{array}\right\} = \text{weight}$$

$$= \text{mass} \times \text{acceleration}$$

$$= 0.2\,\text{kg} \times 9.81\,\text{m/s}^2$$

$$= \textbf{1.962 N}$$

1.4 Work

The **unit of work or energy** is the **joule (J)** where one joule is one newton metre. The joule is defined as the work done or energy transferred when a force of one newton is exerted through a distance of one metre in the direction of the force. Thus

$$\text{work done on a body, in joules, } \boxed{W = Fs}$$

where F is the force in newtons and s is the distance in metres moved by the body in the direction of the force. Energy is the capacity for doing work.

1.5 Power

The **unit of power** is the watt (W) where one watt is one joule per second. Power is defined as the rate of doing work or transferring energy. Thus,

$$\text{power, in watts, } \boxed{P = \dfrac{W}{t}}$$

where W is the work done or energy transferred, in joules, and t is the time, in seconds. Thus,

$$\text{energy, in joules, } \boxed{W = Pt}$$

Problem 4. A portable machine requires a force of 200 N to move it. How much work is done if the machine is moved 20 m and what average power is utilized if the movement takes 25 s?

Work done = force × distance

$$= 200\,\text{N} \times 20\,\text{m}$$

$$= \textbf{4000 Nm or 4 kJ}$$

BTEC National Study Guide: Engineering. See page 325 for order details of individual texts

248

$$\text{Power} = \frac{\text{work done}}{\text{time taken}}$$

$$= \frac{4000\,\text{J}}{25\,\text{s}} = 160\,\text{J/s} = 160\,\text{W}$$

Problem 5. A mass of 1000 kg is raised through a height of 10 m in 20 s. What is (a) the work done and (b) the power developed?

(a) Work done = force × distance

and force = mass × acceleration

Hence, work done $= (1000\,\text{kg} \times 9.81\,\text{m/s}^2) \times (10\,\text{m})$

$= 98\,100\,\text{Nm}$

$= \textbf{98.1\,kNm}$ or $\textbf{98.1\,kJ}$

(b) $\text{Power} = \dfrac{\text{work done}}{\text{time taken}} = \dfrac{98100\,\text{J}}{20\,\text{s}}$

$= 4905\,\text{J/s} = \textbf{4905\,W}$ or $\textbf{4.905\,kW}$

Now try the following exercise

Exercise 1   Further problems on charge, force, work and power

(Take $g = 9.81\,\text{m/s}^2$ where appropriate)

1 What quantity of electricity is carried by 6.24×10^{21} electrons? [1000 C]

2 In what time would a current of 1 A transfer a charge of 30 C? [30 s]

3 A current of 3 A flows for 5 minutes. What charge is transferred? [900 C]

4 How long must a current of 0.1 A flow so as to transfer a charge of 30 C? [5 minutes]

5 What force is required to give a mass of 20 kg an acceleration of 30 m/s²? [600 N]

6 Find the accelerating force when a car having a mass of 1.7 Mg increases its speed with a constant acceleration of 3 m/s² [5.1 kN]

7 A force of 40 N accelerates a mass at 5 m/s². Determine the mass. [8 kg]

8 Determine the force acting downwards on a mass of 1500 g suspended on a string. [14.72 N]

9 A force of 4 N moves an object 200 cm in the direction of the force. What amount of work is done? [8 J]

10 A force of 2.5 kN is required to lift a load. How much work is done if the load is lifted through 500 cm? [12.5 kJ]

11 An electromagnet exerts a force of 12 N and moves a soft iron armature through a distance of 1.5 cm in 40 ms. Find the power consumed. [4.5 W]

12 A mass of 500 kg is raised to a height of 6 m in 30 s. Find (a) the work done and (b) the power developed. [(a) 29.43 kNm (b) 981 W]

1.6   Electrical potential and e.m.f.

The **unit of electric potential** is the volt (V), where one volt is one joule per coulomb. One volt is defined as the difference in potential between two points in a conductor which, when carrying a current of one ampere, dissipates a power of one watt, i.e.

$$\text{volts} = \frac{\text{watts}}{\text{amperes}} = \frac{\text{joules/second}}{\text{amperes}}$$

$$= \frac{\text{joules}}{\text{ampere seconds}} = \frac{\text{joules}}{\text{coulombs}}$$

A change in electric potential between two points in an electric circuit is called a **potential difference**. The **electromotive force (e.m.f.)** provided by a source of energy such as a battery or a generator is measured in volts.

1.7   Resistance and conductance

The **unit of electric resistance** is the **ohm(Ω)**, where one ohm is one volt per ampere. It is defined as the resistance between two points in a conductor when a constant electric potential of one volt applied

---

BTEC National Study Guide: Engineering. See page 325 for order details of individual texts

249

at the two points produces a current flow of one ampere in the conductor. Thus,

$$\text{resistance, in ohms} \quad \boxed{R = \frac{V}{I}}$$

where V is the potential difference across the two points, in volts, and I is the current flowing between the two points, in amperes.

The reciprocal of resistance is called **conductance** and is measured in siemens (S). Thus

$$\text{conductance, in siemens} \quad \boxed{G = \frac{1}{R}}$$

where R is the resistance in ohms.

Problem 6.   Find the conductance of a conductor of resistance: (a) $10\,\Omega$ (b) $5\,k\Omega$ (c) $100\,m\Omega$.

(a) Conductance $G = \dfrac{1}{R} = \dfrac{1}{10}$ siemen $= \mathbf{0.1\,S}$

(b) $G = \dfrac{1}{R} = \dfrac{1}{5 \times 10^3}\,S = 0.2 \times 10^{-3}\,S = \mathbf{0.2\,mS}$

(c) $G = \dfrac{1}{R} = \dfrac{1}{100 \times 10^{-3}}\,S = \dfrac{10^3}{100}\,S = \mathbf{10\,S}$

1.8   Electrical power and energy

When a direct current of I amperes is flowing in an electric circuit and the voltage across the circuit is V volts, then

$$\text{power, in watts} \quad \boxed{P = VI}$$

Electrical energy = Power × time

$$= \textbf{\textit{VIt} joules}$$

Although the unit of energy is the joule, when dealing with large amounts of energy, the unit used is the **kilowatt hour (kWh)** where

$$1\,kWh = 1000\,\text{watt hour}$$

$$= 1000 \times 3600\,\text{watt seconds or joules}$$

$$= 3\,600\,000\,J$$

Problem 7.   A source e.m.f. of 5 V supplies a current of 3 A for 10 minutes. How much energy is provided in this time?

Energy = power × time, and power = voltage × current. Hence

$$\textbf{Energy} = VIt = 5 \times 3 \times (10 \times 60)$$

$$= 9000\,\text{Ws or J} = \mathbf{9\,kJ}$$

Problem 8.   An electric heater consumes 1.8 MJ when connected to a 250 V supply for 30 minutes. Find the power rating of the heater and the current taken from the supply.

$$\text{Power} = \frac{\text{energy}}{\text{time}} = \frac{1.8 \times 10^6\,J}{30 \times 60\,s}$$

$$= 1000\,J/s = 1000\,W$$

i.e. **power rating of heater = 1 kW**

$$\text{Power } P = VI, \text{ thus } I = \frac{P}{V} = \frac{1000}{250} = 4\,A$$

Hence the current taken from the supply is 4 A.

Now try the following exercise

Exercise 2   Further problems on e.m.f., resistance, conductance, power and energy

1 Find the conductance of a resistor of resistance (a) $10\,\Omega$ (b) $2\,k\Omega$ (c) $2\,m\Omega$
 [(a) 0.1 S (b) 0.5 mS (c) 500 S]

2 A conductor has a conductance of $50\,\mu S$. What is its resistance? [20 kΩ]

3 An e.m.f. of 250 V is connected across a resistance and the current flowing through the resistance is 4 A. What is the power developed? [1 kW]

4 450 J of energy are converted into heat in 1 minute. What power is dissipated? [7.5 W]

5 A current of 10 A flows through a conductor and 10 W is dissipated. What p.d. exists across the ends of the conductor? [1 V]

BTEC National Study Guide: Engineering. See page 325 for order details of individual texts

250

6 A battery of e.m.f. 12 V supplies a current of 5 A for 2 minutes. How much energy is supplied in this time? [7.2 kJ]

7 A d.c. electric motor consumes 36 MJ when connected to a 250 V supply for 1 hour. Find the power rating of the motor and the current taken from the supply. [10 kW, 40 A]

1.9 Summary of terms, units and their symbols

Quantity	Quantity Symbol	Unit	Unit Symbol
Length	l	metre	m
Mass	m	kilogram	kg
Time	t	second	s
Velocity	v	metres per second	m/s or $\mathrm{m\,s^{-1}}$
Acceleration	a	metres per second squared	m/s^2 or $\mathrm{m\,s^{-2}}$
Force	F	newton	N
Electrical charge or quantity	Q	coulomb	C
Electric current	I	ampere	A
Resistance	R	ohm	Ω
Conductance	G	siemen	S
Electromotive force	E	volt	V
Potential difference	V	volt	V
Work	W	joule	J
Energy	E (or W)	joule	J
Power	P	watt	W

Now try the following exercises

Exercise 3 Short answer questions on units associated with basic electrical quantities

1 What does 'SI units' mean?

2 Complete the following:

Force = ... × ......

3 What do you understand by the term 'potential difference'?

4 Define electric current in terms of charge and time

5 Name the units used to measure:
(a) the quantity of electricity
(b) resistance
(c) conductance

6 Define the coulomb

7 Define electrical energy and state its unit

8 Define electrical power and state its unit

9 What is electromotive force?

10 Write down a formula for calculating the power in a d.c. circuit

11 Write down the symbols for the following quantities:
(a) electric charge   (b) work
(c) e.m.f.   (d) p.d.

12 State which units the following abbreviations refer to:
(a) A   (b) C   (c) J   (d) N   (e) m

Exercise 4 Multi-choice questions on units associated with basic electrical quantities (Answers on page 375)

1 A resistance of 50 kΩ has a conductance of:
(a) 20 S   (b) 0.02 S
(c) 0.02 mS   (d) 20 kS

2 Which of the following statements is incorrect?
(a) 1 N = 1 kg m/s^2 (b) 1 V = 1 J/C
(c) 30 mA = 0.03 A   (d) 1 J = 1 N/m

3 The power dissipated by a resistor of 10 Ω when a current of 2 A passes through it is:
(a) 0.4 W   (b) 20 W   (c) 40 W   (d) 200 W

4 A mass of 1200 g is accelerated at 200 cm/s^2 by a force. The value of the force required is:
(a) 2.4 N   (b) 2400 N
(c) 240 kN   (d) 0.24 N

5 A charge of 240 C is transferred in 2 minutes. The current flowing is:
(a) 120 A   (b) 480 A   (c) 2 A   (d) 8 A

6 A current of 2 A flows for 10 h through a 100 Ω resistor. The energy consumed by the resistor is:

BTEC National Study Guide: Engineering. See page 325 for order details of individual texts

251

(a) 0.5 kWh   (b) 4 kWh

(c) 2 kWh   (d) 0.02 kWh

7 The unit of quantity of electricity is the:
  (a) volt   (b) coulomb

  (c) ohm   (d) joule

8 Electromotive force is provided by:
  (a) resistance's
  (b) a conducting path
  (c) an electric current
  (d) an electrical supply source

9 The coulomb is a unit of:
  (a) power
  (b) voltage
  (c) energy
  (d) quantity of electricity

10 In order that work may be done:
  (a) a supply of energy is required
  (b) the circuit must have a switch
  (c) coal must be burnt
  (d) two wires are necessary

11 The ohm is the unit of:
  (a) charge   (b) resistance

  (c) power   (d) current

12 The unit of current is the:
  (a) volt   (b) coulomb

  (c) joule   (d) ampere

BTEC National Study Guide: Engineering. See page 325 for order details of individual texts

252

2

An introduction to electric circuits

At the end of this chapter you should be able to:

- appreciate that engineering systems may be represented by block diagrams
- recognize common electrical circuit diagram symbols
- understand that electric current is the rate of movement of charge and is measured in amperes
- appreciate that the unit of charge is the coulomb
- calculate charge or quantity of electricity Q from $Q = It$
- understand that a potential difference between two points in a circuit is required for current to flow
- appreciate that the unit of p.d. is the volt
- understand that resistance opposes current flow and is measured in ohms
- appreciate what an ammeter, a voltmeter, an ohmmeter, a multimeter and a C.R.O. measure
- distinguish between linear and non-linear devices
- state Ohm's law as $V = IR$ or $I = V/R$ or $R = V/I$
- use Ohm's law in calculations, including multiples and sub-multiples of units
- describe a conductor and an insulator, giving examples of each
- appreciate that electrical power P is given by $P = VI = I^2R = V^2/R$ watts
- calculate electrical power
- define electrical energy and state its unit
- calculate electrical energy
- state the three main effects of an electric current, giving practical examples of each
- explain the importance of fuses in electrical circuits

2.1 Electrical/electronic system block diagrams

An electrical/electronic **system** is a group of components connected together to perform a desired function. Figure 2.1 shows a simple public address system, where a microphone is used to collect acoustic energy in the form of sound pressure waves and converts this to electrical energy in the form of small voltages and currents; the signal from the microphone is then amplified by means of an electronic circuit containing transistors/integrated circuits before it is applied to the loudspeaker.

BTEC National Study Guide: Engineering. See page 325 for order details of individual texts

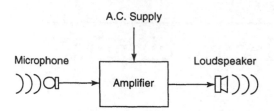

Figure 2.1

A **sub-system** is a part of a system which performs an identified function within the whole system; the amplifier in Fig. 2.1 is an example of a sub-system

A **component** or **element** is usually the simplest part of a system which has a specific and well-defined function – for example, the microphone in Fig. 2.1

The illustration in Fig. 2.1 is called a block diagram and electrical/electronic systems, which can often be quite complicated, can be better understood when broken down in this way. It is not always necessary to know precisely what is inside each sub-system in order to know how the whole system functions.

As another example of an engineering system, Fig. 2.2 illustrates a temperature control system containing a heat source (such as a gas boiler), a fuel controller (such as an electrical solenoid valve), a thermostat and a source of electrical energy. The system of Fig. 2.2 can be shown in block diagram form as in Fig. 2.3; the thermostat compares the

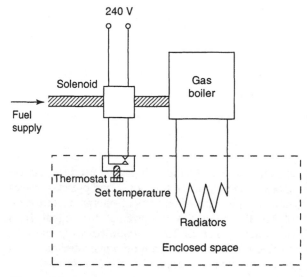

Figure 2.2

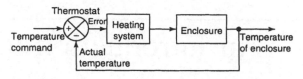

Figure 2.3

actual room temperature with the desired temperature and switches the heating on or off.

There are many types of engineering systems. A **communications system** is an example, where a local area network could comprise a file server, coaxial cable, network adapters, several computers and a laser printer; an **electromechanical system** is another example, where a car electrical system could comprise a battery, a starter motor, an ignition coil, a contact breaker and a distributor. All such systems as these may be represented by block diagrams.

2.2   Standard symbols for electrical components

Symbols are used for components in electrical circuit diagrams and some of the more common ones are shown in Fig. 2.4

2.3   Electric current and quantity of electricity

All **atoms** consist of **protons, neutrons** and **electrons**. The protons, which have positive electrical charges, and the neutrons, which have no electrical charge, are contained within the **nucleus**. Removed from the nucleus are minute negatively charged particles called electrons. Atoms of different materials differ from one another by having different numbers of protons, neutrons and electrons. An equal number of protons and electrons exist within an atom and it is said to be electrically balanced, as the positive and negative charges cancel each other out. When there are more than two electrons in an atom the electrons are arranged into **shells** at various distances from the nucleus.

All atoms are bound together by powerful forces of attraction existing between the nucleus and its electrons. Electrons in the outer shell of an atom, however, are attracted to their nucleus less powerfully than are electrons whose shells are nearer the nucleus.

BTEC National Study Guide: Engineering. See page 325 for order details of individual texts

254

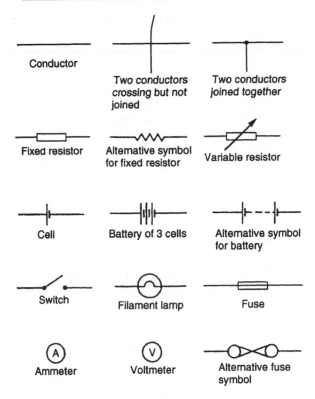

Conductor

Two conductors crossing but not joined

Two conductors joined together

Fixed resistor

Alternative symbol for fixed resistor

Variable resistor

Cell

Battery of 3 cells

Alternative symbol for battery

Switch

Filament lamp

Fuse

Ammeter

Voltmeter

Alternative fuse symbol

Figure 2.4

It is possible for an atom to lose an electron; the atom, which is now called an **ion**, is not now electrically balanced, but is positively charged and is thus able to attract an electron to itself from another atom. Electrons that move from one atom to another are called free electrons and such random motion can continue indefinitely. However, if an electric pressure or **voltage** is applied across any material there is a tendency for electrons to move in a particular direction. This movement of free electrons, known as **drift**, constitutes an electric current flow. **Thus current is the rate of movement of charge**.

Conductors are materials that contain electrons that are loosely connected to the nucleus and can easily move through the material from one atom to another.

Insulators are materials whose electrons are held firmly to their nucleus.

The unit used to measure the **quantity of electrical charge Q** is called the **coulomb C** (where 1 coulomb = 6.24×10^{18} electrons)

If the drift of electrons in a conductor takes place at the rate of one coulomb per second the resulting

current is said to be a current of one ampere.

Thus   1 ampere = 1 coulomb per second or

$$1\,A = 1\,C/s$$

Hence 1 coulomb = 1 ampere second or

$$1\,C = 1\,As$$

Generally, if I is the current in amperes and t the time in seconds during which the current flows, then $I \times t$ represents the quantity of electrical charge in coulombs, i.e. quantity of electrical charge transferred,

$$Q = I \times t \text{ coulombs}$$

> **Problem 1.** What current must flow if 0.24 coulombs is to be transferred in 15 ms?

Since the quantity of electricity, $Q = It$, then

$$I = \frac{Q}{t} = \frac{0.24}{15 \times 10^{-3}} = \frac{0.24 \times 10^3}{15}$$

$$= \frac{240}{15} = 16\,A$$

> **Problem 2.** If a current of 10 A flows for four minutes, find the quantity of electricity transferred.

Quantity of electricity, $Q = It$ coulombs. $I = 10\,A$ and $t = 4 \times 60 = 240\,s$. Hence

$$Q = 10 \times 240 = 2400\,C$$

Now try the following exercise

> **Exercise 5   Further problems on charge**
>
> 1 In what time would a current of 10 A transfer a charge of 50 C ?   [5 s]
>
> 2 A current of 6 A flows for 10 minutes. What charge is transferred ?   [3600 C]
>
> 3 How long must a current of 100 mA flow so as to transfer a charge of 80 C? [13 min 20 s]

BTEC National Study Guide: Engineering. See page 325 for order details of individual texts

255

2.4   Potential difference and resistance

For a continuous current to flow between two points in a circuit a **potential difference (p.d.)** or **voltage**, *V*, is required between them; a complete conducting path is necessary to and from the source of electrical energy. The unit of p.d. is the **volt, V**.

Figure 2.5 shows a cell connected across a filament lamp. Current flow, by convention, is considered as flowing from the positive terminal of the cell, around the circuit to the negative terminal.

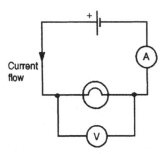

Figure 2.5

The flow of electric current is subject to friction. This friction, or opposition, is called **resistance R** and is the property of a conductor that limits current. The unit of resistance is the **ohm**; 1 ohm is defined as the resistance which will have a current of 1 ampere flowing through it when 1 volt is connected across it,

i.e.
$$\text{resistance } R = \frac{\text{Potential difference}}{\text{current}}$$

2.5   Basic electrical measuring instruments

An **ammeter** is an instrument used to measure current and must be connected **in series** with the circuit. Figure 2.5 shows an ammeter connected in series with the lamp to measure the current flowing through it. Since all the current in the circuit passes through the ammeter it must have a very **low resistance**.

A **voltmeter** is an instrument used to measure p.d. and must be connected **in parallel** with the part of the circuit whose p.d. is required. In Fig. 2.5, a voltmeter is connected in parallel with the lamp to measure the p.d. across it. To avoid a significant

current flowing through it a voltmeter must have a very **high resistance**.

An **ohmmeter** is an instrument for measuring resistance.

A **multimeter**, or universal instrument, may be used to measure voltage, current and resistance. An 'Avometer' is a typical example.

The **cathode ray oscilloscope (CRO)** may be used to observe waveforms and to measure voltages and currents. The display of a CRO involves a spot of light moving across a screen. The amount by which the spot is deflected from its initial position depends on the p.d. applied to the terminals of the CRO and the range selected. The displacement is calibrated in 'volts per cm'. For example, if the spot is deflected 3 cm and the volts/cm switch is on 10 V/cm then the magnitude of the p.d. is 3 cm × 10 V/cm, i.e. 30 V.

(See Chapter 10 for more detail about electrical measuring instruments and measurements.)

2.6   Linear and non-linear devices

Figure 2.6 shows a circuit in which current I can be varied by the variable resistor R_2. For various settings of R_2, the current flowing in resistor R_1, displayed on the ammeter, and the p.d. across R_1, displayed on the voltmeter, are noted and a graph is plotted of p.d. against current. The result is shown in Fig. 2.7(a) where the straight line graph passing through the origin indicates that current is directly proportional to the p.d. Since the gradient, i.e. (p.d.)/(current) is constant, resistance R_1 is constant. A resistor is thus an example of a **linear device**.

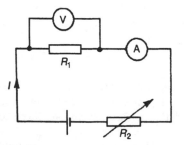

Figure 2.6

If the resistor R_1 in Fig. 2.6 is replaced by a component such as a lamp then the graph shown in Fig. 2.7(b) results when values of p.d. are noted for various current readings. Since the gradient is

BTEC National Study Guide: Engineering. See page 325 for order details of individual texts

256

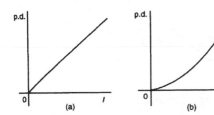

Figure 2.7

changing, the lamp is an example of a **non-linear device**.

2.7 Ohm's law

Ohm's law states that the current I flowing in a circuit is directly proportional to the applied voltage V and inversely proportional to the resistance R, provided the temperature remains constant. Thus,

$$I = \frac{V}{R} \text{ or } V = IR \text{ or } R = \frac{V}{I}$$

Problem 3.   The current flowing through a resistor is 0.8 A when a p.d. of 20 V is applied. Determine the value of the resistance.

From Ohm's law,

$$\text{resistance } R = \frac{V}{I} = \frac{20}{0.8} = \frac{200}{8} = 25\,\Omega$$

2.8 Multiples and sub-multiples

Currents, voltages and resistances can often be very large or very small. Thus multiples and sub-multiples of units are often used, as stated in chapter 1. The most common ones, with an example of each, are listed in Table 2.1

Problem 4.   Determine the p.d. which must be applied to a $2\,k\Omega$ resistor in order that a current of 10 mA may flow.

Resistance $R = 2\,k\Omega = 2 \times 10^3 = 2000\,\Omega$

$$\text{Current } I = 10\,\text{mA} = 10 \times 10^{-3}\,\text{A}$$

$$\text{or } \frac{10}{10^3}\,\text{A or } \frac{10}{1000}\,\text{A} = 0.01\,\text{A}$$

From Ohm's law, potential difference,

$$V = IR = (0.01)(2000) = \mathbf{20\,V}$$

Problem 5.   A coil has a current of 50 mA flowing through it when the applied voltage is 12 V. What is the resistance of the coil?

$$\text{Resistance, } R = \frac{V}{I} = \frac{12}{50 \times 10^{-3}}$$

$$= \frac{12 \times 10^3}{50} = \frac{12\,000}{50} = \mathbf{240\,\Omega}$$

Table 2.1

Prefix	Name	Meaning	Example
M	mega	multiply by 1 000 000 (i.e. $\times 10^6$)	$2\,M\Omega = 2\,000\,000\,\text{ohms}$
k	kilo	multiply by 1000 (i.e. $\times 10^3$)	$10\,kV = 10\,000\,\text{volts}$
m	milli	divide by 1000 (i.e. $\times 10^{-3}$)	$25\,\text{mA} = \dfrac{25}{1000}\,\text{A}$ $= 0.025\,\text{amperes}$
μ	micro	divide by 1 000 000 (i.e. $\times 10^{-6}$)	$50\,\mu V = \dfrac{50}{1\,000\,000}\,\text{V}$ $= 0.000\,05\,\text{volts}$

BTEC National Study Guide: Engineering. See page 325 for order details of individual texts

257

Problem 6. A 100 V battery is connected across a resistor and causes a current of 5 mA to flow. Determine the resistance of the resistor. If the voltage is now reduced to 25 V, what will be the new value of the current flowing?

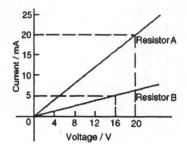

Figure 2.8

$$\text{Resistance } R = \frac{V}{I} = \frac{100}{5 \times 10^{-3}} = \frac{100 \times 10^3}{5}$$

$$= 20 \times 10^3 = 20\,k\Omega$$

Current when voltage is reduced to 25 V,

$$I = \frac{V}{R} = \frac{25}{20 \times 10^3} = \frac{25}{20} \times 10^{-3} = 1.25\,mA$$

Problem 7. What is the resistance of a coil which draws a current of (a) 50 mA and (b) 200 μA from a 120 V supply?

(a) Resistance $R = \dfrac{V}{I} = \dfrac{120}{50 \times 10^{-3}}$

$$= \frac{120}{0.05} = \frac{12\,000}{5}$$

$$= 2400\,\Omega \text{ or } 2.4\,k\Omega$$

(b) Resistance $R = \dfrac{120}{200 \times 10^{-6}} = \dfrac{120}{0.0002}$

$$= \frac{1\,200\,000}{2} = 600\,000\,\Omega$$

$$\text{or } 600\,k\Omega \text{ or } 0.6\,M\Omega$$

Problem 8. The current/voltage relationship for two resistors A and B is as shown in Fig. 2.8 Determine the value of the resistance of each resistor.

For resistor A,

$$R = \frac{V}{I} = \frac{20\,V}{20\,mA} = \frac{20}{0.02} = \frac{2000}{2}$$

$$= 1000\,\Omega \text{ or } 1\,k\Omega$$

For resistor B,

$$R = \frac{V}{I} = \frac{16\,V}{5\,mA} = \frac{16}{0.005} = \frac{16\,000}{5}$$

$$= 3200\,\Omega \text{ or } 3.2\,k\Omega$$

Now try the following exercise

Exercise 6 Further problems on Ohm's law

1 The current flowing through a heating element is 5 A when a p.d. of 35 V is applied across it. Find the resistance of the element. [7 Ω]

2 A 60 W electric light bulb is connected to a 240 V supply. Determine (a) the current flowing in the bulb and (b) the resistance of the bulb. [(a) 0.25 A (b) 960 Ω]

3 Graphs of current against voltage for two resistors P and Q are shown in Fig. 2.9 Determine the value of each resistor. [2 mΩ, 5 mΩ]

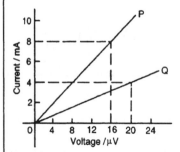

Figure 2.9

4 Determine the p.d. which must be applied to a 5 kΩ resistor such that a current of 6 mA may flow. [30 V]

2.9 Conductors and insulators

A **conductor** is a material having a low resistance which allows electric current to flow in it. All metals

BTEC National Study Guide: Engineering. See page 325 for order details of individual texts

258

are conductors and some examples include copper, aluminium, brass, platinum, silver, gold and carbon.

An **insulator** is a material having a high resistance which does not allow electric current to flow in it. Some examples of insulators include plastic, rubber, glass, porcelain, air, paper, cork, mica, ceramics and certain oils.

2.10 Electrical power and energy

Electrical power

Power P in an electrical circuit is given by the product of potential difference V and current I, as stated in Chapter 1. The unit of power is the **watt, W**.

Hence

$$\boxed{P = V \times I \text{ watts}} \qquad (1)$$

From Ohm's law, $V = IR$. Substituting for V in equation (1) gives:

$$P = (IR) \times I$$

i.e.

$$\boxed{P = I^2 R \text{ watts}}$$

Also, from Ohm's law, $I = V/R$. Substituting for I in equation (1) gives:

$$P = V \times \frac{V}{R}$$

i.e.

$$\boxed{P = \frac{V^2}{R} \text{ watts}}$$

There are thus three possible formulae which may be used for calculating power.

Problem 9. A 100 W electric light bulb is connected to a 250 V supply. Determine (a) the current flowing in the bulb, and (b) the resistance of the bulb.

Power $P = V \times I$, from which, current $I = \dfrac{P}{V}$

(a) Current $I = \dfrac{100}{250} = \dfrac{10}{25} = \dfrac{2}{5} = \mathbf{0.4\,A}$

(b) Resistance $R = \dfrac{V}{I} = \dfrac{250}{0.4} = \dfrac{2500}{4} = \mathbf{625\,\Omega}$

Problem 10. Calculate the power dissipated when a current of 4 mA flows through a resistance of 5 kΩ.

$$\begin{aligned}
\textbf{Power } P = I^2 R &= (4 \times 10^{-3})^2 (5 \times 10^3) \\
&= 16 \times 10^{-6} \times 5 \times 10^3 \\
&= 80 \times 10^{-3} \\
&= \mathbf{0.08\,W} \text{ or } \mathbf{80\,mW}
\end{aligned}$$

Alternatively, since $I = 4 \times 10^{-3}$ and $R = 5 \times 10^3$ then from Ohm's law, voltage

$$V = IR = 4 \times 10^{-3} \times 5 \times 10^3 = 20\,\text{V}$$

Hence,

$$\begin{aligned}
\textbf{power } P = V \times I &= 20 \times 4 \times 10^{-3} \\
&= \mathbf{80\,mW}
\end{aligned}$$

Problem 11. An electric kettle has a resistance of 30 Ω. What current will flow when it is connected to a 240 V supply? Find also the power rating of the kettle.

$$\text{Current, } I = \frac{V}{R} = \frac{240}{30} = \mathbf{8\,A}$$

$$\begin{aligned}
\text{Power, } P = VI &= 240 \times 8 = 1920\,\text{W} \\
&= \mathbf{1.92\,kW} = \text{power rating of kettle}
\end{aligned}$$

Problem 12. A current of 5 A flows in the winding of an electric motor, the resistance of the winding being 100 Ω. Determine (a) the p.d. across the winding, and (b) the power dissipated by the coil.

(a) Potential difference across winding,

$$V = IR = 5 \times 100 = \mathbf{500\,V}$$

(b) Power dissipated by coil,

$$\begin{aligned}
P = I^2 R &= 5^2 \times 100 \\
&= \mathbf{2500\,W} \text{ or } \mathbf{2.5\,kW}
\end{aligned}$$

$$\begin{aligned}
\text{(Alternatively, } P = V \times I &= 500 \times 5 \\
&= \mathbf{2500\,W} \text{ or } \mathbf{2.5\,kW})
\end{aligned}$$

BTEC National Study Guide: Engineering. See page 325 for order details of individual texts

259

Problem 13. The hot resistance of a 240 V filament lamp is 960 Ω. Find the current taken by the lamp and its power rating.

From Ohm's law,

$$\text{current } I = \frac{V}{R} = \frac{240}{960}$$

$$= \frac{24}{96} = \frac{1}{4}\text{A or } \mathbf{0.25\,A}$$

Power rating $P = VI = (240)\left(\frac{1}{4}\right) = \mathbf{60\,W}$

Electrical energy

Electrical energy = power × time

If the power is measured in watts and the time in seconds then the unit of energy is watt-seconds or **joules**. If the power is measured in kilowatts and the time in hours then the unit of energy is **kilowatt-hours**, often called the '**unit of electricity**'. The 'electricity meter' in the home records the number of kilowatt-hours used and is thus an energy meter.

Problem 14. A 12 V battery is connected across a load having a resistance of 40 Ω. Determine the current flowing in the load, the power consumed and the energy dissipated in 2 minutes.

$$\text{Current } I = \frac{V}{R} = \frac{12}{40} = \mathbf{0.3\,A}$$

Power consumed, $P = VI = (12)(0.3) = \mathbf{3.6\,W}$.

Energy dissipated = power × time

$$= (3.6\,\text{W})(2 \times 60\,\text{s})$$

$$= \mathbf{432\,J} \text{ (since} 1\,\text{J} = 1\,\text{Ws)}$$

Problem 15. A source of e.m.f. of 15 V supplies a current of 2 A for 6 minutes. How much energy is provided in this time?

Energy = power × time, and power = voltage × current. Hence

$$\text{energy} = VIt = 15 \times 2 \times (6 \times 60)$$

$$= 10\,800\,\text{Ws or J} = \mathbf{10.8\,kJ}$$

Problem 16. Electrical equipment in an office takes a current of 13 A from a 240 V supply. Estimate the cost per week of electricity if the equipment is used for 30 hours each week and 1 kWh of energy costs 6p.

$$\text{Power} = VI \text{ watts} = 240 \times 13$$

$$= 3120\,\text{W} = 3.12\,\text{kW}$$

Energy used per week = power × time

$$= (3.12\,\text{kW}) \times (30\,\text{h})$$

$$= 93.6\,\text{kWh}$$

Cost at 6p per kWh = 93.6 × 6 = 561.6p. Hence **weekly cost of electricity = £5.62**

Problem 17. An electric heater consumes 3.6 MJ when connected to a 250 V supply for 40 minutes. Find the power rating of the heater and the current taken from the supply.

$$\text{Power} = \frac{\text{energy}}{\text{time}} = \frac{3.6 \times 10^6\,\text{J}}{40 \times 60\,\text{s}} \text{ (or W)} = 1500\,\text{W}$$

i.e. Power rating of heater = **1.5 kW**.

$$\text{Power } P = VI,$$

$$\text{thus } I = \frac{P}{V} = \frac{1500}{250} = 6\,\text{A}$$

Hence the current taken from the supply is **6 A**.

Problem 18. Determine the power dissipated by the element of an electric fire of resistance 20 Ω when a current of 10 A flows through it. If the fire is on for 6 hours determine the energy used and the cost if 1 unit of electricity costs 6.5p.

$$\text{Power } P = I^2 R = 10^2 \times 20$$

$$= 100 \times 20 = \mathbf{2000\,W} \text{ or } \mathbf{2\,kW}.$$

(Alternatively, from Ohm's law,

$$V = IR = 10 \times 20 = 200\,\text{V},$$

hence power

$$P = V \times I = 200 \times 10 = 2000\,\text{W} = 2\,\text{kW}).$$

BTEC National Study Guide: Engineering. See page 325 for order details of individual texts

260

Energy used in 6 hours = power × time = 2 kW × 6 h = **12 kWh**.

1 unit of electricity = 1 kWh; hence the number of units used is 12. Cost of energy = 12 × 6.5 = **78p**

Problem 19. A business uses two 3 kW fires for an average of 20 hours each per week, and six 150 W lights for 30 hours each per week. If the cost of electricity is 6.4p per unit, determine the weekly cost of electricity to the business.

Energy = power × time.

Energy used by one 3 kW fire in 20 hours = 3 kW × 20 h = 60 kWh.

Hence weekly energy used by two 3 kW fires = 2 × 60 = 120 kWh.

Energy used by one 150 W light for 30 hours = 150 W × 30 h = 4500 Wh = 4.5 kWh.

Hence weekly energy used by six 150 W lamps = 6 × 4.5 = 27 kWh.

Total energy used per week = 120 + 27 = 147 kWh.

1 unit of electricity = 1 kWh of energy. Thus weekly cost of energy at 6.4p per kWh = 6.4 × 147 = 940.8p = **£9.41**.

Now try the following exercise

Exercise 7   Further problems on power and energy

1 The hot resistance of a 250 V filament lamp is 625 Ω. Determine the current taken by the lamp and its power rating.   [0.4 A, 100 W]

2 Determine the resistance of a coil connected to a 150 V supply when a current of (a) 75 mA (b) 300 μA flows through it.
[(a) 2 kΩ (b) 0.5 MΩ]

3 Determine the resistance of an electric fire which takes a current of 12 A from a 240 V supply. Find also the power rating of the fire and the energy used in 20 h.
[20 Ω, 2.88 kW, 57.6 kWh]

4 Determine the power dissipated when a current of 10 mA flows through an appliance having a resistance of 8 kΩ.   [0.8 W]

5 85.5 J of energy are converted into heat in 9 s. What power is dissipated?   [9.5 W]

6 A current of 4 A flows through a conductor and 10 W is dissipated. What p.d. exists across the ends of the conductor?   [2.5 V]

7 Find the power dissipated when:
(a) a current of 5 mA flows through a resistance of 20 kΩ
(b) a voltage of 400 V is applied across a 120 kΩ resistor
(c) a voltage applied to a resistor is 10 kV and the current flow is 4 mA
[(a) 0.5 W (b) 1.33 W (c) 40 W]

8 A battery of e.m.f. 15 V supplies a current of 2 A for 5 min. How much energy is supplied in this time?   [9 kJ]

9 A d.c. electric motor consumes 72 MJ when connected to 400 V supply for 2 h 30 min. Find the power rating of the motor and the current taken from the supply. [8 kW, 20 A]

10 A p.d. of 500 V is applied across the winding of an electric motor and the resistance of the winding is 50 Ω. Determine the power dissipated by the coil.   [5 kW]

11 In a household during a particular week three 2 kW fires are used on average 25 h each and eight 100 W light bulbs are used on average 35 h each. Determine the cost of electricity for the week if 1 unit of electricity costs 7p.   [£12.46]

12 Calculate the power dissipated by the element of an electric fire of resistance 30 Ω when a current of 10 A flows in it. If the fire is on for 30 hours in a week determine the energy used. Determine also the weekly cost of energy if electricity costs 6.5p per unit.
[3 kW, 90 kWh, £5.85]

2.11   Main effects of electric current

The three main effects of an electric current are:

(a) magnetic effect
(b) chemical effect
(c) heating effect

Some practical applications of the effects of an electric current include:

BTEC National Study Guide: Engineering. See page 325 for order details of individual texts

261

Magnetic effect: bells, relays, motors, generators, transformers, telephones, car-ignition and lifting magnets (see Chapter 8)

Chemical effect: primary and secondary cells and electroplating (see Chapter 4)

Heating effect: cookers, water heaters, electric fires, irons, furnaces, kettles and soldering irons

2.12 Fuses

A **fuse** is used to prevent overloading of electrical circuits. The fuse, which is made of material having a low melting point, utilizes the heating effect of an electric current. A fuse is placed in an electrical circuit and if the current becomes too large the fuse wire melts and so breaks the circuit. A circuit diagram symbol for a fuse is shown in Fig. 2.1, on page 11.

> **Problem 20.** If 5 A, 10 A and 13 A fuses are available, state which is most appropriate for the following appliances which are both connected to a 240 V supply: (a) Electric toaster having a power rating of 1 kW (b) Electric fire having a power rating of 3 kW.

Power $P = VI$, from which, current $I = \dfrac{P}{V}$

(a) For the toaster,

$$\text{current } I = \frac{P}{V} = \frac{1000}{240} = \frac{100}{24} = 4.17\,\text{A}$$

Hence a **5 A fuse** is most appropriate

(b) For the fire,

$$\text{current } I = \frac{P}{V} = \frac{3000}{240} = \frac{300}{24} = 12.5\,\text{A}$$

Hence a **13 A fuse** is most appropriate

Now try the following exercises

Exercise 8   Further problem on fuses

1 A television set having a power rating of 120 W and electric lawnmower of power rating 1 kW are both connected to a 250 V supply. If 3 A, 5 A and 10 A fuses are available state which is the most appropriate for each appliance.   [3 A, 5 A]

Exercise 9   Short answer questions on the introduction to electric circuits

1 Draw the preferred symbols for the following components used when drawing electrical circuit diagrams:
  (a) fixed resistor   (b) cell
  (c) filament lamp   (d) fuse
  (e) voltmeter

2 State the unit of
  (a) current
  (b) potential difference
  (c) resistance

3 State an instrument used to measure
  (a) current
  (b) potential difference
  (c) resistance

4 What is a multimeter?

5 State Ohm's law

6 Give one example of
  (a) a linear device
  (b) a non-linear device

7 State the meaning of the following abbreviations of prefixes used with electrical units:
  (a) k   (b) μ   (c) m   (d) M

8 What is a conductor? Give four examples

9 What is an insulator? Give four examples

10 Complete the following statement:
   'An ammeter has a ... resistance and must be connected ... with the load'

11 Complete the following statement:
   'A voltmeter has a ... resistance and must be connected ... with the load'

12 State the unit of electrical power. State three formulae used to calculate power

---

BTEC National Study Guide: Engineering. See page 325 for order details of individual texts

262

13 State two units used for electrical energy

14 State the three main effects of an electric current and give two examples of each

15 What is the function of a fuse in an electrical circuit?

Exercise 10   Multi-choice problems on the introduction to electric circuits (Answers on page 375)

1 60 μs is equivalent to:
(a) 0.06 s   (b) 0.00006 s
(c) 1000 minutes   (d) 0.6 s

2 The current which flows when 0.1 coulomb is transferred in 10 ms is:
(a) 1 A   (b) 10 A
(c) 10 mA   (d) 100 mA

3 The p.d. applied to a 1 kΩ resistance in order that a current of 100 μA may flow is:
(a) 1 V   (b) 100 V   (c) 0.1 V   (d) 10 V

4 Which of the following formulae for electrical power is incorrect?

(a) VI (b) $\dfrac{V}{I}$ (c) I^2R (d) $\dfrac{V^2}{R}$

5 The power dissipated by a resistor of 4 Ω when a current of 5 A passes through it is:
(a) 6.25 W   (b) 20 W
(c) 80 W   (d) 100 W

6 Which of the following statements is true?
(a) Electric current is measured in volts
(b) 200 kΩ resistance is equivalent to 2 MΩ
(c) An ammeter has a low resistance and must be connected in parallel with a circuit

(d) An electrical insulator has a high resistance

7 A current of 3 A flows for 50 h through a 6 Ω resistor. The energy consumed by the resistor is:
(a) 0.9 kWh   (b) 2.7 kWh
(c) 9 kWh   (d) 27 kWh

8 What must be known in order to calculate the energy used by an electrical appliance?
(a) voltage and current
(b) current and time of operation
(c) power and time of operation
(d) current and resistance

9 Voltage drop is the:
(a) maximum potential
(b) difference in potential between two points
(c) voltage produced by a source
(d) voltage at the end of a circuit

10 A 240 V, 60 W lamp has a working resistance of:
(a) 1400 ohm   (b) 60 ohm
(c) 960 ohm   (d) 325 ohm

11 The largest number of 100 W electric light bulbs which can be operated from a 240 V supply fitted with a 13 A fuse is:
(a) 2   (b) 7   (c) 31   (d) 18

12 The energy used by a 1.5 kW heater in 5 minutes is:
(a) 5 J   (b) 450 J
(c) 7500 J   (d) 450 000 J

13 When an atom loses an electron, the atom:
(a) becomes positively charged
(b) disintegrates
(c) experiences no effect at all
(d) becomes negatively charged

BTEC National Study Guide: Engineering. See page 325 for order details of individual texts

263

3

Resistance variation

At the end of this chapter you should be able to:

- appreciate that electrical resistance depends on four factors

- appreciate that resistance $R = \rho l / a$, where ρ is the resistivity

- recognize typical values of resistivity and its unit

- perform calculations using $R = \rho l / a$

- define the temperature coefficient of resistance, α

- recognize typical values for α

- perform calculations using $R_\theta = R_0(1 + \alpha\theta)$

- determine the resistance and tolerance of a fixed resistor from its colour code

- determine the resistance and tolerance of a fixed resistor from its letter and digit code

---

3.1 Resistance and resistivity

The resistance of an electrical conductor depends on four factors, these being: (a) the length of the conductor, (b) the cross-sectional area of the conductor, (c) the type of material and (d) the temperature of the material. Resistance, R, is directly proportional to length, l, of a conductor, i.e. $R \propto l$. Thus, for example, if the length of a piece of wire is doubled, then the resistance is doubled.

Resistance, R, is inversely proportional to cross-sectional area, a, of a conductor, i.e. $R \propto 1/a$. Thus, for example, if the cross-sectional area of a piece of wire is doubled then the resistance is halved.

Since $R \propto l$ and $R \propto 1/a$ then $R \propto l/a$. By inserting a constant of proportionality into this relationship the type of material used may be taken into account. The constant of proportionality is known as the **resistivity** of the material and is given the symbol ρ (Greek rho). Thus,

$$\text{resistance} \quad \boxed{R = \frac{\rho l}{a} \text{ ohms}}$$

ρ is measured in ohm metres (Ω m). The value of the resistivity is that resistance of a unit cube of the material measured between opposite faces of the cube.

Resistivity varies with temperature and some typical values of resistivities measured at about room temperature are given below:

Copper $1.7 \times 10^{-8}\ \Omega$ m (or $0.017\,\mu\Omega$ m)

Aluminium $2.6 \times 10^{-8}\ \Omega$ m (or $0.026\,\mu\Omega$ m)

Carbon (graphite) $10 \times 10^{-8}\ \Omega$ m ($0.10\,\mu\Omega$ m)

BTEC National Study Guide: Engineering. See page 325 for order details of individual texts

264

Glass $1 \times 10^{10}\,\Omega\,\text{m}$ (or $10^4\,\mu\Omega\,\text{m}$)

Mica $1 \times 10^{13}\,\Omega\,\text{m}$ (or $10^7\,\mu\Omega\,\text{m}$)

Note that good conductors of electricity have a low value of resistivity and good insulators have a high value of resistivity.

Problem 1. The resistance of a 5 m length of wire is 600 Ω. Determine (a) the resistance of an 8 m length of the same wire, and (b) the length of the same wire when the resistance is 420 Ω.

(a) Resistance, R, is directly proportional to length, l, i.e. $R \propto l$. Hence, $600\,\Omega \propto 5\,\text{m}$ or $600 = (k)(5)$, where k is the coefficient of proportionality.

Hence, $k = \dfrac{600}{5} = 120$

When the length l is 8 m, then resistance $R = kl = (120)(8) = \mathbf{960\,\Omega}$

(b) When the resistance is 420 Ω, $420 = kl$, from which,

length $l = \dfrac{420}{k} = \dfrac{420}{120} = \mathbf{3.5\,m}$

Problem 2. A piece of wire of cross-sectional area $2\,\text{mm}^2$ has a resistance of 300 Ω. Find (a) the resistance of a wire of the same length and material if the cross-sectional area is $5\,\text{mm}^2$, (b) the cross-sectional area of a wire of the same length and material of resistance 750 Ω.

Resistance R is inversely proportional to cross-sectional area, a, i.e. $R \propto 1/a$

Hence $300\,\Omega \propto \frac{1}{2}\text{mm}^2$ or $300 = (k)(\frac{1}{2})$,

from which, the coefficient of proportionality, $k = 300 \times 2 = 600$

(a) When the cross-sectional area $a = 5\,\text{mm}^2$ then

$R = (k)(\frac{1}{5})$

$= (600)(\frac{1}{5}) = \mathbf{120\,\Omega}$

(Note that resistance has decreased as the cross-sectional is increased.)

(b) When the resistance is 750 Ω then

$750 = (k)\left(\dfrac{1}{a}\right)$

from which

cross-sectional area, $a = \dfrac{k}{750} = \dfrac{600}{750}$

$= \mathbf{0.8\,mm^2}$

Problem 3. A wire of length 8 m and cross-sectional area $3\,\text{mm}^2$ has a resistance of 0.16 Ω. If the wire is drawn out until its cross-sectional area is $1\,\text{mm}^2$, determine the resistance of the wire.

Resistance R is directly proportional to length l, and inversely proportional to the cross-sectional area, a, i.e.

$R \propto l/a$ or $R = k(l/a)$, where k is the coefficient of proportionality.

Since $R = 0.16$, $l = 8$ and $a = 3$, then $0.16 = (k)(8/3)$, from which $k = 0.16 \times 3/8 = 0.06$

If the cross-sectional area is reduced to 1/3 of its original area then the length must be tripled to 3×8, i.e. 24 m

New resistance $R = k\left(\dfrac{l}{a}\right) = 0.06\left(\dfrac{24}{1}\right)$

$= \mathbf{1.44\,\Omega}$

Problem 4. Calculate the resistance of a 2 km length of aluminium overhead power cable if the cross-sectional area of the cable is $100\,\text{mm}^2$. Take the resistivity of aluminium to be $0.03 \times 10^{-6}\,\Omega\,\text{m}$.

Length $l = 2\,\text{km} = 2000\,\text{m}$, area $a = 100\,\text{mm}^2 = 100 \times 10^{-6}\,\text{m}^2$ and resistivity $\rho = 0.03 \times 10^{-6}\,\Omega\,\text{m}$.

Resistance $R = \dfrac{\rho l}{a}$

$= \dfrac{(0.03 \times 10^{-6}\,\Omega\,\text{m})(2000\,\text{m})}{(100 \times 10^{-6}\,\text{m}^2)}$

$= \dfrac{0.03 \times 2000}{100}\,\Omega = \mathbf{0.6\,\Omega}$

Problem 5. Calculate the cross-sectional area, in mm^2, of a piece of copper wire, 40 m in length and having a resistance of 0.25 Ω. Take the resistivity of copper as $0.02 \times 10^{-6}\,\Omega\,\text{m}$.

BTEC National Study Guide: Engineering. See page 325 for order details of individual texts

265

Resistance $R = \rho l/a$ hence cross-sectional area

$$a = \frac{\rho l}{R} = \frac{(0.02 \times 10^{-6}\,\Omega\,\mathrm{m})(40\,\mathrm{m})}{0.25\,\Omega}$$

$$= 3.2 \times 10^{-6}\,\mathrm{m}^2$$

$$= (3.2 \times 10^{-6}) \times 10^6\,\mathrm{mm}^2 = \mathbf{3.2\,mm^2}$$

Problem 6. The resistance of 1.5 km of wire of cross-sectional area 0.17 mm^2 is 150 Ω. Determine the resistivity of the wire.

Resistance, $R = \rho l/a$ hence

$$\text{resistivity } \rho = \frac{Ra}{l}$$

$$= \frac{(150\,\Omega)(0.17 \times 10^{-6}\,\mathrm{m}^2)}{(1500\,\mathrm{m})}$$

$$= \mathbf{0.017 \times 10^{-6}\,\Omega\,m}$$

$$\text{or } \mathbf{0.017\,\mu\Omega\,m}$$

Problem 7. Determine the resistance of 1200 m of copper cable having a diameter of 12 mm if the resistivity of copper is $1.7 \times 10^{-8}\,\Omega\,\mathrm{m}$.

Cross-sectional area of cable,

$$a = \pi r^2 = \pi \left(\frac{12}{2}\right)^2$$

$$= 36\pi\,\mathrm{mm}^2 = 36\pi \times 10^{-6}\,\mathrm{m}^2$$

$$\text{Resistance } R = \frac{\rho l}{a}$$

$$= \frac{(1.7 \times 10^{-8}\,\Omega\,\mathrm{m})(1200\,\mathrm{m})}{(36\pi \times 10^{-6}\,\mathrm{m}^2)}$$

$$= \frac{1.7 \times 1200 \times 10^6}{10^8 \times 36\pi}\,\Omega$$

$$= \frac{1.7 \times 12}{36\pi}\,\Omega = \mathbf{0.180\,\Omega}$$

Now try the following exercise

Exercise 11 Further problems on resistance and resistivity

1 The resistance of a 2 m length of cable is 2.5 Ω. Determine (a) the resistance of a 7 m length of the same cable and (b) the length of the same wire when the resistance is 6.25 Ω.
[(a) 8.75 Ω (b) 5 m]

2 Some wire of cross-sectional area 1 mm^2 has a resistance of 20 Ω.
Determine (a) the resistance of a wire of the same length and material if the cross-sectional area is 4 mm^2, and (b) the cross-sectional area of a wire of the same length and material if the resistance is 32 Ω
[(a) 5 Ω (b) 0.625 mm^2]

3 Some wire of length 5 m and cross-sectional area 2 mm^2 has a resistance of 0.08 Ω. If the wire is drawn out until its cross-sectional area is 1 mm^2, determine the resistance of the wire.
[0.32 Ω]

4 Find the resistance of 800 m of copper cable of cross-sectional area 20 mm^2. Take the resistivity of copper as 0.02 $\mu\Omega$ m
[0.8 Ω]

5 Calculate the cross-sectional area, in mm^2, of a piece of aluminium wire 100 m long and having a resistance of 2 Ω. Take the resistivity of aluminium as $0.03 \times 10^{-6}\,\Omega$ m [1.5 mm^2]

6 The resistance of 500 m of wire of cross-sectional area 2.6 mm^2 is 5 Ω. Determine the resistivity of the wire in $\mu\Omega$ m
[0.026 $\mu\Omega$ m]

7 Find the resistance of 1 km of copper cable having a diameter of 10 mm if the resistivity of copper is $0.017 \times 10^{-6}\,\Omega$ m [0.216 Ω]

3.2 Temperature coefficient of resistance

In general, as the temperature of a material increases, most conductors increase in resistance, insulators decrease in resistance, whilst the resistance of some special alloys remain almost constant.

The **temperature coefficient of resistance** of a material is the increase in the resistance of a 1 Ω

BTEC National Study Guide: Engineering. See page 325 for order details of individual texts

266

resistor of that material when it is subjected to a rise of temperature of 1°C. The symbol used for the temperature coefficient of resistance is α (Greek alpha). Thus, if some copper wire of resistance 1 Ω is heated through 1°C and its resistance is then measured as 1.0043 Ω then $\alpha = 0.0043 \, \Omega/\Omega°C$ for copper. The units are usually expressed only as 'per °C', i.e. $\alpha = 0.0043/°C$ for copper. If the 1 Ω resistor of copper is heated through 100°C then the resistance at 100°C would be $1 + 100 \times 0.0043 = 1.43 \, \Omega$ Some typical values of temperature coefficient of resistance measured at 0°C are given below:

Copper	0.0043/°C
Nickel	0.0062/°C
Constantan	0
Aluminium	0.0038/°C
Carbon	−0.00048/°C
Eureka	0.00001/°C

(Note that the negative sign for carbon indicates that its resistance falls with increase of temperature.)

If the resistance of a material at 0°C is known the resistance at any other temperature can be determined from:

$$R_\theta = R_0(1 + \alpha_0\theta)$$

where R_0 = resistance at 0°C

R_θ = resistance at temperature θ°C

α_0 = temperature coefficient of resistance
at 0°C

Problem 8. A coil of copper wire has a resistance of 100 Ω when its temperature is 0°C. Determine its resistance at 70°C if the temperature coefficient of resistance of copper at 0°C is 0.0043/°C.

Resistance $R_\theta = R_0(1 + \alpha_0\theta)$. Hence resistance at 100°C,

$$R_{100} = 100[1 + (0.0043)(70)]$$
$$= 100[1 + 0.301]$$
$$= 100(1.301) = \mathbf{130.1 \, \Omega}$$

Problem 9. An aluminium cable has a resistance of 27 Ω at a temperature of 35°C. Determine its resistance at 0°C. Take the temperature coefficient of resistance at 0°C to be 0.0038/°C.

Resistance at θ°C, $R_\theta = R_0(1 + \alpha_0\theta)$. Hence resistance at 0°C,

$$R_0 = \frac{R_\theta}{(1 + \alpha_0\theta)} = \frac{27}{[1 + (0.0038)(35)]}$$
$$= \frac{27}{1 + 0.133}$$
$$= \frac{27}{1.133} = \mathbf{23.83 \, \Omega}$$

Problem 10. A carbon resistor has a resistance of 1 kΩ at 0°C. Determine its resistance at 80°C. Assume that the temperature coefficient of resistance for carbon at 0°C is −0.0005/°C.

Resistance at temperature θ°C,

$$R_\theta = R_0(1 + \alpha_0\theta)$$

i.e.

$$R_\theta = 1000[1 + (-0.0005)(80)]$$
$$= 1000[1 - 0.040] = 1000(0.96) = \mathbf{960 \, \Omega}$$

If the resistance of a material at room temperature (approximately 20°C), R_{20}, and the temperature coefficient of resistance at 20°C, α_{20}, are known then the resistance R_θ at temperature θ°C is given by:

$$R_\theta = R_{20}[1 + \alpha_{20}(\theta - 20)]$$

Problem 11. A coil of copper wire has a resistance of 10 Ω at 20°C. If the temperature coefficient of resistance of copper at 20°C is 0.004/°C determine the resistance of the coil when the temperature rises to 100°C.

Resistance at θ°C,

$$R_\theta = R_{20}[1 + \alpha_{20}(\theta - 20)]$$

BTEC National Study Guide: Engineering. See page 325 for order details of individual texts

267

Hence resistance at 100°C,

$$R_{100} = 10[1 + (0.004)(100 - 20)]$$
$$= 10[1 + (0.004)(80)]$$
$$= 10[1 + 0.32]$$
$$= 10(1.32) = \mathbf{13.2\ \Omega}$$

Problem 12. The resistance of a coil of aluminium wire at 18°C is 200 Ω. The temperature of the wire is increased and the resistance rises to 240 Ω. If the temperature coefficient of resistance of aluminium is 0.0039/°C at 18°C determine the temperature to which the coil has risen.

Let the temperature rise to θ°C. Resistance at θ°C,

$$R_\theta = R_{18}[1 + \alpha_{18}(\theta - 18)]$$

i.e.

$$240 = 200[1 + (0.0039)(\theta - 18)]$$
$$240 = 200 + (200)(0.0039)(\theta - 18)$$
$$240 - 200 = 0.78(\theta - 18)$$
$$40 = 0.78(\theta - 18)$$
$$\frac{40}{0.78} = \theta - 18$$
$$51.28 = \theta - 18,\ \text{from which,}$$
$$\theta = 51.28 + 18 = 69.28°C$$

Hence the temperature of the coil increases to 69.28°C

If the resistance at 0°C is not known, but is known at some other temperature θ_1, then the resistance at any temperature can be found as follows:

$$R_1 = R_0(1 + \alpha_0\theta_1)$$
and
$$R_2 = R_0(1 + \alpha_0\theta_2)$$

Dividing one equation by the other gives:

$$\boxed{\frac{R_1}{R_2} = \frac{1 + \alpha_0\theta_1}{1 + \alpha_0\theta_2}}$$

where R_2 = resistance at temperature θ_2

Problem 13. Some copper wire has a resistance of 200 Ω at 20°C. A current is passed through the wire and the temperature rises to 90°C. Determine the resistance of the wire at 90°C, correct to the nearest ohm, assuming that the temperature coefficient of resistance is 0.004/°C at 0°C.

$$R_{20} = 200\ \Omega,\ \alpha_0 = 0.004/°C$$

and

$$\frac{R_{20}}{R_{90}} = \frac{[1 + \alpha_0(20)]}{[1 + \alpha_0(90)]}$$

Hence

$$R_{90} = \frac{R_{20}[1 + 90\alpha_0]}{[1 + 20\alpha_0]}$$
$$= \frac{200[1 + 90(0.004)]}{[1 + 20(0.004)]}$$
$$= \frac{200[1 + 0.36]}{[1 + 0.08]}$$
$$= \frac{200(1.36)}{(1.08)} = \mathbf{251.85\ \Omega}$$

i.e. the resistance of the wire at 90°C is 252 Ω, correct to the nearest ohm

---

Now try the following exercises

Exercise 12   Further problems on the temperature coefficient of resistance

1 A coil of aluminium wire has a resistance of 50 Ω when its temperature is 0°C. Determine its resistance at 100°C if the temperature coefficient of resistance of aluminium at 0°C is 0.0038/°C   [69 Ω]

2 A copper cable has a resistance of 30 Ω at a temperature of 50°C. Determine its resistance at 0°C. Take the temperature coefficient of resistance of copper at 0°C as 0.0043/°C   [24.69 Ω]

3 The temperature coefficient of resistance for carbon at 0°C is −0.00048/°C. What is the significance of the minus sign? A carbon resistor has a resistance of 500 Ω at 0°C. Determine its resistance at 50°C.   [488 Ω]

BTEC National Study Guide: Engineering. See page 325 for order details of individual texts

268

4 A coil of copper wire has a resistance of 20 Ω at 18°C. If the temperature coefficient of resistance of copper at 18°C is 0.004/°C, determine the resistance of the coil when the temperature rises to 98°C [26.4 Ω]

5 The resistance of a coil of nickel wire at 20°C is 100 Ω. The temperature of the wire is increased and the resistance rises to 130 Ω. If the temperature coefficient of resistance of nickel is 0.006/°C at 20°C, determine the temperature to which the coil has risen.

[70°C]

6 Some aluminium wire has a resistance of 50 Ω at 20°C. The wire is heated to a temperature of 100°C. Determine the resistance of the wire at 100°C, assuming that the temperature coefficient of resistance at 0°C is 0.004/°C

[64.8 Ω]

7 A copper cable is 1.2 km long and has a cross-sectional area of 5 mm². Find its resistance at 80°C if at 20°C the resistivity of copper is 0.02×10^{-6} Ω m and its temperature coefficient of resistance is 0.004/°C [5.95 Ω]

3.3 Resistor colour coding and ohmic values

(a) Colour code for fixed resistors

The colour code for fixed resistors is given in Table 3.1

(i) For a **four-band fixed resistor** (i.e. resistance values with two significant figures):
yellow-violet-orange-red indicates 47 k Ω with a tolerance of ±2%
(Note that the first band is the one nearest the end of the resistor)

(ii) For a **five-band fixed resistor** (i.e. resistance values with three significant figures): red-yellow-white-orange-brown indicates 249 k Ω with a tolerance of ±1%
(Note that the fifth band is 1.5 to 2 times wider than the other bands)

Table 3.1

Colour	Significant Figures	Multiplier	Tolerance
Silver	–	10^{-2}	±10%
Gold	–	10^{-1}	±5%
Black	0	1	–
Brown	1	10	±1%
Red	2	10^2	±2%
Orange	3	10^3	–
Yellow	4	10^4	–
Green	5	10^5	±0.5%
Blue	6	10^6	±0.25%
Violet	7	10^7	±0.1%
Grey	8	10^8	–
White	9	10^9	–
None	–	–	±20%

Problem 14. Determine the value and tolerance of a resistor having a colour coding of: orange-orange-silver-brown.

The first two bands, i.e. orange-orange, give 33 from Table 3.1
The third band, silver, indicates a multiplier of 10^2 from Table 3.1, which means that the value of the resistor is $33 \times 10^{-2} = 0.33$ Ω
The fourth band, i.e. brown, indicates a tolerance of ±1% from Table 3.1 Hence a colour coding of orange-orange-silver-brown represents a resistor of value **0.33 Ω with a tolerance of ±1%**

Problem 15. Determine the value and tolerance of a resistor having a colour coding of: brown-black-brown.

The first two bands, i.e. brown-black, give 10 from Table 3.1
The third band, brown, indicates a multiplier of 10 from Table 3.1, which means that the value of the resistor is $10 \times 10 = 100$ Ω
There is no fourth band colour in this case; hence, from Table 3.1, the tolerance is ±20% Hence a colour coding of brown-black-brown represents a resistor of value **100 Ω with a tolerance of ±20%**

Problem 16. Between what two values should a resistor with colour coding brown-black-brown-silver lie?

BTEC National Study Guide: Engineering. See page 325 for order details of individual texts

269

From Table 3.1, brown-black-brown-silver indicates 10×10, i.e. $100\,\Omega$, with a tolerance of $\pm 10\%$ This means that the value could lie between

$$(100 - 10\% \text{ of } 100)\,\Omega$$

and $$(100 + 10\% \text{ of } 100)\,\Omega$$

i.e. brown-black-brown-silver indicates any value **between 90 Ω and 110 Ω**

Problem 17. Determine the colour coding for a $47\,\text{k}\,\Omega$ having a tolerance of $\pm 5\%$.

From Table 3.1, $47\,\text{k}\,\Omega = 47 \times 10^3$ has a colour coding of yellow-violet-orange. With a tolerance of $\pm 5\%$, the fourth band will be gold. Hence $47\,\text{k}\,\Omega \pm 5\%$ has a colour coding of: **yellow-violet-orange-gold**.

Problem 18. Determine the value and tolerance of a resistor having a colour coding of: orange-green-red-yellow-brown.

---

orange-green-red-yellow-brown is a five-band fixed resistor and from Table 3.1, indicates: $352 \times 10^4\,\Omega$ with a tolerance of $\pm 1\%$ $352 \times 10^4\,\Omega = 3.52 \times 10^6\,\Omega$, i.e. $3.52\,\text{M}\,\Omega$

Hence orange-green-red-yellow-brown indicates **3.52 M Ω $\pm 1\%$**

(b) Letter and digit code for resistors

Another way of indicating the value of resistors is the letter and digit code shown in Table 3.2

Table 3.2

Resistance Value	Marked as:
$0.47\,\Omega$	R47
$1\,\Omega$	1R0
$4.7\,\Omega$	4R7
$47\,\Omega$	47R
$100\,\Omega$	100R
$1\,\text{k}\,\Omega$	1K0
$10\,\text{k}\,\Omega$	10 K
$10\,\text{M}\,\Omega$	10 M

Tolerance is indicated as follows: $F = \pm 1\%$, $G = \pm 2\%$, $J = \pm 5\%$, $K = \pm 10\%$ and $M = \pm 20\%$ Thus, for example,

$$\text{R33M} = 0.33\,\Omega \pm 20\%$$

$$\text{4R7K} = 4.7\,\Omega \pm 10\%$$

$$\text{390RJ} = 390\,\Omega \pm 5\%$$

Problem 19. Determine the value of a resistor marked as 6K8F.

From Table 3.2, 6K8F is equivalent to: **6.8 k Ω $\pm 1\%$**

Problem 20. Determine the value of a resistor marked as 4M7M.

From Table 3.2, 4M7M is equivalent to: **4.7 M Ω $\pm 20\%$**

Problem 21. Determine the letter and digit code for a resistor having a value of $68\,\text{k}\,\Omega \pm 10\%$.

From Table 3.2, $68\,\text{k}\,\Omega \pm 10\%$ has a letter and digit code of: **68 KK**

Now try the following exercises

Exercise 13 Further problems on resistor colour coding and ohmic values

1 Determine the value and tolerance of a resistor having a colour coding of: blue-grey-orange-red   [$68\,\text{k}\,\Omega \pm 2\%$]

2 Determine the value and tolerance of a resistor having a colour coding of: yellow-violet-gold   [$4.7\,\Omega \pm 20\%$]

3 Determine the value and tolerance of a resistor having a colour coding of: blue-white-black-black-gold   [$690\,\Omega \pm 5\%$]

4 Determine the colour coding for a $51\,\text{k}\,\Omega$ resistor having a tolerance of $\pm 2\%$ [green-brown-orange-red]

BTEC National Study Guide: Engineering. See page 325 for order details of individual texts

270

5 Determine the colour coding for a $1\,M\Omega$ resistor having a tolerance of $\pm10\%$
[brown-black-green-silver]

6 Determine the range of values expected for a resistor with colour coding: red-black-green-silver
[$1.8\,M\Omega$ to $2.2\,M\Omega$]

7 Determine the range of values expected for a resistor with colour coding: yellow-black-orange-brown
[$39.6\,k\Omega$ to $40.4\,k\Omega$]

8 Determine the value of a resistor marked as
(a) R22G (b) 4K7F
[(a) $0.22\,\Omega \pm 2\%$ (b) $4.7\,k\Omega \pm 1\%$]

9 Determine the letter and digit code for a resistor having a value of $100\,k\Omega \pm 5\%$
[100 KJ]

10 Determine the letter and digit code for a resistor having a value of $6.8\,M\Omega \pm 20\%$
[6 M8 M]

Exercise 14 Short answer questions on resistance variation

1 Name four factors which can effect the resistance of a conductor

2 If the length of a piece of wire of constant cross-sectional area is halved, the resistance of the wire is . . . . . .

3 If the cross-sectional area of a certain length of cable is trebled, the resistance of the cable is . . . . . .

4 What is resistivity? State its unit and the symbol used.

5 Complete the following:

Good conductors of electricity have a . . . . . . value of resistivity and good insulators have a . . . . . . value of resistivity

6 What is meant by the 'temperature coefficient of resistance ? State its units and the symbols used.

7 If the resistance of a metal at $0°C$ is R_0, R_θ is the resistance at $\theta°C$ and α_0 is the temperature coefficient of resistance at $0°C$ then: $R_\theta = $ . . . . . .

---

8 Explain briefly the colour coding on resistors

9 Explain briefly the letter and digit code for resistors

Exercise 15 Multi-choice questions on resistance variation (Answers on page 375)

1 The unit of resistivity is:
(a) ohms
(b) ohm millimetre
(c) ohm metre
(d) ohm/metre

2 The length of a certain conductor of resistance $100\,\Omega$ is doubled and its cross-sectional area is halved. Its new resistance is:
(a) $100\,\Omega$ (b) $200\,\Omega$
(c) $50\,\Omega$ (d) $400\,\Omega$

3 The resistance of a $2\,km$ length of cable of cross-sectional area $2\,mm^2$ and resistivity of $2 \times 10^{-8}\,\Omega m$ is:
(a) $0.02\,\Omega$ (b) $20\,\Omega$
(c) $0.02\,m\Omega$ (d) $200\,\Omega$

4 A piece of graphite has a cross-sectional area of $10\,mm^2$. If its resistance is $0.1\,\Omega$ and its resistivity $10 \times 10^8\,\Omega\,m$, its length is:
(a) $10\,km$ (b) $10\,cm$
(c) $10\,mm$ (d) $10\,m$

5 The symbol for the unit of temperature coefficient of resistance is:
(a) $\Omega/°C$ (b) Ω
(c) $°C$ (d) $\Omega/\Omega°C$

6 A coil of wire has a resistance of $10\,\Omega$ at $0°C$. If the temperature coefficient of resistance for the wire is $0.004/°C$, its resistance at $100°C$ is:
(a) $0.4\,\Omega$ (b) $1.4\,\Omega$
(c) $14\,\Omega$ (d) $10\,\Omega$

7 A nickel coil has a resistance of $13\,\Omega$ at $50°C$. If the temperature coefficient of resistance at $0°C$ is $0.006/°C$, the resistance at $0°C$ is:
(a) $16.9\,\Omega$ (b) $10\,\Omega$
(c) $43.3\,\Omega$ (d) $0.1\,\Omega$

BTEC National Study Guide: Engineering. See page 325 for order details of individual texts

271

8 A colour coding of red-violet-black on a resistor indicates a value of:

    (a) $27\,\Omega \pm 20\%$ (b) $270\,\Omega$

    (c) $270\,\Omega \pm 20\%$ (d) $27\,\Omega \pm 10\%$

9 A resistor marked as 4K7G indicates a value of:

    (a) $47\,\Omega \pm 20\%$ (b) $4.7\,\mathrm{k}\Omega \pm 20\%$

    (c) $0.47\,\Omega \pm 10\%$ (d) $4.7\,\mathrm{k}\Omega \pm 2\%$

BTEC National Study Guide: Engineering. See page 325 for order details of individual texts

272

5

Series and parallel networks

At the end of this chapter you should be able to:

- calculate unknown voltages, current and resistances in a series circuit
- understand voltage division in a series circuit
- calculate unknown voltages, currents and resistances in a parallel network
- calculate unknown voltages, currents and resistances in series-parallel networks
- understand current division in a two-branch parallel network
- describe the advantages and disadvantages of series and parallel connection of lamps

5.1 Series circuits

Figure 5.1 shows three resistors R_1, R_2 and R_3 connected end to end, i.e. in series, with a battery source of V volts. Since the circuit is closed a current I will flow and the p.d. across each resistor may be determined from the voltmeter readings V_1, V_2 and V_3.

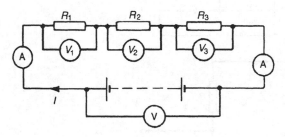

Figure 5.1

In a series circuit

(a) the current I is the same in all parts of the circuit and hence the same reading is found on each of the ammeters shown, and

(b) the sum of the voltages V_1, V_2 and V_3 is equal to the total applied voltage, V,

i.e.
$$V = V_1 + V_2 + V_3$$

From Ohm's law: $V_1 = IR_1$, $V_2 = IR_2$, $V_3 = IR_3$ and $V = IR$ where R is the total circuit resistance. Since $V = V_1 + V_2 + V_3$ then $IR = IR_1 + IR_2 + IR_3$. Dividing throughout by I gives

$$R = R_1 + R_2 + R_3$$

Thus for a series circuit, the total resistance is obtained by adding together the values of the separate resistance's.

Problem 1. For the circuit shown in Fig. 5.2, determine (a) the battery voltage V, (b) the total resistance of the circuit, and (c) the values of resistors R_1, R_2 and R_3, given that the p.d.'s across R_1, R_2 and R_3 are 5 V, 2 V and 6 V respectively.

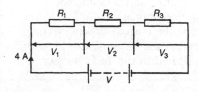

Figure 5.2

(a) Battery voltage $V = V_1 + V_2 + V_3$

$$= 5 + 2 + 6 = \mathbf{13\,V}$$

BTEC National Study Guide: Engineering. See page 325 for order details of individual texts

273

(b) Total circuit resistance $R = \dfrac{V}{I} = \dfrac{13}{4} = 3.25\,\Omega$

(c) Resistance $R_1 = \dfrac{V_1}{I} = \dfrac{5}{4} = 1.25\,\Omega$

Resistance $R_2 = \dfrac{V_2}{I} = \dfrac{2}{4} = 0.5\,\Omega$

Resistance $R_3 = \dfrac{V_3}{I} = \dfrac{6}{4} = 1.5\,\Omega$

(Check: $R_1 + R_2 + R_3 = 1.25 + 0.5 + 1.5 = 3.25\,\Omega = R$)

Problem 2. For the circuit shown in Fig. 5.3, determine the p.d. across resistor R_3. If the total resistance of the circuit is $100\,\Omega$, determine the current flowing through resistor R_1. Find also the value of resistor R_2.

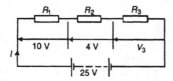

Figure 5.3

P.d. across R_3, $V_3 = 25 - 10 - 4 = \mathbf{11\,V}$

Current $I = \dfrac{V}{R} = \dfrac{25}{100} = \mathbf{0.25\,A}$,

which is the current flowing in each resistor

Resistance $R_2 = \dfrac{V_2}{I} = \dfrac{4}{0.25} = \mathbf{16\,\Omega}$

Problem 3. A 12 V battery is connected in a circuit having three series-connected resistors having resistance's of $4\,\Omega$, $9\,\Omega$ and $11\,\Omega$. Determine the current flowing through, and the p.d. across the $9\,\Omega$ resistor. Find also the power dissipated in the $11\,\Omega$ resistor.

The circuit diagram is shown in Fig. 5.4

Total resistance $R = 4 + 9 + 11 = 24\,\Omega$

Current $I = \dfrac{V}{R} = \dfrac{12}{24} = \mathbf{0.5\,A}$,

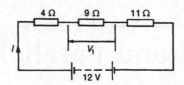

Figure 5.4

which is the current in the $9\,\Omega$ resistor.
P.d. across the $9\,\Omega$ resistor,

$$V_1 = I \times 9 = 0.5 \times 9 = \mathbf{4.5\,V}$$

Power dissipated in the $11\,\Omega$ resistor,

$$P = I^2 R = (0.5)^2(11)$$
$$= (0.25)(11) = \mathbf{2.75\,W}$$

5.2 Potential divider

The voltage distribution for the circuit shown in Fig. 5.5(a) is given by:

$$V_1 = \left(\frac{R_1}{R_1 + R_2}\right) V \text{ and } V_2 = \left(\frac{R_2}{R_1 + R_2}\right) V$$

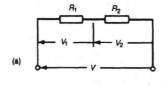

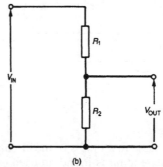

Figure 5.5

The circuit shown in Fig. 5.5(b) is often referred to as a **potential divider** circuit. Such a circuit can consist of a number of similar elements in series connected across a voltage source, voltages

BTEC National Study Guide: Engineering. See page 325 for order details of individual texts

274

being taken from connections between the elements. Frequently the divider consists of two resistors as shown in Fig. 5.5(b), where

$$V_{\text{OUT}} = \left(\frac{R_2}{R_1 + R_2}\right) V_{\text{IN}}$$

Problem 4.   Determine the value of voltage V shown in Fig. 5.6

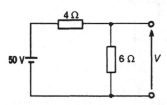

Figure 5.6

Figure 5.6 may be redrawn as shown in Fig. 5.7, and

$$\text{voltage } V = \left(\frac{6}{6+4}\right)(50) = 30\,\text{V}$$

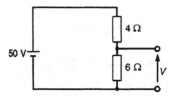

Figure 5.7

Problem 5.   Two resistors are connected in series across a 24 V supply and a current of 3 A flows in the circuit. If one of the resistors has a resistance of 2 Ω determine (a) the value of the other resistor, and (b) the p.d. across the 2 Ω resistor. If the circuit is connected for 50 hours, how much energy is used?

The circuit diagram is shown in Fig. 5.8

(a) Total circuit resistance

$$R = \frac{V}{I} = \frac{24}{3} = 8\,\Omega$$

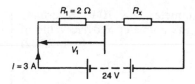

Figure 5.8

Value of unknown resistance,

$$R_x = 8 - 2 = 6\,\Omega$$

(b) P.d. across 2 Ω resistor,

$$V_1 = IR_1 = 3 \times 2 = 6\,\text{V}$$

Alternatively, from above,

$$V_1 = \left(\frac{R_1}{R_1 + R_x}\right) \text{V}$$

$$= \left(\frac{2}{2+6}\right)(24) = 6\,\text{V}$$

Energy used = power × time

$$= (V \times I) \times t$$

$$= (24 \times 3\,\text{W})(50\,\text{h})$$

$$= 3600\,\text{Wh} = \mathbf{3.6\,kWh}$$

Now try the following exercise

Exercise 19   Further problems on series circuits

1 The p.d's measured across three resistors connected in series are 5 V, 7 V and 10 V, and the supply current is 2 A. Determine (a) the supply voltage, (b) the total circuit resistance and (c) the values of the three resistors.
   [(a) 22 V (b) 11 Ω (c) 2.5 Ω, 3.5 Ω, 5 Ω]

2 For the circuit shown in Fig. 5.9, determine the value of V_1. If the total circuit resistance is 36 Ω determine the supply current and the value of resistors R_1, R_2 and R_3
   [10 V, 0.5 A, 20 Ω, 10 Ω, 6 Ω]

3 When the switch in the circuit in Fig. 5.10 is closed the reading on voltmeter 1 is 30 V

BTEC National Study Guide: Engineering. See page 325 for order details of individual texts

275

and that on voltmeter 2 is 10 V. Determine the reading on the ammeter and the value of resistor R_x [4 A, 2.5 Ω]

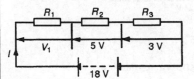

Figure 5.9

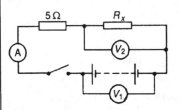

Figure 5.10

4 Calculate the value of voltage V in Fig. 5.11 [45 V]

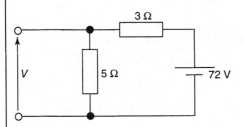

Figure 5.11

5 Two resistors are connected in series across an 18 V supply and a current of 5 A flows. If one of the resistors has a value of 2.4 Ω determine (a) the value of the other resistor and (b) the p.d. across the 2.4 Ω resistor.
[(a) 1.2 Ω (b) 12 V]

5.3 Parallel networks

Figure 5.12 shows three resistors, R_1, R_2 and R_3 connected across each other, i.e. in parallel, across a battery source of V volts.

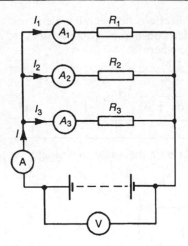

Figure 5.12

In a parallel circuit:

(a) the sum of the currents I_1, I_2 and I_3 is equal to the total circuit current, I,

i.e. $\boxed{I = I_1 + I_2 + I_3}$ and

(b) the source p.d., V volts, is the same across each of the resistors.

From Ohm's law:

$$I_1 = \frac{V}{R_1}, \; I_2 = \frac{V}{R_2}, \; I_3 = \frac{V}{R_3} \text{ and } I = \frac{V}{R}$$

where R is the total circuit resistance. Since

$$I = I_1 + I_2 + I_3 \text{ then } \frac{V}{R} = \frac{V}{R_1} + \frac{V}{R_2} + \frac{V}{R_3}$$

Dividing throughout by V gives:

$$\boxed{\frac{1}{R} = \frac{1}{R_1} + \frac{1}{R_2} + \frac{1}{R_3}}$$

This equation must be used when finding the total resistance R of a parallel circuit. For the special case of **two resistors in parallel**

$$\frac{1}{R} = \frac{1}{R_1} + \frac{1}{R_2} = \frac{R_2 + R_1}{R_1 R_2}$$

Hence $\boxed{R = \frac{R_1 R_2}{R_1 + R_2}} \quad \left(\text{i.e. } \frac{\text{product}}{\text{sum}}\right)$

BTEC National Study Guide: Engineering. See page 325 for order details of individual texts

276

Problem 6. For the circuit shown in Fig. 5.13, determine (a) the reading on the ammeter, and (b) the value of resistor R_2.

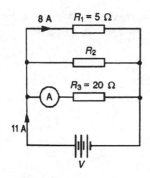

Figure 5.13

P.d. across R_1 is the same as the supply voltage V
Hence supply voltage, $V = 8 \times 5 = 40\,\text{V}$

(a) Reading on ammeter,

$$I = \frac{V}{R_3} = \frac{40}{20} = 2\,\text{A}$$

(b) Current flowing through $R_2 = 11 - 8 - 2 = 1\,\text{A}$. Hence

$$R_2 = \frac{V}{I_2} = \frac{40}{1} = 40\,\Omega$$

Problem 7. Two resistors, of resistance $3\,\Omega$ and $6\,\Omega$, are connected in parallel across a battery having a voltage of $12\,\text{V}$. Determine (a) the total circuit resistance and (b) the current flowing in the $3\,\Omega$ resistor.

The circuit diagram is shown in Fig. 5.14

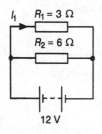

Figure 5.14

(a) The total circuit resistance R is given by

$$\frac{1}{R} = \frac{1}{R_1} + \frac{1}{R_2} = \frac{1}{3} + \frac{1}{6} = \frac{2+1}{6} = \frac{3}{6}$$

Since $\dfrac{1}{R} = \dfrac{3}{6}$ then $\mathbf{R = 2\,\Omega}$

(Alternatively,

$$R = \frac{R_1 R_2}{R_1 + R_2} = \frac{3 \times 6}{3 + 6} = \frac{18}{9} = 2\,\Omega)$$

(b) Current in the $3\,\Omega$ resistance,

$$I_1 = \frac{V}{R_1} = \frac{12}{3} = 4\,\text{A}$$

Problem 8. For the circuit shown in Fig. 5.15, find (a) the value of the supply voltage V and (b) the value of current I.

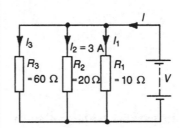

Figure 5.15

(a) P.d. across $20\,\Omega$ resistor $= I_2 R_2 = 3 \times 20 = 60\,\text{V}$, hence supply voltage $\mathbf{V = 60\,\text{V}}$ since the circuit is connected in parallel

(b) Current $I_1 = \dfrac{V}{R_1} = \dfrac{60}{10} = 6\,\text{A}$, $I_2 = 3\,\text{A}$

and $I_3 = \dfrac{V}{R_3} = \dfrac{60}{60} = 1\,\text{A}$

Current $I = I_1 + I_2 + I_3$ hence
$\mathbf{I} = 6 + 3 + 1 = \mathbf{10\,\text{A}}$.
Alternatively,

$$\frac{1}{R} = \frac{1}{60} + \frac{1}{20} + \frac{1}{10} = \frac{1 + 3 + 6}{60} = \frac{10}{60}$$

Hence total resistance

$$R = \frac{60}{10} = 6\,\Omega, \text{ and current}$$

$$\mathbf{I} = \frac{V}{R} = \frac{60}{6} = \mathbf{10\,\text{A}}$$

BTEC National Study Guide: Engineering. See page 325 for order details of individual texts

277

Problem 9. Given four $1\,\Omega$ resistors, state how they must be connected to give an overall resistance of (a) $\frac{1}{4}\,\Omega$ (b) $1\,\Omega$ (c) $1\frac{1}{3}\,\Omega$ (d) $2\frac{1}{2}\,\Omega$, all four resistors being connected in each case.

(a) **All four in parallel** (see Fig. 5.16), since

$$\frac{1}{R} = \frac{1}{1} + \frac{1}{1} + \frac{1}{1} + \frac{1}{1} = \frac{4}{1} \text{ i.e. } R = \frac{1}{4}\,\Omega$$

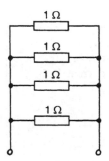

Figure 5.16

(b) **Two in series, in parallel with another two in series** (see Fig. 5.17), since $1\,\Omega$ and $1\,\Omega$ in series gives $2\,\Omega$, and $2\,\Omega$ in parallel with $2\,\Omega$ gives

$$\frac{2 \times 2}{2 + 2} = \frac{4}{4} = 1\,\Omega$$

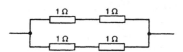

Figure 5.17

(c) **Three in parallel, in series with one** (see Fig. 5.18), since for the three in parallel,

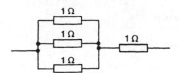

Figure 5.18

$$\frac{1}{R} = \frac{1}{1} + \frac{1}{1} + \frac{1}{1} = \frac{3}{1},$$

i.e. $R = \frac{1}{3}\,\Omega$ and $\frac{1}{3}\,\Omega$ in series with $1\,\Omega$ gives $1\frac{1}{3}\,\Omega$

(d) **Two in parallel, in series with two in series** (see Fig. 5.19), since for the two in parallel

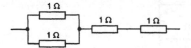

Figure 5.19

$$R = \frac{1 \times 1}{1 + 1} = \frac{1}{2}\,\Omega,$$

and $\frac{1}{2}\,\Omega$, $1\,\Omega$ and $1\,\Omega$ in series gives $2\frac{1}{2}\,\Omega$

Problem 10. Find the equivalent resistance for the circuit shown in Fig. 5.20

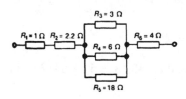

Figure 5.20

R_3, R_4 and R_5 are connected in parallel and their equivalent resistance R is given by

$$\frac{1}{R} = \frac{1}{3} + \frac{1}{6} + \frac{1}{18} = \frac{6 + 3 + 1}{18} = \frac{10}{18}$$

hence $R = (18/10) = 1.8\,\Omega$. The circuit is now equivalent to four resistors in series and the **equivalent circuit resistance** $= 1 + 2.2 + 1.8 + 4 = \mathbf{9\,\Omega}$

Problem 11. Resistances of $10\,\Omega$, $20\,\Omega$ and $30\,\Omega$ are connected (a) in series and (b) in parallel to a 240 V supply. Calculate the supply current in each case.

(a) The series circuit is shown in Fig. 5.21
The equivalent resistance
$R_T = 10\,\Omega + 20\,\Omega + 30\,\Omega = 60\,\Omega$

Supply current $I = \dfrac{V}{R_T} = \dfrac{240}{60} = \mathbf{4\,A}$

BTEC National Study Guide: Engineering. See page 325 for order details of individual texts

278

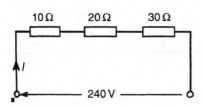

Figure 5.21

(b) The parallel circuit is shown in Fig. 5.22
The equivalent resistance R_T of $10\,\Omega$, $20\,\Omega$ and $30\,\Omega$ resistance's connected in parallel is given by:

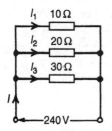

Figure 5.22

$$\frac{1}{R_T} = \frac{1}{10} + \frac{1}{20} + \frac{1}{30} = \frac{6+3+2}{60} = \frac{11}{60}$$

hence $R_T = \frac{60}{11}\,\Omega$

Supply current

$$I = \frac{V}{R_T} = \frac{240}{\frac{60}{11}} = \frac{240 \times 11}{60} = \mathbf{44\,A}$$

(Check:

$$I_1 = \frac{V}{R_1} = \frac{240}{10} = 24\,\text{A},$$

$$I_2 = \frac{V}{R_2} = \frac{240}{20} = 12\,\text{A}$$

and $I_3 = \frac{V}{R_3} = \frac{240}{30} = \mathbf{8\,A}$

For a parallel circuit $I = I_1 + I_2 + I_3$
$= 24 + 12 + 8 = \mathbf{44\,A}$, as above)

5.4 Current division

For the circuit shown in Fig. 5.23, the total circuit resistance, R_T is given by

$$R_T = \frac{R_1 R_2}{R_1 + R_2}$$

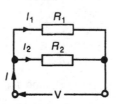

Figure 5.23

and $\qquad V = IR_T = I\left(\dfrac{R_1 R_2}{R_1 + R_2}\right)$

Current $\quad I_1 = \dfrac{V}{R_1} = \dfrac{I}{R_1}\left(\dfrac{R_1 R_2}{R_1 + R_2}\right)$

$$= \left(\frac{R_2}{R_1 + R_2}\right)(I)$$

Similarly,

current $\quad I_2 = \dfrac{V}{R_2} = \dfrac{I}{R_2}\left(\dfrac{R_1 R_2}{R_1 + R_2}\right)$

$$= \left(\frac{R_1}{R_1 + R_2}\right)(I)$$

Summarising, with reference to Fig. 5.23

$$\boxed{I_1 = \left(\frac{R_2}{R_1 + R_2}\right)(I)}$$

and $\qquad \boxed{I_2 = \left(\dfrac{R_1}{R_1 + R_2}\right)(I)}$

Problem 12. For the series-parallel arrangement shown in Fig. 5.24, find (a) the supply current, (b) the current flowing through each resistor and (c) the p.d. across each resistor.

BTEC National Study Guide: Engineering. See page 325 for order details of individual texts

279

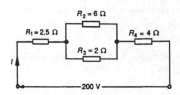

Figure 5.24

(a) The equivalent resistance R_x of R_2 and R_3 in parallel is:

$$R_x = \frac{6 \times 2}{6 + 2} == 1.5\,\Omega$$

The equivalent resistance R_T of R_1, R_x and R_4 in series is:

$$R_T = 2.5 + 1.5 + 4 = 8\,\Omega$$

Supply current

$$I = \frac{V}{R_T} = \frac{200}{8} = 25\,\text{A}$$

(b) The current flowing through R_1 and R_4 is 25 A. The current flowing through

$$R_2 = \left(\frac{R_3}{R_2 + R_3}\right)I = \left(\frac{2}{6 + 2}\right)25$$

$$= 6.25\,\text{A}$$

The current flowing through

$$R_3 = \left(\frac{R_2}{R_2 + R_3}\right)I$$

$$= \left(\frac{6}{6 + 2}\right)25 = 18.75\,\text{A}$$

(Note that the currents flowing through R_2 and R_3 must add up to the total current flowing into the parallel arrangement, i.e. 25 A)

(c) The equivalent circuit of Fig. 5.24 is shown in Fig. 5.25

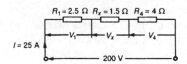

Figure 5.25

p.d. across R_1, i.e.

$$V_1 = IR_1 = (25)(2.5) = \mathbf{62.5\,V}$$

p.d. across R_x, i.e.

$$V_x = IR_x = (25)(1.5) = \mathbf{37.5\,V}$$

p.d. across R_4, i.e.

$$V_4 = IR_4 = (25)(4) = \mathbf{100\,V}$$

Hence the p.d. across R_2

$$= \text{p.d. across } R_3 = \mathbf{37.5\,V}$$

Problem 13. For the circuit shown in Fig. 5.26 calculate (a) the value of resistor R_x such that the total power dissipated in the circuit is 2.5 kW, (b) the current flowing in each of the four resistors.

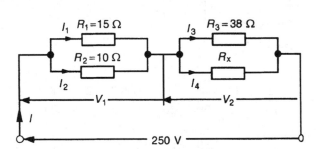

Figure 5.26

(a) Power dissipated $P = VI$ watts, hence

$$2500 = (250)(I)$$

i.e. $I = \dfrac{2500}{250} = 10\,\text{A}$

From Ohm's law,

$$R_T = \frac{V}{I} = \frac{250}{10} = 25\,\Omega,$$

where R_T is the equivalent circuit resistance. The equivalent resistance of R_1 and R_2 in parallel is

$$\frac{15 \times 10}{15 + 10} = \frac{150}{25} = 6\,\Omega$$

The equivalent resistance of resistors R_3 and R_x in parallel is equal to $25\,\Omega - 6\,\Omega$, i.e. $19\,\Omega$.

BTEC National Study Guide: Engineering. See page 325 for order details of individual texts

280

There are three methods whereby R_x can be determined.

Method 1

The voltage $V_1 = IR$, where R is $6\,\Omega$, from above, i.e. $V_1 = (10)(6) = 60\,\text{V}$. Hence

$$V_2 = 250\,\text{V} - 60\,\text{V} = 190\,\text{V}$$

$$= \text{p.d. across } R_3$$

$$= \text{p.d. across } R_x$$

$$I_3 = \frac{V_2}{R_3} = \frac{190}{38} = 5\,\text{A}.$$

Thus $I_4 = 5\,\text{A}$ also, since $I = 10\,\text{A}$. Thus

$$\mathbf{R_x} = \frac{V_2}{I_4} = \frac{190}{5} = \mathbf{38\,\Omega}$$

Method 2

Since the equivalent resistance of R_3 and R_x in parallel is $19\,\Omega$,

$$19 = \frac{38R_x}{38 + R_x} \quad \left(\text{i.e. } \frac{\text{product}}{\text{sum}} \right)$$

Hence

$$19(38 + R_x) = 38R_x$$

$$722 + 19R_x = 38R_x$$

$$722 = 38R_x - 19R_x = 19R_x$$

$$= 19R_x$$

Thus $$\mathbf{R_x} = \frac{722}{19} = \mathbf{38\,\Omega}$$

Method 3

When two resistors having the same value are connected in parallel the equivalent resistance is always half the value of one of the resistors. Thus, in this case, since $R_T = 19\,\Omega$ and $R_3 = 38\,\Omega$, then $R_x = 38\,\Omega$ could have been deduced on sight.

(b) Current $I_1 = \left(\dfrac{R_2}{R_1 + R_2} \right) I$

$$= \left(\frac{10}{15 + 10} \right) (10)$$

$$= \left(\frac{2}{5} \right) (10) = \mathbf{4\,A}$$

Current $I_2 = \left(\dfrac{R_1}{R_1 + R_2} \right) I = \left(\dfrac{15}{15 + 10} \right)$ (10)

$$= \left(\frac{3}{5} \right) (10) = \mathbf{6\,A}$$

From part (a), method 1, $\mathbf{I_3 = I_4 = 5\,A}$

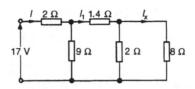

Problem 14.   For the arrangement shown in Fig. 5.27, find the current I_x.

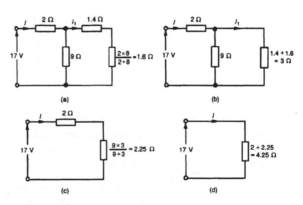

Figure 5.27

Commencing at the right-hand side of the arrangement shown in Fig. 5.27, the circuit is gradually reduced in stages as shown in Fig. 5.28(a)–(d).

Figure 5.28

From Fig. 5.28(d),

$$I = \frac{17}{4.25} = 4\,\text{A}$$

From Fig. 5.28(b),

$$I_1 = \left(\frac{9}{9+3} \right) (I) = \left(\frac{9}{12} \right) (4) = 3\,\text{A}$$

From Fig. 5.27

$$I_x = \left(\frac{2}{2+8} \right) (I_1) = \left(\frac{2}{10} \right) (3) = \mathbf{0.6\,A}$$

BTEC National Study Guide: Engineering. See page 325 for order details of individual texts

281

Now try the following exercise

Exercise 20   Further problems on parallel networks

1 Resistances of 4 Ω and 12 Ω are connected in parallel across a 9 V battery. Determine (a) the equivalent circuit resistance, (b) the supply current, and (c) the current in each resistor.

   [(a) 3 Ω (b) 3 A (c) 2.25 A, 0.75 A]

2 For the circuit shown in Fig. 5.29 determine (a) the reading on the ammeter, and (b) the value of resistor R   [2.5 A, 2.5 Ω]

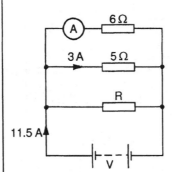

Figure 5.29

3 Find the equivalent resistance when the following resistances are connected (a) in series (b) in parallel (i) 3 Ω and 2 Ω (ii) 20 kΩ and 40 kΩ (iii) 4 Ω, 8 Ω and 16 Ω (iv) 800 Ω, 4 kΩ and 1500 Ω

   [(a) (i) 5 Ω   (ii) 60 kΩ
         (iii) 28 Ω   (iv) 6.3 kΩ
    (b) (i) 1.2 Ω   (ii) 13.33 kΩ
         (iii) 2.29 Ω (iv) 461.54 kΩ]

4 Find the total resistance between terminals A and B of the circuit shown in Fig. 5.30(a)   [8 Ω]

5 Find the equivalent resistance between terminals C and D of the circuit shown in Fig. 5.30(b)   [27.5 Ω]

6 Resistors of 20 Ω, 20 Ω and 30 Ω are connected in parallel. What resistance must be added in series with the combination to obtain a total resistance of 10 Ω. If the com-

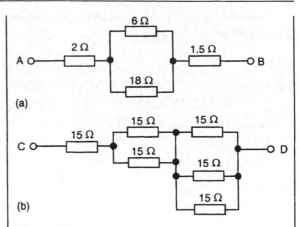

(a)

(b)

Figure 5.30

plete circuit expends a power of 0.36 kW, find the total current flowing.

   [2.5 Ω, 6 A]

7 (a) Calculate the current flowing in the 30 Ω resistor shown in Fig. 5.31 (b) What additional value of resistance would have to be placed in parallel with the 20 Ω and 30 Ω resistors to change the supply current to 8 A, the supply voltage remaining constant.

   [(a) 1.6 A (b) 6 Ω]

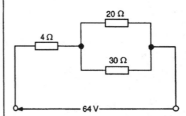

Figure 5.31

8 For the circuit shown in Fig. 5.32, find (a) V_1, (b) V_2, without calculating the current flowing.   [(a) 30 V (b) 42 V]

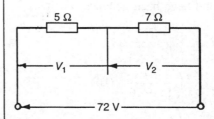

Figure 5.32

BTEC National Study Guide: Engineering. See page 325 for order details of individual texts

282

9 Determine the currents and voltages indicated in the circuit shown in Fig. 5.33

$[I_1 = 5\,\text{A}, I_2 = 2.5\,\text{A}, I_3 = 1\frac{2}{3}\,\text{A}, I_4 = \frac{5}{6}\,\text{A}$
$I_5 = 3\,\text{A}, I_6 = 2\,\text{A}, V_1 = 20\,\text{V}, V_2 = 5\,\text{V},$
$V_3 = 6\,\text{V}]$

10 Find the current I in Fig. 5.34   [1.8 A]

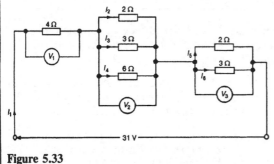

Figure 5.33

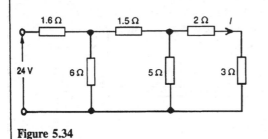

Figure 5.34

5.5 Wiring lamps in series and in parallel

Series connection

Figure 5.35 shows three lamps, each rated at 240 V, connected in series across a 240 V supply.

(i) Each lamp has only (240/3) V, i.e. 80 V across it and thus each lamp glows dimly.

(ii) If another lamp of similar rating is added in series with the other three lamps then each lamp

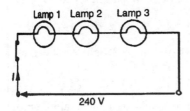

Figure 5.35

now has (240/4) V, i.e. 60 V across it and each now glows even more dimly.

(iii) If a lamp is removed from the circuit or if a lamp develops a fault (i.e. an open circuit) or if the switch is opened, then the circuit is broken, no current flows, and the remaining lamps will not light up.

(iv) Less cable is required for a series connection than for a parallel one.

The series connection of lamps is usually limited to decorative lighting such as for Christmas tree lights.

Parallel connection

Figure 5.36 shows three similar lamps, each rated at 240 V, connected in parallel across a 240 V supply.

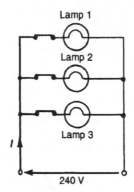

Figure 5.36

(i) Each lamp has 240 V across it and thus each will glow brilliantly at their rated voltage.

(ii) If any lamp is removed from the circuit or develops a fault (open circuit) or a switch is opened, the remaining lamps are unaffected.

(iii) The addition of further similar lamps in parallel does not affect the brightness of the other lamps.

(iv) More cable is required for parallel connection than for a series one.

The parallel connection of lamps is the most widely used in electrical installations.

> Problem 15. If three identical lamps are connected in parallel and the combined resistance is 150 Ω, find the resistance of one lamp.

BTEC National Study Guide: Engineering. See page 325 for order details of individual texts

283

Let the resistance of one lamp be R, then

$$\frac{1}{150} = \frac{1}{R} + \frac{1}{R} + \frac{1}{R} = \frac{3}{R},$$

from which, $R = 3 \times 150 = \mathbf{450\,\Omega}$

Problem 16. Three identical lamps A, B and C are connected in series across a 150 V supply. State (a) the voltage across each lamp, and (b) the effect of lamp C failing.

(a) Since each lamp is identical and they are connected in series there is 150/3 V, i.e. **50 V** across each.

(b) If lamp C fails, i.e. open circuits, no current will flow and **lamps A and B will not operate**.

Now try the following exercises

Exercise 21   Further problems on wiring lamps in series and in parallel

1 If four identical lamps are connected in parallel and the combined resistance is $100\,\Omega$, find the resistance of one lamp. [$400\,\Omega$]

2 Three identical filament lamps are connected (a) in series, (b) in parallel across a 210 V supply. State for each connection the p.d. across each lamp. [(a) 70 V (b) 210 V]

Exercise 22   Short answer questions on series and parallel networks

1 Name three characteristics of a series circuit

2 Show that for three resistors R_1, R_2 and R_3 connected in series the equivalent resistance R is given by $R = R_1 + R_2 + R_3$

3 Name three characteristics of a parallel network

4 Show that for three resistors R_1, R_2 and R_3 connected in parallel the equivalent resistance R is given by

$$\frac{1}{R} = \frac{1}{R_1} + \frac{1}{R_2} + \frac{1}{R_3}$$

5 Explain the potential divider circuit

6 Compare the merits of wiring lamps in (a) series (b) parallel

---

Exercise 23   Multi-choice questions on series and parallel networks (Answers on page 375)

1 If two $4\,\Omega$ resistors are connected in series the effective resistance of the circuit is:
(a) $8\,\Omega$ (b) $4\,\Omega$ (c) $2\,\Omega$ (d) $1\,\Omega$

2 If two $4\,\Omega$ resistors are connected in parallel the effective resistance of the circuit is:
(a) $8\,\Omega$ (b) $4\,\Omega$ (c) $2\,\Omega$ (d) $1\,\Omega$

3 With the switch in Fig. 5.37 closed, the ammeter reading will indicate:
(a) 1 A (b) 75 A (c) $\frac{1}{3}$ A (d) 3 A

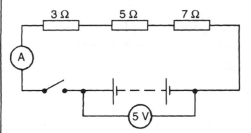

Figure 5.37

4 The effect of connecting an additional parallel load to an electrical supply source is to increase the
(a) resistance of the load
(b) voltage of the source
(c) current taken from the source
(d) p.d. across the load

5 The equivalent resistance when a resistor of $\frac{1}{3}\,\Omega$ is connected in parallel with a $\frac{1}{4}\,\Omega$ resistance is:
(a) $\frac{1}{7}\,\Omega$ (b) $7\,\Omega$ (c) $\frac{1}{12}\,\Omega$ (d) $\frac{3}{4}\,\Omega$

6 With the switch in Fig. 5.38 closed the ammeter reading will indicate:
(a) 108 A (b) $\frac{1}{3}$ A (c) 3 A (d) $4\frac{3}{5}$ A

7 A $6\,\Omega$ resistor is connected in parallel with the three resistors of Fig. 5.38. With the

BTEC National Study Guide: Engineering. See page 325 for order details of individual texts

284

switch closed the ammeter reading will indicate:
(a) $\frac{3}{4}$ A   (b) 4 A   (c) $\frac{1}{4}$ A   (d) $1\frac{1}{3}$ A

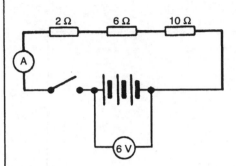

Figure 5.38

8 A $10\,\Omega$ resistor is connected in parallel with a $15\,\Omega$ resistor and the combination in series with a $12\,\Omega$ resistor. The equivalent resistance of the circuit is:
(a) $37\,\Omega$ (b) $18\,\Omega$ (c) $27\,\Omega$ (d) $4\,\Omega$

9 When three $3\,\Omega$ resistors are connected in parallel, the total resistance is:
(a) $3\,\Omega$ (b) $9\,\Omega$
(c) $1\,\Omega$ (d) $0.333\,\Omega$

10 The total resistance of two resistors R_1 and R_2 when connected in parallel is given by:

(a) $R_1 + R_2$ (b) $\dfrac{1}{R_1} + \dfrac{1}{R_2}$

(c) $\dfrac{R_1 + R_2}{R_1 R_2}$ (d) $\dfrac{R_1 R_2}{R_1 + R_2}$

11 If in the circuit shown in Fig. 5.39, the reading on the voltmeter is 5 V and the reading on the ammeter is 25 mA, the resistance of resistor R is:
(a) $0.005\,\Omega$ (b) $5\,\Omega$
(c) $125\,\Omega$ (d) $200\,\Omega$

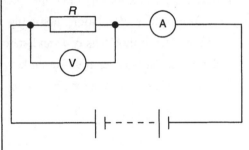

Figure 5.39

BTEC National Study Guide: Engineering. See page 325 for order details of individual texts

285

6

Capacitors and capacitance

At the end of this chapter you should be able to:

- describe an electrostatic field
- appreciate Coulomb's law
- define electric field strength E and state its unit
- define capacitance and state its unit
- describe a capacitor and draw the circuit diagram symbol
- perform simple calculations involving $C = Q/V$ and $Q = It$
- define electric flux density D and state its unit
- define permittivity, distinguishing between ε_0, ε_r and ε
- perform simple calculations involving

$$D = \frac{Q}{A}, E = \frac{V}{d} \text{ and } \frac{D}{E} = \varepsilon_0 \varepsilon_r$$

- understand that for a parallel plate capacitor,

$$C = \frac{\varepsilon_0 \varepsilon_r A (n - 1)}{d}$$

- perform calculations involving capacitors connected in parallel and in series
- define dielectric strength and state its unit
- state that the energy stored in a capacitor is given by $W = \frac{1}{2}CV^2$ joules
- describe practical types of capacitor
- understand the precautions needed when discharging capacitors

6.1 Electrostatic field

Figure 6.1 represents two parallel metal plates, A and B, charged to different potentials. If an electron that has a negative charge is placed between the plates, a force will act on the electron tending to push it away from the negative plate B towards the positive plate, A. Similarly, a positive charge would be acted on by a force tending to move it toward

the negative plate. Any region such as that shown between the plates in Fig. 6.1, in which an electric charge experiences a force, is called an **electrostatic field**. The direction of the field is defined as that of the force acting on a positive charge placed in the field. In Fig. 6.1, the direction of the force is from the positive plate to the negative plate. Such a field may be represented in magnitude and direction by **lines of electric force** drawn between the charged surfaces. The closeness of the lines is

BTEC National Study Guide: Engineering. See page 325 for order details of individual texts

286

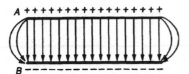

Figure 6.1

an indication of the field strength. Whenever a p.d. is established between two points, an electric field will always exist.

Figure 6.2(a) shows a typical field pattern for an isolated point charge, and Fig. 6.2(b) shows the field pattern for adjacent charges of opposite polarity. Electric lines of force (often called electric flux lines) are continuous and start and finish on point charges; also, the lines cannot cross each other. When a charged body is placed close to an uncharged body, an induced charge of opposite sign appears on the surface of the uncharged body. This is because lines of force from the charged body terminate on its surface.

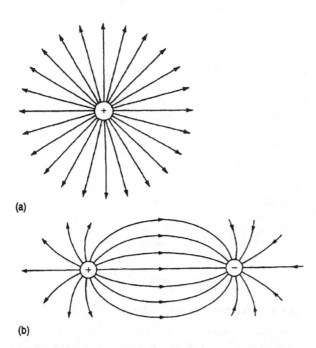

(a)

(b)

Figure 6.2

The concept of field lines or lines of force is used to illustrate the properties of an electric field. However, it should be remembered that they are only aids to the imagination.

The **force of attraction or repulsion** between two electrically charged bodies is proportional to

the magnitude of their charges and inversely proportional to the square of the distance separating them, i.e.

$$\text{force} \propto \frac{q_1 q_2}{d^2}$$

or

$$\boxed{\textbf{force} = k\,\frac{q_1 q_2}{d^2}}$$

where constant $k \approx 9 \times 10^9$. This is known as **Coulomb's law**.

Hence the force between two charged spheres in air with their centres 16 mm apart and each carrying a charge of $+1.6\,\mu\text{C}$ is given by:

$$\text{force} = k\frac{q_1 q_2}{d^2} \approx (9 \times 10^9)\frac{(1.6 \times 10^{-6})^2}{(16 \times 10^{-3})^2}$$

$$= \textbf{90 newtons}$$

6.2 Electric field strength

Figure 6.3 shows two parallel conducting plates separated from each other by air. They are connected to opposite terminals of a battery of voltage V volts. There is therefore an electric field in the space between the plates. If the plates are close together, the electric lines of force will be straight and parallel and equally spaced, except near the edge where fringing will occur (see Fig. 6.1). Over the area in which there is negligible fringing,

$$\boxed{\textbf{Electric field strength, } E = \frac{V}{d} \text{ volts/metre}}$$

where d is the distance between the plates. Electric field strength is also called **potential gradient**.

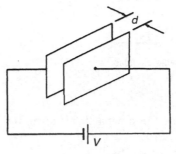

Figure 6.3

BTEC National Study Guide: Engineering. See page 325 for order details of individual texts

287

6.3 Capacitance

Static electric fields arise from electric charges, electric field lines beginning and ending on electric charges. Thus the presence of the field indicates the presence of equal positive and negative electric charges on the two plates of Fig. 6.3. Let the charge be $+Q$ coulombs on one plate and $-Q$ coulombs on the other. The property of this pair of plates which determines how much charge corresponds to a given p.d. between the plates is called their capacitance:

$$\text{capacitance } C = \frac{Q}{V}$$

The **unit of capacitance** is the **farad** F (or more usually $\mu F = 10^{-6} F$ or $pF = 10^{-12} F$), which is defined as the capacitance when a p.d. of one volt appears across the plates when charged with one coulomb.

6.4 Capacitors

Every system of electrical conductors possesses capacitance. For example, there is capacitance between the conductors of overhead transmission lines and also between the wires of a telephone cable. In these examples the capacitance is undesirable but has to be accepted, minimized or compensated for. There are other situations where capacitance is a desirable property.

Devices specially constructed to possess capacitance are called **capacitors** (or condensers, as they used to be called). In its simplest form a capacitor consists of two plates which are separated by an insulating material known as a **dielectric**. A capacitor has the ability to store a quantity of static electricity.

The symbols for a fixed capacitor and a variable capacitor used in electrical circuit diagrams are shown in Fig. 6.4

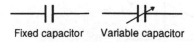

Fixed capacitor   Variable capacitor

Figure 6.4

The **charge Q** stored in a capacitor is given by:

$$Q = I \times t \text{ coulombs}$$

where I is the current in amperes and t the time in seconds.

Problem 1.   (a) Determine the p.d. across a $4\,\mu F$ capacitor when charged with $5\,mC$ (b) Find the charge on a $50\,pF$ capacitor when the voltage applied to it is $2\,kV$.

(a) $C = 4\,\mu F = 4 \times 10^{-6}\,F$ and $Q = 5\,mC = 5 \times 10^{-3}\,C$.

Since $C = \dfrac{Q}{V}$ then $V = \dfrac{Q}{C} = \dfrac{5 \times 10^{-3}}{4 \times 10^{-6}}$

$$= \frac{5 \times 10^{6}}{4 \times 10^{3}} = \frac{5000}{4}$$

Hence p.d. $V = 1250\,V$ or $1.25\,kV$

(b) $C = 50\,pF = 50 \times 10^{-12}\,F$ and $V = 2\,kV = 2000\,V$

$$Q = CV = 50 \times 10^{-12} \times 2000$$

$$= \frac{5 \times 2}{10^{8}} = 0.1 \times 10^{-6}$$

Hence, charge $Q = 0.1\,\mu C$

Problem 2.   A direct current of $4\,A$ flows into a previously uncharged $20\,\mu F$ capacitor for $3\,ms$. Determine the p.d. between the plates.

$I = 4\,A$, $C = 20\,\mu F = 20 \times 10^{-6}\,F$ and $t = 3\,ms = 3 \times 10^{-3}\,s$. $Q = It = 4 \times 3 \times 10^{-3}\,C$.

$$V = \frac{Q}{C} = \frac{4 \times 3 \times 10^{-3}}{20 \times 10^{-6}}$$

$$= \frac{12 \times 10^{6}}{20 \times 10^{3}} = 0.6 \times 10^{3} = 600\,V$$

Hence, the p.d. between the plates is $600\,V$

Problem 3.   A $5\,\mu F$ capacitor is charged so that the p.d. between its plates is $800\,V$. Calculate how long the capacitor can provide an average discharge current of $2\,mA$.

$C = 5\,\mu F = 5 \times 10^{-6}\,F$, $V = 800\,V$ and $I = 2\,mA = 2 \times 10^{-3}\,A$.
$Q = CV = 5 \times 10^{-6} \times 800 = 4 \times 10^{-3}\,C$

BTEC National Study Guide: Engineering. See page 325 for order details of individual texts

288

Also, $Q = It$. Thus,

$$t = \frac{Q}{I} = \frac{4 \times 10^{-3}}{2 \times 10^{-3}} = 2\,\text{s}$$

Hence, the capacitor can provide an average discharge current of 2 mA for 2 s.

Now try the following exercise

Exercise 24   Further problems on capacitors and capacitance

1 Find the charge on a 10 μF capacitor when the applied voltage is 250 V   [2.5 mC]

2 Determine the voltage across a 1000 pF capacitor to charge it with 2 μC   [2 kV]

3 The charge on the plates of a capacitor is 6 mC when the potential between them is 2.4 kV. Determine the capacitance of the capacitor.   [2.5 μF]

4 For how long must a charging current of 2 A be fed to a 5 μF capacitor to raise the p.d. between its plates by 500 V.   [1.25 ms]

5 A direct current of 10 A flows into a previously uncharged 5 μF capacitor for 1 ms. Determine the p.d. between the plates.   [2 kV]

6 A 16 μF capacitor is charged at a constant current of 4 μA for 2 min. Calculate the final p.d. across the capacitor and the corresponding charge in coulombs.   [30 V, 480 μC]

7 A steady current of 10 A flows into a previously uncharged capacitor for 1.5 ms when the p.d. between the plates is 2 kV. Find the capacitance of the capacitor.   [7.5 μF]

6.5 Electric flux density

Unit flux is defined as emanating from a positive charge of 1 coulomb. Thus electric flux ψ is measured in coulombs, and for a charge of Q coulombs, the flux $\psi = Q$ coulombs.

Electric flux density D is the amount of flux passing through a defined area A that is perpendicular to the direction of the flux:

---

electric flux density, $D = \dfrac{Q}{A}$ coulombs/metre^2

Electric flux density is also called **charge density**, σ.

6.6 Permittivity

At any point in an electric field, the electric field strength E maintains the electric flux and produces a particular value of electric flux density D at that point. For a field established in **vacuum** (or for practical purposes in air), the ratio D/E is a constant ε_0, i.e.

$$\frac{D}{E} = \varepsilon_0$$

where ε_0 is called the **permittivity of free space** or the free space constant. The value of ε_0 is 8.85×10^{-12} F/m.

When an insulating medium, such as mica, paper, plastic or ceramic, is introduced into the region of an electric field the ratio of D/E is modified:

$$\frac{D}{E} = \varepsilon_0 \varepsilon_r$$

where ε_r, the **relative permittivity** of the insulating material, indicates its insulating power compared with that of vacuum:

---

relative permittivity,

$$\varepsilon_r = \frac{\text{flux density in material}}{\text{flux density in vacuum}}$$

ε_r has no unit. Typical values of ε_r include air, 1.00; polythene, 2.3; mica, 3–7; glass, 5–10; water, 80; ceramics, 6–1000.

The product $\varepsilon_0 \varepsilon_r$ is called the **absolute permittivity**, ε, i.e.

$$\varepsilon = \varepsilon_0 \varepsilon_r$$

BTEC National Study Guide: Engineering. See page 325 for order details of individual texts

289

The insulating medium separating charged surfaces is called a **dielectric**. Compared with conductors, dielectric materials have very high resistivities. They are therefore used to separate conductors at different potentials, such as capacitor plates or electric power lines.

Problem 4. Two parallel rectangular plates measuring 20 cm by 40 cm carry an electric charge of 0.2 μC. Calculate the electric flux density. If the plates are spaced 5 mm apart and the voltage between them is 0.25 kV determine the electric field strength.

Area $= 20\,\text{cm} \times 40\,\text{cm} = 800\,\text{cm}^2 = 800 \times 10^{-4}\,\text{m}^2$
and charge $Q = 0.2\,\mu\text{C} = 0.2 \times 10^{-6}\,\text{C}$,
Electric flux density

$$D = \frac{Q}{A} = \frac{0.2 \times 10^{-6}}{800 \times 10^{-4}} = \frac{0.2 \times 10^4}{800 \times 10^6}$$

$$= \frac{2000}{800} \times 10^{-6} = 2.5\,\mu\text{C/m}^2$$

Voltage $V = 0.25\,\text{kV} = 250\,\text{V}$ and plate spacing,
$d = 5\,\text{mm} = 5 \times 10^{-3}\,\text{m}$.
Electric field strength

$$E = \frac{V}{d} = \frac{250}{5 \times 10^{-3}} = 50\,\text{kV/m}$$

Problem 5. The flux density between two plates separated by mica of relative permittivity 5 is 2 μC/m². Find the voltage gradient between the plates.

Flux density $D = 2\,\mu\text{C/m}^2 = 2 \times 10^{-6}\,\text{C/m}^2$,
$\varepsilon_0 = 8.85 \times 10^{-12}\,\text{F/m}$ and $\varepsilon_r = 5$.
$D/E = \varepsilon_0 \varepsilon_r$, hence **voltage gradient**,

$$E = \frac{D}{\varepsilon_0 \varepsilon_r} = \frac{2 \times 10^{-6}}{8.85 \times 10^{-12} \times 5}\,\text{V/m}$$

$$= 45.2\,\text{kV/m}$$

Problem 6. Two parallel plates having a p.d. of 200 V between them are spaced 0.8 mm apart. What is the electric field strength? Find also the electric flux density when the dielectric between the plates is (a) air, and (b) polythene of relative permittivity 2.3

Electric field strength

$$E = \frac{V}{d} = \frac{200}{0.8 \times 10^{-3}} = 250\,\text{kV/m}$$

(a) For air: $\varepsilon_r = 1$ and $\dfrac{D}{E} = \varepsilon_0 \varepsilon_r$

Hence **electric flux density**

$$D = E\varepsilon_0 \varepsilon_r$$

$$= (250 \times 10^3 \times 8.85 \times 10^{-12} \times 1)\,\text{C/m}^2$$

$$= 2.213\,\mu\text{C/m}^2$$

(b) For polythene, $\varepsilon_r = 2.3$

Electric flux density

$$D = E\varepsilon_0 \varepsilon_r$$

$$= (250 \times 10^3 \times 8.85 \times 10^{-12} \times 2.3)\,\text{C/m}^2$$

$$= 5.089\,\mu\text{C/m}^2$$

Now try the following exercise

Exercise 25 Further problems on electric field strength, electric flux density and permittivity

(Where appropriate take ε_0 as 8.85×10^{-12} F/m)

1 A capacitor uses a dielectric 0.04 mm thick and operates at 30 V. What is the electric field strength across the dielectric at this voltage?
[750 kV/m]

2 A two-plate capacitor has a charge of 25 C. If the effective area of each plate is 5 cm² find the electric flux density of the electric field.
[50 kC/m²]

3 A charge of 1.5 μC is carried on two parallel rectangular plates each measuring 60 mm by 80 mm. Calculate the electric flux density. If the plates are spaced 10 mm apart and the voltage between them is 0.5 kV determine the electric field strength.
[312.5 μC/m², 50 kV/m]

4 Two parallel plates are separated by a dielectric and charged with 10 μC. Given that the

---

BTEC National Study Guide: Engineering. See page 325 for order details of individual texts

290

area of each plate is $50\,\text{cm}^2$, calculate the electric flux density in the dielectric separating the plates. [$2\,\text{mC/m}^2$]

5 The electric flux density between two plates separated by polystyrene of relative permittivity 2.5 is $5\,\mu\text{C/m}^2$. Find the voltage gradient between the plates. [$226\,\text{kV/m}$]

6 Two parallel plates having a p.d. of 250 V between them are spaced 1 mm apart. Determine the electric field strength. Find also the electric flux density when the dielectric between the plates is (a) air and (b) mica of relative permittivity 5
[$250\,\text{kV/m}$ (a) $2.213\,\mu\text{C/m}^2$ (b) $11.063\,\mu\text{C/m}^2$]

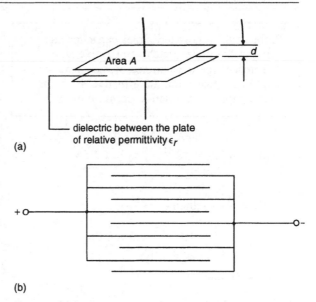

(a)

(b)

Figure 6.5

6.7 The parallel plate capacitor

For a parallel-plate capacitor, as shown in Fig. 6.5(a), experiments show that capacitance C is proportional to the area A of a plate, inversely proportional to the plate spacing d (i.e. the dielectric thickness) and depends on the nature of the dielectric:

$$\textbf{Capacitance, } C = \frac{\varepsilon_0 \varepsilon_r A}{d} \textbf{ farads}$$

where $\varepsilon_0 = 8.85 \times 10^{-12}$ F/m (constant)

ε_r = relative permittivity

A = area of one of the plates, in m^2, and

d = thickness of dielectric in m

Another method used to increase the capacitance is to interleave several plates as shown in Fig 6.5(b). Ten plates are shown, forming nine capacitors with a capacitance nine times that of one pair of plates.
If such an arrangement has n plates then capacitance $C \propto (n-1)$. Thus capacitance

$$C = \frac{\varepsilon_0 \varepsilon_r A (n-1)}{d} \textbf{ farads}$$

Problem 7. (a) A ceramic capacitor has an effective plate area of $4\,\text{cm}^2$ separated by 0.1 mm of ceramic of relative permittivity 100. Calculate the capacitance of the capacitor in picofarads. (b) If the capacitor in part (a) is given a charge of $1.2\,\mu\text{C}$ what will be the p.d. between the plates?

(a) Area $A = 4\,\text{cm}^2 = 4 \times 10^{-4}\,\text{m}^2$,
$d = 0.1\,\text{mm} = 0.1 \times 10^{-3}\,\text{m}$,

$\varepsilon_0 = 8.85 \times 10^{-12}$ F/m and $\varepsilon_r = 100$

Capacitance,

$$C = \frac{\varepsilon_0 \varepsilon_r A}{d} \text{ farads}$$

$$= \frac{8.85 \times 10^{-12} \times 100 \times 4 \times 10^{-4}}{0.1 \times 10^{-3}} \text{ F}$$

$$= \frac{8.85 \times 4}{10^{10}} \text{ F}$$

$$= \frac{8.85 \times 4 \times 10^{12}}{10^{10}} \text{ pF} = \textbf{3540 pF}$$

(b) $Q = CV$ thus

$$V = \frac{Q}{C} = \frac{1.2 \times 10^{-6}}{3540 \times 10^{-12}} \text{ V} = \textbf{339 V}$$

BTEC National Study Guide: Engineering. See page 325 for order details of individual texts

291

Problem 8.   A waxed paper capacitor has two parallel plates, each of effective area $800\,\text{cm}^2$. If the capacitance of the capacitor is 4425 pF determine the effective thickness of the paper if its relative permittivity is 2.5

$A = 800\,\text{cm}^2 = 800 \times 10^{-4}\,\text{m}^2 = 0.08\,\text{m}^2$, $C = 4425\,\text{pF} = 4425 \times 10^{-12}\,\text{F}$, $\varepsilon_0 = 8.85 \times 10^{-12}\,\text{F/m}$ and $\varepsilon_r = 2.5$. Since

$$C = \frac{\varepsilon_0 \varepsilon_A A}{d} \text{ then } d = \frac{\varepsilon_0 \varepsilon_r A}{C}$$

$$= \frac{8.85 \times 10^{-12} \times 2.5 \times 0.08}{4425 \times 10^{-12}}$$

$$= 0.0004\,\text{m}$$

Hence, the thickness of the paper is 0.4 mm.

Problem 9.   A parallel plate capacitor has nineteen interleaved plates each 75 mm by 75 mm separated by mica sheets 0.2 mm thick. Assuming the relative permittivity of the mica is 5, calculate the capacitance of the capacitor.

$n = 19$ thus $n - 1 = 18$, $A = 75 \times 75 = 5625\,\text{mm}^2 = 5625 \times 10^{-6}\,\text{m}^2$, $\varepsilon_r = 5$, $\varepsilon_0 = 8.85 \times 10^{-12}\,\text{F/m}$ and $d = 0.2\,\text{mm} = 0.2 \times 10^{-3}\,\text{m}$. Capacitance,

$$C = \frac{\varepsilon_0 \varepsilon_r A (n - 1)}{d}$$

$$= \frac{8.85 \times 10^{-12} \times 5 \times 5625 \times 10^{-6} \times 18}{0.2 \times 10^{-3}}\,\text{F}$$

$$= \mathbf{0.0224\,\mu F} \text{ or } \mathbf{22.4\,nF}$$

Now try the following exercise

Exercise 26   Further problems on parallel plate capacitors

(Where appropriate take ε_0 as 8.85×10^{-12} F/m)

1 A capacitor consists of two parallel plates each of area $0.01\,\text{m}^2$, spaced 0.1 mm in air. Calculate the capacitance in picofarads.   [885 pF]

2 A waxed paper capacitor has two parallel plates, each of effective area $0.2\,\text{m}^2$. If the capacitance is 4000 pF determine the effective thickness of the paper if its relative permittivity is 2   [0.885 mm]

3 Calculate the capacitance of a parallel plate capacitor having 5 plates, each 30 mm by 20 mm and separated by a dielectric 0.75 mm thick having a relative permittivity of 2.3   [65.14 pF]

4 How many plates has a parallel plate capacitor having a capacitance of 5 nF, if each plate is 40 mm by 40 mm and each dielectric is 0.102 mm thick with a relative permittivity of 6.   [7]

5 A parallel plate capacitor is made from 25 plates, each 70 mm by 120 mm interleaved with mica of relative permittivity 5. If the capacitance of the capacitor is 3000 pF determine the thickness of the mica sheet.   [2.97 mm]

6 A capacitor is constructed with parallel plates and has a value of 50 pF. What would be the capacitance of the capacitor if the plate area is doubled and the plate spacing is halved?   [200 pF]

7 The capacitance of a parallel plate capacitor is 1000 pF. It has 19 plates, each 50 mm by 30 mm separated by a dielectric of thickness 0.40 mm. Determine the relative permittivity of the dielectric.   [1.67]

8 The charge on the square plates of a multiplate capacitor is 80 μC when the potential between them is 5 kV. If the capacitor has twenty-five plates separated by a dielectric of thickness 0.102 mm and relative permittivity 4.8, determine the width of a plate.   [40 mm]

9 A capacitor is to be constructed so that its capacitance is 4250 pF and to operate at a p.d. of 100 V across its terminals. The dielectric is to be polythene ($\varepsilon_r = 2.3$) which, after allowing a safety factor, has a dielectric strength of 20 MV/m. Find (a) the thickness of the polythene needed, and (b) the area of a plate.   [(a) 0.005 mm (b) $10.44\,\text{cm}^2$]

BTEC National Study Guide: Engineering. See page 325 for order details of individual texts

292

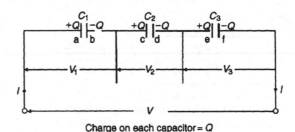

Figure 6.7

6.8 Capacitors connected in parallel and series

(a) Capacitors connected in parallel

Figure 6.6 shows three capacitors, C_1, C_2 and C_3, connected in parallel with a supply voltage V applied across the arrangement.

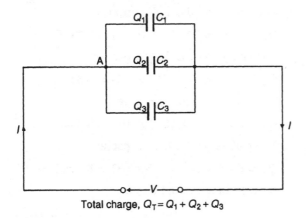

Figure 6.6

When the charging current I reaches point A it divides, some flowing into C_1, some flowing into C_2 and some into C_3. Hence the total charge $Q_T (= I \times t)$ is divided between the three capacitors. The capacitors each store a charge and these are shown as Q_1, Q_2 and Q_3 respectively. Hence

$$Q_T = Q_1 + Q_2 + Q_3$$

But $Q_T = CV$, $Q_1 = C_1V$, $Q_2 = C_2V$ and $Q_3 = C_3V$. Therefore $CV = C_1V + C_2V + C_3V$ where C is the total equivalent circuit capacitance, i.e.

$$C = C_1 + C_2 + C_3$$

It follows that for n parallel-connected capacitors,

$$\boxed{C = C_1 + C_2 + C_3 \ldots \ldots + C_n}$$

i.e. the equivalent capacitance of a group of parallel-connected capacitors is the sum of the capacitances of the individual capacitors. (Note that this formula is similar to that used for **resistors** connected in **series**).

(b) Capacitors connected in series

Figure 6.7 shows three capacitors, C_1, C_2 and C_3, connected in series across a supply voltage V. Let the p.d. across the individual capacitors be V_1, V_2 and V_3 respectively as shown.

Let the charge on plate 'a' of capacitor C_1 be $+Q$ coulombs. This induces an equal but opposite charge of $-Q$ coulombs on plate 'b'. The conductor between plates 'b' and 'c' is electrically isolated from the rest of the circuit so that an equal but opposite charge of $+Q$ coulombs must appear on plate 'c', which, in turn, induces an equal and opposite charge of $-Q$ coulombs on plate 'd', and so on.

Hence when capacitors are connected in series the charge on each is the same. In a series circuit:

$$V = V_1 + V_2 + V_3$$

Since $V = \dfrac{Q}{C}$ then $\dfrac{Q}{C} = \dfrac{Q}{C_1} + \dfrac{Q}{C_2} + \dfrac{Q}{C_3}$

where C is the total equivalent circuit capacitance, i.e.

$$\frac{1}{C} = \frac{1}{C_1} + \frac{1}{C_2} + \frac{1}{C_3}$$

It follows that for n series-connected capacitors:

$$\boxed{\frac{1}{C} = \frac{1}{C_1} + \frac{1}{C_2} + \frac{1}{C_3} + \ldots + \frac{1}{C_n}}$$

i.e. for series-connected capacitors, the reciprocal of the equivalent capacitance is equal to the sum of the reciprocals of the individual capacitances. (Note that this formula is similar to that used for **resistors** connected in **parallel**).

For the special case of **two capacitors in series:**

$$\frac{1}{C} = \frac{1}{C_1} + \frac{1}{C_2} = \frac{C_2 + C_1}{C_1 C_2}$$

BTEC National Study Guide: Engineering. See page 325 for order details of individual texts

293

Hence

$$C = \frac{C_1 C_2}{C_1 + C_2} \qquad \left(\text{i.e. } \frac{\text{product}}{\text{sum}}\right)$$

Problem 10. Calculate the equivalent capacitance of two capacitors of $6\,\mu\text{F}$ and $4\,\mu\text{F}$ connected (a) in parallel and (b) in series.

(a) In parallel, equivalent capacitance,
$$C = C_1 + C_2 = 6\,\mu\text{F} + 4\,\mu\text{F} = \mathbf{10\,\mu F}$$

(b) In series, equivalent capacitance C is given by:

$$C = \frac{C_1 C_2}{C_1 + C_2}$$

This formula is used for the special case of **two** capacitors in series. Thus

$$C = \frac{6 \times 4}{6 + 4} = \frac{24}{10} = \mathbf{2.4\,\mu F}$$

Problem 11. What capacitance must be connected in series with a $30\,\mu\text{F}$ capacitor for the equivalent capacitance to be $12\,\mu\text{F}$?

Let $C = 12\,\mu\text{F}$ (the equivalent capacitance), $C_1 = 30\,\mu\text{F}$ and C_2 be the unknown capacitance. For two capacitors in series

$$\frac{1}{C} = \frac{1}{C_1} + \frac{1}{C_2}$$

Hence

$$\frac{1}{C_2} = \frac{1}{C} - \frac{1}{C_1} = \frac{C_1 - C}{CC_1}$$

and

$$C_2 = \frac{CC_1}{C_1 - C} = \frac{12 \times 30}{30 - 12} = \frac{360}{18} = \mathbf{20\,\mu F}$$

Problem 12. Capacitance's of $1\,\mu\text{F}$, $3\,\mu\text{F}$, $5\,\mu\text{F}$ and $6\,\mu\text{F}$ are connected in parallel to a direct voltage supply of $100\,\text{V}$. Determine (a) the equivalent circuit capacitance, (b) the total charge and (c) the charge on each capacitor.

(a) The equivalent capacitance C for four capacitors in parallel is given by:

$$C = C_1 + C_2 + C_3 + C_4$$

i.e. $C = 1 + 3 + 5 + 6 = \mathbf{15\,\mu F}$

(b) Total charge $Q_T = CV$ where C is the equivalent circuit capacitance i.e.

$$Q_T = 15 \times 10^{-6} \times 100 = 1.5 \times 10^{-3} C$$
$$= \mathbf{1.5\,mC}$$

(c) The charge on the $1\,\mu\text{F}$ capacitor

$$Q_1 = C_1 V = 1 \times 10^{-6} \times 100 = \mathbf{0.1\,mC}$$

The charge on the $3\,\mu\text{F}$ capacitor

$$Q_2 = C_2 V = 3 \times 10^{-6} \times 100 = \mathbf{0.3\,mC}$$

The charge on the $5\,\mu\text{F}$ capacitor

$$Q_3 = C_3 V = 5 \times 10^{-6} \times 100 = \mathbf{0.5\,mC}$$

The charge on the $6\,\mu\text{F}$ capacitor

$$Q_4 = C_4 V = 6 \times 10^{-6} \times 100 = \mathbf{0.6\,mC}$$

[Check: In a parallel circuit

$$Q_T = Q_1 + Q_2 + Q_3 + Q_4.$$
$$Q_1 + Q_2 + Q_3 + Q_4 = 0.1 + 0.3 + 0.5 + 0.6$$
$$= 1.5\,\text{mC} = Q_T]$$

Problem 13. Capacitance's of $3\,\mu\text{F}$, $6\,\mu\text{F}$ and $12\,\mu\text{F}$ are connected in series across a $350\,\text{V}$ supply. Calculate (a) the equivalent circuit capacitance, (b) the charge on each capacitor, and (c) the p.d. across each capacitor.

The circuit diagram is shown in Fig. 6.8.

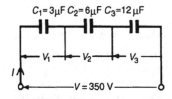
$C_1 = 3\,\mu\text{F} \quad C_2 = 6\,\mu\text{F} \quad C_3 = 12\,\mu\text{F}$

Figure 6.8

(a) The equivalent circuit capacitance C for three capacitors in series is given by:

$$\frac{1}{C} = \frac{1}{C_1} + \frac{1}{C_2} + \frac{1}{C_3}$$

i.e. $\dfrac{1}{C} = \dfrac{1}{3} + \dfrac{1}{6} + \dfrac{1}{12} = \dfrac{4 + 2 + 1}{12} = \dfrac{7}{12}$

BTEC National Study Guide: Engineering. See page 325 for order details of individual texts

294

Hence the equivalent circuit capacitance

$$C = \frac{12}{7} = 1\frac{5}{7}\,\mu\text{F or } \mathbf{1.714\,\mu F}$$

(b) Total charge $Q_T = CV$, hence

$$Q_T = \frac{12}{7} \times 10^{-6} \times 350$$

$$= 600\,\mu\text{C or } 0.6\,\text{mC}$$

Since the capacitors are connected in series 0.6 mC is the charge on each of them.

(c) The voltage across the 3 μF capacitor,

$$V_1 = \frac{Q}{C_1}$$

$$= \frac{0.6 \times 10^{-3}}{3 \times 10^{-6}} = \mathbf{200\,V}$$

The voltage across the 6 μF capacitor,

$$V_2 = \frac{Q}{C_2}$$

$$= \frac{0.6 \times 10^{-3}}{6 \times 10^{-6}} = \mathbf{100\,V}$$

The voltage across the 12 μF capacitor,

$$V_3 = \frac{Q}{C_3}$$

$$= \frac{0.6 \times 10^{-3}}{12 \times 10^{-6}} = \mathbf{50\,V}$$

[Check: In a series circuit $V = V_1 + V_2 + V_3$. $V_1 + V_2 + V_3 = 200 + 100 + 50 = 350\,\text{V} =$ supply voltage]

In practice, capacitors are rarely connected in series unless they are of the same capacitance. The reason for this can be seen from the above problem where the lowest valued capacitor (i.e. 3 μF) has the highest p.d. across it (i.e. 200 V) which means that if all the capacitors have an identical construction they must all be rated at the highest voltage.

Problem 14. For the arrangement shown in Fig. 6.9 find (a) the equivalent capacitance of the circuit, (b) the voltage across QR, and (c) the charge on each capacitor.

(a) 2 μF in parallel with 3 μF gives an equivalent capacitance of $2\,\mu\text{F} + 3\,\mu\text{F} = 5\,\mu\text{F}$. The circuit is now as shown in Fig. 6.10.

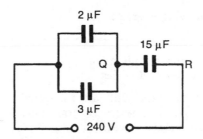

Figure 6.9

The **equivalent capacitance** of 5 μF in series with 15 μF is given by

$$\frac{5 \times 15}{5 + 15}\,\mu\text{F} = \frac{75}{20}\,\mu\text{F} = \mathbf{3.75\,\mu F}$$

(b) The charge on each of the capacitors shown in Fig. 6.10 will be the same since they are connected in series. Let this charge be Q coulombs.

Then $\qquad Q = C_1 V_1 = C_2 V_2$

i.e. $\qquad 5V_1 = 15V_2$

$$V_1 = 3V_2 \qquad (1)$$

Also $\quad V_1 + V_2 = 240\,\text{V}$

Hence $3V_2 + V_2 = 240\,\text{V}$ from equation (1)

Thus $\qquad V_2 = 60\,\text{V}$ and $V_1 = 180\,\text{V}$

Hence the voltage across QR is 60 V

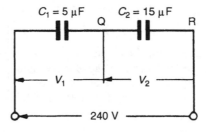

Figure 6.10

(c) The charge on the 15 μF capacitor is

$$C_2 V_2 = 15 \times 10^{-6} \times 60 = \mathbf{0.9\,mC}$$

The charge on the 2 μF capacitor is

$$2 \times 10^{-6} \times 180 = \mathbf{0.36\,mC}$$

The charge on the 3 μF capacitor is

$$3 \times 10^{-6} \times 180 = \mathbf{0.54\,mC}$$

BTEC National Study Guide: Engineering. See page 325 for order details of individual texts

295

Now try the following exercise

Exercise 27   Further problems on capacitors in parallel and series

1   Capacitors of $2\,\mu F$ and $6\,\mu F$ are connected (a) in parallel and (b) in series. Determine the equivalent capacitance in each case.
[(a) $8\,\mu F$ (b) $1.5\,\mu F$]

2   Find the capacitance to be connected in series with a $10\,\mu F$ capacitor for the equivalent capacitance to be $6\,\mu F$ [$15\,\mu F$]

3   What value of capacitance would be obtained if capacitors of $0.15\,\mu F$ and $0.10\,\mu F$ are connected (a) in series and (b) in parallel
[(a) $0.06\,\mu F$ (b) $0.25\,\mu F$]

4   Two $6\,\mu F$ capacitors are connected in series with one having a capacitance of $12\,\mu F$. Find the total equivalent circuit capacitance. What capacitance must be added in series to obtain a capacitance of $1.2\,\mu F$?   [$2.4\,\mu F$, $2.4\,\mu F$]

5   Determine the equivalent capacitance when the following capacitors are connected (a) in parallel and (b) in series:
(i) $2\,\mu F$, $4\,\mu F$ and $8\,\mu F$
(ii) $0.02\,\mu F$, $0.05\,\mu F$ and $0.10\,\mu F$
(iii) $50\,pF$ and $450\,pF$
(iv) $0.01\,\mu F$ and $200\,pF$

[(a)   (i) $14\,\mu F$ (ii) $0.17\,\mu F$
(iii) $500\,pF$ (iv) $0.0102\,\mu F$
(b)   (i) $1.143\,\mu F$ (ii) $0.0125\,\mu F$
(iii) $45\,pF$ (iv) $196.1\,pF$]

6   For the arrangement shown in Fig. 6.11 find (a) the equivalent circuit capacitance and (b) the voltage across a $4.5\,\mu F$ capacitor.
[(a) $1.2\,\mu F$ (b) $100\,V$]

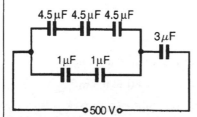

Figure 6.11

7   Three $12\,\mu F$ capacitors are connected in series across a $750\,V$ supply. Calculate (a) the equivalent capacitance, (b) the

charge on each capacitor and (c) the p.d. across each capacitor.
[(a) $4\,\mu F$ (b) $3\,mC$ (c) $250\,V$]

8   If two capacitors having capacitances of $3\,\mu F$ and $5\,\mu F$ respectively are connected in series across a $240\,V$ supply, determine (a) the p.d. across each capacitor and (b) the charge on each capacitor.
[(a) $150\,V$, $90\,V$ (b) $0.45\,mC$ on each]

9   In Fig. 6.12 capacitors P, Q and R are identical and the total equivalent capacitance of the circuit is $3\,\mu F$. Determine the values of P, Q and R [$4.2\,\mu F$ each]

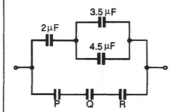

Figure 6.12

10   Capacitances of $4\,\mu F$, $8\,\mu F$ and $16\,\mu F$ are connected in parallel across a $200\,V$ supply. Determine (a) the equivalent capacitance, (b) the total charge and (c) the charge on each capacitor.
[(a) $28\,\mu F$ (b) $5.6\,mC$
(c) $0.8\,mC$, $1.6\,mC$, $3.2\,mC$]

11   A circuit consists of two capacitors P and Q in parallel, connected in series with another capacitor R. The capacitances of P, Q and R are $4\,\mu F$, $12\,\mu F$ and $8\,\mu F$ respectively. When the circuit is connected across a $300\,V$ d.c. supply find (a) the total capacitance of the circuit, (b) the p.d. across each capacitor and (c) the charge on each capacitor.
[(a) $5.33\,\mu F$ (b) $100\,V$ across P, $100\,V$ across Q, $200\,V$ across R (c) $0.4\,mC$ on P, $1.2\,mC$ on Q, $1.6\,mC$ on R]

6.9   Dielectric strength

The maximum amount of field strength that a dielectric can withstand is called the dielectric strength of the material. Dielectric strength,

$$E_m = \frac{V_m}{d}$$

BTEC National Study Guide: Engineering. See page 325 for order details of individual texts

296

Problem 15. A capacitor is to be constructed so that its capacitance is $0.2\,\mu F$ and to take a p.d. of $1.25\,kV$ across its terminals. The dielectric is to be mica which, after allowing a safety factor of 2, has a dielectric strength of $50\,MV/m$. Find (a) the thickness of the mica needed, and (b) the area of a plate assuming a two-plate construction. (Assume ε_r for mica to be 6).

(a) Dielectric strength,

$$E = \frac{V}{d}$$

i.e. $$d = \frac{V}{E} = \frac{1.25 \times 10^3}{50 \times 10^6}\,m$$

$$= 0.025\,mm$$

(b) Capacitance,

$$C = \frac{\varepsilon_0 \varepsilon_r A}{d}$$

hence

$$\text{area } A = \frac{Cd}{\varepsilon_0 \varepsilon_r} = \frac{0.2 \times 10^{-6} \times 0.025 \times 10^{-3}}{8.85 \times 10^{-12} \times 6}\,m^2$$

$$= 0.09416\,m^2 = 941.6\,cm^2$$

6.10 Energy stored in capacitors

The energy, W, stored by a capacitor is given by

$$W = \frac{1}{2}CV^2 \text{ joules}$$

Problem 16. (a) Determine the energy stored in a $3\,\mu F$ capacitor when charged to $400\,V$ (b) Find also the average power developed if this energy is dissipated in a time of $10\,\mu s$.

(a) **Energy stored**

$$W = \frac{1}{2}CV^2 \text{ joules} = \frac{1}{2} \times 3 \times 10^{-6} \times 400^2$$

$$= \frac{3}{2} \times 16 \times 10^{-2} = 0.24\,J$$

(b) **Power** $= \frac{\text{energy}}{\text{time}} = \frac{0.24}{10 \times 10^{-6}}\,W = 24\,kW$

Problem 17. A $12\,\mu F$ capacitor is required to store $4\,J$ of energy. Find the p.d. to which the capacitor must be charged.

Energy stored

$$W = \frac{1}{2}CV^2$$

hence $$V^2 = \frac{2W}{C}$$

and p.d. $$V = \sqrt{\frac{2W}{c}} = \sqrt{\frac{2 \times 4}{12 \times 10^{-6}}}$$

$$= \sqrt{\frac{2 \times 10^6}{3}} = 816.5\,V$$

Problem 18. A capacitor is charged with $10\,mC$. If the energy stored is $1.2\,J$ find (a) the voltage and (b) the capacitance.

Energy stored $W = \frac{1}{2}CV^2$ and $C = Q/V$. Hence

$$W = \frac{1}{2}\left(\frac{Q}{V}\right)V^2$$

$$= \frac{1}{2}QV \text{ from which}$$

$$V = \frac{2W}{Q}$$

$$Q = 10\,mC = 10 \times 10^{-3}\,C$$

and $$W = 1.2\,J$$

(a) Voltage

$$V = \frac{2W}{Q} = \frac{2 \times 1.2}{10 \times 10^{-3}} = 0.24\,kV \text{ or } 240\,V$$

(b) Capacitance

$$C = \frac{Q}{V} = \frac{10 \times 10^{-3}}{240}\,F = \frac{10 \times 10^6}{240 \times 10^3}\,\mu F$$

$$= 41.67\,\mu F$$

BTEC National Study Guide: Engineering. See page 325 for order details of individual texts

297

Now try the following exercise

Exercise 28 Further problems on energy stored in capacitors

(Assume $\varepsilon_0 = 8.85 \times 10^{-12}$ F/m)

1 When a capacitor is connected across a 200 V supply the charge is $4\,\mu$C. Find (a) the capacitance and (b) the energy stored

[(a) $0.02\,\mu$F (b) 0.4 mJ]

2 Find the energy stored in a $10\,\mu$F capacitor when charged to 2 kV   [20 J]

3 A 3300 pF capacitor is required to store 0.5 mJ of energy. Find the p.d. to which the capacitor must be charged.   [550 V]

4 A capacitor is charged with 8 mC. If the energy stored is 0.4 J find (a) the voltage and (b) the capacitance.   [(a) 100 V (b) $80\,\mu$F]

5 A capacitor, consisting of two metal plates each of area 50 cm^2 and spaced 0.2 mm apart in air, is connected across a 120 V supply. Calculate (a) the energy stored, (b) the electric flux density and (c) the potential gradient

[(a) $1.593\,\mu$J (b) $5.31\,\mu$C/m^2 (c) 600 kV/m]

6 A bakelite capacitor is to be constructed to have a capacitance of $0.04\,\mu$F and to have a steady working potential of 1 kV maximum. Allowing a safe value of field stress of 25 MV/m find (a) the thickness of bakelite required, (b) the area of plate required if the relative permittivity of bakelite is 5, (c) the maximum energy stored by the capacitor and (d) the average power developed if this energy is dissipated in a time of $20\,\mu$s.

[(a) 0.04 mm (b) 361.6 cm^2
(c) 0.02 J   (d) 1 kW]

6.11 Practical types of capacitor

Practical types of capacitor are characterized by the material used for their dielectric. The main types include: variable air, mica, paper, ceramic, plastic, titanium oxide and electrolytic.

1. Variable air capacitors. These usually consist of two sets of metal plates (such as aluminium), one fixed, the other variable. The set of moving plates rotate on a spindle as shown by the end view of Fig. 6.13.

As the moving plates are rotated through half a revolution, the meshing, and therefore the capacitance, varies from a minimum to a maximum value. Variable air capacitors are used in radio and electronic circuits where very low losses are required, or where a variable capacitance is needed. The maximum value of such capacitors is between 500 pF and 1000 pF.

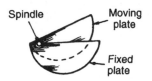

Figure 6.13

2. Mica capacitors. A typical older type construction is shown in Fig. 6.14.

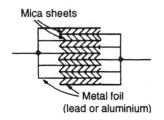

Figure 6.14

Usually the whole capacitor is impregnated with wax and placed in a bakelite case. Mica is easily obtained in thin sheets and is a good insulator. However, mica is expensive and is not used in capacitors above about $0.2\,\mu$F. A modified form of mica capacitor is the silvered mica type. The mica is coated on both sides with a thin layer of silver which forms the plates. Capacitance is stable and less likely to change with age. Such capacitors have a constant capacitance with change of temperature, a high working voltage rating and a long service life and are used in high frequency circuits with fixed values of capacitance up to about 1000 pF.

3. Paper capacitors. A typical paper capacitor is shown in Fig. 6.15 where the length of the roll corresponds to the capacitance required.

The whole is usually impregnated with oil or wax to exclude moisture, and then placed in a plastic or aluminium container for protection.

BTEC National Study Guide: Engineering. See page 325 for order details of individual texts

298

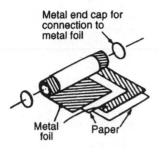

Figure 6.15

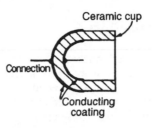

Figure 6.17

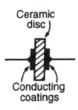

Figure 6.18

Paper capacitors are made in various working voltages up to about 150 kV and are used where loss is not very important. The maximum value of this type of capacitor is between 500 pF and 10 μF. Disadvantages of paper capacitors include variation in capacitance with temperature change and a shorter service life than most other types of capacitor.

4. **Ceramic capacitors**. These are made in various forms, each type of construction depending on the value of capacitance required. For high values, a tube of ceramic material is used as shown in the cross section of Fig. 6.16. For smaller values the cup construction is used as shown in Fig. 6.17, and for still smaller values the disc construction shown in Fig. 6.18 is used. Certain ceramic materials have a very high permittivity and this enables capacitors of high capacitance to be made which are of small physical size with a high working voltage rating. Ceramic capacitors are available in the range 1 pF to 0.1 μF and may be used in high frequency electronic circuits subject to a wide range of temperatures.

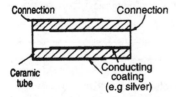

Figure 6.16

5. **Plastic capacitors**. Some plastic materials such as polystyrene and Teflon can be used as dielectrics. Construction is similar to the paper capacitor but using a plastic film instead of paper. Plastic capacitors operate well under conditions of high temperature, provide a precise value of capacitance, a very long service life and high reliability.

6. **Titanium oxide capacitors** have a very high capacitance with a small physical size when used at a low temperature.

7 **Electrolytic capacitors**. Construction is similar to the paper capacitor with aluminium foil used for the plates and with a thick absorbent material, such as paper, impregnated with an electrolyte (ammonium borate), separating the plates. The finished capacitor is usually assembled in an aluminium container and hermetically sealed. Its operation depends on the formation of a thin aluminium oxide layer on the positive plate by electrolytic action when a suitable direct potential is maintained between the plates. This oxide layer is very thin and forms the dielectric. (The absorbent paper between the plates is a conductor and does not act as a dielectric.) Such capacitors **must always be used on d.c.** and must be connected with the correct polarity; if this is not done the capacitor will be destroyed since the oxide layer will be destroyed. Electrolytic capacitors are manufactured with working voltage from 6 V to 600 V, although accuracy is generally not very high. These capacitors possess a much larger capacitance than other types of capacitors of similar dimensions due to the oxide film being only a few microns thick. The fact that they can be used only on d.c. supplies limit their usefulness.

BTEC National Study Guide: Engineering. See page 325 for order details of individual texts

299

6.12 Discharging capacitors

When a capacitor has been disconnected from the supply it may still be charged and it may retain this charge for some considerable time. Thus precautions must be taken to ensure that the capacitor is automatically discharged after the supply is switched off. This is done by connecting a high value resistor across the capacitor terminals.

Now try the following exercises

Exercise 29   Short answer questions on capacitors and capacitance

1 Explain the term 'electrostatics'

2 Complete the statements:

Like charges . . . . . . ; unlike charges . . . . . .

3 How can an 'electric field' be established between two parallel metal plates?

4 What is capacitance?

5 State the unit of capacitance

6 Complete the statement:

$$\text{Capacitance} = \frac{\ldots\ldots}{\ldots\ldots}$$

7 Complete the statements:
   (a) $1\,\mu F = \ldots F$ (b) $1\,pF = \ldots F$

8 Complete the statement:

Electric field strength $E = \dfrac{\ldots\ldots}{\ldots\ldots}$

9 Complete the statement:

Electric flux density $D = \dfrac{\ldots\ldots}{\ldots\ldots}$

10 Draw the electrical circuit diagram symbol for a capacitor

11 Name two practical examples where capacitance is present, although undesirable

12 The insulating material separating the plates of a capacitor is called the . . . . . .

13 10 volts applied to a capacitor results in a charge of 5 coulombs. What is the capacitance of the capacitor?

14 Three $3\,\mu F$ capacitors are connected in parallel. The equivalent capacitance is. . . .

15 Three $3\,\mu F$ capacitors are connected in series. The equivalent capacitance is. . . .

16 State a disadvantage of series-connected capacitors

17 Name three factors upon which capacitance depends

18 What does 'relative permittivity' mean?

19 Define 'permittivity of free space'

20 What is meant by the 'dielectric strength' of a material?

21 State the formula used to determine the energy stored by a capacitor

22 Name five types of capacitor commonly used

23 Sketch a typical rolled paper capacitor

24 Explain briefly the construction of a variable air capacitor

25 State three advantages and one disadvantage of mica capacitors

26 Name two disadvantages of paper capacitors

27 Between what values of capacitance are ceramic capacitors normally available

28 What main advantages do plastic capacitors possess?

29 Explain briefly the construction of an electrolytic capacitor

30 What is the main disadvantage of electrolytic capacitors?

31 Name an important advantage of electrolytic capacitors

32 What safety precautions should be taken when a capacitor is disconnected from a supply?

Exercise 30   Multi-choice questions on capacitors and capacitance (Answers on page 375)

1 Electrostatics is a branch of electricity concerned with
   (a) energy flowing across a gap between conductors
   (b) charges at rest
   (c) charges in motion
   (d) energy in the form of charges

BTEC National Study Guide: Engineering. See page 325 for order details of individual texts

300

2 The capacitance of a capacitor is the ratio
   (a) charge to p.d. between plates
   (b) p.d. between plates to plate spacing
   (c) p.d. between plates to thickness of dielectric
   (d) p.d. between plates to charge

3 The p.d. across a $10\,\mu F$ capacitor to charge it with $10\,mC$ is
   (a) $10\,V$ (b) $1\,kV$
   (c) $1\,V$ (d) $10\,V$

4 The charge on a $10\,pF$ capacitor when the voltage applied to it is $10\,kV$ is
   (a) $100\,\mu C$ (b) $0.1\,C$
   (c) $0.1\,\mu C$ (d) $0.01\,\mu C$

5 Four $2\,\mu F$ capacitors are connected in parallel. The equivalent capacitance is
   (a) $8\,\mu F$ (b) $0.5\,\mu F$
   (c) $2\,\mu F$ (d) $6\,\mu F$

6 Four $2\,\mu F$ capacitors are connected in series. The equivalent capacitance is
   (a) $8\,\mu F$ (b) $0.5\,\mu F$
   (c) $2\,\mu F$ (d) $6\,\mu F$

7 State which of the following is false.
   The capacitance of a capacitor
   (a) is proportional to the cross-sectional area of the plates
   (b) is proportional to the distance between the plates
   (c) depends on the number of plates

   (d) is proportional to the relative permittivity of the dielectric

8 Which of the following statement is false?
   (a) An air capacitor is normally a variable type
   (b) A paper capacitor generally has a shorter service life than most other types of capacitor
   (c) An electrolytic capacitor must be used only on a.c. supplies
   (d) Plastic capacitors generally operate satisfactorily under conditions of high temperature

9 The energy stored in a $10\,\mu F$ capacitor when charged to $500\,V$ is
   (a) $1.25\,mJ$ (b) $0.025\,\mu J$
   (c) $1.25\,J$ (d) $1.25\,C$

10 The capacitance of a variable air capacitor is at maximum when
   (a) the movable plates half overlap the fixed plates
   (b) the movable plates are most widely separated from the fixed plates
   (c) both sets of plates are exactly meshed
   (d) the movable plates are closer to one side of the fixed plate than to the other

11 When a voltage of $1\,kV$ is applied to a capacitor, the charge on the capacitor is $500\,nC$. The capacitance of the capacitor is:
   (a) $2 \times 10^9\,F$ (b) $0.5\,pF$
   (c) $0.5\,mF$ (d) $0.5\,nF$

BTEC National Study Guide: Engineering. See page 325 for order details of individual texts

301

7

Magnetic circuits

At the end of this chapter you should be able to:

- describe the magnetic field around a permanent magnet
- state the laws of magnetic attraction and repulsion for two magnets in close proximity
- define magnetic flux, Φ, and magnetic flux density, B, and state their units
- perform simple calculations involving $B = \Phi/A$
- define magnetomotive force, F_m, and magnetic field strength, H, and state their units
- perform simple calculations involving $F_m = NI$ and $H = NI/l$
- define permeability, distinguishing between μ_0, μ_r and μ
- understand the B–H curves for different magnetic materials
- appreciate typical values of μ_r
- perform calculations involving $B = \mu_0\mu_r H$
- define reluctance, S, and state its units
- perform calculations involving

$$ S = \frac{\text{m.m.f.}}{\Phi} = \frac{l}{\mu_0\mu_r A} $$

- perform calculations on composite series magnetic circuits
- compare electrical and magnetic quantities
- appreciate how a hysteresis loop is obtained and that hysteresis loss is proportional to its area

7.1 Magnetic fields

A **permanent magnet** is a piece of ferromagnetic material (such as iron, nickel or cobalt) which has properties of attracting other pieces of these materials. A permanent magnet will position itself in a north and south direction when freely suspended. The north-seeking end of the magnet is called the **north pole, N**, and the south-seeking end the **south pole, S**.

The area around a magnet is called the **magnetic field** and it is in this area that the effects of the magnetic force produced by the magnet can be detected. A magnetic field cannot be seen, felt, smelt or heard and therefore is difficult to represent. Michael Faraday suggested that the magnetic field could be represented pictorially, by imagining the field to consist of **lines of magnetic flux**, which enables investigation of the distribution and density of the field to be carried out.

The distribution of a magnetic field can be investigated by using some iron filings. A bar magnet is placed on a flat surface covered by, say, cardboard, upon which is sprinkled some iron filings. If the

BTEC National Study Guide: Engineering. See page 325 for order details of individual texts

302

cardboard is gently tapped the filings will assume a pattern similar to that shown in Fig. 7.1. If a number of magnets of different strength are used, it is found that the stronger the field the closer are the lines of magnetic flux and vice versa. Thus a magnetic field has the property of exerting a force, demonstrated in this case by causing the iron filings to move into the pattern shown. The strength of the magnetic field decreases as we move away from the magnet. It should be realized, of course, that the magnetic field is three dimensional in its effect, and not acting in one plane as appears to be the case in this experiment.

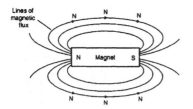

Figure 7.1

If a compass is placed in the magnetic field in various positions, the direction of the lines of flux may be determined by noting the direction of the compass pointer. The direction of a magnetic field at any point is taken as that in which the north-seeking pole of a compass needle points when suspended in the field. The direction of a line of flux is from the north pole to the south pole on the outside of the magnet and is then assumed to continue through the magnet back to the point at which it emerged at the north pole. Thus such lines of flux always form complete closed loops or paths, they never intersect and always have a definite direction.

The laws of magnetic attraction and repulsion can be demonstrated by using two bar magnets. In Fig. 7.2(a), **with unlike poles adjacent, attraction takes place.** Lines of flux are imagined to contract and the magnets try to pull together. The magnetic field is strongest in between the two magnets, shown by the lines of flux being close together. In Fig. 7.2(b), **with similar poles adjacent (i.e. two north poles), repulsion occurs,** i.e. the two north poles try to push each other apart, since magnetic flux lines running side by side in the same direction repel.

7.2 Magnetic flux and flux density

Magnetic flux is the amount of magnetic field (or the number of lines of force) produced by a

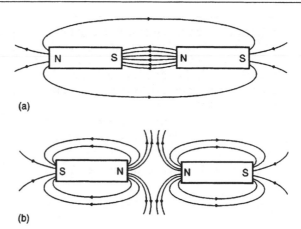

(a)

(b)

Figure 7.2

magnetic source. The symbol for magnetic flux is Φ (Greek letter 'phi'). The unit of magnetic flux is the **weber, Wb**

Magnetic flux density is the amount of flux passing through a defined area that is perpendicular to the direction of the flux:

$$\textbf{Magnetic flux density} = \frac{\textbf{magnetic flux}}{\textbf{area}}$$

The symbol for magnetic flux density is B. The unit of magnetic flux density is the tesla, T, where $1\,T = 1\,Wb/m^2$. Hence

$$B = \frac{\Phi}{A} \textbf{ tesla}$$

where $A(m^2)$ is the area

Problem 1.   A magnetic pole face has a rectangular section having dimensions 200 mm by 100 mm. If the total flux emerging from the pole is 150 μWb, calculate the flux density.

Flux $\Phi = 150\,\mu Wb = 150 \times 10^{-6}\,Wb$
Cross sectional area $A = 200 \times 100 = 20\,000\,mm^2 = 20\,000 \times 10^{-6}\,m^2$.

$$\text{Flux density, } B = \frac{\Phi}{A} = \frac{150 \times 10^{-6}}{20\,000 \times 10^{-6}}$$

$$= \textbf{0.0075 T} \text{ or } \textbf{7.5 mT}$$

BTEC National Study Guide: Engineering. See page 325 for order details of individual texts

Problem 2.   The maximum working flux density of a lifting electromagnet is 1.8 T and the effective area of a pole face is circular in cross-section. If the total magnetic flux produced is 353 mWb, determine the radius of the pole face.

Flux density $B = 1.8\,\text{T}$ and flux $\Phi = 353\,\text{mWb} = 353 \times 10^{-3}\,\text{Wb}$.

Since $B = \Phi/A$, cross-sectional area $A = \Phi/B$

$$= \frac{353 \times 10^{-3}}{1.8}\,\text{m}^2 = 0.1961\,\text{m}^2$$

The pole face is circular, hence area $= \pi r^2$, where r is the radius. Hence $\pi r^2 = 0.1961$ from which, $r^2 = 0.1961/\pi$ and radius $r = \sqrt{(0.1961/\pi)} = 0.250\,\text{m}$ i.e. **the radius of the pole face is 250 mm**.

7.3   Magnetomotive force and magnetic field strength

Magnetomotive force (m.m.f.) is the cause of the existence of a magnetic flux in a magnetic circuit,

$$\boxed{\textbf{m.m.f. } F_\text{m} = NI \textbf{ amperes}}$$

where N is the number of conductors (or turns) and I is the current in amperes. The unit of mmf is sometimes expressed as 'ampere-turns'. However since 'turns' have no dimensions, the S.I. unit of m.m.f. is the ampere.

Magnetic field strength (or **magnetising force**),

$$\boxed{H = \frac{NI}{l} \textbf{ ampere per metre}}$$

where l is the mean length of the flux path in metres. Thus

$$\boxed{\textbf{m.m.f.} = NI = Hl \textbf{ amperes}}$$

Problem 3.   A magnetising force of 8000 A/m is applied to a circular magnetic circuit of mean diameter 30 cm by passing a current through a coil wound on the circuit. If the coil is uniformly wound around the circuit and has 750 turns, find the current in the coil.

$H = 8000\,\text{A/m}$, $l = \pi d = \pi \times 30 \times 10^{-2}\,\text{m}$ and $N = 750$ turns. Since $H = NI/l$, then

$$I = \frac{Hl}{N} = \frac{8000 \times \pi \times 30 \times 10^{-2}}{750}$$

Thus, **current $I = 10.05\,\text{A}$**

Now try the following exercise

Exercise 31   Further problems on magnetic circuits

1 What is the flux density in a magnetic field of cross-sectional area 20 cm^2 having a flux of 3 mWb?   [1.5 T]

2 Determine the total flux emerging from a magnetic pole face having dimensions 5 cm by 6 cm, if the flux density is 0.9 T   [2.7 mWb]

3 The maximum working flux density of a lifting electromagnet is 1.9 T and the effective area of a pole face is circular in cross-section. If the total magnetic flux produced is 611 mWb determine the radius of the pole face. [32 cm]

4 An electromagnet of square cross-section produces a flux density of 0.45 T. If the magnetic flux is 720 µWb find the dimensions of the electromagnet cross-section.   [4 cm by 4 cm]

5 Find the magnetic field strength applied to a magnetic circuit of mean length 50 cm when a coil of 400 turns is applied to it carrying a current of 1.2 A   [960 A/m]

6 A solenoid 20 cm long is wound with 500 turns of wire. Find the current required to establish a magnetising force of 2500 A/m inside the solenoid.   [1 A]

7 A magnetic field strength of 5000 A/m is applied to a circular magnetic circuit of mean diameter 250 mm. If the coil has 500 turns find the current in the coil.   [7.85 A]

7.4   Permeability and B–H curves

For air, or any non-magnetic medium, the ratio of magnetic flux density to magnetising force is a constant, i.e. $B/H = $ a constant. This constant is

BTEC National Study Guide: Engineering. See page 325 for order details of individual texts

304

μ_0, the **permeability of free space** (or the magnetic space constant) and is equal to $4\pi \times 10^{-7}$ H/m, i.e. **for air, or any non-magnetic medium**, the ratio

$$\boxed{\frac{B}{H} = \mu_0}$$

(Although all non-magnetic materials, including air, exhibit slight magnetic properties, these can effectively be neglected.)
For all media other than free space,

$$\boxed{\frac{B}{H} = \mu_0 \mu_r}$$

where u_r is the relative permeability, and is defined as

$$\boxed{\mu_r = \frac{\text{flux density in material}}{\text{flux density in a vacuum}}}$$

μ_r varies with the type of magnetic material and, since it is a ratio of flux densities, it has no unit. From its definition, μ_r for a vacuum is 1.
$\mu_0 \mu_r = \mu$, called the **absolute permeability**

By plotting measured values of flux density B against magnetic field strength H, a **magnetisation curve** (or **B–H curve**) is produced. For non-magnetic materials this is a straight line. Typical curves for four magnetic materials are shown in Fig. 7.3

The **relative permeability** of a ferromagnetic material is proportional to the slope of the B–H curve and thus varies with the magnetic field strength. The approximate range of values of relative permeability μ_r for some common magnetic materials are:

Cast iron $\mu_r = 100–250$
Mild steel $\mu_r = 200–800$
Silicon iron $\mu_r = 1000–5000$
Cast steel $\mu_r = 300–900$
Mumetal $\mu_r = 200–5000$
Stalloy $\mu_r = 500–6000$

Problem 4. A flux density of 1.2 T is produced in a piece of cast steel by a magnetising force of 1250 A/m. Find the relative permeability of the steel under these conditions.

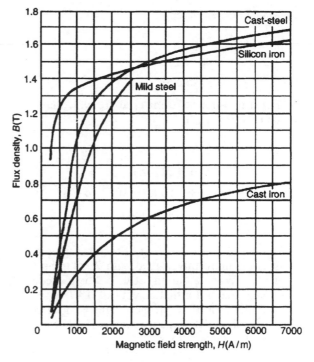

Figure 7.3

For a magnetic material: $B = \mu_0 \mu_r H$

i.e. $\mu_r = \dfrac{B}{\mu_0 H} = \dfrac{1.2}{(4\pi \times 10^{-7})(1250)} = \mathbf{764}$

Problem 5. Determine the magnetic field strength and the m.m.f. required to produce a flux density of 0.25 T in an air gap of length 12 mm.

For air: $B = \mu_0 H$ (since $\mu_r = 1$)
Magnetic field strength,

$$H = \frac{B}{\mu_0} = \frac{0.25}{4\pi \times 10^{-7}} = \mathbf{198\,940\ A/m}$$

m.m.f. $= Hl = 198\,940 \times 12 \times 10^{-3} = \mathbf{2387\,A}$

Problem 6. A coil of 300 turns is wound uniformly on a ring of non-magnetic material. The ring has a mean circumference of 40 cm and a uniform cross-sectional area of 4 cm². If the current in the coil is 5 A, calculate (a) the magnetic field strength, (b) the flux density and (c) the total magnetic flux in the ring.

BTEC National Study Guide: Engineering. See page 325 for order details of individual texts

305

(a) Magnetic field strength

$$H = \frac{NI}{l} = \frac{300 \times 5}{40 \times 10^{-2}}$$

$$= 3750 \, \text{A/m}$$

(b) For a non-magnetic material $\mu_r = 1$, thus flux density $B = \mu_0 H$

i.e. $\qquad B = 4\pi \times 10^{-7} \times 3750$

$$= 4.712 \, \text{mT}$$

(c) Flux $\Phi = BA = (4.712 \times 10^{-3})(4 \times 10^{-4})$

$$= 1.885 \, \mu\text{Wb}$$

Problem 7. An iron ring of mean diameter 10 cm is uniformly wound with 2000 turns of wire. When a current of 0.25 A is passed through the coil a flux density of 0.4 T is set up in the iron. Find (a) the magnetising force and (b) the relative permeability of the iron under these conditions.

$l = \pi d = \pi \times 10 \, \text{cm} = \pi \times 10 \times 10^{-2} \, \text{m}$,
$N = 2000$ turns, $I = 0.25 \, \text{A}$ and $B = 0.4 \, \text{T}$

(a) $\quad H = \dfrac{NI}{l} = \dfrac{2000 \times 0.25}{\pi \times 10 \times 10^{-2}}$

$$= 1592 \, \text{A/m}$$

(b) $\quad B = \mu_0 \mu_r H$, hence μ_r

$$= \frac{B}{\mu_0 H} = \frac{0.4}{(4\pi \times 10^{-7})(1592)} = 200$$

Problem 8. A uniform ring of cast iron has a cross-sectional area of $10 \, \text{cm}^2$ and a mean circumference of 20 cm. Determine the m.m.f. necessary to produce a flux of 0.3 mWb in the ring. The magnetisation curve for cast iron is shown on page 71.

$A = 10 \, \text{cm}^2 = 10 \times 10^{-4} \text{m}^2$, $l = 20 \, \text{cm} = 0.2 \, \text{m}$ and $\Phi = 0.3 \times 10^{-3} \, \text{Wb}$.

Flux density $B = \dfrac{\Phi}{A} = \dfrac{0.3 \times 10^{-3}}{10 \times 10^{-4}} = 0.3 \, \text{T}$

From the magnetisation curve for cast iron on page 71, when $B = 0.3 \, \text{T}$, $H = 1000 \, \text{A/m}$, hence **m.m.f.** $= Hl = 1000 \times 0.2 = \textbf{200 A}$

A tabular method could have been used in this problem. Such a solution is shown below in Table 1.

Problem 9. From the magnetisation curve for cast iron, shown on page 71, derive the curve of μ_r against H.

$B = \mu_0 \mu_r H$, hence

$$\mu_r = \frac{B}{\mu_0 H} = \frac{1}{\mu_0} \times \frac{B}{H}$$

$$= \frac{10^7}{4\pi} \times \frac{B}{H}$$

A number of co-ordinates are selected from the B–H curve and μ_r is calculated for each as shown in Table 2.

Table 1

Part of circuit	Material	Φ (Wb)	$A(m^2)$	$B = \dfrac{\Phi}{A}(T)$	H from graph	$l(m)$	m.m.f. $= Hl(A)$
Ring	Cast iron	0.3×10^{-3}	10×10^{-4}	0.3	1000	0.2	200

Table 2

$B(T)$	0.04	0.13	0.17	0.30	0.41	0.49	0.60	0.68	0.73	0.76	0.79
$H(A/m)$	200	400	500	1000	1500	2000	3000	4000	5000	6000	7000
$\mu_r = \dfrac{10^7}{4\pi} \times \dfrac{B}{H}$	159	259	271	239	218	195	159	135	116	101	90

BTEC National Study Guide: Engineering. See page 325 for order details of individual texts

306

μ_r is plotted against H as shown in Fig. 7.4. The curve demonstrates the change that occurs in the relative permeability as the magnetising force increases.

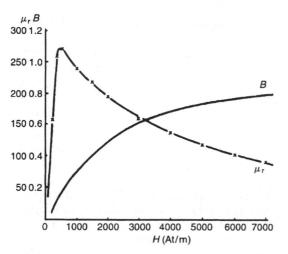

Figure 7.4

Now try the following exercise

Exercise 32   Further problems on magnetic circuits

(Where appropriate, assume $\mu_0 = 4\pi \times 10^{-7}$ H/m)

1 Find the magnetic field strength and the magnetomotive force needed to produce a flux density of 0.33 T in an air-gap of length 15 mm.
[(a) 262 600 A/m (b) 3939 A]

2 An air-gap between two pole pieces is 20 mm in length and the area of the flux path across the gap is 5 cm². If the flux required in the air-gap is 0.75 mWb find the m.m.f. necessary.
[23 870 A]

3 (a) Determine the flux density produced in an air-cored solenoid due to a uniform magnetic field strength of 8000 A/m (b) Iron having a relative permeability of 150 at 8000 A/m is inserted into the solenoid of part (a). Find the flux density now in the solenoid.
[(a) 10.05 mT (b) 1.508 T]

4 Find the relative permeability of a material if the absolute permeability is 4.084×10^{-4} H/m.
[325]

5 Find the relative permeability of a piece of silicon iron if a flux density of 1.3 T is produced by a magnetic field strength of 700 A/m
[1478]

6 A steel ring of mean diameter 120 mm is uniformly wound with 1 500 turns of wire. When a current of 0.30 A is passed through the coil a flux density of 1.5 T is set up in the steel. Find the relative permeability of the steel under these conditions.
[1000]

7 A uniform ring of cast steel has a cross-sectional area of 5 cm² and a mean circumference of 15 cm. Find the current required in a coil of 1200 turns wound on the ring to produce a flux of 0.8 mWb. (Use the magnetisation curve for cast steel shown on page 71)
[0.60 A]

8 (a) A uniform mild steel ring has a diameter of 50 mm and a cross-sectional area of 1 cm². Determine the m.m.f. necessary to produce a flux of 50 μWb in the ring. (Use the B–H curve for mild steel shown on page 71) (b) If a coil of 440 turns is wound uniformly around the ring in Part (a) what current would be required to produce the flux?
[(a) 110 A (b) 0.25 A]

9 From the magnetisation curve for mild steel shown on page 71, derive the curve of relative permeability against magnetic field strength. From your graph determine (a) the value of μ_r when the magnetic field strength is 1200 A/m, and (b) the value of the magnetic field strength when μ_r is 500
[(a) 590–600 (b) 2000]

7.5   Reluctance

Reluctance S (or R_M) is the 'magnetic resistance' of a magnetic circuit to the presence of magnetic flux. **Reluctance,**

$$S = \frac{F_M}{\Phi} = \frac{NI}{\Phi} = \frac{Hl}{BA} = \frac{l}{(B/H)A} = \frac{l}{\mu_0 \mu_r A}$$

The unit of reluctance is $1/H$ (or H^{-1}) or A/Wb.

Ferromagnetic materials have a low reluctance and can be used as **magnetic screens** to prevent magnetic fields affecting materials within the screen.

BTEC National Study Guide: Engineering. See page 325 for order details of individual texts

307

Problem 10. Determine the reluctance of a piece of mumetal of length 150 mm and cross-sectional area 1800 mm^2 when the relative permeability is 4000. Find also the absolute permeability of the mumetal.

Reluctance,

$$S = \frac{l}{\mu_0 \mu_r A}$$

$$= \frac{150 \times 10^{-3}}{(4\pi \times 10^{-7})(4000)(1800 \times 10^{-6})}$$

$$= \mathbf{16\,580/H}$$

Absolute permeability,

$$\mu = \mu_0 \mu_r = (4\pi \times 10^{-7})(4000)$$

$$= \mathbf{5.027 \times 10^{-3} \ H/m}$$

Problem 11. A mild steel ring has a radius of 50 mm and a cross-sectional area of 400 mm^2. A current of 0.5 A flows in a coil wound uniformly around the ring and the flux produced is 0.1 mWb. If the relative permeability at this value of current is 200 find (a) the reluctance of the mild steel and (b) the number of turns on the coil.

$l = 2\pi r = 2 \times \pi \times 50 \times 10^{-3}$m, $A = 400 \times 10^{-6}$m^2, $I = 0.5$ A, $\Phi = 0.1 \times 10^{-3}$ Wb and $\mu_r = 200$

(a) **Reluctance,**

$$S = \frac{l}{\mu_0 \mu_r A}$$

$$= \frac{2 \times \pi \times 50 \times 10^{-3}}{(4\pi \times 10^{-7})(200)(400 \times 10^{-6})}$$

$$= \mathbf{3.125 \times 10^6/H}$$

(b) $S = \dfrac{\text{m.m.f.}}{\Phi}$ from which m.m.f.

$$= S\Phi \quad \text{i.e.} \quad NI = S\Phi$$

Hence, number of terms

$$N = \frac{S\Phi}{I} = \frac{3.125 \times 10^6 \times 0.1 \times 10^{-3}}{0.5}$$

$$= \mathbf{625 \ turns}$$

Now try the following exercise

Exercise 33 Further problems on magnetic circuits

(Where appropriate, assume $\mu_0 = \pi \times 10^{-7}$H/m)

1 Part of a magnetic circuit is made from steel of length 120 mm, cross sectional area 15 cm^2 and relative permeability 800. Calculate (a) the reluctance and (b) the absolute permeability of the steel. [(a) 79 580/H (b) 1 mH/m]

2 A mild steel closed magnetic circuit has a mean length of 75 mm and a cross-sectional area of 320.2 mm^2. A current of 0.40 A flows in a coil wound uniformly around the circuit and the flux produced is 200 μWb. If the relative permeability of the steel at this value of current is 400 find (a) the reluctance of the material and (b) the number of turns of the coil. [(a) 466 000/H (b) 233]

7.6 Composite series magnetic circuits

For a series magnetic circuit having n parts, the **total reluctance** S is given by: $S = S_1 + S_2 + \ldots + S_n$ (This is similar to resistors connected in series in an electrical circuit)

Problem 12. A closed magnetic circuit of cast steel contains a 6 cm long path of cross-sectional area 1 cm^2 and a 2 cm path of cross-sectional area 0.5 cm^2. A coil of 200 turns is wound around the 6 cm length of the circuit and a current of 0.4 A flows. Determine the flux density in the 2 cm path, if the relative permeability of the cast steel is 750.

For the 6 cm long path:

$$\text{Reluctance } S_1 = \frac{l_1}{\mu_0 \mu_r A_1}$$

$$= \frac{6 \times 10^{-2}}{(4\pi \times 10^{-7})(750)(1 \times 10^{-4})}$$

$$= 6.366 \times 10^5/H$$

BTEC National Study Guide: Engineering. See page 325 for order details of individual texts

308

For the 2 cm long path:

$$\text{Reluctance } S_2 = \frac{l_2}{\mu_0\mu_r A_2}$$

$$= \frac{2 \times 10^{-2}}{(4\pi \times 10^{-7})(750)(0.5 \times 10^{-4})}$$

$$= 4.244 \times 10^5/\text{H}$$

Total circuit reluctance $S = S_1 + S_2$
$= (6.366 + 4.244) \times 10^5 = 10.61 \times 10^5/\text{H}$

$$S = \frac{\text{m.m.f}}{\Phi} \text{ i.e. } \Phi = \frac{\text{m.m.f.}}{S} = \frac{NI}{S}$$

$$= \frac{200 \times 0.4}{10.61 \times 10^5} = 7.54 \times 10^{-5}\,\text{Wb}$$

Flux density in the 2 cm path,

$$B = \frac{\Phi}{A} = \frac{7.54 \times 10^{-5}}{0.5 \times 10^{-4}} = \mathbf{1.51\,T}$$

Problem 13. A silicon iron ring of cross-sectional area $5\,\text{cm}^2$ has a radial air gap of 2 mm cut into it. If the mean length of the silicon iron path is 40 cm calculate the magnetomotive force to produce a flux of 0.7 mWb. The magnetisation curve for silicon is shown on page 71.

There are two parts to the circuit – the silicon iron and the air gap. The total m.m.f. will be the sum of the m.m.f.'s of each part.

For the silicon iron:

$$B = \frac{\Phi}{A} = \frac{0.7 \times 10^{-3}}{5 \times 10^{-4}} = 1.4\,\text{T}$$

From the B–H curve for silicon iron on page 71, when $B = 1.4\,\text{T}$, $H = 1650\,\text{At/m}$ Hence the m.m.f. for the iron path $= Hl = 1650 \times 0.4 = 660\,\text{A}$

For the air gap:

The flux density will be the same in the air gap as in the iron, i.e. 1.4 T (This assumes no leakage or fringing occurring). For air,

$$H = \frac{B}{\mu_0} = \frac{1.4}{4\pi \times 10^{-7}} = 1\,114\,000\,\text{A/m}$$

Hence the m.m.f. for the air gap $= Hl = 1\,114\,000 \times 2 \times 10^{-3} = 2228\,\text{A}$.

Total m.m.f. to produce a flux of 0.6 mWb $= 660 + 2228 = \mathbf{2888\,A}$.

A tabular method could have been used as shown at the bottom of the page.

Problem 14. Figure 7.5 shows a ring formed with two different materials – cast steel and mild steel. The dimensions are:

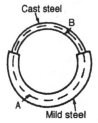

Cast steel

Mild steel

Figure 7.5

	mean length	cross-sectional area
Mild steel	400 mm	500 mm^2
Cast steel	300 mm	312.5 mm^2

Find the total m.m.f. required to cause a flux of 500 µWb in the magnetic circuit.
Determine also the total circuit reluctance.

Part of circuit	Material	$\Phi(\text{Wb})$	$A(m^2)$	$B(T)$	$H(A/m)$	$l(m)$	$\text{Ł m.m.f.} = \text{Ł}Hl(A)$
Ring	Silicon iron	0.7×10^{-3}	5×10^{-4}	1.4	1650 (from graph)	0.4	660
Air-gap	Air	0.7×10^{-3}	5×10^{-4}	1.4	$\dfrac{1.4}{4\pi \times 10^{-7}}$ $= 1\,114\,000$	2×10^{-3}	2228
						Total:	**2888 A**

BTEC National Study Guide: Engineering. See page 325 for order details of individual texts

309

Part of circuit	Material	Φ(Wb)	A(m^2)	$B(T)$ (= Φ/A)	H(A/m) (from graphs page 71)	$l(m)$	m.m.f. $= Hl(A)$
A	Mild steel	500×10^{-6}	500×10^{-6}	1.0	1400	400×10^{-3}	560
B	Cast steel	500×10^{-6}	312.5×10^{-6}	1.6	4800	300×10^{-3}	1440
						Total:	**2000 A**

A tabular solution is shown above.

$$\left. \begin{array}{c} \textbf{Total circuit} \\ \textbf{reluctance} \end{array} \right\} S = \frac{\text{m.m.f.}}{\Phi}$$

$$= \frac{2000}{500 \times 10^{-6}} = \textbf{4} \times \textbf{10}^6/\textbf{H}$$

Problem 15. A section through a magnetic circuit of uniform cross-sectional area 2 cm^2 is shown in Fig. 7.6. The cast steel core has a mean length of 25 cm. The air gap is 1 mm wide and the coil has 5000 turns. The B–H curve for cast steel is shown on page 71. Determine the current in the coil to produce a flux density of 0.80 T in the air gap, assuming that all the flux passes through both parts of the magnetic circuit.

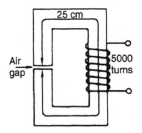

Figure 7.6

For the cast steel core, when $B = 0.80$ T, $H = 750$ A/m (from page 71).

Reluctance of core $S_1 = \dfrac{l_1}{\mu_0 \mu_r A_1}$ and

since $B = \mu_0 \mu_r H$, then $\mu_r = \dfrac{B}{\mu_0 H}$.

$$S_1 = \frac{l_1}{\mu_0 \left(\dfrac{B}{\mu_0 H}\right) A_1} = \frac{l_1 H}{B A_1}$$

$$= \frac{(25 \times 10^{-2})(750)}{(0.8)(2 \times 10^{-4})} = 1\,172\,000/\text{H}$$

For the air gap:

Reluctance, $S_2 = \dfrac{l_2}{\mu_0 \mu_r A_2}$

$$= \frac{l_2}{\mu_0 A_2} \text{ (since } \mu_r = 1 \text{ for air)}$$

$$= \frac{1 \times 10^{-3}}{(4\pi \times 10^{-7})(2 \times 10^{-4})}$$

$$= 3\,979\,000/\text{H}$$

Total circuit reluctance

$$S = S_1 + S_2 = 1\,172\,000 + 3\,979\,000$$

$$= 5\,151\,000/\text{H}$$

Flux $\Phi = BA = 0.80 \times 2 \times 10^{-4} = 1.6 \times 10^{-4}$ Wb

$$S = \frac{\text{m.m.f.}}{\Phi},$$

thus

$$\text{m.m.f.} = S\Phi \text{ hence } NI = S\Phi$$

and

$$\textbf{current } \textbf{\textit{I}} = \frac{S\Phi}{N} = \frac{(5\,151\,000)(1.6 \times 10^{-4})}{5000}$$

$$= \textbf{0.165 A}$$

Now try the following exercise

Exercise 34 Further problems on composite series magnetic circuits

1 A magnetic circuit of cross-sectional area 0.4 cm^2 consists of one part 3 cm long, of material having relative permeability 1200, and a second part 2 cm long of material having relative permeability 750. With a 100 turn coil

---

BTEC National Study Guide: Engineering. See page 325 for order details of individual texts

310

carrying 2 A, find the value of flux existing in the circuit. [0.195 mWb]

2 (a) A cast steel ring has a cross-sectional area of 600 mm^2 and a radius of 25 mm. Determine the mmf necessary to establish a flux of 0.8 mWb in the ring. Use the B–H curve for cast steel shown on page 71. (b) If a radial air gap 1.5 mm wide is cut in the ring of part (a) find the m.m.f. now necessary to maintain the same flux in the ring. [(a) 270 A (b)1860 A]

3 A closed magnetic circuit made of silicon iron consists of a 40 mm long path of cross-sectional area 90 mm^2 and a 15 mm long path of cross-sectional area 70 mm^2. A coil of 50 turns is wound around the 40 mm length of the circuit and a current of 0.39 A flows. Find the flux density in the 15 mm length path if the relative permeability of the silicon iron at this value of magnetising force is 3 000. [1.59 T]

4 For the magnetic circuit shown in Fig. 7.7 find the current I in the coil needed to produce a flux of 0.45 mWb in the air-gap. The silicon iron magnetic circuit has a uniform cross-sectional area of 3 cm^2 and its magnetisation curve is as shown on page 71. [0.83 A]

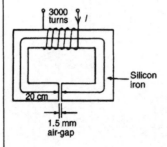

Figure 7.7

5 A ring forming a magnetic circuit is made from two materials; one part is mild steel of mean length 25 cm and cross-sectional area 4 cm^2, and the remainder is cast iron of mean length 20 cm and cross-sectional area 7.5 cm^2. Use a tabular approach to determine the total m.m.f. required to cause a flux of 0.30 mWb in the magnetic circuit. Find also the total reluctance of the circuit. Use the magnetisation curves shown on page 71. [550 A, 18.3 × 10^5/H]

6 Figure 7.8 shows the magnetic circuit of a relay. When each of the air gaps are 1.5 mm wide find the mmf required to produce a flux density of 0.75 T in the air gaps. Use the B–H curves shown on page 71. [2970 A]

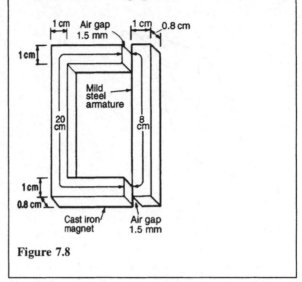

Figure 7.8

7.7 Comparison between electrical and magnetic quantities

Electrical circuit	Magnetic circuit
e.m.f. E (V)	m.m.f. F_m (A)
current I (A)	flux Φ (Wb)
resistance R (Ω)	reluctance S (H^{-1})
$I = \dfrac{E}{R}$	$\Phi = \dfrac{m.m.f.}{S}$
$R = \dfrac{\rho l}{A}$	$S = \dfrac{l}{\mu_0 \mu_r A}$

7.8 Hysteresis and hysteresis loss

Hysteresis loop

Let a ferromagnetic material which is completely demagnetised, i.e. one in which $B = H = 0$ be subjected to increasing values of magnetic field strength H and the corresponding flux density B measured. The resulting relationship between B and H is shown by the curve Oab in Fig. 7.9. At a

BTEC National Study Guide: Engineering. See page 325 for order details of individual texts

311

particular value of H, shown as Oy, it becomes difficult to increase the flux density any further. The material is said to be saturated. Thus **by** is the **saturation flux density**.

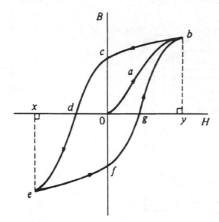

Figure 7.9

If the value of H is now reduced it is found that the flux density follows curve **bc**. When H is reduced to zero, flux remains in the iron. This **remanent flux density** or **remanence** is shown as **Oc** in Fig. 7.9. When H is increased in the opposite direction, the flux density decreases until, at a value shown as **Od**, the flux density has been reduced to zero. The magnetic field strength **Od** required to remove the residual magnetism, i.e. reduce B to zero, is called the **coercive force**.

Further increase of H in the reverse direction causes the flux density to increase in the reverse direction until saturation is reached, as shown by curve **de**. If H is varied backwards from **Ox** to **Oy**, the flux density follows the curve **efgb**, similar to curve **bcde**.

It is seen from Fig. 7.9 that the flux density changes lag behind the changes in the magnetic field strength. This effect is called **hysteresis**. The closed figure **bcdefgb** is called the **hysteresis loop** (or the B/H loop).

Hysteresis loss

A disturbance in the alignment of the domains (i.e. groups of atoms) of a ferromagnetic material causes energy to be expended in taking it through a cycle of magnetisation. This energy appears as heat in the specimen and is called the **hysteresis loss**

The energy loss associated with hysteresis is proportional to the area of the hysteresis loop.

The area of a hysteresis loop varies with the type of material. The area, and thus the energy loss, is much greater for hard materials than for soft materials.

Figure 7.10 shows typical hysteresis loops for:

(a) **hard material**, which has a high remanence Oc and a large coercivity **Od**

(b) **soft steel**, which has a large remanence and small coercivity

(c) **ferrite**, this being a ceramic-like magnetic substance made from oxides of iron, nickel, cobalt, magnesium, aluminium and mangenese; the hysteresis of ferrite is very small.

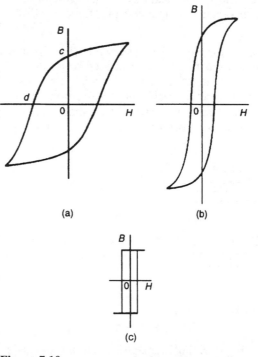

Figure 7.10

For a.c.-excited devices the hysteresis loop is repeated every cycle of alternating current. Thus a hysteresis loop with a large area (as with hard steel) is often unsuitable since the energy loss would be considerable. Silicon steel has a narrow hysteresis loop, and thus small hysteresis loss, and is suitable for transformer cores and rotating machine armatures.

BTEC National Study Guide: Engineering. See page 325 for order details of individual texts

312

Now try the following exercises

Exercise 35   Short answer questions on magnetic circuits

1 What is a permanent magnet?

2 Sketch the pattern of the magnetic field associated with a bar magnet. Mark the direction of the field.

3 Define magnetic flux

4 The symbol for magnetic flux is ... and the unit of flux is the ...

5 Define magnetic flux density

6 The symbol for magnetic flux density is ... and the unit of flux density is ...

7 The symbol for m.m.f. is ... and the unit of m.m.f. is the ...

8 Another name for the magnetising force is ...... ; its symbol is ... and its unit is ...

9 Complete the statement:

$$\frac{\text{flux density}}{\text{magnetic field strength}} = \ldots$$

10 What is absolute permeability?

11 The value of the permeability of free space is ...

12 What is a magnetisation curve?

13 The symbol for reluctance is ... and the unit of reluctance is ...

14 Make a comparison between magnetic and electrical quantities

15 What is hysteresis?

16 Draw a typical hysteresis loop and on it identify:
   (a) saturation flux density
   (b) remanence
   (c) coercive force

17 State the units of (a) remanence (b) coercive force

18 How is magnetic screening achieved?

19 Complete the statement: magnetic materials have a ... reluctance;non-magnetic materials have a .... reluctance

20 What loss is associated with hysteresis?

Exercise 36   Multi-choice questions on magnetic circuits (Answers on page 375)

1 The unit of magnetic flux density is the:
   (a) weber   (b) weber per metre
   (c) ampere per metre   (d) tesla

2 The total flux in the core of an electrical machine is 20 mWb and its flux density is 1 T. The cross-sectional area of the core is:
   (a) 0.05 m^2 (b) 0.02 m^2
   (c) 20 m^2 (d) 50 m^2

3 If the total flux in a magnetic circuit is 2 mWb and the cross-sectional area of the circuit is 10 cm^2, the flux density is:
   (a) 0.2 T   (b) 2 T   (c) 20 T   (d) 20 mT

Questions 4 to 8 refer to the following data: A coil of 100 turns is wound uniformly on a wooden ring. The ring has a mean circumference of 1 m and a uniform cross-sectional area of 10 cm^2. The current in the coil is 1 A.

4 The magnetomotive force is:
   (a) 1 A   (b) 10 A   (c) 100 A   (d) 1000 A

5 The magnetic field strength is:
   (a) 1 A/m   (b) 10 A/m
   (c) 100 A/m   (d) 1000 A/m

6 The magnetic flux density is:
   (a) 800 T   (b) 8.85 × 10^{-10} T
   (c) 4π × 10^{-7} T   (d) 40π μT

7 The magnetic flux is:
   (a) 0.04π μWb   (b) 0.01 Wb
   (c) 8.85 μWb   (d) 4π μWb

8 The reluctance is:

   (a) $\dfrac{10^8}{4\pi}$ H^{-1} (b) 1000 H^{-1}

   (c) $\dfrac{2.5}{\pi} \times 10^9$ H^{-1} (d) $\dfrac{10^8}{8.85}$ H^{-1}

9 Which of the following statements is false?
   (a) For non-magnetic materials reluctance is high
   (b) Energy loss due to hysteresis is greater for harder magnetic materials than for softer magnetic materials
   (c) The remanence of a ferrous material is measured in ampere/metre

BTEC National Study Guide: Engineering. See page 325 for order details of individual texts

313

(d) Absolute permeability is measured in henrys per metre

10 The current flowing in a 500 turn coil wound on an iron ring is 4 A. The reluctance of the circuit is 2×10^6 H. The flux produced is:

(a) 1 Wb   (b) 1000 Wb

(c) 1 mWb   (d) 62.5 μWb

11 A comparison can be made between magnetic and electrical quantities. From the following list, match the magnetic quantities with their equivalent electrical quantities.

(a) current   (b) reluctance

(c) e.m.f.   (d) flux

(e) m.m.f.   (f) resistance

12 The effect of an air gap in a magnetic circuit is to:

(a) increase the reluctance

(b) reduce the flux density

(c) divide the flux

(d) reduce the magnetomotive force

13 Two bar magnets are placed parallel to each other and about 2 cm apart, such that the south pole of one magnet is adjacent to the north pole of the other. With this arrangement, the magnets will:

(a) attract each other

(b) have no effect on each other

(c) repel each other

(d) lose their magnetism

BTEC National Study Guide: Engineering. See page 325 for order details of individual texts

314

TEN STEPS TO A GREAT IVA

What is the IVA?

IVA stands for **Integrated Vocational Assignment**. This is a specific piece of work you will do for your BTEC National qualification.

The IVA is set by Edexcel, marked by your tutors and the assessment is checked by Edexcel. The IVA is **compulsory**. You cannot gain the complete award unless you attempt it. Obviously, though, you should do a lot more than just attempt it! Indeed, it is sensible to aim as high as you can. You might even surprise yourself.

This guide gives you hints and tips on researching and completing your IVA so that you will target all your efforts productively. In other words, you won't waste time doing things that aren't needed or you weren't intended to do! This doesn't mean that you can get by without doing any work at all. It does mean that you will get the maximum benefit for the work that you do.

Step 1: Understanding the basics

The IVA is a set of tasks you have to do. The tasks only relate to one or two specific units. These are identified on the front cover of the IVA. You will only be expected to complete tasks after you have learned about the unit(s) in class.

The IVA *must* be all your own work. If you have to do part of the work as a member of a group then the conclusions you write must be your own. If any part of the work has been done with someone else this must be clearly stated. This also means that you should not share your ideas or your researched information with anyone or copy anyone else's work

The IVA is not an examination. It is a series of tasks that you have to do to check that you understand the information you have learned. If you can demonstrate that you can apply and use this information in more than one situation and make informed judgements then you will gain a higher grade. You will be expected to research your own information to add to the work you have done in class. However, you must always list and identify your sources and never try to pass them off as you own work. How to do this is shown under Step 4.

You can produce your IVA over a period of time. Your tutor will tell you how long you have to complete it when it is issued. Make sure you know your deadlines for each stage and for any reviews that you have with your tutor. These will be included on a **Centre IVA Issue Sheet** that your tutor will give you. It also includes information about the resources you can use and support that is available to you. Keep this sheet safely and enter all the dates into your diary or onto your wall planner immediately. It is also sensible to enter a 'warning' a week before each important date, to remind yourself that it is looming!

Always remember that if you have any worries or concerns about your IVA then you should talk to your tutor. Don't wait for the next review date to do this – especially if the problem is serious.

1

BTEC National Study Guide: Engineering. See page 325 for order details of individual texts

315

> **Help yourself . . .**
>
> . . . by making sure you possess a diary or wall planner on which you can write deadline dates when you receive your Centre IVA issue sheet.

Step 2: Obtaining your IVA

You are unlikely to be expected to start your IVA until you have completed most, if not all, of the unit(s) to which it relates. However, you might be given it sooner so that you know what to expect and you can see the actual tasks you will have to answer.

You can see the IVA at any time, yourself, by logging onto the Edexcel website at www.edexcel.org.uk . Click on to 'qualifications', then select 'BTEC National' then click on the subject you are studying. The document you want is entitled *IVA – Learner Instructions*. It is normally quite short, between 8 and 10 pages, and contains the following information.

- The title page, which gives you

  – the level and title of your BTEC National qualification
  – the subject
  – the unit(s) to which the IVA relates
  – the date of issue and specification to which it relates. Ask your tutor if you are not sure whether this matches your course.

- Full instructions for completing and presenting the IVA. This is on page 2. It is very important that you read this carefully.

- Your assignment tasks and a copy of the assessment criteria grid(s). You will find out more about these under Step 3.

> **Help yourself . . .**
>
> . . . by starting a special IVA file that includes the IVA, the Centre IVA issue sheet and any specific notes your tutor gives you relating to the IVA.

Step 3: Understanding the tasks

This is the most important step of all. If you don't understand what you have to do to answer a question then you are very unlikely to get a good grade. You may do a lot of work but much of it may be irrelevant or – more likely – you will miss out important information.

It is quite normal for students to panic when they first read a set of assignment tasks! For this reason you are likely to be introduced to your IVA in a special session held by your tutor. Although your tutor cannot do the work for you (obviously!) you are allowed to receive guidance and can discuss general ideas, just like you would for an internal assessment. Your tutor can also answer any queries you have and give you ongoing advice and support in your review sessions to help you to do your best.

All IVAs are written in a certain format, or design.

- They start with a scenario or context to 'set the scene'. This may be quite short – just a few lines – or take up most of a page.

BTEC National Study Guide: Engineering. See page 325 for order details of individual texts

316

- Below this are several tasks. Each task usually starts with some introductory or background information and is then divided into lettered sub-sections.

- You are often expected to provide your answer in a specific document, such as a report, a letter, a leaflet, a table or a summary.

- At the end of each task you will see the unit number and assessment criteria covered by that task, eg Unit 2, P1, M1, D1. In this case it would mean that particular task related to Unit 2 and your answer must focus on providing evidence against the first assessment criterion under each of the pass, merit and distinction columns. You can match up this information in the assessment criteria grid(s). Your tutor will show you how to do this if you are not sure.

You will not be expected to do all the tasks at once. Let's assume you have been told to start with Task 1. There are two things you can do to make sure you understand *exactly* what you have to do.

1 Break the task down into chunks and analyse it.

2 Complete a task checklist before you start work.

You will read how to do this in Steps 4 and 5.

Help yourself . . .

. . . by first reading all the tasks you will have to do to get the overall picture and then reading – far more carefully – the first task you have to do. Then note down anything that puzzles you or that you do not understand.

Step 4: Analyse the task

Although IVAs aren't meant to be daunting or difficult to understand, it can be useful to know what to do if you do experience any problems. If a scenario or a task is short it is normally easier to understand. If it is long it may be more difficult. This is because there is more 'additional' information and if you miss any of this, it may affect your grade.

If there is a lot of information don't expect to understand it fully the first time you read it. Just read it to get a general impression. Then read it again, more slowly, to get the meaning. It is often helpful to go through it again, much more thoroughly, to identify the important words. This is called **task analysis**. The aim is to identify:

- the **background information** – which sets the scene or the context. You need to understand this for the task to make sense

- the **command words**, such as 'describe' or 'explain' – which tell you what you have to do. You *must* obey these when you answer the questions. If you are unsure what any of these words mean, check back to the explanation in *The Smart Way to Achieve Your BTEC National* at the start of this book

- other **specific instructions** which tell you what you have to do – such as 'provide three examples' or 'write a report'

- any important **topic words** which give you the subject of the task.

Finally, make sure you now understand the purpose of the task you have to do and the audience you are preparing it for. Both these factors affect the way you will structure and present your answer.

BTEC National Study Guide: Engineering. See page 325 for order details of individual texts

317

Task 1: Prove your understanding of the IVA

Edexcel issues an assessment called an IVA that covers the whole of either one or two units of a BTEC National programme. This tests all learners nationally on the same set of tasks. <u>Produce a short report</u> which identifies <u>your own tasks in relation to your IVA</u>. <u>Your report should include:</u>

a A <u>brief</u> **description** <u>of the IVA.</u>

b An **explanation** <u>of the main instructions given to learners.</u> This <u>must include</u> the **identification** <u>of</u> <u>three</u> <u>requirements which ensure that each IVA is the student's own original work.</u>

c <u>Your own plan</u> <u>for producing your IVA which shows how you have</u> **analysed** <u>your options and provides</u> **justifications** <u>for the decisions you have made.</u>

Background information which sets the scene.

To produce a short report, and what the report should include are both <u>instructions</u>. <u>Your own tasks in relation to the IVA</u> are topic words

'Brief' is an instruction, 'of the IVA' is the topic. 'Description' and 'explanation' are both **command words**. 'Must include' is an instruction but 'identification' is a command word. The remaining words are topic words except for 'three' which is an instruction.

'Your own plan' is an instruction. The remaining words give you the topic. This must involve 'analysis' and 'justification', so these are both **command words**.

Help yourself . . .

. . . by practising task analysis yourself.

In agreement with your tutor, select **one** task in the IVA you have been issued and carry out the following tasks.

a Identify the background information, command words, instructions and topic words that it contains. You can use any combination of colour or highlighting (such as bold or underscore) that you find easiest to understand.

b Explain the purpose of that task and identify your audience. Then say how these two factors will influence your answer.

c Compare your ideas with those of other members of your group.

Step 5: Completing a task checklist

This will confirm if you really do understand what you have to do. Simply read the following list. If you can complete the column on the right with ticks then you understand the task. If you can't then you must resolve the problem before you start work.

BTEC National Study Guide: Engineering. See page 325 for order details of individual texts

318

Checklist for understanding your IVA task		✓ or x
Read the scenario or context that 'sets the scene'	Does it make sense? Do you understand all the words used? Can you identify the key words? Would it help you to highlight these? Could you accurately explain the scenario or context to someone else, using your own words?	
Read the task you have to do and then analyse it	Have you carried out task analysis? Can you identify the background information? Can you identify *all* the command words? Can you identify *all* the instructions? Do you understand the topics? Can you clearly state what you have to do, using your own words? Do you know how to set out the document(s) you have to produce?	
Do you know the purpose of the task and have you identified your audience?	Can you explain the reason for doing this task? Who is your audience? How will these two factors affect your answer?	
Check the evidence statement at the bottom of the task and check this against the assessment criteria grid	Do you know the grades you can get for this task? Can you see how the command words differ within the task to cover merit and distinction questions? Are you *certain* that you know what is meant by each command word?	

- If you don't understand a word that is used then look in a dictionary or check the list of command words and their meanings given in *The Smart Way to Achieve your BTEC National*.

- If there is any instruction that you do not understand, such as how to set out a document that is required, talk to your tutor.

- If there is any aspect of the topic that you missed when it was covered in class then talk to your tutor about obtaining the information you need.

Help yourself . . .

. . . copy the checklist and complete it for the first task on your list. Remember that you *must* obtain help if you still cannot understand anything about the task you have to do.

Step 6: Planning your work

Completing any task(s) will take some time. You have to allow enough time for obtaining the information, deciding what to use, getting it into the right order and writing it up. You also need to bear in mind the review date(s) agreed with your tutor – as well as all the other college and personal commitments you have! It is therefore sensible to make a plan.

- The IVA is designed to cover the unit content and each task covers different parts of the unit. You can check which parts of a unit are covered by a particular task by looking at the key words. These will relate to the assessment criteria for the unit and the unit specification, which gives detailed information on the content.

BTEC National Study Guide: Engineering. See page 325 for order details of individual texts

319

- Next estimate how long it will take you to find the information you need. You will do this more accurately if you identify your information sources. Although this will obviously depend on the format of your IVA and the task you are doing you will probably want to refer to

  - notes you have been given in class
  - your course textbook
  - two or three library books or journals
  - some online resources.

  If you are researching for a project or need to use evidence from a particular event then you may need to arrange to talk to people to get their views. You must therefore allow enough time to obtain your information.

- Decide how long it is likely to take to sort through your information before you can start to write your first draft answer.

- Allow time for rereading and revising your answer and then for checking the way you have presented the information.

- Decide how many hours a week you will need to spend on your IVA to stay on schedule.

- Split these up into sensible sessions. Longer than two or three hours is too much – you won't work well when you're tired. Shorter than half an hour isn't much good unless you've a specific small job to do.

- Identify times during the week when you will do the work and mark these in your diary or on your wall planner, eg Tuesday 5 pm – 7 pm. Then stick to them! If an emergency means you can't work at that time remember that you then need to reschedule these hours at another time to keep on target!

Help yourself . . .

. . . by always allowing more time than you think you will need, never less. You should also find a quiet place to work, where you can concentrate. Now make out your plan for the first task you have to do. Aim to finish a week early to allow time for slippage.

Step 7: Researching, storing and selecting your information

Problems with researching are always linked to the quality and quantity of information. For information to be good quality it needs to relate directly to the topic. You also need to understand it! Quantity is also important. If you only rely on your course notes then you are unlikely to produce original work and this will affect your grade, but too much information is very confusing and you are likely to get bogged down trying to decide what to use.

Start by listing all the potential sources of information you can use. These will depend largely upon the type of task you are doing and the information you need.

- If you are looking for books you are best to aim for two or three that specifically cover the topic. Check this by looking in the index when you are in the library, then skim the text to make sure it is written at the right level and that you find the style 'user-friendly'. You are wise to schedule in a prompt visit to your college library – particularly if there are many students doing the same IVA as you!

- If you are searching online you will have far more success if you learn how to do advanced searches on websites such as Google. It is also important to keep focused and not get distracted by interesting but irrelevant information you come across as you search! If you need help searching on line, talk to the IT resource staff at college.

- If you need to visit organisations or interview someone then prepare well in advance. Make the arrangement and then draft a list of questions. If you want to take a tape recorder, first check this is acceptable.

BTEC National Study Guide: Engineering. See page 325 for order details of individual texts

320

- If you are preparing a presentation that involves other people in your group arrange a first meeting to decide your roles and responsibilities. Check in your library for useful guidelines on preparing and giving a presentation.

- Buy a box file and label it. If you are broke use an empty cardboard box! Put in every scrap of information that might be helpful for your IVA. If your IVA covers two units then you might find it helpful to keep the information that relates to each one in separate folders.

- Make sure that all the information you put into your box file is dated and labelled with its source (see below). This includes any photocopies you have taken or print-outs you have made.

- Have a cut-off date when you stop collecting information and start to write. If you don't, you can easily find yourself running out of time to complete the task.

- Only select the most relevant information after re-reading the task *and* your task analysis. It's often easiest to start by spreading out all your information on a large table (or the floor!). Then select everything you think you might need and put the rest away.

- Read through your information and make draft notes to answer the question. *Don't* copy out reams of information – note down the source of the information instead. Remember that most of your IVA must be in your own words.

- Make sure you only include relevant information and that you re-word or adapt information to match the task you are doing. It is very tempting to 'cut and paste' lots of information, particularly from the Internet, just because you found it! A good trick is to keep looking back to the question at regular intervals to keep yourself focused and *never* include everything 'just 'cos it's there'! Remember that marks are always awarded for quality of work, not quantity!

Help yourself . . .

. . . by being self-disciplined when you are looking for information. This means not getting distracted, *always* noting down the source of information you print out or photocopy and *always* storing it safely so you can find it again!

Step 8: Identifying your sources

You must do this if you quote from any source. If you forget then you could be guilty of plagiarism. This is a serious academic crime as it is assumed that you were trying to pass off someone else's work as your own. It is so serious that some colleges and universities have installed special software to catch plagiarists!

Your tutor or your college library will be able to give you detailed information on citing references. If not, use the following as your guide.

In the text:

- Always put quoted information in quotation marks. Mark Twain said 'There are lies, damned lies and statistics.'

- If you refer to an author put their name and then the date and/or page number in brackets. Chaffey (2002) argues that . . . .

At the end of the task, in your bibliography, list your references in alphabetical order of author. Put the title in bold or in italics so that it stands out.

- If your source is a newspaper or magazine, state the name of the author(s), year of publication in brackets, title of the article, the title of the publication, volume or date, pages of the article eg Gascoigne, C (2005) **Leading from the front**, Sunday Times Smarter Business, 6 February 2005, page 7.

- If your source is a book, give the author(s), date of publication in brackets, title and the publisher eg Chaffey, D (2002) **E-Business and E-Commerce Management**, Prentice Hall, page 25.

BTEC National Study Guide: Engineering. See page 325 for order details of individual texts

321

- If your source is from the Internet then you should give enough information for your tutor to be able to find the article online. However, you are also wise to keep your print-out as Internet sites are regularly updated and you may need proof of your information. It is recommended that you give the name of the person or organisation responsible for the article or site, the title of the document, the word Internet in square brackets, the URL and the date you accessed the information. This is the address line that shows on screen and is normally printed at the bottom of the page eg Sport England, **What the 2012 Olympics would do for the UK**, [Internet], http://www.sportengland.org/index/news_and_media/olympics_2012/2012_uk.htm [Accessed 7 February 2005]

Help yourself . . .

. . . by checking if there is a course or college guide to citing references. Ask your tutor or librarian if you are not sure. Alternatively you can test your research skills by finding information online. Type 'Harvard referencing' into any search engine. This is the most usual method used by students at university.

Step 9: Writing and presenting your IVA

The first thing to do is to plan your answer. Re-read your task analysis to refresh your memory. Check carefully the command words, the instructions and the topic words. Make sure you know what type of document you have to produce and how to set it out.

There are two ways in which you can plan your answer. Use the one that is most natural for you:

1 Write a list of all the information you want to include. Then put it into the correct order. Decide what will go in the introduction, what in the middle of the answer and what your conclusion will be.

2 Write the question in the middle of the page and write your information around it. Link the information with arrows so you end up with different themes. Decide the best order to introduce each theme and how these will be reflected in your paragraphs.

If you find that you are missing any information write this on a 'to do' list. You can still plan and draft your answer. Your 'to do' list is to make certain you don't forget to find out the remaining details.

Decide the approach you want to use. For example, if you have to contrast and compare two things then you could write all about one and then the other; alternatively you could describe each one and then analyse the similarities and differences afterwards. *Neither is right or wrong* – do the one you find easier. If you find that it then doesn't work very well when you start to draft your answer, be prepared to change it.

Don't think that you need to write in a more flowery or grandiose style than you normally do. In fact, there are lots of pitfalls if you do this – such as using the wrong word or writing a complex sentence that no-one can understand! Instead, keep your writing style simple and only use words you understand. If you also keep your sentences relatively short but vary the length a little then your answer will also be more interesting and easier to read.

Don't expect to write the answers to merit and distinction level questions quickly. These are deliberately written to make you think! Look back at the command words information and examples in *The Smart Way to Achieve your BTEC National* if you are struggling. Then draft your answer as best you can and discuss your ideas with your tutor at your next review meeting. This might help to put you on the right track again.

The type of task and your audience will determine your writing style. If you are asked to prepare a formal business document such as a report it is better to use a quite formal writing style. In this case try to write using the third person. This means you don't say 'I think that ' but 'it is considered that' or 'it would appear that'. Equally you wouldn't say 'You can do this by . . .' but 'This could be done by . . . '. The situation is different, though, if you are preparing an informal account, such as an article for a staff newsletter. In every document, though, you should avoid using slang or contracted words (eg can't or hasn't) and *never* use the abbreviated words or jargon that you would use in a text message or if you were talking to your friends.

BTEC National Study Guide: Engineering. See page 325 for order details of individual texts

322

Leave your work alone for a day or two before you make a final check. This way you are more likely to spot errors. You may also find this easier to do if you take a print-out rather than read it on screen. Check it against the question. Have you obeyed all the command words? Have you included everything that was asked for? Is the information given in a logical order?

Now check the presentation and your writing style. Have you set out the document correctly? Is it in the right style? For example a letter or report must be set out in the right format and not written as an essay style answer. Is the grammar correct? Is every word spelt properly? Don't rely on your spellchecker here. It cannot tell the difference between 'hear' and 'here' or 'there' and 'their'! Word processing packages are also very limited in their ability to correct grammatical errors, so never assume that you don't need to check your work carefully yourself. If you are preparing a draft print-out to discuss with your tutor it is useful to use wide margins and double spacing then you have plenty of room to note down comments.

Make sure you have included a sheet with all your references on it. It is usually easier to compile this as you go – rather than create these at the end when some notes will be buried under a mountain of paper.

Finally check that the presentation of your IVA matches *all* the requirements set out on page 2 of your *Instructions for Learners completing IVAs*. For example, you must not put your work into plastic pockets or into a box file or a lever arch file. You also need to put a cover sheet on the front and sign a declaration that all the work you are submitting is your own.

Help yourself . . .

. . . by asking someone you trust to read through your work and make comments. This can be a close friend or a family member but shouldn't be a fellow student who is doing the same IVA as you. If your friend or relative can't understand what you are trying to say then it is probably true that your tutor will have the same problem!

Step 10: Is this the best you can do?

It always seems a tragedy when students just miss a better grade because of carelessness or silly mistakes. As a final check, before you give in your work, run through the following list. Only hand in your work when, hand on heart, you know you honestly couldn't do any more.

- You have incorporated all the suggestions and ideas that you discussed with your tutor at your review meetings.
- You have answered every part of every task and there are no gaps or omissions.
- You have addressed all the command words correctly and taken account of all the instructions.
- You have checked the spelling, punctuation and layout.
- You have checked and double-checked that all the references are included.
- All your pages are numbered and your name is on every sheet.
- You have followed every other instruction for completing and presenting your work. Do a final check of page 2 of your *Instructions for Learners completing IVAs* before you hand in your work. For example, are all your pages in the right order and are they securely fastened together?

Help yourself . . .

. . . by handing in your work before the deadline and then relaxing! Once you have done your best and submitted your work you cannot then alter the grade for that particular piece of work. Remember, though, that the grade you achieve is very important feedback for future work you will do. Learn from your mistakes and build on your successes – and your work will always continue to improve.

BTEC National Study Guide: Engineering. See page 325 for order details of individual texts

323

BTEC National Study Guide: Engineering. See page 325 for order details of individual texts

324

BTEC National Study Guide

ENGINEERING

The Units in this Study Guide are taken from a variety of books. If you found any to be of help, then follow the instructions to purchase a copy.

Science for Technicians comes from

BTEC National Engineering
by Mike Tooley and Lloyd Dingle published by Newnes

Unit 2 Computer Systems comes from

BTEC National IT Practitioners
by Sharon Yull and Howard Anderson, published by Newnes

If you liked this book, and would like to order a full copy, either go to your local bookshop and quote the ISBN number: 0 7506 5166 0 or order online at www.newnespress.com

Mechanical Principles comes from

Mechanical Engineering: BTEC National Option Units
by Alan Darbyshire, published by Newnes

If you liked this book, and would like to order a full copy, either go to your local bookshop and quote the ISBN number: 0 7506 5761 8 or order online at www.newnespress.com

Basic Electrical and Electronic Engineering Principles comes from

Electrical and Electronic Principles and Technology
by John Bird, published by Newnes

If you liked this book, and would like to order a full copy, either go to your local bookshop and quote the ISBN number: 0 7506 6550 5 or order online at www.newnespress.com